CORELDRAW 4
A USER'S GUIDE

About the Author

ALAN BALFE originally trained as a programmer on mainframe computers and then went on to work in industry for a number of years. Later he worked for a small software company when IBM launched the PC. He went on to teach in Further Education for some time, before becoming a journalist with one of the UK's leading computer magazines. Today he is a full-time author and freelance journalist, as well as being Technical Director of CDR, the Official Independent Organization for CorelDRAW Users, and of the PageMaker User Group. His time is mainly spent in writing books, providing technical support in beta testing hardware and software for major manufacturers. He has had a number of books published on a range of software and hardware topics and has been one of the judges of the CorelDRAW World Design Contest.

■

Colour plate section: reproduced by kind permission of Corel Corporation. It shows the winners of the 1993 CorelDRAW World Design Contest and demonstrates what can be achieved using CorelDRAW.

■

Front cover: The graphic depicted on the front cover is reproduced by kind permission of Corel Corporation. It is by Georgina Curry and is the winner of the 'Best of the Show' award in the 1993 fourth annual CorelDRAW World Design Contest.
Entry details can be obtained from :
Corel Corporation,
1600 Carling Avenue, Ottawa, Ontario, Canada, K1Z 8RT.

CORELDRAW! 4

A USER'S GUIDE

ALAN BALFE

PRENTICE HALL

New York · London · Toronto · Sydney · Tokyo · Singapore

First published 1993 by Prentice Hall International (UK) Ltd
Campus 400, Maylands Avenue
Hemel Hempstead
Hertfordshire, HP2 7EZ
A division of Simon & Schuster International Group

NOTICE
The author and the publisher have used their best efforts to prepare the book, including the computer examples contained in it. The computer examples have been tested. The authors and the publishers make no warranty, implicit or explicit, about the documentation. The authors and the publishers will not be liable under any circumstances for any direct or indirect damages arising from any use, direct or indirect of the documentation or the computer examples contained in this book.

Printed and bound in Great Britain by
Redwood Books, Trowbridge

Library of Congress Cataloging-in-Publication Data

Available from the publishers.

British Library Cataloguing in Publication Data

*A catalogue record for this book is available
from the British Library*

ISBN 0-13-207770-1

1 2 3 4 5   97 96 95 94 93

Dedication

This is for Wendy Bunting, the publishing assistant at Prentice Hall.
She does an unenviable job that everyone, not least me, takes for granted.

TRADEMARKS

CorelCHART, CorelDRAW, CorelMOSAIC, CorelMOVE, CorelPHOTO-PAINT, CorelSHOW and CorelTRACE are all registered trademarks of Corel Corporation.

Microsoft, MS-DOS and Windows are all registered trademarks of Microsoft Corporation.

Aldus and PageMaker are registered trademarks of Aldus Corporation.

Adobe Type Manager, PostScript and Encapsulated PostScript are registered trademarks of Adobe Systems Incorporated.

All other products are trademarks of their respective companies.

CONTENTS

CONTENTS

FOREWORD

Since its initial release in January of 1989, CorelDRAW has become the most talked-about PC graphics software package in the world. CorelDRAW has become the standard in the PC illustration and graphics arena. Today, it is easy to understand why the program has received so much favourable attention, including over 90 major industry awards to date - include "Best Drawing Software", Windows Users UK 1993, "Best Graphics Package for Business", PC Today UK 1993, and "Readers Award, Best Overall Software Purchase: Graphics", PC User UK 1993. No other graphics package offers so many powerful features, so much value, and so much fun in one box.

With the release of CorelDRAW 3 in May of 1992, a new era in PC Graphics was launched. The "All-In-One Graphics Solution" had arrived. Now, one year later, this theme has evolved with CorelDRAW 4! CorelDRAW 4 includes everything that was in Version 3 plus hundreds of new features, innovations, added functionality, plus a new 2-Dimensional animation module. The release of CorelDRAW 4 marks the beginning of another era in PC Graphics! The best has just got better!!

It has been simply an amazing year for the CorelDRAW development team here in Ottawa, Canada. Inspiring thoughts and innovative ideas sprung up almost daily over the course of the last year and CorelDRAW is now more powerful, intuitive, fun and value-packed than ever before. The obvious question that is asked continually is "Where do all the ideas come from?" The answer is simply "Lots of places". Corel's Director of Graphics Software, Susan Wimmer, answers, "Naturally, we keep an eye on the competition, and of course we always respond to our user's suggestions for enhancements, but at the heart of our creative process is a simple philosophy - Look to the future beyond the horizons and then reach for it. It's all about human potential and our desire to enhance the artistic potential of every CorelDRAW user. We set no limits on our ideas, and want our users to live with creative limits as well."

It's hard to believe the amount of work that takes place in just one year of development. You simply will not believe what has been added to CorelDRAW 4. The flagship module, CorelDRAW itself, now a complete desktop publishing tool, is packed with exciting new illustration features, has vastly improved precision drawing tools, and has numerous additional import and export filters. CorelDRAW is the only software you need for illustration, DTP and technical drawing. But that's

CorelDRAW 4 - A Users Guide

just the beginning... we don't stop with CorelDRAW. All of the modules in the package have been redesigned with uniform interfaces so it's now easier than ever to learn and use the applications.

CorelCHART now lets you perform calculations in the Data Manager, you can choose from over 45 financial and mathematical formulae, you can print directly from the Data Manager and you can access all CorelDRAW fills and outlines, including patterns, fountain fills and textures.

CorelPHOTO-PAINT has undergone some major renovations also. CorelPHOTO-PAINT is now easier to use and more fun than ever before. There are 14 image correction filters, 20 Artistic filters, and now you can imitate the oil and pointillism styles of Van Gogh and Seurat, and use the new canvas layer to create a realistic textured background.

CorelSHOW lets you create presentations that are more spectacular than ever before. With the graphical guidelines, the ability to play animations in a frame, add transition effects to singular objects within a frame and the availability of user cues, CorelSHOW lets you develop complete presentations right on screen.

CorelMOVE is the most recent module to join the CorelDRAW suite of applications. CorelMOVE is a path-based animation package that allows users to combine sound and graphics to produce 2-dimensional multimedia animations. Extensive libraries of professionally designed actors and props are included for convenience or you can work with vector illustrations produced in CorelDRAW or props and single-cel actors made in CorelPHOTO-PAINT. CorelMOVE sets your imagination in motion.

CorelDRAW 4 now features over 750 fonts, both TrueType and Adobe Type 1, including 650 Bitstream and ITC fonts. In keeping with Corel's philosophy of giving users everything they would imagine, every box of CorelDRAW 4 includes 2 CD-ROM discs that are brimming with fonts, more than 18,000 Clip-Art images, animations and sound libraries.

To provide a forum for showcasing the spectacular works of art that are created each year with CorelDRAW, Corel Corporation hosts the Annual World Design Contest which is now recognised as the foremost computer art competition in the world. The contest is open to all registered users of CorelDRAW. This year's contest came to a spectacular finale at the Gala Awards Night, dubbed the Academy Awards of Graphics, here in Ottawa on May 20th. The contest featured designers, graphic artists and technical illustrators from all over the world. In total there were well over 4,000 entries received and the Grand Final winner - "Indian Headdress" - is beautifully displayed on the front cover of this book, and the winners of the other categories are included in the colour plates section.

At the Gala Night, which was attended by over 900 guests, Corel Corporation was thrilled to award Georgina Currie from Phoenix, Arizona, a 2 kilogram bar of gold - worth over $22,500 - and her winning entry will feature in all CorelDRAW International print advertising and promotions during 1993-94.

Next year's contest is expected to be even more spectacular and Corel Corporation is eager to see what users of CorelDRAW from all over the world will think of next. So put your thinking cap on, gather your creative energies, summon your artistic talent, compile your technical knowledge and get to work. Send in your entries and that gold bar could be yours next May!

From the perspective of someone who has lived and breathed CorelDRAW since its inception almost five years ago, Alan Balfe will certainly help you to build your skills and maximise the power of CorelDRAW with this book. It was a pleasure to assist someone so keenly interested in Corel Corporation and CorelDRAW and I know that you will find his words in this book both helpful and inspiring. Whether you are a power user, an occasional player or a rookie to graphics software, this book will be a great companion. Thank you, Alan, for your never-ending support, enthusiasm and dedication to Corel. I look forward to CorelDRAW 5 : A User's Guide!

Katie Marriott
International Marketing,
Corel Corporation

PREFACE

CorelDRAW continues to go from strength to strength, it wins awards and prizes like nobody's business and it remains the world's best selling computer graphics package. With the release of CorelDRAW 4 this entire process will continue unabated. You can expect to see the program win yet more prizes left, right and centre.

CorelDRAW 4 gives you yet another quantum leap in graphic capability. You can now do things that you only thought possible. As always Corel Corporation has listened to the users of its product and incorporated the best elements from people's wish lists into the new version. I know of no other company which pays such close attention to its customer's desires and needs. Long may they continue to do so.

With CorelDRAW 4, Corel Corporation have taken another step towards completed integrated software that will do the whole job for you.

You now have a graphics programs, CorelDRAW itself, that contains complete DTP facilities with multiple pages, text styles, tabs and indents and what-have-you.

You have CorelCHART which will produce dynamic and vibrant charts from just about any kind of data you care to throw at it. You can change the graph, the layout, the typefaces, the colours, just about anything you want.

You have CorelSHOW, the slide show presentation program in which you can include static files, sounds and animations.

You have CorelMOVE, the animation program. This allows you to create your own animations simply and quickly.

You have CorelMOSAIC, the graphic file manager par excellence. It has been improved and enhanced and now offers multiple windows and full support for Kodak Photo-CD.

You have Corel TRACE, the bitmap to vector format converter. It too has been rewritten, improved and enhanced.

You have CorelPHOTO-PAINT, the bitmap editor program. Again it has been rewritten and streamlined.

All the programs now share certain common features, e.g. they all use the same print dialogue box and their tools have been rationalised and improved. At the same time the program take ups no more room than CorelDRAW 3 did. Don't expect to produce masterpieces with CorelDRAW in an instant - you won't even though the interface of the program is much the same as in version 3.0 There are a lot of new features sitting waiting for you to discover.

This book is going to concentrate on the basics of CorelDRAW 4.0. It will take a brief look at some of the associated programs but they will be covered fully in another book. In addition there will be a CorelDRAW 4 Advanced Users Guide that delves into the full capabilities of CorelDRAW 4. Why so many books? Because it is simply not possible to cover everything in one book.

Before going any further I must publicly thank a number of people for their help and support while writing this book.

Viki Williams, my editor at Prentice Hall, is the real driving force behind this book. Without her it simply wouldn't exist.

Wendy Bunting at Prentice Hall. This book is dedicated to her.

Katie Marriott, at Corel Corporation, who kindly did the foreword for this book and provided me with lots of information.

The entire Quality Assurance team at Corel, especially Bill Cullen, who had the unenviable task of beta testing the program and making sure it is ready for launch in time.

Malcolm Brown, at Star Micronics, for providing the latest Star LaserPrinter 5 which was used to print out this book and for helping with general printing problems.

Last but definitely not least, Pat, my wife, who proof-reads all my manuscripts and corrects my bad grammar and spelling mistakes. Any that remain are my fault not hers.

Alan Balfe

CONVENTIONS

The following section details how keystrokes, commands and actions will be shown in this book.

MAIN KEYS

The names of all keys will be shown, in Bold, exactly as they appear on the keyboard, e.g. **G**, **S**, **L**, **I**, etc.

CURSOR KEYS

The major cursor keys are shown in Bold exactly as they appear, e.g. **PgUp**, **Home**, **Ins**, **Del**. The minor cursor keys, i.e. the arrow keys, are denoted by their actions, e.g. **Left**, **Right**, **Up** and **Down**. You may use either the true cursor keys, that block of ten keys between the main keypad and the Numeric keypad, or the keys on the Numeric Keypad itself - provided you do not have the **Num Lock** turned on.

ADDITIONAL KEYS

Those keys which have a specific function are also shown in Bold, again exactly as they appear on the keyboard, e.g. **Ctrl**, **Enter**, **Backspace**. Function keys are always shown as they appear, e.g. **F2**, **F8**, **F12** again in bold.

KEY COMBINATIONS

Where it is necessary for you to press two or more keys together these will be shown joined by a hyphen. For example, **Ctrl-F12** means that you press and hold the **Ctrl** key and then press **F12**, **Ctrl-Alt-Del** means that you press all three keys together.

Where the keys are meant to be pressed sequentially they will be shown in Bold but without the hyphen. Thus **Ctrl F12** means that you press and release **Ctrl** before pressing and releasing **F12**. **Shift-F10 F** means that you press and hold **Shift** and then press **F10**, before releasing both and then pressing **F**.

12

ENTERING COMMANDS

Throughout this book anything that you have to type verbatim will appear in Bold. For example, the phrase enter **SETUP** means that you have to type **SETUP** and then press the **Enter** key.

MS-DOS and Windows commands will also appear in Bold, for example **COPY A:*.*** or **ATTRIB C:\DOS*.EXE**. Where you are required to supply a word, phrase or filename it will appear enclosed in square brackets. For example, **MD C:\WINDOWS\[directory]** means that you enter **MD C:\WINDOWS** followed by a directory name of your choice, but excluding the brackets.

USING THE MOUSE

Where you are required to press a mouse button the text will say, for example, click on **File** and then on **Open**. This means that you move the mouse pointer to the File menu and then click once so that the menu pops-down. You then click on the word Open in that menu.

ASSUMPTIONS

For various reasons it is necessary that I make a number of assumptions about your basic hardware, your disk drives and directories and your familiarity with using the computer system. Using a computer is a very personal thing and your system is liable to be different to mine and it will contain different software. Therefore, before we go any further here is a list of the assumptions that this book makes and what they imply. Likewise the following section provides definitions of various commands and actions for those who are unfamiliar with using computers.

FAMILIARITY WITH WINDOWS

This book assumes that you are reasonably familiar with the Windows 3.1 operating environment and what it does. However, it also assumes that you are not totally conversant with every aspect of Windows and the initial exercises that this book contains reflect this. The exercises start with very simple steps, including, for example, full details of how to open menus and select a command, but as you progress through the book the exercises become more complex, until by the final set of exercises the detailed step by step approach will no longer be used.

FAMILIARITY WITH MS-DOS

This book assumes that you are using MS-DOS 5.0 as your main operating system and that you are reasonably familiar with the major commands that the operating system contains.

HARD DISK IS DRIVE-C

Throughout this book it is assumed that you are using a hard disk and that this is Drive-C. The reason for doing so is that every hard disk based computer that runs under MS-DOS must have Drive-C in order to boot. Except in special circumstances this book will not prompt you to supply a drive designator: if you wish to use an alternative disk at any point you should include the drive letter before any filename.

TEXT KNOWLEDGE

This book assumes that you know the difference between upper and lower case letters, i.e. A, B, C are upper case while a, b, c are lower case.

USING A MOUSE

The final assumption is that you know how to use a mouse and that you have one connected to your machine. In order to use CorelDRAW properly you must have a mouse. Trying to use the program without one is so nonsensical as to be totally impractical.

Because the majority of people are right handed this book must reflect that and it therefore presupposes that you are right handed. If you are left handed you can either use the mouse in your left hand, which is possible although awkward, or you can change the mouse buttons in the Windows Control Panel so that they act the other way round. Therefore please bear in mind that when you see the words 'click once' it refers to the right hand button - but if you have reversed these then it means the left hand one.

TERMINOLOGY

The following section gives brief definitions of phrases, terms and specific words that will appear in this book. For a more detailed and comprehensive description see the Glossary at the back of the book.

ALT DEFINITION

The **Alt** key is that one which is normally found just to the left of the space bar on the majority of U.K. AT keyboards. The key allows you to generate alternative characters using the numeric keypad. In addition the key is used by Windows to activate menus and commands.

BEZIER CURVE

A Bezier Curve is a special type of line that you can change various aspects of very easily. The line is shown, in certain resolutions, with two or more small square 'handles', called Nodes, appended to it. By moving one of these handles it is possible to change the aspect of the line. Using Bezier curves you can do things to and with lines that are just not possible otherwise.

BITMAP

A bit map refers specifically to a graphic file format. Any file that is bit mapped contains a list of all the pixels that the file contains, along with their attributes. Bitmap files therefore tend to be fairly large. The most common bitmap formats are PCX and TIF.

CLICKING

This refers to a mouse action and it simply means moving the mouse pointer, usually shown on screen as a white arrowhead, to the object you want and then clicking the left hand mouse button once.

CLIP-ART

Pre-drawn images that are available from a wide variety of sources. For example, there are over 12,000 images supplied with CorelDRAW 3.0. The way you use these brings up the spectre of copyright law which is too complex to go into here. Basically, you can use any clip-art that is supplied with CorelDRAW for your own use, even if that involves incorporating it into design work. What you cannot do is sell the clip-art by itself. See Appendix B for more details.

CTRL DEFINITION

The **Ctrl** key is the one normally found at the extreme left hand edge of the keyboard, on the same line as the spacebar. The key produces a signal that allows specific actions to be generated by the software.

CUT

Within Windows applications it is possible to select an object, or group of objects, e.g. lines of text, and then transfer this to the Clipboard before deleting it from the original document. This copy and delete action is called cutting. You can use **Shift-Del** as a shortcut.

DIALOGUE BOXES

A dialogue box is a pop up box within Windows that allows you to set preferences from a predetermined list of options. Once you have made your selection you click on **OK** or press **Enter** to accept your choice and action it.

DOUBLE CLICK

This simply means pressing the right hand mouse button twice, in rapid succession. If you don't click fast enough then nothing happens. You can change the speed of the double click using the Control Panel of Windows.

CORELDRAW 4 - A USERS GUIDE

DRAGGING

This is a mouse action. It means clicking on an object and then, while still holding down the mouse button, moving the mouse and so dragging the object around the screen.

EXPORT

To export a file means to save that file in a format different from that in which it was loaded or created. For example, in CorelDRAW you can open a .CDR file (Corel Draw's own format) and then save that graphic, or selected parts of it, as a PCX file or any other format for which you have a filter installed.

FLOPPY DISK

A floppy disk is a small disk of Mylar, coated with a magnetisable resin, that is used for storing small amounts of data. Floppy disks are prone to damage and thus should be handled carefully.

HARD DISK

A hard disk is a self-contained unit that contains a number of aluminium disks, called platters, coated with a magnetisable material. The unit also contains a Read/Write head assembly that floats just above the platters. Hard disks can be susceptible to damage caused by jolting and banging and thus you should always take care to park the heads before moving any computer fitted with a hard disk. This action moves the Read/Write heads to a safe position and then locks them in place so that they cannot impact the platters. These days most hard disks self-park the heads.

Please Note: You cannot use CorelDRAW without a hard disk - even if you run it from the CD-ROM. The program is so large and the files it can create so complex that you must have a hard disk to run the program. Equally the speed of your hard disk will affect how the program runs. CorelDRAW is the most disk-intensive program that I know of and a slow disk will slow it down considerably. Equally you should ensure that you have at least 8 Mb of free space on your disk before you create any graphics with CorelDRAW - you might not need that much all the time but there will be occasions when you do.

IMPORT

This means to load a file in a different format into an existing document so as to combine a number of files together. For example, in CorelDRAW you can create a picture then insert a piece of clip-art or another .CDR image and then combine the two to make a single graphic. Importing files is especially important with graphic programs because it allows you to build complex graphics from simpler elements. CorelDRAW will allow you to import a large range of different graphic file formats.

LIST BOXES

A list box is a pop down box that contains a list of items from which you can choose any one item. For example all Windows menus are list boxes from which you select a single command that you wish to action.

MOUSE

A mouse is an input device that is used in conjunction with, or occasionally, instead of the keyboard. Within the Windows environment you can use the keyboard and the mouse in conjunction to do things much faster than using either device by itself. Please Note: To use CorelDRAW properly you must have a mouse and this book assumes that you do so.

OBJECT ORIENTATED GRAPHIC

An object orientated graphic is one where the program keeps track of what objects are where by reasoning. For example, a filled square may be recorded as 'there is a black bordered square, having sides x units long, positioned at x,y which is filled with yellow'. Because the information is recorded in this fashion object orientated files can be much smaller than bit mapped ones. However, because object orientated files tend to be much more complex than bit mapped ones the files tend to be much larger. CorelDRAW normally uses only object orientated files.

CORELDRAW 4 - A USERS GUIDE

OPEN

To load a file into an application.

PASTE

Within Windows this means to insert the contents of the Clipboard at the current cursor position. You can use the shortcut **Shift-Ins** in all Windows programs.

PIXEL

A pixel, also called picture element, is the smallest area of the screen that can be independently illuminated. The number of pixels on your monitor depends on the quality of the monitor and its type, e.g. VGA monitors generally have more pixels than CGA ones.

POINT SIZES

All type is traditionally measured in Points, a single point being one Seventy Second of an inch, and this refers to the height of the characters. Until recently and the advent of laser printers all type in computer applications was measured, normally, in Pitch - the number of characters that could be squeezed into a one inch horizontal space.

POSTSCRIPT

PostScript is a form of computer language used by printers. It was invented by Adobe and it allows whole pages to be printed at high speed because it is not concerned with individual characters. All PostScript printers must therefore have a large amount of on-board RAM to handle the calculations necessary for describing and printing the page. This is especially true when using CorelDRAW - any printer must have at least 2 Mb of on-board RAM if you want to print graphics larger than A5 in a reasonable period of time.

SAVE

The action of writing a file from the current application to a disk for permanent or temporary storage using the default filename and extension. The keyboard shortcut is usually **Ctrl-S**.

SAVE AS

The action of saving a file from the current application to the disk using an alternative filename and/or extension. The keyboard shortcut is **Alt-F A**.

UNDO

To cancel the last operation. Many applications have an undo facility and how they work varies from program to program but all of them will at least allow you to annul the last act, whether it is an operation or a action, that you performed, e.g. because of an error. The keyboard shortcut is always **Alt-Backspace**.

WINDOWS

The operating system front end developed by Microsoft to enhance MS-DOS. The Windows environment is bright, colourful, intuitive and a joy to use. The most fundamentally important software development since the development of the original IBM PC and the creation of MS-DOS.

WYSIWYG

The acronym for What You See Is What You Get which is normally used to refer to word processors, though it also applies to graphic programs - especially to CorelDRAW. Basically the acronym means that any changes you make to the document will cause the display to reflect that change. The level of WYSIWYG depends on the program concerned and the quality of the monitor display and its controller. To get the best from CorelDRAW you will need, at the very least, a 16-bit VGA colour monitor running in Super VGA mode.

Equipment used

Whenever I write a book I always try to use machines that are readily available to everyone. For the purposes of this book I used the following:

a. My own personal computer. This is an AT clone made by MCA who are based in Luton. However, because I need a powerful machine it has been greatly enhanced. The machine is basically an 80486 running at 33 Mhz but it has 16 Mb of RAM, which will shortly be upgraded to 32 Mb, and a 660 Mb SCSI hard disk, partitioned into five 128 Mb logical drives. It also has a Sound Blaster Pro board which drives the CD-ROM. The monitor is a 17" Panasonic which I run at 1024 by 768 resolution with 256 colours driven by a Trident 8900C card.

    The machine runs MS-DOS 6.0 and Windows 3.1 and has been specially configured to run both at optimum levels. Windows reports 34,159 Kb of Free Memory and 86% Free Resources.

b. My standby machine is also an 80486 running at 33 Mhz. This has a Sound Blaster Pro card, a Toshiba CD-ROM drive, a 120 Mb IDE drive and 8 Mb of RAM. Unfortunately it only has a VGA monitor, driven by a VRAM II card, which I still need to upgrade. It too runs under MS-DOS 6 and Windows 3.1.

c. My own printer, a Star Micronics LaserPrinter 4 StarPage, fitted with 3 Mb of RAM. This is a PostScript clone and has been fitted with the new EPROM chips which allows it to accept downloaded Abode Type 1 fonts and TrueType fonts. It has served me very well for the last two years, during which time it has had over 25,000 pieces of paper through it - that's about 10 times the standard throughput. It has no problems printing anything from CorelDRAW.

d. A Star LaserPrinter 5 TrueImage and PostScript printer was used to produce the CRC for this book. Thanks to Start Micronics for loaning it.

VERSIONS

Corel Corporation's adherence to the pursuit of excellence has always underlined the way that the company operates. This philosophy means that you, the user, can always be sure that the company is working in your best interest to improve and enhance the software. In addition Corel has always asked for user input to new versions and they have always tried to incorporate new features based on what you have asked for. That policy continues to this day. Over the past three years there have been four major versions of the program and a number of minor upgrades.

JANUARY 1989 - CORELDRAW 1.0 RELEASED

The program had grown out of a need for quality graphics and had been developed in-house by Corel programmers. Once the program was launched demand outstripped supply by a factor of ten to one.

MARCH 1989 - VERSION 1.01

A minor upgrade that involved some program improvements and fixes. New features included the creation of a backup file when saving, the capability to draw rectangles and ellipses from the centre and an expansion of the Clip-Art library. In addition the File Menu was enhanced, the ability to handle up to 1024 nodes was added, plotter support was added, drawing of curved objects was improved, and the Illustrator import filter was improved. In addition there were a number of minor fixes.

APRIL 1989 - VERSION 1.02

The second minor upgrade which included more fixes and enhancements. The primary new feature was the ability to import IBM's PIF format files. Improvements included enhancement of the WMF export, screen views were improved, the handling of groups of objects was improved, printing to non-PostScript printers was improved. PostScript printing was also enhanced to allow images to automatically centre on the page, and the ability to reduce an image to 10% of its original size was also incorporated. PostScript export was improved and a number of fixes were included.

CORELDRAW 4 - A USERS GUIDE

JULY 1989 - CORELDRAW 1.10

The first major revision of the program was released and many new features were added. These included new fonts allowing a total of 102 different fonts from 35 typefaces; the WFNBoss font conversion utility; Windows Clipboard support to allow transfer across and between Windows programs; additional Clip-Art libraries, most of it licensed from producers; CGM import and export filters; SCODL export filter.

In addition the program included a range of improvements over previous versions which included reading TIFF Version 5.0 files, improvements to the drawing screen, the Preview Selected Only option was enhanced, the PCX import filter was improved, cropping of TIFF and PCX images was modified, Preview mode was enhanced and printing fountain fills on PostScript printers was improved. In addition there were a number of fixes from version 1.02.

FEBRUARY 1990 - VERSION 1.11

A minor upgrade that added some new features but which was primarily concerned with improving the previous version. The new features were DXF import and export; GEM import and export; WPG export capability and Video Show export. The improvements included better text spacing, correction of the A4 page size default; improved printing of dotted and dashed lines on PostScript printers. There were also a few minor fixes.

MAY 1990 - CORELDRAW 1.20

This was the second major revision of the program and a number of new features were added including the CorelTRACE conversion utility; Adobe Illustrator AI export filter, HPGL import and export filters; Mac PICT import and export filters. Improvements included the ability to copy bitmaps to the Windows Clipboard; pasting images from the Clipboard; improvements to the TIFF and PCX filters; enhancement to the EPS filter and improved display capabilities.

November 1990 - CorelDRAW 2.00

The first major revision level change to the program. It included a huge range of improvements and enhancements, far too many to list here. Essentially the entire program was rewritten, not least so that it would run exclusively under Windows 3.0.
The main new features were importing of colour bitmaps including BMP files; ability to create typefaces and symbols; printing enhancements included fountain fill definitions defined by the user; the ability to include file information in the print out; printing of multiple copies; major improvements to PostScript printing; Print Merge feature added; new page set-ups. Also included were the ability to move objects using numerical values; tenth of a degree increments for rotation of objects; transformation clearing.

A complete new menu was added - the Effects menu - that included the ability to manipulate object envelopes, perspective, blends and extrusions.

Object arrangements were enhanced and improved; there were grid and guideline enhancements; on-screen colour palette; full screen preview mode. Pattern and arrow creation from within CorelDRAW was added; the Preferences menu and dialogue boxes were enhanced; macro capability was deleted.

There were a whole host of new improvements to all of the tools and their functionality including keyboard nudges using both the Pointer and Node edit tools; Bezier curve drawing. Typeface preview was enhanced dramatically with the ability to display two characters, a range of size units, text spacing enhancements, Paragraph text capability and rapid access to the Symbol Libraries.

Improvements to the Pen tool included quick selection of some sizes; custom dashing; user defined arrows; custom outline colours. The Fill tool improvements included changes to the custom fills, bitmap fills, vector fills and fountain fills.

In addition there were major improvements to the associated programs and files. The Symbol Libraries were expanded to include over 3000 objects and the user was given the ability to add addition symbols. The Clip-Art libraries were massively enhanced and now included over 750 images organised into 14 library files accessible via Mosaic.

CorelDRAW 4 - A Users Guide

Mosaic itself was included for the first time. This is the graphic file manager utility that allows handling of multiple CDR files.

CorelTRACE was improved as was WFNBoss.

The manuals were completely rewritten and the video was redone.

May 1992 - CorelDRAW 3.0

CorelDRAW 3.0 was the first program to be totally Windows 3.1 compatible - not even Microsoft's own products can lay claim to that. Full colour editing, Blends, Extrude, Text Handling, you name it, it had it. In fact there was so much new that it would take pages to itemise it all. The floppy version of the program included 153 TrueType fonts, 4,600 symbol and clip-art images. If you used the CD-ROM version you had an additional 100 TrueType fonts, all 253 fonts in Abode Type 1 format, over 14,000 Symbol and Clip-Art images and over 100 Autodesk animation files.

CorelTRACE, the program that allows you to convert from bitmapped images to vectored ones. Full handling of GIF and TGA files was included.

CorelMOSAIC, the graphics file handling utility par excellence, had been dramatically enhanced. It could handle just about every graphics file format you care to mention; AI, BMP, CCH, CDR, DIB, EPS, GIF, PCC, PCX, SHW, SHB, TIF and TGA, all of them in full colour and at a speed that you wouldn't have thought possible.

CorelCHART was new. It allowed you to create dynamic graphical presentations from data and images. It includes its own built in data manager and the range of graph types it can generate is enormous - all of them interactively.

CorelPHOTO-PAINT was also new. It had been licenced from Z-Soft and it allowed you to do things with bitmapped images that are simply incredible.

CorelSHOW is a full blown, super-enhanced presentation graphics program. Forget about doing simple slides, this would allow you to run complete animations and slides as a single presentation. You can include sound too.

MAY 1993 - CORELDRAW 4

CorelDRAW has been further enhanced and improved. The package now contains Chart, Draw, Mosaic, Move, Photo-Paint, Show and Trace. The program interfaces of each are more closely integrated so that the tools are much the same in each application. There are now over 18,000 clip-art images and 750 fonts, also more than 125 animations and over 400 cartoon figures for CorelMOVE.

OVERALL ENHANCEMENTS

Interface Enhancements Overall, tighter integration of applications, and interfaces.

CorelDRAW Roll-up management, Preview of fonts in text roll-up. Multiple levels of undo: user specified number of levels. Drag and Drop Symbols allow quick and easy assembly of diagrams. Use of right mouse button for object menus.

CorelPHOTO-PAINT Roll-ups for tools, colours and fills.

Printing and Separations Modules share a common printing engine for enhanced printing and colour separations. On-screen print preview. Control of emulsion side (up/down). Automatic trapping. Output calibration bar, densitometer scale and device colour compensation curve. Enhanced colour separations with on screen preview of separation channels, separations on both PostScript and non-PostScript devices, optionally convert spot colours to CMYK, Monitor calibration and Auto-trapping.

Enhanced PrePress Controls including Grey component replacement, UnderColor removal, Black Point control, Dot Gain compensation, Colour Calibration and Control of registration marks.

Libraries Over 3000 additional clip-art images for use in CorelDRAW, CorelCHART and CorelPHOTO-PAINT. Now over 750 fonts in total - 650 fonts come from Bitstream, a leading font foundry known for the quality of their fonts. Extensive collection of over 125 animations, and over 400 cartoon figures for CorelMOVE actors and props. An additional 71 FLI animations. Sounds and a Multi-media tutorial.

CorelDRAW 4 - A Users Guide

CorelDRAW Desktop Publishing Features

Perform graphics oriented DTP all from within CorelDRAW! Create multi-page newsletters, brochures and documents without leaving CorelDRAW. Professionally designed templates provide a framework for newsletters, flyers, letterheads and other common applications. Create document wide layouts using the master pages. Text controls. Flow paragraph text from frame to frame. Imported text from popular word processors will automatically generate new frames and pages to fit. Envelope paragraph text to allow text to wrap around objects or inside a graphic. Complete control of Bullets, Tabs and Indents with any of over 5000 symbols as a bullet.

Vastly improved colour separations. Includes auto-trapping. Monitor calibration.

CorelDRAW Artistic Features

Quickly and easily add artistic effects with Powerlines - create lines with shapes. Create lines with variable width and shape with or without a tablet. Support for pressure sensitive tablets. Add both fill and outline to a Power line. Edit lines anytime.

Textures that imitate natural phenomena like marble or water using fractal textures. Over 30,000 variations possible on each of more than 40 textures that can automatically rescale with object. New Fills including custom fountain fills - multiple colours and Contour and conical fills.

Styles to allow easier management of complex drawings. Rapidly reformat documents with styles controlling graphic appearance, paragraph and artistic text. Use professionally designed templates to create newsletters, flyers, invitations etc.

Weld - create new objects by joining the outlines of existing objects.

CorelDRAW Technical Illustration Features

Use CorelDRAW to create floor plans, landscape designs and more.

Cloning - Create clones of a master object; as the master changes, so do clones.

Attach data to objects, keep track of costs, materials etc. by attaching information to an object, automatically consolidate data to calculate totals. Node Edit Enhancements. Drag and Drop Symbol manipulation. Dimensioning.

CORELCHART

Enhanced Data Manager Reduce or eliminate the need for a separate spreadsheet. Over 40 mathematical and financial formulae. Print directly from within the data manager. Format cells individually.

Improved Fills and Printing Output directly from within CorelCHART. Shares Draw printing and colour separation engine. Uses algorithmic textures from CorelDRAW.

CORELSHOW

Enhanced Frame Control Slides come alive with transitions which can be applied to each object with on/off transitions, each of which can be previewed. Change the shape of a frame. Animations play within a frame. Multiple backgrounds per presentation.

Cues Create interactive presentations, responding to your audience. Allow branching and complete control of a running show with simple scripting. Any object or action can act as a cue.

Timelines Rapidly assemble a multimedia presentation. Allow synchronisation of frames, slides, sounds and animations.

Miscellaneous Support for FLI/FLC, Quicktime for Windows, CorelMOVE animations.

CORELDRAW 4 - A USERS GUIDE

CORELPHOTO-PAINT

Image Editing Easily input images directly into CorelPHOTO-PAINT. Direct scanner support. Support of Twain interface. Enhanced image correction filters. Support of popular scanners.

Painting New artistic features for image creation. Canvas or paper texture. Brushes and filters to imitate artistic styles. Brush strokes. Dots. Fountain fills. Improved masking.

Output Monitor calibration. Colour calibration. Colour separations.

CORELMOVE

CorelMOVE creates multimedia animations containing sound, graphics and 2D animated actors. These animations are ideal for presentations, entertainment and interactive demos. CorelMOVE animations consist of animated actors which move along a path; each actor can also cycle through a number of cels.

Create Animations Easily Libraries and familiar tools to get you started. Extensive libraries of professionally designed actors and props. Just point and click to assemble your own animations.

Path based animations let you control where the actors go - simply sketch out a line for the actor to follow. Add or delete nodes of the path, and automatically smooth and distribute points. Start with a rough sketch, and use the tools to create a polished look.

Create multi-cel actors easily using the familiar tools of CorelDRAW. Provides the convenience and flexibility of working with vector illustrations. Use CorelPHOTO-PAINT to create props and single-cel actors.

Choose from 14 transitions for props, to allow text and graphics to appear and disappear. Add any .WAV sound file into your animation. Customise the sounds using the CorelMOVE Sound Editor. Import existing animations from .FLC and .AVI formats. Export to FLC, AVI formats, or use the standalone player to distribute your animations.

Powerful and complete animation tools Use CorelDRAW and CorelPHOTO-PAINT tools to create actors. Graphical timelines allow co-ordination of actors, sounds and props. Turn objects on or off, and control when they enter and exit a scene. Specialised tools for actor creation include Onion Skin, so that previous cel is visible during the creation of a new cel. Tweening allows automatic generation of new cels while the actor is rotated, scaled and flipped.

Synchronise actor's motions to specific frames using the Cel Synchroniser. Create interactive animations using menu driven cues. Any object can act as a button. Pause or stop the animation, or branch to a new animation.

Extensive libraries of professionally designed animations include mix and match elements.

CORELTRACE

Complete Document Conversion in one package.

Direct scanning support Scan and trace from within the same module. Direct scanner support. Support of Twain interface. Support of popular scanners. Use CorelPHOTO-PAINT to touch up scanned bitmaps before tracing.

Optical Character Recognition Create editable text from scanned images. Automatically recognises text from scanned images. Maintains position on page. Special optimisations for faxed documents and dot matrix output. Form processing identifies text, layout of forms and graphics - all in one step.

Enhanced Tracing On screen colour feedback; works with up to 24 bit colour. Allow use of CorelPHOTO-PAINT to touch up scanned bitmaps before tracing. Straighten horizontal and vertical lines. New tracing methods: woodcut creates a half toned traced image with lines drawn across it at a specified angle. Silhouette traces outlines of a selected area and creates an object filled with specified colour. Select area to be traced using a marquee selection, or by choosing similar colours (magic wand selection). Save images directly as .BMP, .TXT (text files) or .EPS (traced files). OLE client. Multiple levels of undo.

CorelDRAW 4 - A Users Guide

CorelMOSAIC

Organise and visually manage files. Create catalogues of non-compressed files to easily track and organise artwork. Catalogues store a thumbnail image of files, along with any keywords, and pointers to the files. This makes it easy to group related files together without necessarily physically moving them around, and provides improved performance when dealing with large amounts of clip-art.

Create archives of compressed files to conserve disk space. Display multiple windows simultaneously (like the Windows File Manager) to compare catalogues and libraries. Drag and Drop files from one window to another to quickly copy or move files between catalogues and libraries. Drag and Drop between libraries to simplify document management. Start applications from within Mosaic - both Corel programs and other applications.

1. BEFORE YOU START

In order to get the best from CorelDRAW, or from any other program for that matter, you have to have your computer properly organised. This means that you have to have enough memory and free contiguous disk space at the very least. The vast majority of problems that people encounter when running CorelDRAW are due to the fact that their computers are not configured properly in the first place.

One of the main problems that people have today is a lack of knowledge of MS-DOS. After all why should they know how to use it? The machine will normally come from the dealer already set up, the operating system will have been installed, in some cases Windows will have been installed and maybe other software too. Therefore everything should be okay. Kindly note the word 'should'. Unfortunately what should be and what actually is can be two vastly different things.

It's a bit like owning a car. I can drive my car, and have been doing so for years, but I can't do any major repairs to it. I have no mechanical ability whatsoever. But I can change the tyres, replace the fan belt, put in oil, petrol and water and so on. I've even replaced an engine on one occasion - albeit with someone else giving me directions. The point is that I don't know how to fix the car - I pay someone else to do that. The problem arises with the person being paid. How do you know that they will repair the car correctly? The answer is, very often, that you don't. You have to go on hearsay and other people's opinions.

The same thing applies to computers. Generally speaking you have to rely on someone else to make it work correctly. But how do you know that they will? Unfortunately you cannot. And that causes a major problem. I get a number of calls each week that usually begin with "I have the dealer here. Can you talk him through what he has to do?" I always want to answer "Why? You're paying him to do it not me" but I never do. Unfortunately there seem to be a lot of people who call themselves dealers and/or consultants who think that just because they can run a program that's all they need to know. This doesn't apply to everyone, there are a number of dealers who take a pride in what they do and they will always put the customer first. If you can find one of them they are worth their weight in gold.

Having got all that off my chest, as it were, we can now get on with this chapter which is divided into four parts:

CorelDRAW 4 - A Users Guide

a. MS-DOS and machine configuration.
This includes a sample CONFIG.SYS and AUTOEXEC.BAT file and looks at the various ways that the computer can be set up.

b. Disk management.
This will quickly run through basic good disk management and hard disk utilities, what to do with them and when.

c. Windows 3.1.
A quick overview of Windows and the INI file.

d. Fonts and more fonts.
The different types of fonts, how to install and use them.

You don't have to read any of it if you don't want to but I suggest that you do because it has been condensed down from countless user questions and so it will give you a head start. However, none of the sections are intended to be definitive. There are a number of good books around about each part - I've written a some of them myself - that will cover the elements in much greater detail than there is room to do here. What the sections will give you is sufficient overview so that you can configure your machine for yourself or at the very least check what your dealer has done.

MS-DOS and Configuration

Both my computers run under MS-DOS 6.0 and before that they used version 5.0. I've been using 6.0 for some months - I helped beta test it - and it hasn't given me any problems. The transition from 5.0 to 6.0 was fairly faultless apart from a minor problem with the MemMaker, and that was partly my fault.

The advantage of MS-DOS 6.0 is that it virtually configures the machine for you and it is intended to integrate fully with Windows 3.1. The problem with it is that it configures itself! I know this sounds like a contradiction but it isn't. Whenever anything configures itself it is likely to cause you problems simply because no two computers are the same. The result is that with MS-DOS 6.0 you have to play around a little with the CONFIG.SYS and AUTOEXEC.BAT to tweak them.

Installing MS-DOS 6.0 is simple, just run the SETUP program. However, make sure you do a Custom Setup. Never, but never, allow anything to do a complete installation all by itself - otherwise you don't know what's going on. It's your computer and you should know what happening with it. Therefore you should always use Custom Setup - the same thing applies to CorelDRAW.

Once you have installed MS-DOS you find that you have a new CONFIG.SYS and AUTOEXEC.BAT. Check these out and save them to a floppy disk. The next thing to do is run the MemMaker program. This will reconfigure your CONFIG.SYS and optimise the memory for you. Just type **MEMMAKER** and follow the instructions that will appear on screen. It's actually very good and the closest thing to a valid self-configuration program that you can currently get.

Once the program has run you can then edit the new CONFIG.SYS again and then rerun MemMaker. You may need to do this about three times but the law of diminishing returns applies and thereafter it's not worth running it again. At the end of the day you are never going to get it perfect anyway so you just have to aim for the best you can get.

Consider this, it is the CONFIG.SYS off my main system after going through the process above.

```
FILES=30
BUFFERS=10,0
DEVICE=C:\DOS\HIMEM.SYS
DEVICE=C:\DOS\EMM386.EXE NOEMS
DOS=HIGH,UMB
DEVICEHIGH /L:2,12048 =C:\DOS\SETVER.EXE
DEVICEHIGH /L:2,5888 =C:\DOS\RAMDRIVE.SYS 4096/E
DEVICEHIGH /L:2,10960 =C:\DOS\SBPCD.SYS /D:MSCD001 /P:220
COUNTRY=044,,C:\DOS\COUNTRY.SYS
FCBS=16,8
LASTDRIVE=I
STACKS=9,256
SHELL=C:\DOS\COMMAND.COM C:\DOS\ /P
```

The machine has 16 Mb of RAM and a Sound Blaster Pro card which drives the CD-ROM. The SCSI hard disk is transparent to the operating system and so it doesn't need anything special. The order that the lines appear in is very important - not many people realise that but it is true. This is what it means:

FILES refers to the maximum number of separate files that MS-DOS can have open at any one time, in this case 30. If you are using a file intensive program, e.g. a database, then this number will probably need to be increased. The problem with it is that each additional file you add uses memory. By default the operating system is intended to use 8 files, the absolute minimum. Every additional file over and above that takes up 39 bytes of memory. Not a lot really but the 30 files above means that the amount of base memory used is increased by nearly 1 Kb. As Windows is memory intensive you need to keep as much of it free as possible.

BUFFERS is a sort of poor man's disk cache. You have to have a minimum number based on the type of processor you are using and the amount of memory plus the type of hard disk. When you install Windows it should default to 10 buffers which is all it needs because SMARTDRV, a real disk caching program, makes the buffers command largely redundant - although not totally. Each buffer takes up 528 bytes of the base memory, so a value of 10 takes up over 5 Kb of RAM.

HIMEM.SYS is vital if you want to use Windows because it is a memory manager. It has to be loaded as a device. By putting it directly after the files and buffers you are allowing the memory to be used to the best advantage. Himem must be the first device that you load and it cannot be loaded into high memory because it is Himem that makes the high memory available.

DOS=HIGH,UMB loads the main part of the operating system in high memory - that part of the memory above the 640 Kb base limit and below the 1 Mb extended memory range. The UMB part of the line means Upper Memory Blocks. If you omit this part of the line then you cannot place other device drivers into the upper memory area.

EMM386 is only needed on computers based on the 80386 cr 80486 Intel chips. The line must follow the previous one. It provides access to the high memory area again and it is this which manages how the memory is allocated and used. The command has a huge range of possible parameters which we're not going to go into here. The only parameter I use is NOEMS which means no expanded memory. This is because Windows works best with extended memory.

SETVER is needed to operate the CD-ROM drive. It is a special file that causes some programs to be given false information about things. You can actually edit it from the system prompt if you have to. The command is loaded into high memory, that's what the DEVICEHIGH means, but it doesn't take up much room. The extra values after the device high are simply the locations in memory that the file is loaded to. I use MemMaker to define them.

The next line, **RAMDRIVE**, creates a virtual drive using memory. Don't use this if you have less than 16 Mb of RAM on your machine. If you have only 8 Mb of memory then leave as much of it free as possible and Windows will use nearly all of it. If you have less than 8 Mb of RAM then the best thing you can do is go and buy some memory and add it to your computer. You can run Windows with 4 Mb of memory but it's like driving a car with the hand brake on all the time. In my case I create a 4 Mb Ramdrive, which is actually a bit small, and then I use it as the temporary storage area. At times this causes some programs to crash because I run out of space. CorelDRAW in particular can create temporary files of 10 Mb or more. The /E parameter means the Ramdrive uses extended memory.

CorelDRAW 4 - A Users Guide

The next line initialises the Sound Blaster card and allows it to run the CD-ROM drive.

COUNTRY simply sets the national characteristics of the system, in this case it sets it to the U.K. so I can get a £ sign by pressing Shift-3.

FCBS stands for File Control Blocks. These are data structures that MS-DOS needs and the number specifies how many can be used at any one time. The values on my system are the defaults that MS-DOS set up and as they work I've never bothered to change them.

LASTDRIVE is necessary if you have more than 5 drives connected to your computer. MS-DOS will handle up to five drives automatically, Drive-A and B are floppies, Drive-C is the first partition of a hard disk - the one that the machine boots from. Drive-D and E can be anything. In my case because my hard disk is partitioned into 128 Mb chunks it uses the letters C to G. The Ramdrive is Drive-H and the CD-ROM is Drive-I. So you have to tell MS-DOS that this is how many drives it has to handle. Don't be tempted to add extra drive letters because each one uses memory.

STACKS is used by Windows. Under version 3.0 you had to have this set to 0,0 but Windows 3.1 wants 9,256 so that's what it gets.

The final line, **SHELL**, simply sets the parameters by which Windows can recognise where the command system file is. Whether you include it or not is optional.

That's the CONFIG.SYS sorted. All in all it is fairly basic and as standard as you are liable to get, the only odd bits are the Ramdrive and Sound Blaster lines.

The second configuration file is the AUTOEXEC.BAT and there is even less likelihood of there being a standard one of these because no two people use the same things in the same order. For reference mine reads:

```
@ECHO OFF
CLS
PATH C:\DOS;C:\;C:\WINDOWS;C:\UTIL;C:\WWORD;C:\ALDUS
LH /L:2,46576 C:\DOS\MSCDEX /V /M:15 /D:MSCD001
LH /L:0;2,42400 /S C:\DOS\SMARTDRV.EXE
```

```
LH /L:2,15904 C:\DOS\KEYB UK,,C:\DOS\KEYBOARD.SYS
LH /L:2,13984 C:\DOS\SHARE.EXE
MD H:\TEMP
SET TEMP=H:\TEMP
REM SET TEMP=C:\TEMP
SET BLASTER=A220 I7 D1 T4
SET SOUND=C:\SBPRO
C:\DOS\SBP-SET /M:15 /VOC:15 /CD:15 /FM:15
PROMPT $P$G
VERIFY ON
CLS
PATH
DIR/W
```

The first line simply stops the screen displaying things and the second clears the screen. The rest are what is important, at least as far as my machine is concerned.

The **PATH** line simply includes those sub-directories that I need to be able to access. Notice that each one also has a drive letter - necessary if you use multiple drives.

The **MSCDEX** line is necessary so I can use the CD-ROM, it actually refers to the MS-DOS Extensions. I've never amended it, that's the way it was added when I first installed the CD-ROM drive. The **LH** means Load High, i.e. into the high memory area. Again the values are memory locations. Under MS-DOS 5.0 I wasn't able to get the MS-DOS Extensions loaded into high memory.

SMARTDRV is the disk caching program that comes with Windows 3.1 and MS-DOS. The one that comes with MS-DOS 6.0 is the latest and so that's the one you should use.

KEYBOARD.SYS is the compliment to the Country line of the CONFIG.SYS.

SHARE allows the running of multiple copies of things like CorelDRAW, Word for Windows and so on. It's essential for CorelDRAW 4.

MD H:\TEMP and **SET TEMP=H:\TEMP** creates a sub-directory called Temp in the Ramdrive and then assigns all temporary files to it.

The **REM** line is a standby. When a program crashes because of lack of space for the temp files I remove the word REM from the front of this line and instead place it in front of the previous two. Then I reboot the machine. Most of the time, though, I can get away with using the Ramdrive for temp storage.

The next three lines are all to do with the Sound Blaster card, setting various parameters for it.

PROMPT PG is fairly standard and causes the system cursor to show the drive letter and the sub-directory.

VERIFY is an internal MS-DOS command that causes it to check that a file has been written properly to the disk. Don't put in a line saying verify off because it is off by default.

The remaining lines just tidy things up whenever the system is rebooted. **DS** is Norton Directory Sort and it makes sure that all files are in alphabetical order. The screen then clears, displays the Path and then the directories of Drive-C.

DISK MANAGEMENT

At long last MS-DOS has a disk defragmenter built into it. It's actually a cut down version of Norton Speed Disk but at least it does allow you to defragment your hard disk. This is probably one of the most important and vital operations that anyone can do with a computer - especially if they want to run CorelDRAW.

MS-DOS Defrag will do the job for you, at a minimum level, sufficiently well for your hard disk to be neat and tidy. If you want better performance you are going to have to buy some disk utilities, either Norton Utilities or PC Tools. Both sets of utilities contain roughly the same basic programs and it becomes purely a matter of choice which one you use. I have both and so I can pick and choose elements from each. I must admit that I prefer PC Tools Compress to Norton's Speed Disk though because it is about four times faster. If you can only afford one set of utilities then you will have to find reviews of them and select whichever you think is the best for your situation.

But why do you need to defragment the hard disk in the first place? That takes a little explanation but the concept is very simple. When MS-DOS writes a file to disk it does so by allocating sectors of the disk to hold the file. The sectors, which are the smallest usable parts of the disk, are allocated in groups of two or four (depending on the type of disk you have) called Clusters. Imagine your disk looked something like this:- the X's are used clusters and the O's are empty ones:

```
XXXOXXXXXXOOOOXXXXXOOOXXXXOXXXOXOOOXXXXOOOOOOXXX
XXXXOOOOOXXXOOOXXOOOXXXXOOXXXOXOXOXOXOXOXOXOXXXOO
OOOOXXXXXXXXXXXXXXXXOOOOOOOOOOOOOOOOOOOOOOOOOOXX
```

Now you want to write a file that takes up twelve clusters. What happens is that MS-DOS places as much of the file in the first empty clusters it can find and then puts another part of the file in the next blank cluster area, then some more of the file is placed in the next set of clusters, and finally the balance of the file is written to the next empty area. So you end up with something like this:

```
XXX**XXXXXXXXXXXX**XXXXXX**XX**XXXXX**XXX**XXX**XXX**OXXXXOOOOOOXXX
XXXXOOOOOXXXOOOXXOOOXXXXOOXXXOXOXOXOXOXOXOXOXXXOO
OOOXXXXXXXXXXXXXXXXOOOOOOOOOOOOOOOOOOOOOOOOOOXX
```

The bold X's are the file that has just been written. That's okay because MS-DOS knows where the file is stored and can therefore access it. But - it takes time to do so because the Read/Write heads of the disk have to physically move to find the necessary clusters when you want to load the file. A file that is stored like this is called Fragmented on Non-contiguous.

A defragmenter program rearranges the files on your hard disk so that all files are stored in adjacent clusters, so on our theoretical disk you could end up with something like this:

XXX**XXXXXXXXXXXXX**XXXXXXXXXXXXXXXXXXXXXXXXXXXXXXXXXXXXXX
XXXXXXXXXXXXXXXXXXXXXXXXXXXXXXXXXXXXXXXXXOOOOOOOOOOOOO
OOOOOOOOOOOOOOOOOOOOOOOOOOOOOOOOOOOOOOOOOOOOOOO

The files are now stored in adjacent clusters, i.e. they are contiguous - which simply means touching, and all the empty clusters, i.e. the free space, are now at the end of the disk. This makes finding and loading files faster. It might only be milliseconds but it's milliseconds per file and over the course of a day the difference is actually measurable.

The first time you run a defragmenter program it can take ages, anything up to an hour depending on the size of the partition and the number of files it contains. But if you run it daily thereafter it can take less than a minute a day. The difference in speed that it gives you is well worth the time.

But what happens when you delete the file you've just written? The answer is you end up with a set of empty clusters in the contiguous area and that causes the problem all over again. The answer is that you run the defragmentation program daily. If you do a lot of file deletion or moving then you run the defragmentation program once you have done so. Get into a routine. At the end of every day, I run PC Tools Compress on all my drives and then I run a batch file that runs MIRROR on the whole lot. (Mirror is another utility that is part of MS-DOS, and PC Tools, that notes where all the files are on the hard disk so you can reinstate any files you accidentally delete.) That means that every morning my hard disks are fully contiguous before I start doing anything. It only takes about five minutes to do all five drives but it is time well spent.

Another reason why defragmenting files is so important has to do with Windows. Any Windows applications, and Windows itself for that matter, will create temporary files as it is operating. These are normally stored in a directory called, logically enough, TEMP. This directory, by the way, should always be sub-tended directly off the root of your hard disk - on Drive-C for preference but it can be another hard disk.

The important thing about TEMP files, they actually have an extension of TMP, is that they **MUST** be contiguous. One of the main reasons for Windows applications crashing is because the program cannot write its temp files into a contiguous space. If you ever get a #5000 series error message from CorelDRAW that's what it means. There isn't enough contiguous disk space for the temp file.

Another thing to bear in mind is the size of temp files. They can be very large depending on what you do. Some CorelDRAW temp files can be anything up to 12 MEGABYTES. I'll grant that this is rare but it can happen, especially if you are using a file with lots of text and complex fill patterns. That means that in order to run CorelDRAW comfortably you should allow at least 10 Mb of free contiguous disk space for the temp files. The key word there is Contiguous. Use MS-DOS Defrag or Norton Speed Disk or PC Tools Compress daily.

While we're on the subject of disks, do yourself a favour and don't use any kind of disk compression program. MS-DOS comes complete with a program called DblSpace which, theoretically, allows you to store more files on your hard disk in the same amount of space by squashing the files into less space. There are also a couple of proprietary program on the market that do the same thing. At best all of these can be considered as stop gap measures but they can never replace a true hard disk.

If you are running out of disk space then buy another hard disk. They are not expensive and they last for a lifetime with a bit of care and attention. Always buy a disk that is larger than your current needs. A good rule of thumb is to work out what size you actually need and then double it. And you should always round the size up - never down.

Consider this. You want a new hard disk that will take MS-DOS, that's 8 Mb if you install all of it; Windows 3.1, that's another 10 Mb or so depending on your system; and CorelDRAW 4, that's roughly 35 Mb give or take a little. Add that lot up and you get 43 Mb. Add to that the Windows Virtual Memory file, which for a 486 system with 8 MB of RAM is around 15 Mb, plus the space necessary for the temp file storage, i.e. 10 to 12 Mb. The total then is 70 Mb near as damn it. That's the basic size you want.

Now double it which gives you 140 Mb. Round it up a little and you have 200 Mb. That's the size of disk you actually want. Right now you only need 70 Mb of it but within a year you could well find yourself needing more space.

A 200 Mb drive will cost you somewhere in the region of £250, depending on how much looking around you are prepared to do. It takes minutes to install and will last you for the life of the computer.

A disk compression program will cost you anything up to half the price of the drive. The problem arises because your disk compression program doesn't in reality actually give you any more space. In addition it slows down your system because the files have to be squished and unsquished behind the scenes as it were. That takes time - a measurable amount when you are dealing with lots of files - and time is at a premium. It also takes much longer to defragment a system that uses file compression techniques.

So the moral of the story is - Buy a new hard disk when you start running out of space. It will serve you much better in the long run. A rule of thumb is that whenever you have 10% or less of your current disk free then you need a new one.

WINDOWS 3.1

Windows sits on top of the operating system, and operates in conjunction with it, which is why it is important to get MS-DOS configured properly first. Once that is done you can get on with installing Windows. Whenever you install Windows you should always load the basic configuration and the standard VGA display option. The reason is that VGA is so standard that it is an absolute. Windows, and every Windows application, will always work in VGA mode so you install this first. When you have Windows up and running you can then add additional drivers for other monitor displays using Windows Setup.

CorelDRAW 4 is designed to run under Windows 3.1 so please don't try running it under earlier versions. If you have a CD-ROM drive and Windows on CD-ROM then the installation is simplicity itself - it takes about 8 minutes! If you are limited to using floppy disks then it takes much longer. (I just wish everything came on CD-ROM!)

There are a couple of things that you should be aware of. Firstly, printer drivers. Most manufacturers now produce specific drivers for their own printers and they will happily supply you with these if you ask for them. In addition Microsoft have updated the PostScript driver. The latest version, at the time of writing, is 3.55. The updated driver is available from Microsoft free of charge - you just have to ask for it. The simplest way to add the new driver is to install Windows as standard, with whatever printer driver you need, and then manually copy the new driver later.

Secondly, Windows 3.1 will automatically install a range of TrueType fonts for you and you have no choice about whether or not they are installed. See the next section for details of fonts.

Thirdly, Windows will automatically install itself for English - American, even though you have asked for something else. So you have to change it later.

1   Once you have Windows installed you should run the Windows Control Panel and then double click on **International**. This will bring up a separate window:

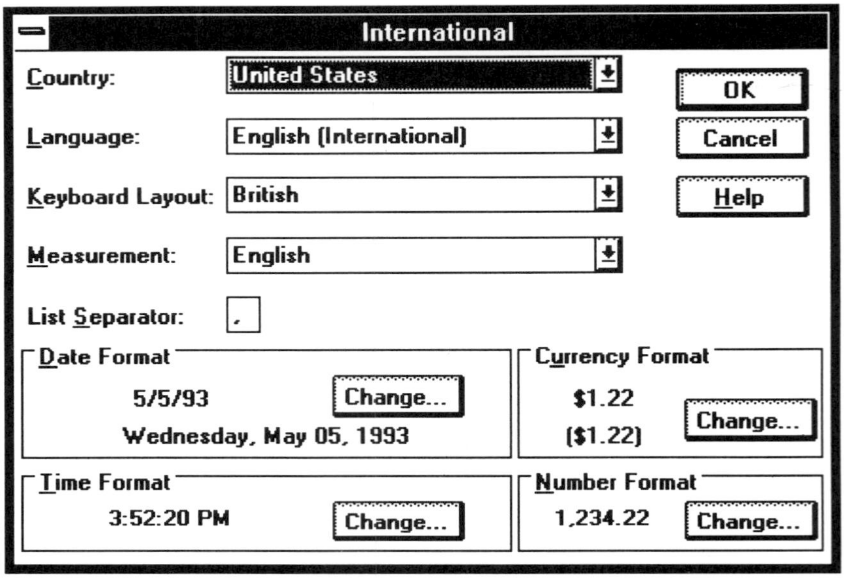

1.01 Control Panel - International

2   Regardless of the fact that you selected to Windows install itself with a U.K. keyboard it will always default to the United States. Therefore you have to change it to United Kingdom. Just press **Up** once, because Country is already highlighted, and then press **Enter**.

You can now configure Windows itself any which way you please. Add additional monitor drivers, using Windows Setup; add more printer drivers, using Control Panel; change the colours, icon spacing and desktop, also using Control Panel.

In addition it is worth adding a new program to the Windows environment - the System Editor. This allows you to amend the CONFIG.SYS, AUTOEXEC.BAT, WIN.INI and SYSTEM.INI quickly and easily. The program is installed on your hard disk automatically but it is not added as an icon.

3   At the Program Manager, press **Alt-F N Enter** or open the **File** menu and then click on **New** then press **Enter**, and a dialogue box appears. Type **System Editor** on the top line, press **Tab** and then type **SYSEDIT.EXE** on the second line. Press **Enter** again.

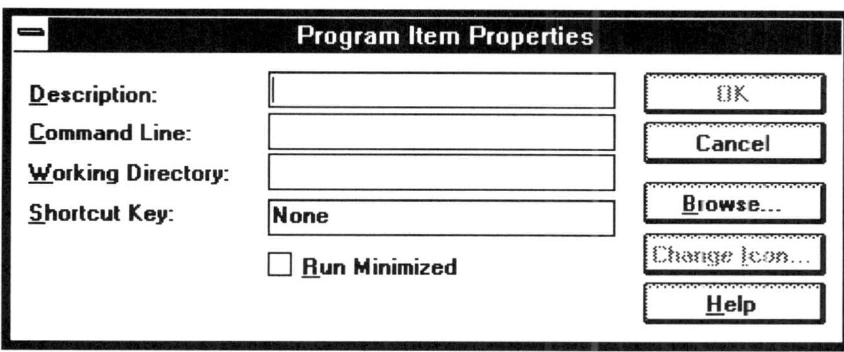

1.02 New Item dialogue box

4   A new icon appears in whatever group window is currently active. You can move or copy this to wherever you wish. Now either double click on the icon or highlight it and then press **Enter**. The full program window will appear.

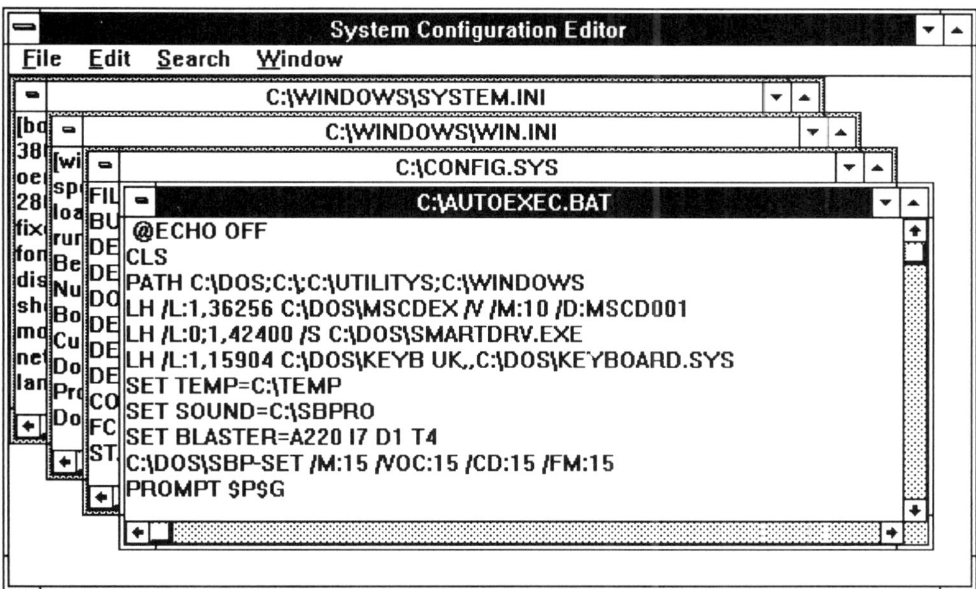

1.03 System Editor window

5   The program window contains four sub-windows, one each for the four system files. Move the **WIN.INI** one to the front. Scroll down through the file until you come to the section that says **[PostScript,LPT1]**. Now you should add a line saying **LandscapeOrient=270**. This causes rotated files to be printed properly.

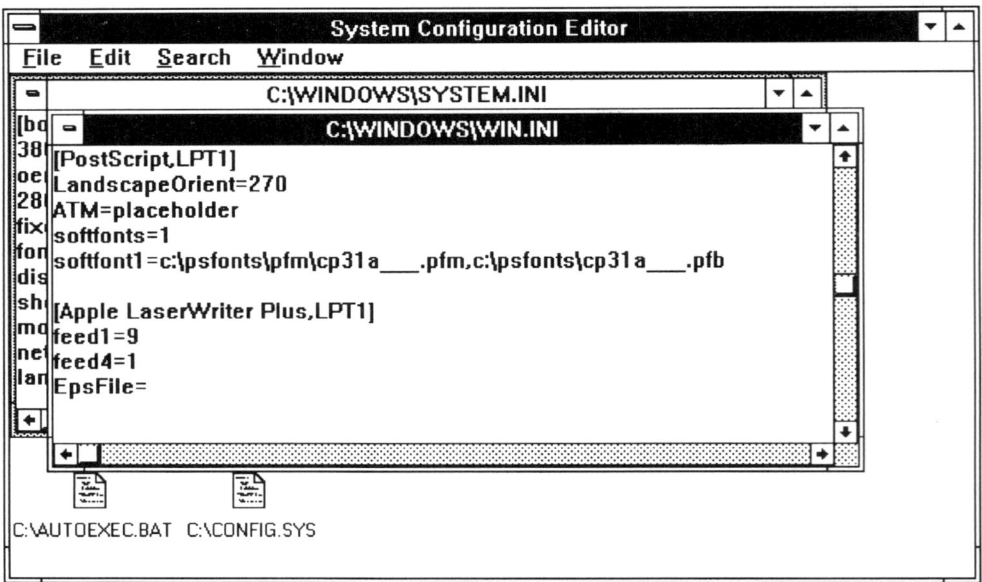

1.04 Line added to WIN.INI

6   You need to add the line to any PostScript printer definition that the WIN.INI contains. You need to add the line especially if you are wanting to print EPS files on a landscape page. If you don't put the line in then the EPS file will be printed in the wrong place on the page and it may also be turned through ninety degrees. Close the system editor once you have saved the file.

One other thing that you should check is the size of the **Virtual Memory**, formerly called the Swapfile, that Windows is using. When you install Windows in the first place it can grab a huge amount of the available disk space for the swapfile - anything up to 25% of the available contiguous space. Generally speaking this will be incorrect and you have to manually amend it.

There are no hard and fast rules about how large the swapfile should be but you should make it at least 10 Mb. I set mine up so that the size of the swapfile, in my case it's around 24 Mb, and the amount of memory that the machine has adds up to the amount of Free Memory displayed in the **Help, About** dialogue box.

7   In Program Manager click on **Help** and then on **About**. A message box appears like this:

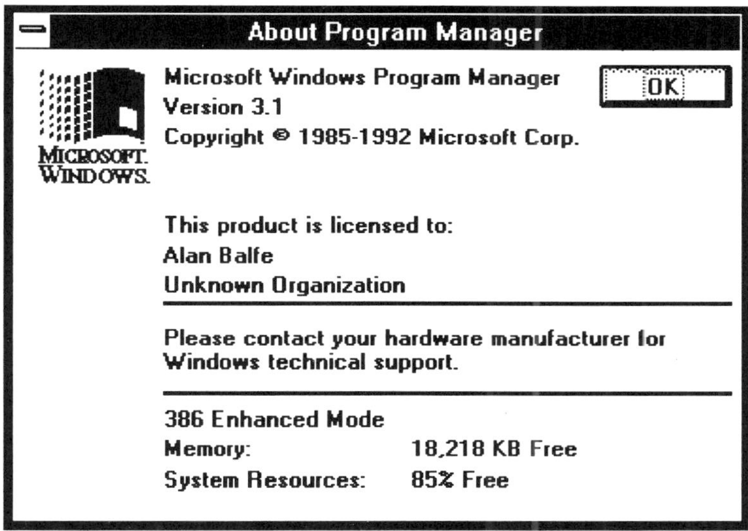

1.05 Help About message box

In the case of my backup machine, which is where the illustration comes from, you can see that there is just under 10 Mb of Free Memory - this figure refers both to the RAM and the swapfile. This particular machine has 7 Mb of free RAM - a figure to bear in mind. (You need to know how much free RAM your own system has.)

8   To change the Virtual Memory size, run **Windows Control Panel** and then double click on **386 Enhanced**. A dialogue box appears:

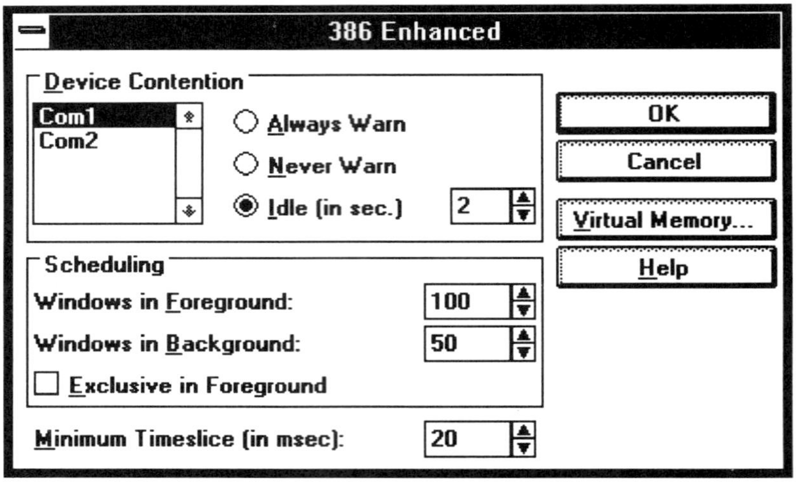

1.06 386 Enhanced dialogue box

9   Click on **Virtual Memory** or press **Alt-V**. A new dialogue box appears. Click
     on **Change** to expand this.

Because there is already a permanent swapfile on this machine, the change option
automatically suggests a temporary one. You don't normally want to do this. You
should create a Permanent swapfile but you must have defragmented your hard disk
first because the swapfile must be in contiguous space. You can place the swapfile
on any partition that is available on your system but it does work better, and gives
you a slight speed advantage, if you place it on Drive-C.

10   Change the value to, say, **10240** and then click on **OK**. A message box will
     appear asking if you are sure you want to do this. Just click on **Yes** or press
     Enter. Then another dialogue box appears telling you that the Windows needs
     to be rebooted. Just press **Enter**.

11   Once Windows reboots click on **Help** and then **About** again. Check the amount
     of free memory. Does the value given equal, roughly, the amount of free RAM
     you have added to the size of the swapfile you have just created? For example,
     I have just created a 10 Mb swapfile and the machine has 7 Mb of free RAM.
     But when I look at Help, About it tells me that I have only got 18,430 Kb of free

memory. Therefore the swapfile is about right. You're never going to get the figure exact but you should be able to get close. The net result is that you have to fiddle around with different swapfile sizes until the value displayed in Help, About is roughly what you know you have.

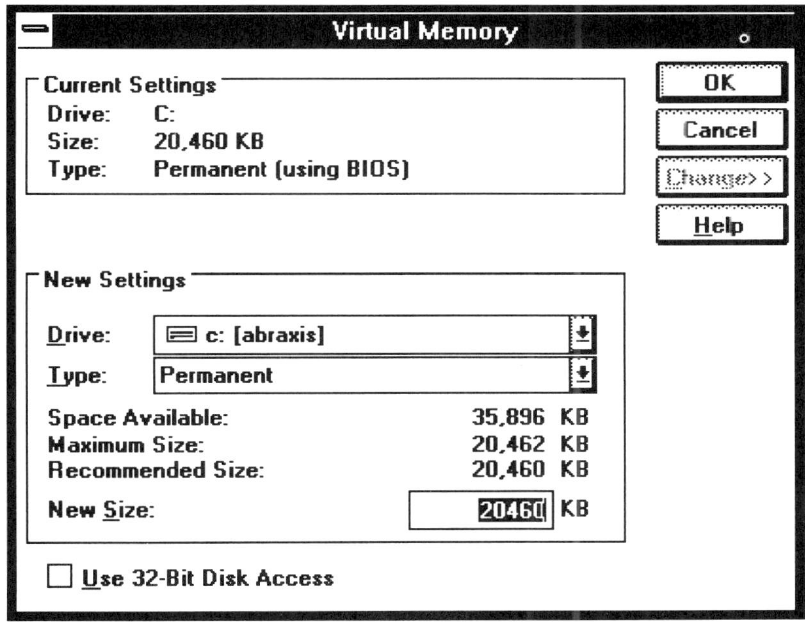

1.07 Virtual Memory dialogue box

Change the swapfile value in small steps, e.g. about 1 Mb at a time, until Windows gets it roughly right. On my main machine the swapfile is 24 Mb. This does not give a true figure but it gives the optimum performance. The problem is that there comes a point where the swapfile can end up being much larger than the amount of free memory reported by Help, About. For example, if I create a 35 Mb swapfile on my main machine then Windows reports 34,202 Kb of free memory. This is smaller than the swapfile itself and this machine has 11 Mb of free RAM!

Ultimately you will probably never get the figure just right but you should be able to get close. You just have to play with it and see what happens. Be wary of creating a swapfile that is too large because that can actually slow Windows down.

You are more likely not to have sufficient space to create the right size of swapfile, most people don't have enough free space on their hard disk to play with lots of different values. The following figures are rough guidelines to swapfile sizes, based on the amount of RAM fitted to a machine, and they have been worked out over a number of months by different people. They are not intended to be hard and fast rules, they are guidelines for you to consider.

4 Mb RAM	8 Mb swapfile
6 Mb RAM	10 Mb swapfile
8 Mb RAM	12 Mb swapfile
10 Mb RAM	15 Mb swapfile
12 Mb RAM	18 Mb swapfile
16 Mb RAM	24 Mb swapfile
20 Mb RAM	26 Mb swapfile
32 Mb RAM	30 Mb swapfile

Obviously you can only create a permanent swapfile is you have sufficient available space but it is strongly recommended that you do make a permanent virtual memory file - it works much better than a temporary one.

Fonts and Typefaces

Before we go any further there is a matter of definition to be cleared up concerning typefaces and fonts. The two words are not interchangeable - they refer to different things.

A Typeface is a design of type created by a person. It encompasses all the variations within that type. Common typeface names are Helvetica, Times Roman, Palatino, Zapf Dingbats. In essence a typeface is a family name, like your surname. Typefaces are usually copyright.

A Font is a sub-set of a typeface. This sub-set can be any variation within the main family. For example, Helvetica Bold and Helvetica Italic are two different fonts. But a font can also be a variation on the size. So Helvetica Bold 10 Point and Helvetica Bold 12 Point are two different fonts. In essence a font is an individual member of the typeface family.

Windows 3.1 comes complete with a range of different types of fonts and typefaces.

Some of these are intended solely for display purposes, they have an extension of .FON. The number of these you have installed will depend on how many monitor drivers you have loaded because you may need different FON files for different resolutions.

Others are downloadable fonts, i.e. ones you can print. Unfortunately these are not really scaleable and they won't work too well if you try to use them at any sizes other than those which they are intended to be used at.

Finally there are TrueType fonts which are fully scaleable, i.e. you can use then at virtually any size.

You cannot select fonts to be loaded during the installation process, they will all be installed automatically and then you have to remove the ones you don't want afterwards.

But before you do that there are some things to consider first. I must say here and now that I don't like TrueType fonts - and I've yet to meet anyone who does - and so this is biased! There are people who use them because they have no choice but they don't necessarily like them. I use Adobe Type Manager instead for the following reasons.

In order for any character of to be displayed on your monitor it has to be drawn on the screen. This process takes a measurable amount of time, albeit that it is so fast you cannot see it in action. In order to do so all fonts and typefaces have built in control points. These define how the line between two adjacent control points will appear - in a similar way to the nodes in CorelDRAW. Adobe Type 1 fonts have 54 control points for each character. TrueType fonts have 72 control points.

Theoretically the more control points there are the better the definition. But the lines between the control points take time to display. In addition the more control points the more memory is required for each character. Because TrueType have a third more control points they can take 30% longer to display - again you won't necessarily see this in action but it is true nonetheless. With a large block of text you may actually see the difference - depending on your monitor and the graphics card you are using.

When it comes to printing the whole thing gets even sillier. All laser printers, and the majority of all other types, will accept Adobe Type 1 fonts sent to them via the Adobe Type Manager. The fonts have to be rendered first and then downloaded as bitmaps but they will print. With PostScript printers the fonts are sent directly, without any rendering.

But what happens with TrueType fonts? If you have a True Image printer, which is highly unlikely because there are only about two manufacturers in the world who make them, then the TrueType fonts will be downloaded as they are. If you have an ordinary non-PostScript printer then the fonts will be rendered to bitmaps and downloaded that way. If you have a PostScript printer then the TrueType fonts will be converted to Adobe Type 1 format for printing!

So, if you don't have a True Image printer the fonts are going to be converted to Adobe Type 1 format anyway but in the meantime they take a lot of memory and resources from your system. In addition, having lots of TrueType fonts installed will slow down your system's performance by a highly noticeable degree whereas ATM fonts won't. So why not just use Adobe Type 1 in the first place?

That's just what I do. I have Adobe Type Manager Version 2.5 and I only use Adobe Type 1 typefaces and fonts. They take less memory and resources than TrueType does, they display faster, they don't need any conversion to print. All in all they are better. You don't have to agree with me, this is a personal preference after all but it is based on how the fonts perform. Make up your own mind. Because I have a CD-ROM drive I can also use the CorelDRAW fonts in ATM format which helps.

There is one other point to bear in mind. There are well over 10,000 Adobe Type 1 fonts currently available, and more are added every week. As yet there are very few TrueType fonts and the majority of the ones that are available are converted fonts rather than ones that have been designed from the ground up. These never work as well as genuine ones - at least in my experience. Every time you convert something you lose some definition and some TrueType fonts have been converted seven times to get them to their current state!

Changing the subject slightly, don't have masses and masses of fonts installed all the time, regardless of which format you use. Just because you have 750 fonts it doesn't mean that you need them all available all the time. Besides which, they are taking up memory and resources. Far better to have a few basic typefaces or fonts loaded all the time and then add others as you need them. Once you have used these remove them again. That way your system will work faster which is the main object of the exercise.

There is also a design point to bear in mind. There is an old 'rule' in design that says that no page should ever have more than half a dozen fonts on it - remember that a font is not just a printing effect but also a size. One thing that people tend to do when they get lots of fonts is use them - generally all of them at the same time. This is bad design and it defeats the object of the exercise. (A page with lots and lots of fonts is called a Printers Pie, by the way, and it dates from the days of using little lead blocks. If these were spilled it was the devil's own job to sort them out.)

When you are designing something using text you also have to be aware of the limitations of the human brain and the way that it interprets text.

To start with you don't read individual characters, except in very special circumstances like when you're reading a foreign language or if you are dyslexic. You read words as a whole. They are called word shapes. The average human brain has more than 4,000 word shapes stored in it. People who don't read much or who have never learned to read properly might only have half that many. People who read a lot may have twice or even three times that many. (Just as an aside, the average person who goes through the British education system only knows about 5,000 words. If you go through the Scottish educational system then you are likely to know 6,000 words! The Scottish education system has always been better than the English one.)

The word shapes are all individually recognisable subject to certain conditions, e.g. the amount of ambient light. Typefaces that have serifs, little squiggely bits at the ends of the characters, are easier to read because they make more distinctive word shapes. Typefaces without serifs make more of an impact but your brain quickly tires of reading them. So you should never use sans serif typefaces, e.g. Helvetica or Avant Garde, for main body text. By all means use them for headings and banners where they are short and punchy and their impact is greatest. (Serif typefaces, by the way, came about as a result of carving letters on stone. The serif allowed the stonemason to tidy up the ends of the lines. There were no sans serif typefaces until the advent of printing.)

Back to reading body text. Your brain works by reading blocks of word shapes which usually contain up to twenty characters. But the brain can only read three and a half of these quickly and then it takes a rest for a split second. So if you have a line of text that contains roughly 60 characters you can read it very fast and your brain rests while your eyes move to the next line. Just to complicate matters further your brain can handle about 60 lines of text per page before it needs to take a longer rest.

That's why legal documents and the small print on contracts are hard to read by the way. They generally have more than 60 characters per line and anything up to 90 lines per page. Your brain literally gets tired of reading it.

The net result of all this is that you need more typefaces with serifs than you do sans serif ones unless you are only going to produce banners and headlines.

Adding and removing fonts

You can add and remove fonts very quickly in Windows using the Control Panel.

1   Run **Windows Control Panel** and double click on **Fonts**. A dialogue box appears. This will list all the typefaces and fonts already installed on your system. Because I use Adobe Type Manager I remove all the fonts except two - MS San Serif and MS Serif. Don't delete these because they are used by Windows itself, the former is the one used for labelling the icons and menus.

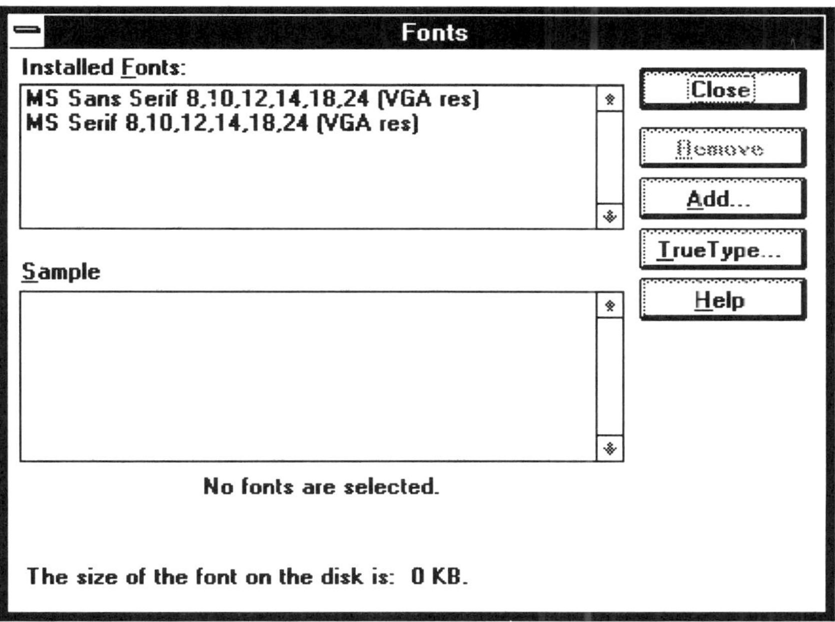

1.08 Fonts dialogue box

2   To remove a typeface just click on it to highlight it and then click on **Remove**. You can remove multiple fonts at the same time if you hold down **Ctrl** while you click on a selection to highlight them all. Alternatively, click on the first font then hold down **Shift** and click on the last one. All the intervening names will be selected.

3   You can add fonts by clicking on **Add**. If you are adding fronts from a floppy disk you will have to log on to the relevant drive. If you want to add fonts that are already on your system then you need to log on to the **\SYSTEM** directory - because that's where they are all stored. Once you log on to the right place the box will change to give you a list of the available fonts.

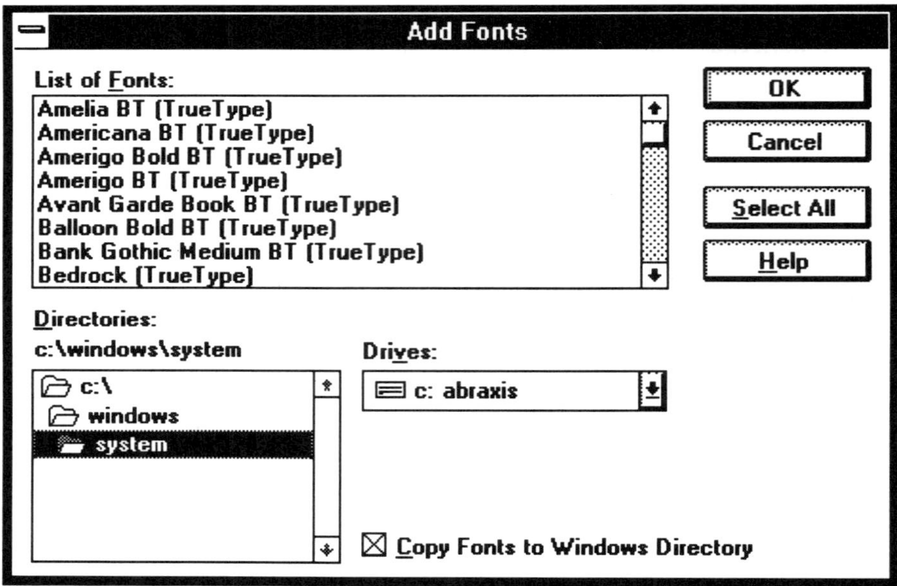

1.09 Listed fonts

4   To add just click on the ones you want and then on **OK**. The dialogue box will close and the fonts will be added to the previous dialogue box.

5   If you want to use TrueType then just close the dialogue box, the TrueType capability is turned on by default. If you don't want to use it then you should click on the button labelled **TrueType** which brings up another dialogue box.

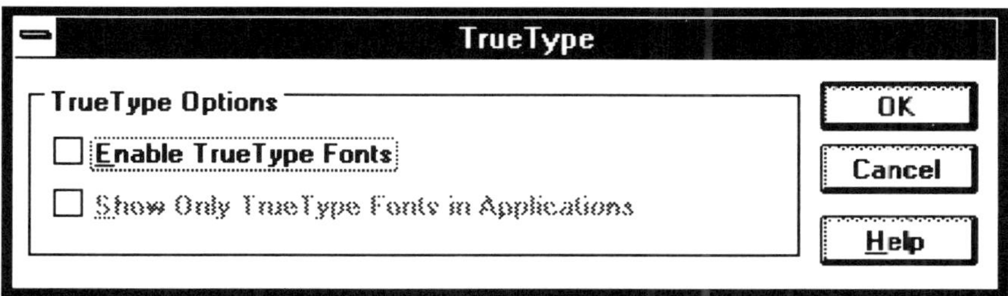

1.10 TrueType dialogue box

6   To turn off TrueType click on **Enable TrueType**. This will turn off the TrueType capability but leave the fonts in place on your hard disk. Click on **OK** to close the dialogue box. Click on **OK** again to close the main dialogue box and the press **Alt-F4** to close the Control Panel.

2. Installation

This book is being written using a beta version of the software and so there may be slight changes between what follows and what you actually have. However, any such change will be very slight and the major areas are unlikely to be different.

The instructions that follow are all based on using the floppy disks to install the program as the CD-ROM version is not available at the time of writing. Be that as it may, installing from either source will be much the same apart from the fact that installation from the CD-ROM is much, much quicker. If you do not have a CD-ROM drive I would strongly advocate that you go and get one - it will be one of the best purchases you ever make. More and more software is becoming available on CD-ROM and as it all has to comply with the same standard you automatically acquire some future proofing.

Before you do any installation make sure you have defragmented your hard disk first. Ideally you also want to do the installation as the only operation in action. In other words don't try doing the installation while you are running a word processor for example.

You can install CorelDRAW in a number of different ways:

So That The Program Runs Directly Off The CD-ROM.

This is useful if you have only a limited amount of disk space but it does bring its own problems. Firstly, you have to have the CD-ROM in the drive at all times which may be inconvenient. Secondly, it is difficult, though not impossible, to install any updates or enhancements that may come along later. Thirdly, the program will be slower simply because a CD-ROM access and transfer time is slower that that of a hard disk. On the whole I would not recommend that you use this option unless you have no other. This option will require a minimum amount of disk space, but it still needs some.

CORELDRAW 4 - A USERS GUIDE

YOU CAN HAVE A FULL INSTALLATION FROM FLOPPY DISKS.

This will install everything on the disks, all the software, a number of fonts and some sample clip-art. You will not get the same thing as if you installed the software from CD-ROM though. CorelDRAW 4 comes with 2 CD-ROM discs - that's a total of more than 1.2 Gigabytes of stuff. For obvious reasons you cannot have all that on floppy disks - it would take over 900 floppy disks! Installing off floppy disks will give you everything that you need to run the software, you simply cannot have most of the additional clip-art and fonts.

While I think of it there is another point to bear in mind. By the terms of the licence agreement you cannot pay anyone to copy things off the CD-ROM for you. If you have a CD-ROM of your own then that's fine but you should not use someone else's. This option will require roughly 35 Mb of free disk space.

YOU CAN HAVE A FULL INSTALLATION OFF THE CD-ROM.

This will give you the same thing as you will get from the floppy disks plus a whole lot more. At the moment, April 1994, I'm not one hundred per cent certain what is going to be on the CD-ROM discs but I do know that it will contain over 750 fonts and 18,000 clip-art images. The latter you won't bother to install - it's better left on the CD-ROM - and you should be able to select which fonts you want placed on your hard disk.

YOU CAN HAVE A CUSTOM INSTALLATION.

This is *always* the preferable option - no matter what the software is. A custom installation allows you to define exactly what you want and where it goes. The previous options are pre-programmed and give you little choice.

This option will require a minimum of 10 Mb of disk space, the equivalent of the Minimum Installation, and a maximum of 35 Mb, the equivalent of a Full Installation.

Regardless of which of the installation options you choose to use remember that you must also allow sufficient disk space for MS-DOS, Windows, the Windows Virtual Memory file and approximately 15 Mb for temp file storage. So even before you install CorelDRAW 4 you may have already used anything up to 50 Mb.

FULL INSTALLATION

The Full Installation takes about 30 minutes and will require roughly 35 Mb of disk space. This installation will also copy all the TrueType fonts to the WINDOWS\SYSTEM directory.

1 All the installation procedures for CorelDRAW require that you have Windows up and running to start with. If you want to do the full installation, place the first floppy disk into the drive and then either open the **File** menu and click on **Run** or simply press **Alt-F R**. In the dialogue box that appears type **A:\SETUP** and then press **Enter**. There will be a slight pause and then the CorelDRAW Setup screen appears:

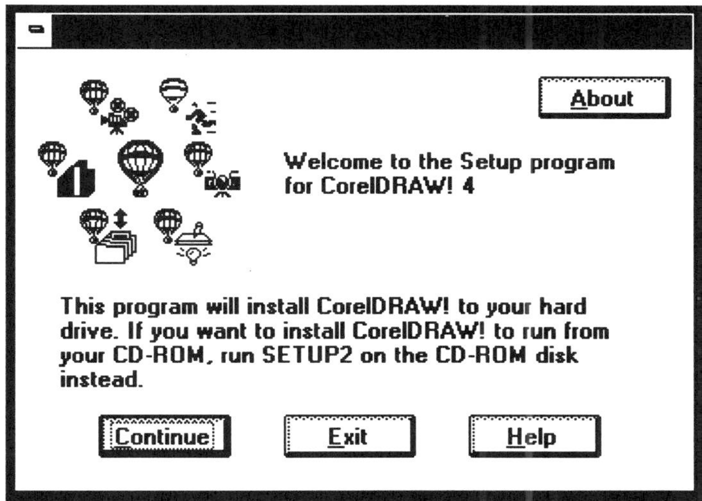

2.01 Installation starts

2 Press **Enter** or click on **Continue**. Another dialogue box appears. This is the personal customisation dialogue box and you have to put in your name and the Serial Number that you will find on the first disk.

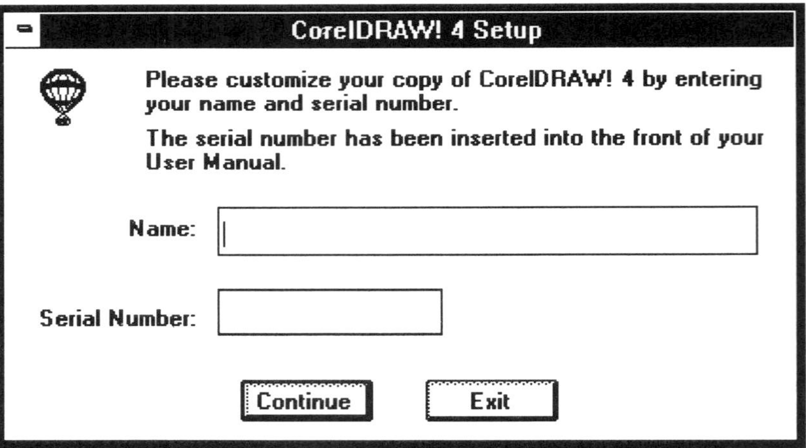

2.02 Installation part ii

3   Once you've entered the required details click on **Continue** or press **Enter** to continue and another dialogue box appears.

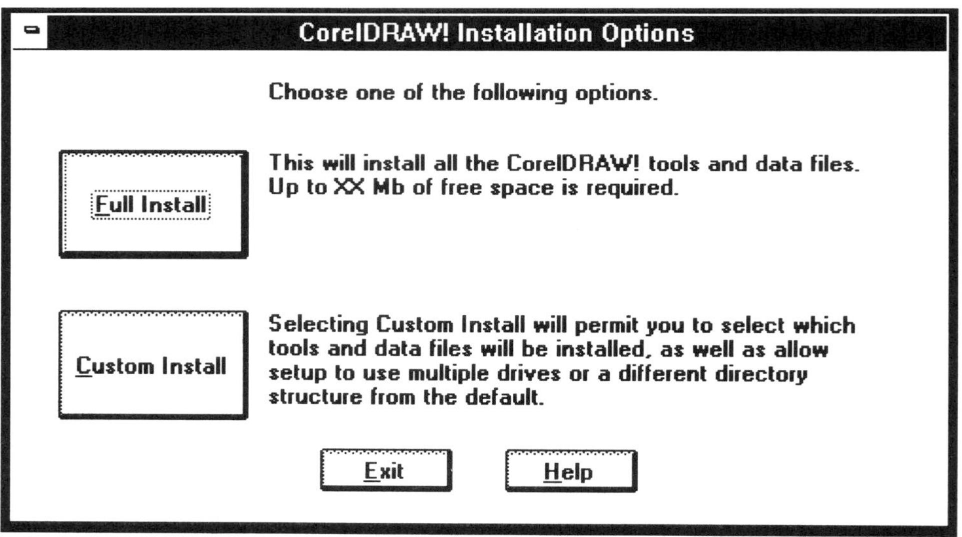

2.03 Installation selection

4   The **Full Installation** option is selected by default so you can just press **Enter** to continue. The Path select dialogue box appears.

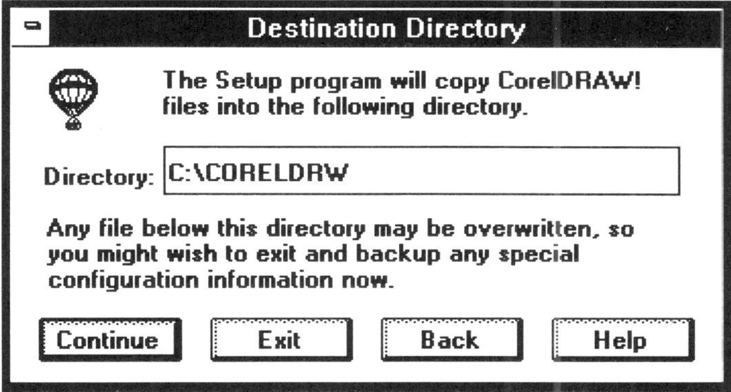

2.04 Path Select dialogue box

5   Click on **Continue** or press **Enter** and the process begins. A message box appears telling you that the program is calculating disk space and then you get a selection box that allows you to choose which Filters, Fonts and Scanner Drivers to install.

2.05 Elements dialogue box

6   Select the main elements you want and then press **Enter** or click on **Continue**. The process of copying the file then begins.

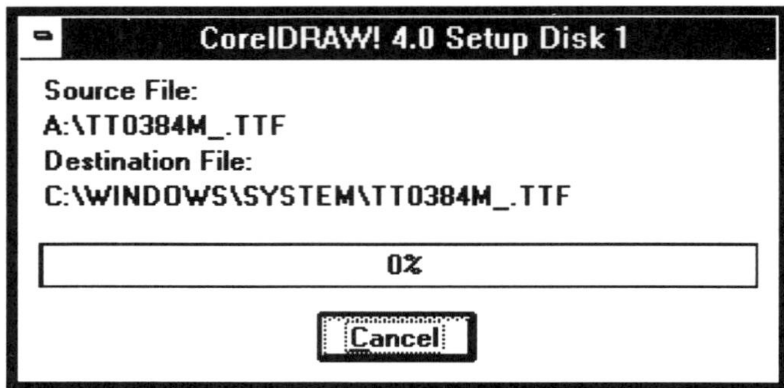

2.06 Installation begins

7   As the program is being installed you will get occasional messages asking you to swap disks. Change the disk and then press **Enter** and the process continues.

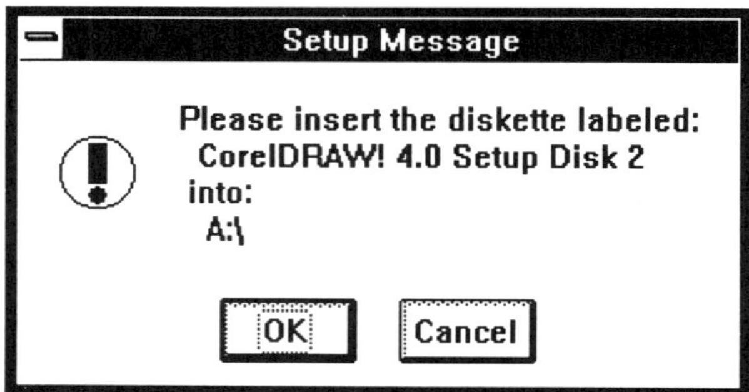

2.07 Swap disk message box

8   You will get then a message box telling you that CorelDRAW is registering the TrueType fonts - assuming you installed them. You don't have to do anything about this - it will vanish once it is completed.

9   Next you get another dialogue box asking you about installing SHARE.EXE.

This is needed for OLE2. If you already have Share loaded, e.g. because you use Word for Windows, then you can skip this by clicking on **Don't Update**. If you do not have Share loaded then click on **Update** or simply press **Enter**. (Don't forget that if you do update your AUTOEXEC.BAT you have to reboot your computer for the change to take effect.)

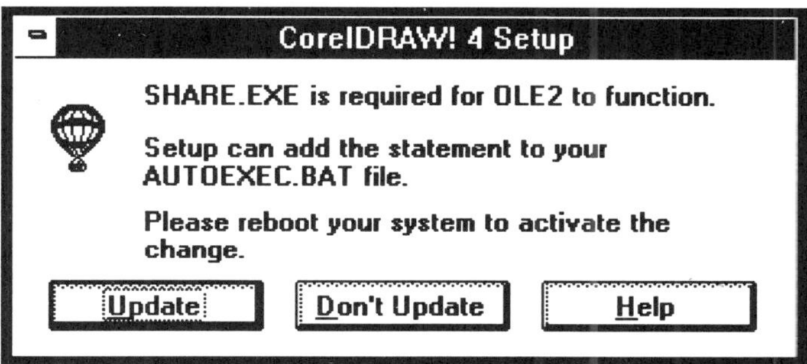

2.08 Share dialogue box

10   Finally you get the setup completion dialogue box and when you close that you will find that you have a new group window containing the icons for all the programs in CorelDRAW 4.

2.09 Installation completed

CUSTOM INSTALLATION

The Custom Installation is the best option to use because it gives you total control over what is installed and where it is put. The installation time varies according to what you select as does the amount of disk space required.

1   If you want to do the custom installation, place the first floppy disk into the drive and then either open the **File** menu and click on **Run** or simply press **Alt-F R**. In the dialogue box that appears type **A:\SETUP** and then press **Enter**. There will be a slight pause and then the CorelDRAW Setup screen appears:

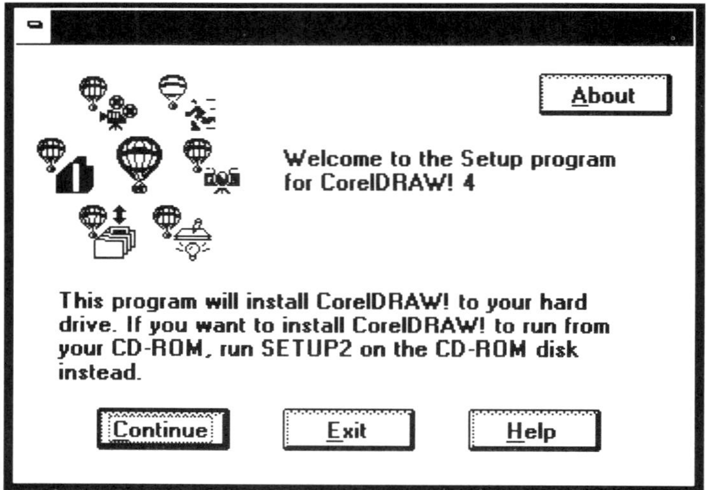

2.10 Installation starts

2   Press **Enter** or click on **Continue**. Another dialogue box appears that requires you to enter your name and the serial number. Type your name on the first line and the serial number, which is written on the first disk, on the second line. Then press **Enter** to continue.

CorelDRAW! 4 Setup

Please customize your copy of CorelDRAW! 4 by entering your name and serial number.

The serial number has been inserted into the front of your User Manual.

Name:

Serial Number:

Continue   Exit

2.11 Serial Number entry

3   You will then get the installation options dialogue box.

CorelDRAW! Installation Options

Choose one of the following options.

Full Install — This will install all the CorelDRAW! tools and data files. Up to XX Mb of free space is required.

Custom Install — Selecting Custom Install will permit you to select which tools and data files will be installed, as well as allow setup to use multiple drives or a different directory structure from the default.

Exit   Help

2.12 Installation Options

4   Click on **Custom Install** and the path selection dialogue box appears. Here you can change the destination drive and directory if you wish. Click on **Continue** or press **Enter**.

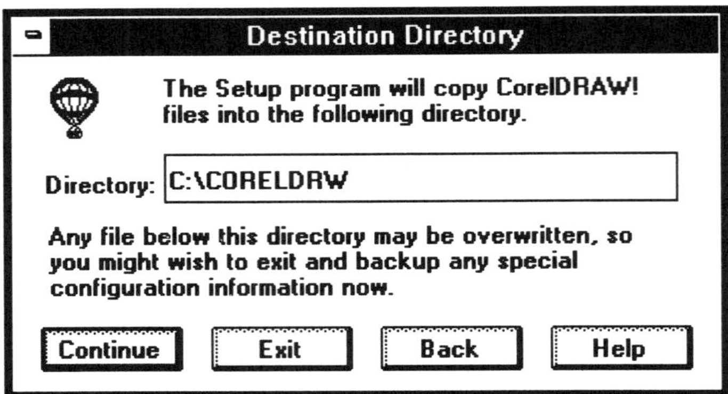

2.13 Path Selection

5   You will get a message box telling you that the program is checking the disk space available and then a new dialogue box wherein you can select a wide range of things.

Choose which applications to install

	All:	Some:	None:		Disk Usage:
CorelDRAW!:	●	○	○	C:\CORELDRW\DRAW	10354 K
CorelCHART!:	●	○	○	C:\CORELDRW\CHART	6198 K
CorelSHOW!:	●	○	○	C:\CORELDRW\SHOW	2736 K
CorelPHOTO-PAINT!:	●	○	○	C:\CORELDRW\PHOTOPNT	2204 K
CorelMOVE!:	●	○	○	C:\CORELDRW\MOVE	2610 K
CorelTRACE!:	●		○	C:\CORELDRW\TRACE	1774 K
CorelMOSAIC!:	●		○	C:\CORELDRW\PROGRAMS	522 K
Root Directory:				C:\CORELDRW	4882 K

Drive: C:
Space Required: 36704 K
Space Available: 51638 K

Continue   Exit   Back   Help

2.14 Custom select dialogue box

6   Everything is selected for you so you have to deselect those elements that you don't want by clicking on **None**. If you click on **Some** for any element then you will get a second level dialogue box.

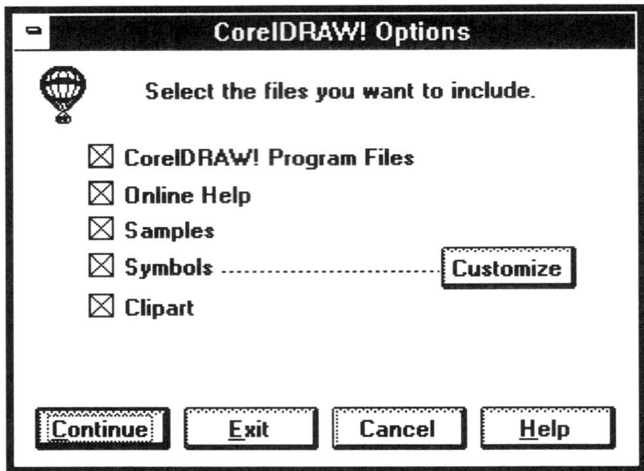

2.15 Second level selection

7   Make whatever selections you want and then click on **Continue**. You'll go back to the previous dialogue box. You can make additional **Some** selections if you wish. Finally click on **Continue** and another dialogue box appears from which you can select filters and fonts:

	All:	Some:	None:		Disk Usage:
Filters:	●	○	○	C:\CORELDRW\PROGRAMS	2882 K
TrueType Fonts:	●	○	○	C:\WINDOWS\SYSTEM	0 K
Scanner Drivers:		○	●	C:\WINDOWS\TWAIN\COREL4	0 K

Drive:	C:
Space Required:	34122 K
Space Available:	49344 K

[Continue]   [Exit]   [Back]   [Help]

2.16 Files dialogue box

8   Again make whatever selections you wish and then click on **Continue**. A message box appears telling you that CorelDRAW is ready to be installed. Press **Enter** or click on **Continue** to move on.

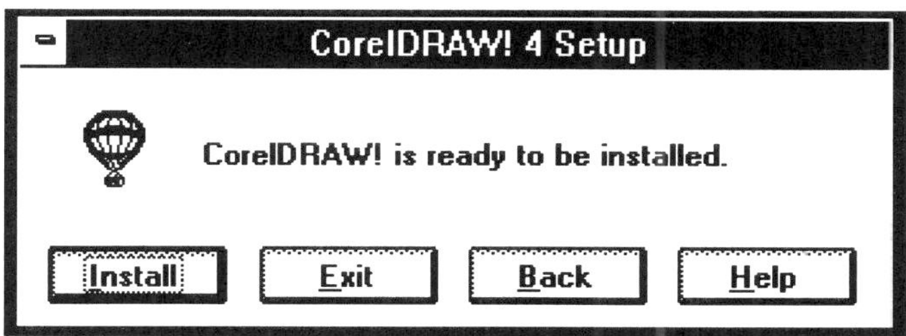

2.17 Ready message box

9   As the installation progresses you will be prompted to swap the disks. Do so and press **Enter** or click on **OK** each time.

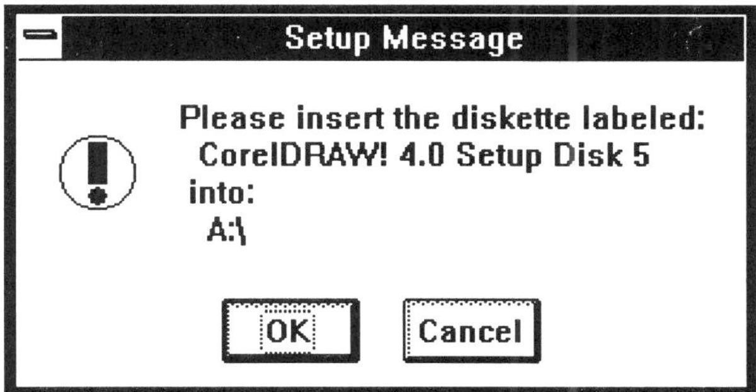

2.18 Swap disk message box

10   Next you get another dialogue box asking you about installing SHARE.EXE. This is needed for OLE2. If you already have Share loaded, e.g. because you use Word for Windows, then you can skip this by clicking on **Don't Update**. If you do not have Share loaded then click on **Update** or simply press **Enter**. (Don't forget that if you do update your AUTOEXEC.BAT you have to reboot your computer for the change to take effect.)

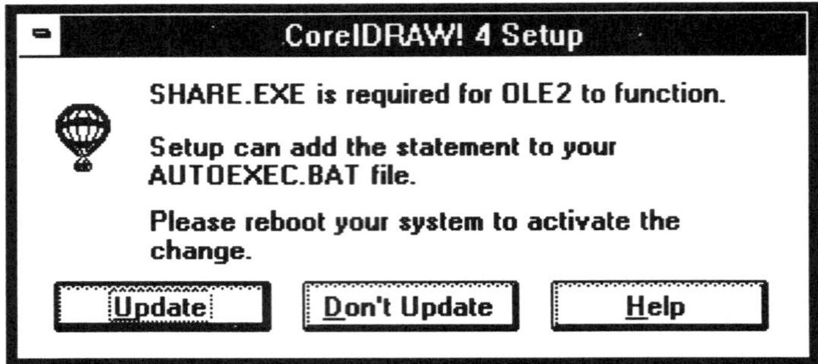

2.19 Share dialogue box

11   Finally you get the setup completion dialogue box and when you close that you will find that you have a new group window containing the icons for all the programs in CorelDRAW 4.

2.20 Installation completed

INSTALLATION PROBLEMS

All in all there are very few problems that you are likely to encounter when installing CorelDRAW, however you may encounter some and these are the most common ones.

THE SETUP PROGRAM LOCKS UP FOR NO APPARENT REASON.

This is usually caused by a memory conflict of some kind. Make sure that you unload any memory resident software from the CONFIG.SYS - virus checker programs are notorious for causing problems by the way, and that you disable any Windows screen savers that might be running and then try again.

THE INSTALLATION TAKES A LONG TIME.

Because the installation is copying lots of files it is dependant on Smartdrive - the MS-DOS and Windows disk cache. Make sure that you have it configured as normal, i.e. don't have any exclusions.

You should also be aware that all floppy disk drives are slow - they are really the oldest remaining part of the original IBM PC system. They are incredibly reliable but they are inherently slow. There is nothing you can do about that.

For some reason that nobody seems to have the answer to, you can find that the performance of the installation on two identical machines can be radically different. For instance installation on my main machine takes much longer than installation on my backup computer even though they are essentially the same thing. Again there is nothing you can do about it.

Normally it should not take longer than about 30 minutes to install CorelDRAW 4 provided you are using Smartdrv as standard.

Setup tells you that you don't have enough disk space even though you know you have.

This occasionally happens if you are trying to install CorelDRAW to a drive other than Drive-C because the latter is nearly full. It's caused by the fact that the installation creates a temporary directory, which it uses to copy files, on the first hard disk. If there isn't enough room for that then you will get a lack of space message. To correct the problem make sure you leave something between 5 and 10 Mb free on Drive-C. It also helps if you have defragmented the drive before you begin.

You repeatedly get a message to supply the same disk.

This usually means that the disk in question is faulty. There is nothing much you can do in this case except get the disk changed by the Corel Support.

Installing off CD-ROM causes problems.

Your CD-ROM drive must ahve an ID number higher than 1. Check your CONFIG.SYS and you'll find a line that laods the necessary driver and which includes a bit saying /ID:x where x is the number of the drive. You need to increase this beyond 1. You may also have to set a switch on the drive itself.

3. CUSTOMISATION

Now that you have CorelDRAW installed, using whichever installation option you desire, the first thing that you need to do is customise the program. There are a huge range of things that can be customised in CorelDRAW - you can do as much or as little as you wish - and this chapter has them all.

1   Double click on the CorelDRAW icon. The program will run and after a slight pause, during which you get the version number and copyright information, it appears on screen.

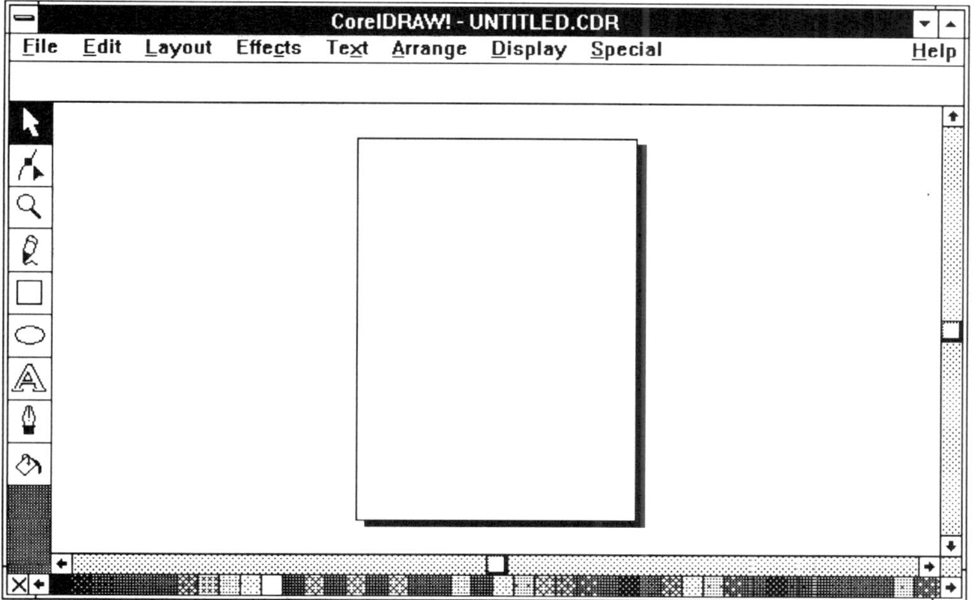

3.01 CorelDRAW as it is installed

There are a whole range of features about CorelDRAW that can be customised and as it is a matter of personal taste - there are no hard and fast rules about what you should or should not do. What follows is the way that I customise CorelDRAW but you need only do what you want yourself.

2   The first thing to do is set the global measurement units. Open the **Layout** menu and then click on **Grid Setup**. A large dialogue box appears:

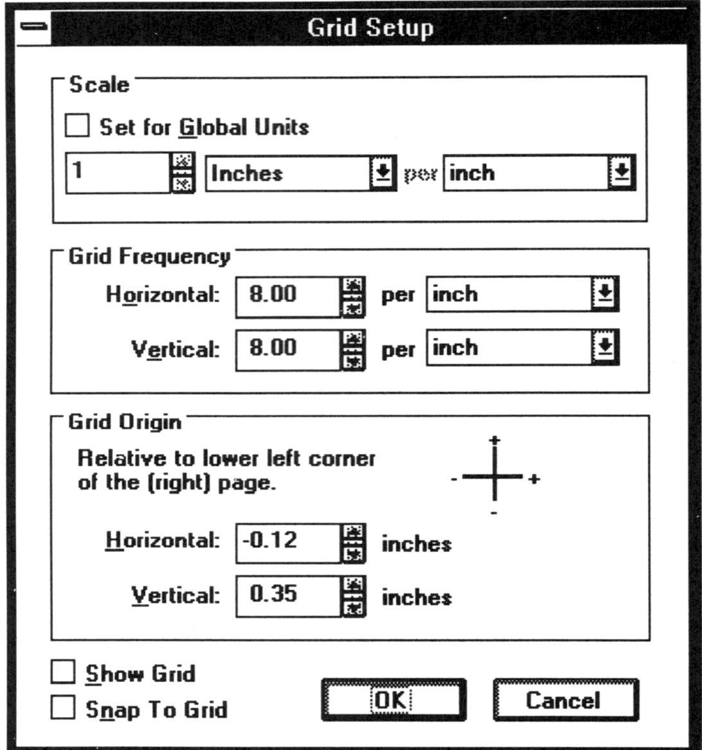

3.02 Grid Setup dialogue box

3   Click on **Set for Global Units** to activate the top line of the dialogue box. I change the measurements to be Millimetres per millimetre. The global units are really intended for people working to scale but they also provide a fast way to change the dialogue boxes. Now all the dialogue boxes that exist within CorelDRAW will default to millimetres hereafter.

4   While you're here you may as well set the **Grid Frequency**. The grid is normally hidden from view but you can have the various tools snap to it automatically. It can be extremely useful. You set the frequency in terms of

units per measurement. This causes people more grief than any other part of CorelDRAW. I want to use a grid that gives me 1 centimetre squares. That means I need a grid frequency of 0.1 per millimetre for both the Horizontal and Vertical frequencies.

5   Change the **Grid Origin** for both the **Horizontal** and **Vertical** origins to **0.0**. That makes the zero point for the rulers lie at the lower left hand corner of the page.

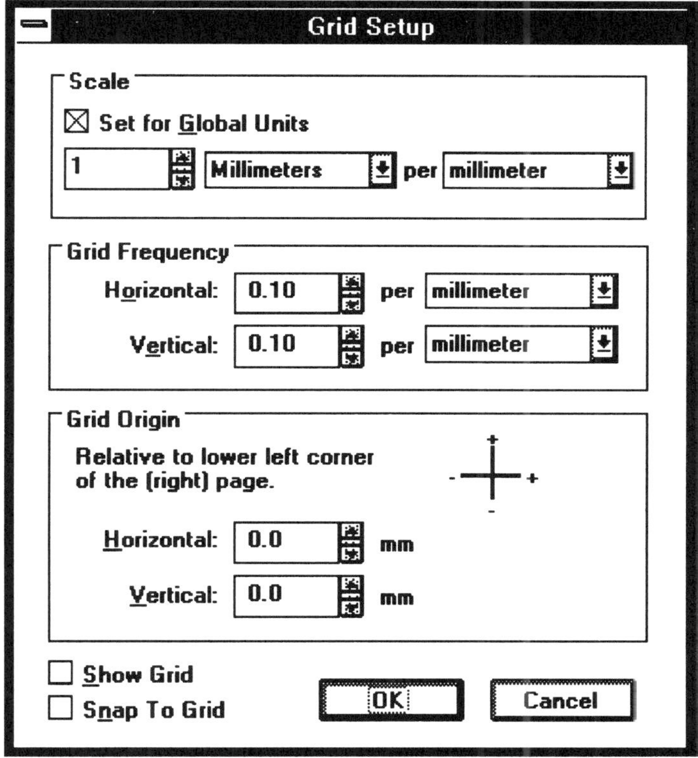

3.03 Grid changed

6   Click on **OK** to close the dialogue box. I never turn on Show Grid or Snap to Grid at this point - preferring to do it as necessary.

Grid Setup

The Grid within CorelDRAW can be very important. The grid itself is an invisible layer, rather like a sheet of transparent graph paper, that sits directly on top of the page on screen. You can modify the grid size at any time as and when necessary. Once you start creating images in CorelDRAW you can have the cursor Snap to the Grid, i.e. the cursor can only be positioned at the grid intersections. This allows you to draw things accurately and precisely. The grid also applies when you move things. The objects being moved can only be placed so that their edges align with the grid intersections.

However, there are occasions when you do not want the grid on, for instance when you are rotating things. In such a case having the cursor move only to the grid intersection points can be a nuisance. Fortunately there is a keyboard shortcut that allows you to turn the Snap to Grid feature on or off. Press **Ctrl-Y** the first time and the feature is turned on, press the two keys again and it will be turned off, press them again and it is back on. In other words the keyboard shortcut is a Toggle, like a light switch it is either on or off.

7   Open the **Layout** menu again and click on **Page Setup**. A dialogue box appears as opposite.

8   This has a new feature. Click on **Set From Printer** and the dialogue box will adopt the current sizes and configuration that you have set for the Windows printer driver. This gives you a quick way to set the parameters. Whenever I use CorelDRAW I normally work with Landscape pages, not always but most of the time, because they fit the screen better. However, CorelDRAW 4 has multiple page capabilities and so that no longer really applies. However, as this chapter is concerned with setting the defaults and, for this book at least, we will mainly be using single pages I suggest that you set it to Landscape for now. It can be changed at any time later.

9   So for now you should have an A4 Landscape page with Full Page and Show Page Border. Click on **OK** once you have that. The page representation on the screen will now change to what you have just set.

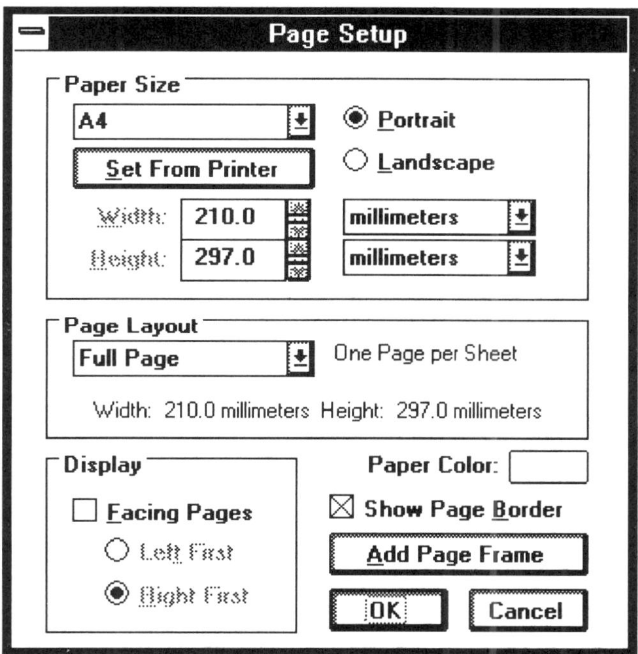

3.04 Page Setup dialogue box

The Page Setup dialogue box in CorelDRAW 4 assumes a much greater importance than it did in earlier versions of the program simply because CorelDRAW 4 now has DTP features and is capable of handling multiple pages. In the dialogue box you can set the page size, the layout, the kind of pages, the paper colour and the paper frame. All of these features we will come back to later. The maximum page size you can have in CorelDRAW by the way is 30 inches (762 millimetres) square.

10   Press **Ctrl-J**, or open the **Display** menu and then click on **Preferences**, and a dialogue box appears.

3.05 Preferences dialogue box

The Preferences dialogue box allows you to set a large range of features for CorelDRAW 4, everything from constrain angles to the mouse functions. As such it can appear a little complex.

11   The first thing to do is set the values for **Place Duplicates**. Within CorelDRAW you can create a copy of anything in a number of different ways. One of the easiest is to create a duplicate which not only copies the selected object but moves the copy to another position on the page - all in a single operation. The value you set here refers to how far above and to the right of the original object the copy will be placed. I normally set the values to 5 millimetres as a default and then change it to something else whenever necessary.

12   The **Nudge** feature can be very useful. Once you have an object on screen you can move it around by dragging it, by using the Move dialogue box, by placing a duplicate or by nudging it. To do the latter you simply select the object and then press one of the arrow keys. The object will move by whatever increment you set for the Nudge here. Moving things using Nudge also overrides the Grid setting by the way. I generally set the nudge value to 1 millimetre. Again

it can be changed quickly and easily whenever you want. The maximum value you can have is 2 inches (50 millimetres) and the minimum is 0.001 inches (0.1 millimetres).

13   The **Constrain Angle** is just that. It is the angle increment that any rotation or skew, including drawing straight lines, can be tied to. When you rotate things you can hold down **Ctrl** and the object being rotated will jump in whatever increment you set here. By default it is set to 15 degrees which is useful. In other words it gives you 24 steps for a full rotation. I rarely need to change this.

Maths co-processor

While we're on the subject of moving and rotating things there is a point to bear in mind. People often ask if they need to have a maths co-processor to run CorelDRAW. The answer is No, the program was not designed to use floating math. That can occasionally cause problems because standard math as performed by the normal chip gets rounded up. The result is that if you nudge something, for instance, a number of times you find that an error begins to creep in due to the rounding problems. Generally speaking you want to move, rotate or nudge things a maximum of about six times - after that the error is likely to appear. You'll notice it when something suddenly stops being in whole numbers. For example, you might nudge something up the page and the values go 10, 11, 12, 13, 14, 15, 15.9. When that happens there is nothing you can do except delete the object at the wrong place and duplicate it a different way.

14   **Mitre Limit** is what affects the appearance of corners. When any two lines, which are part of the same object meet, they will have a bevelled point provided that their angle is less than the mitre limit. Those lines which have an angle greater than the limit will have sharp points. Why is it there? Because you could have a sharp point that extends way beyond the actual lines. By default the mitre limit is set to 10 degrees and I tend to leave it at that except in special circumstances where I want the effect.

15   **Undo Levels** is new in CorelDRAW 4. In previous versions of the program you could always undo the last action but in 4.0 you can now undo multiple actions - the exact number depends on what you set here. The problem is that the

number of undo levels is affected by the amount of memory you have available. By default it is set to 4 which will work fine on any machine with a minimum of 4 Mb of RAM - depending on what you do. As I have 8 Mb of RAM, on the smaller machine, I can change the undo levels to more if I wish but I generally leave it at the default.

16 **Auto-panning** is turned on by default, i.e. it has a cross in the box beside it. What it does is cause the screen display to move as you drag an object or draw a line beyond the extent of the available window space. With the feature turned on, if you drag an object to the top of the screen and then continue dragging the screen display will scroll downwards to accommodate your movements. If you turn auto-panning off then you cannot drag anything beyond the screen edges.

17 **Cross Hair Cursor** is off by default. All the tools in CorelDRAW normally have their own cursor shapes as a result. If you turn this feature on then that facility is lost and all you have is a set of cross hairs, regardless of what tool you are using. Personally I like having the different cursors so I leave it off.

18 **Interruptible Display** is extremely useful and it is turned on by default. What it does is allow you to interrupt the screen redraw by clicking the mouse button or hitting any key. This can be helpful especially when you have complex objects on screen and you want to get on with doing something else. The redraw will resume after a pause if you do nothing else or it will continue after you complete an action. You can redraw the entire window at any time by pressing **Ctrl-W** by the way.

19 **3.x Compatibility Message** is off by default. CorelDRAW 3 and CorelDRAW 4 use line spacing for text in different ways. If you have this option turned on you will get a message when you open a version 3 file that contains text. The dialogue box will give you the option of changing the line spacing to version 4 if you wish. In the normal course of events you are unlikely to notice the difference between the two but it will be visible if you have mixed font types and sizes in any individual string. Turn it on by clicking on it.

20 Click on the button labelled **Curves** and a second level dialogue box appears:

3.06 Curves dialogue box

21 The dialogue box allows you to set the parameters for various actions. Notice that all the settings are determined in pixels - that's because the settings all apply to the screen and so the resolution you are using will also have an effect. By default all the values are set to 5 pixels.

> **Freehand Tracking** controls how closely CorelDRAW follows the movement of the cursor when you are drawing lines in freehand mode, i.e. as normal. The higher the number the more tightly the resulting line will match your movements and the more nodes you have generated, the lower the number the rougher the line but the fewer nodes.

> **Autotrace Tracking** applies when you are tracing a bitmap within CorelDRAW itself. The setting controls how closely the trace conforms to the outline of the bitmap. Lower values will produce a trace that more closely follows the bitmap edges but will generate many more nodes, a higher value will give a less well defined object and fewer nodes. The default of 5 is a good compromise between the two.

> **Corner Threshold** directly affects the nodes that CorelDRAW produces when you are drawing in freehand mode or tracing a bitmap. With a high number you are more likely to create Smooth corner nodes, with a low

number you are more likely to generate Cusp nodes. Again the default of 5 is a good compromise.

Straight Line Threshold affects whether CorelDRAW produces a straight line or a curve when you are drawing in freehand mode or tracing a bitmap. The higher the number the more straight lines you will get.

Auto-Join affects how and when lines will join up to produce closed shapes. Remember that lines can only join at the ends, never in the middle. The lower the number the closer you must position the end of line to the beginning of the previous one for them to join together to produce the closed shape.

Auto-Reduce is a new feature for CorelDRAW 4. When you are node editing you now have to option to remove unnecessary nodes, which is extremely useful, and exactly how many is affected by this setting. The higher the number the more nodes it removes.

Set the values to whatever you wish, personally I leave them all set to 5 and only change them in specific circumstances. Click on **OK** to close the dialogue box and go back to the original one.

22   Click on the button labelled **Display** and another dialogue box appears as opposite.

23   This dialogue box affects the way that things appear on screen and as such it can be used to speed up the display in some areas. **Preview Fountain Stripes** applies to the number of stripes that will appear on screen whenever you use a fountain fill. By default the number is 20, the maximum is 256 and the minimum 2. The lower the number the faster the stripes appear but the more stripy the effect is. I always change this to 25. Why? Because 25 stripes is good enough for a quick view but if I want to see the reality I simply add a 6 to the end of the number. Once I've seen the finished product I can go back to a quick view by removing the 6 and leaving it on 25. The value will also affect fountain fills in any file exported as AI, EPS, CGM, PCT, WMF and all bitmap formats.

3.07 Display dialogue box

Greek Text Below is set in pixels. What it means is that any text that appears on screen and is less than the number of pixels specified high, then the text will not be shown as true text but as pseudo-text made of easy to display symbols. It simply speeds up the display. The default of 9 is okay but if you have a large amount of text on screen you may want to increase the number to make the display faster. Don't forget that because you are greeking text below a certain pixel size, if you zoom in to the text the greeking will no longer apply because it is then a larger pixel size.

Preview Colours depends on the type of graphics card you have and the Windows screen driver in use. In the case of the illustration above it can only use Windows dithering because the screen is set in monochrome to make the screen shots easier to see. The problem is that this limits the number of colours that can be displayed, even in colour, to a maximum of 15 so that colour blends are not very good. On my main machine I have it set to 256-Colour Dithering which gives a decent range of colours.

Optimised Palette for Full Screen Preview loads the palette with pure colours - it is only available when using 256-Colour Display. The colours are actually only displayed properly in full screen preview mode, in the normal course of events the on-screen colours will be dithered.

Curve Flatness changes the way that curves are drawn on screen or on non-PostScript printers. The higher you make the number the faster the curve will draw but the less curved it becomes. For example, a circle will appear as a polygon. The default of 1 is okay for most things.

For reference I set this dialogue box to 25 fountain stripes, 9 pixels for the greeked text and the Normal curve flatness. Click on **OK** to close the dialogue box and go back to the original one.

24   Click on the button labelled **Mouse** and a new dialogue box appears:

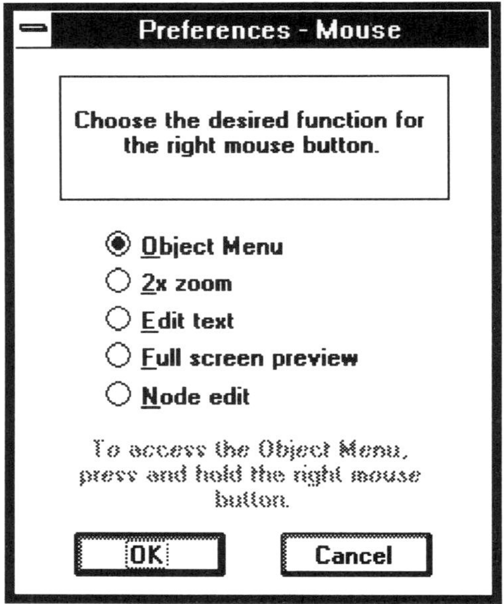

3.08 Mouse dialogue box

25 This dialogue box allows you to set the function for the right mouse button - which would otherwise be redundant. You have a choice of the following:

Object Menu is a new feature that we will come to later.

2x Zoom allows you to zoom in to things quickly. This is the option that I prefer. You can also activate the magnifier by pressing **F2**.

Edit Text activates the text dialogue box, i.e. it is the same as pressing **Ctrl-T**.

Full Screen Preview is the same as pressing **F9**.

Node edit activates the node edit tool which you can also do by pressing **F10**.

Regardless of which action you assign to the right mouse button you can still access the Object Data by holding down the right mouse button and you can still use the right mouse button to create a duplicate of something by moving it and then depressing the button.

Select the option you want to use and then click on **OK** to close the dialogue box and go back to the original.

26 Click on the button labelled **Roll-Ups** and a new dialogue box comes up.

27 This dialogue box allows you to set how the roll-ups will appear the next time you run CorelDRAW. It does not affect the roll-ups this time! Your choices are:

No Roll-Ups which means just that. This is the one I favour because I prefer to open the roll-ups as I need them.

All Roll-Ups Arranged will open all the roll-ups and arrange them in two neat stacks either side of the screen.

Appearance of Roll-Ups on Exit will open the roll-ups next time in exactly the same number and position as you have them when you close CorelDRAW this time.

Current Appearance of Roll-Ups will open the roll-ups exactly as they are right now, i.e. when you activated this dialogue box.

Select whichever option you wish and then click on **OK** to go back to the previous dialogue box.

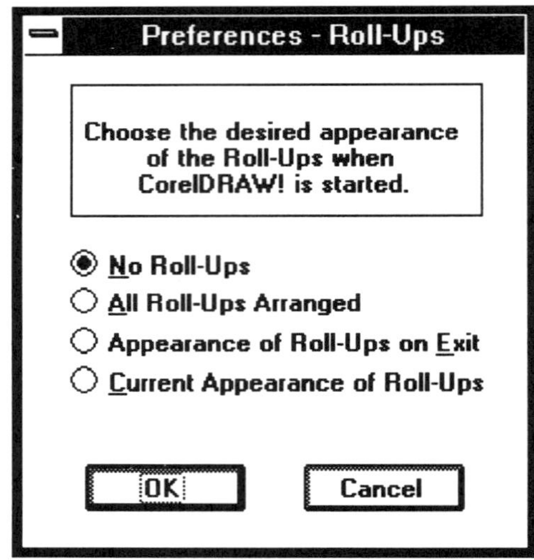

3.09 Roll-up dialogue box

28   Click on the button labelled **Dimension** and you get another dialogue box.

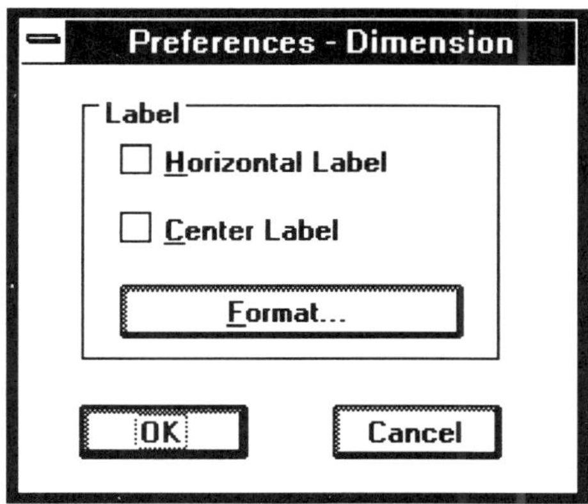

3.10 Dimension dialogue box

29   Dimensions are something else new in CorelDRAW 4. They can be used to measure the exact length of a line. When you use dimension lines you will get a string of text giving you the measurement. The dialogue box allows you to set where this text string will appear.

> **Horizontal Label** sets the text string so that the baseline of the string is always horizontal!
>
> **Centre Label** places the text string midway along the dimension line.

30   You can also change the format of the text string by clicking on **Format**. This will bring up another dialogue box.

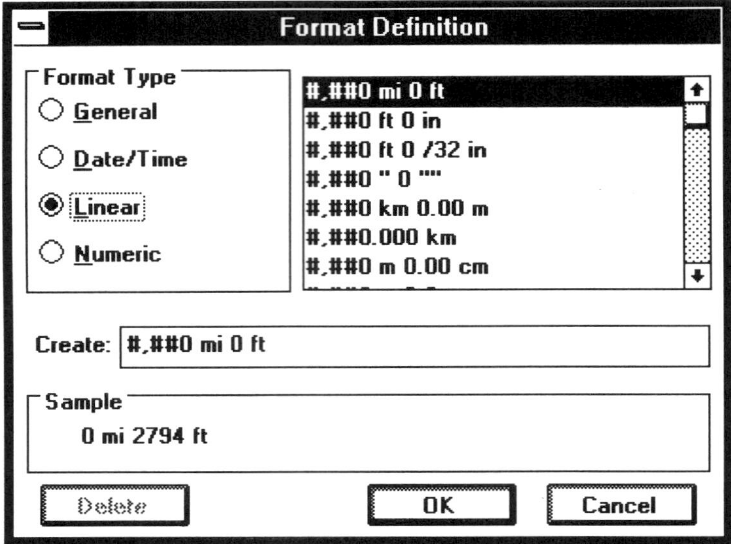

3.11 Dimensions, Format dialogue box

31   Select whichever dimension format you wish - although at this stage you're probably better off leaving it just on **General** until you get used to using the dimensions themselves. Click on **OK** to close the dialogue box.

32   At the main Dimension dialogue box click on **OK** again to close that and go back to the main Preferences dialogue box.

33   That's all the preferences set so click on **OK** to close down the dialogue box.

34   Open the **Display** menu and click on **Show Rulers**. The rulers will appear down the left hand side of the screen and just below the Status Bar at the top. Note that the measurements used for the rulers is whatever you set in the grid Setup dialogue box.

35   Open the **Text** menu and click on **Character**. A message box appears:

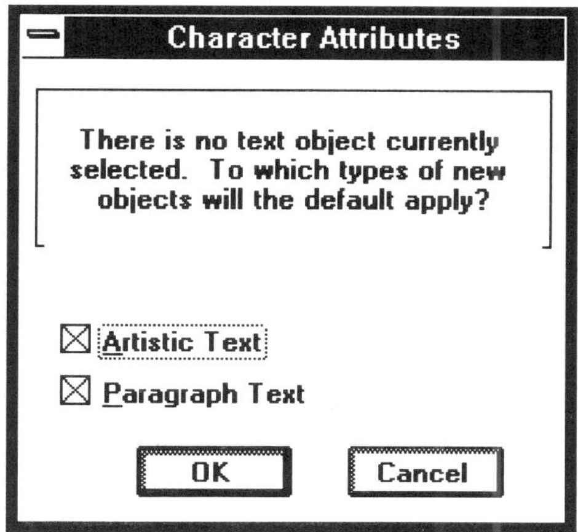

3.12 Character message box

36   This allows you to set the default typeface and size for either Artistic, Paragraph or both sorts of text. I usually set different defaults for each. So click on **Paragraph text** to deselect it and then click on **OK**. A new dialogue box appears.

3.13 Character Attributes dialogue box

37 Set the attributes for the Artistic text to be whatever you want. For artistic text, which I use mainly for banners and headlines, I set it to Helvetica 24 point, normal. Click on **OK** when you've made your choice.

38 Now repeat step 35 and 36 but this time deselect Artistic text. I set the default for Paragraph Text to be Palatino 10 point normal. (The same text that this book is set in.) Set it to whatever you want and then click on **OK**.

39 Open the **Text** menu again and click on **Paragraph**. Again you'll get a message box that allows you to apply the default settings to either Artistic or Paragraph text. Deselect Artistic text and click on **OK** and a dialogue box appears.

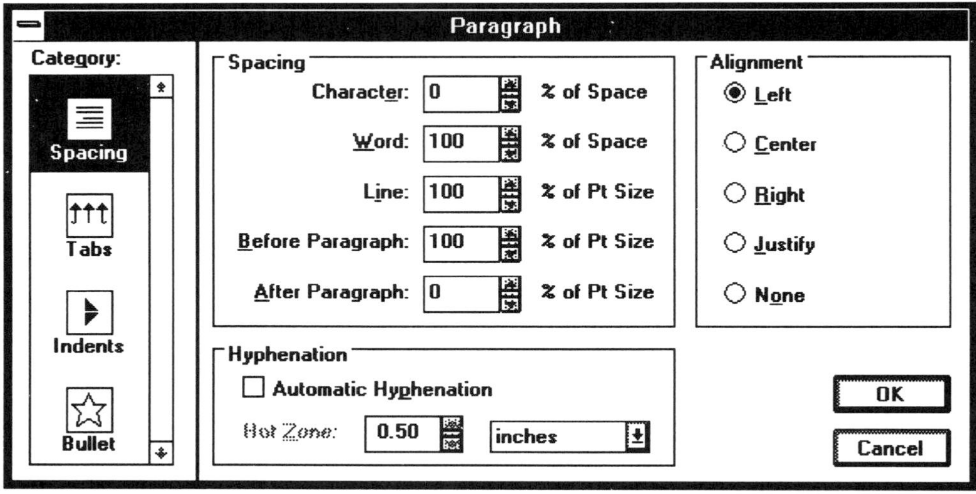

3.14 Paragraph spacing dialogue box

40 This dialogue box allows you to set a range of parameters for the paragraph text, everything from the spacing to bullets, because CorelDRAW 4 now has full DTP capabilities. You can set the spacing and alignment to whatever you feel most comfortable with - there are no hard and fast rules for this, it is purely a matter of personal taste. Make the changes and then click on the **Tabs** icon on the left hand side of the dialogue box and it will change to this:

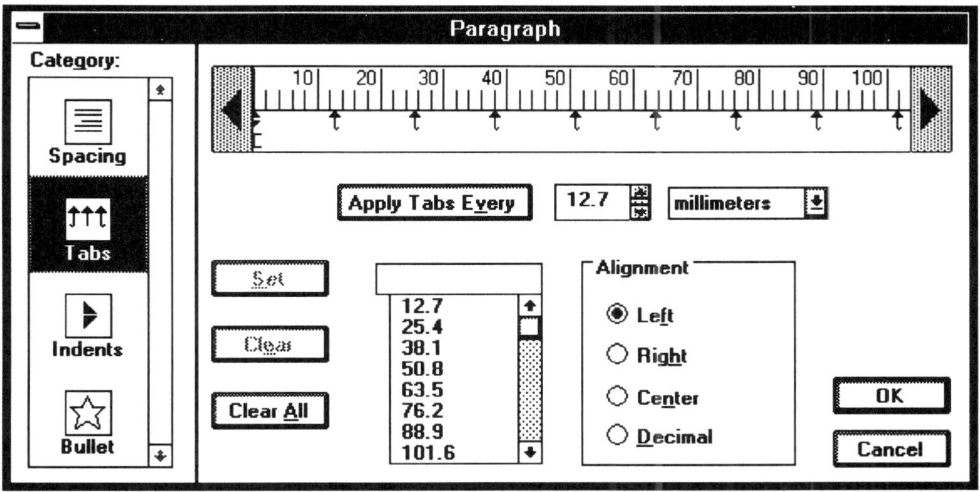

3.15 Tabs dialogue box

41   By default the tabs are set to be placed every half inch, even if you are using millimetres. I prefer to have tabs every 10 millimetres so I click on **Clear All** to remove the existing ones, then change the value in the box beside **Apply Tabs Every** to 10 millimetres before clicking on the button to apply them. I leave them as Left Aligned until I need to change them interactively later.

42   Click on the **Indents** icon on the left and the dialogue box changes again. You won't normally need to do anything with this at this stage but you will use it when you come to defining styles.

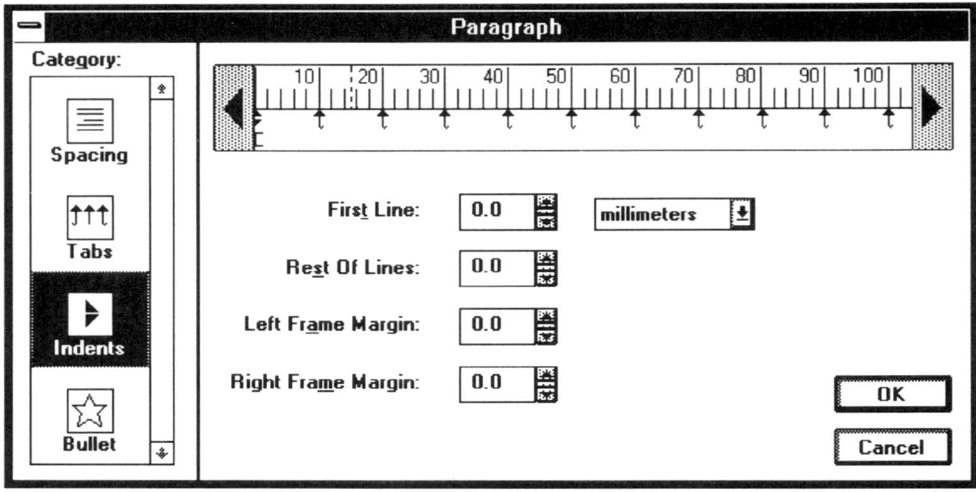

3.16 Indents dialogue box

43 Click on the **Bullet** icon on the left and the dialogue box changes yet again. CorelDRAW is unusual in that it will allow you to use any of the Symbols as a bullet. In other words you can have a choice of over 8,000 possible bullet symbols! Again you don't need them yet.

44 Click on **OK** to close the dialogue box. Open the **Text** menu again and click on **Spell Checker**, this will bring up another dialogue box.

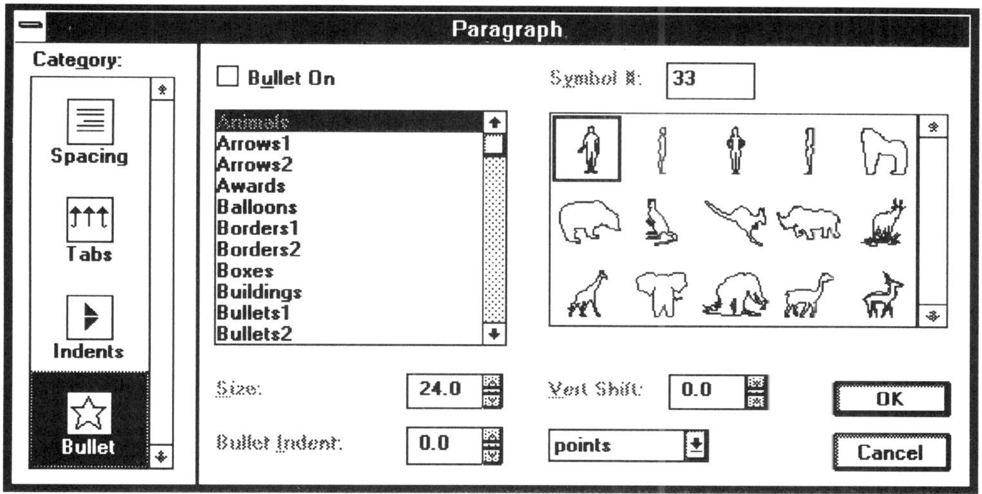

3.17 Bullet dialogue box

3.18 Spell Checker dialogue box

45 As you don't have any text to check at this stage, you are just setting the basic parameters and creating a personal dictionary. Turn on **Always Suggest** so that it has a cross beside it. You can also create your personal dictionary at this time. The spell checker that comes with CorelDRAW is very good and it has an enormous number of words built into it. However it cannot have every word in it, e.g. proper names, legal terms or medical words. These you have to add to a personal dictionary.

46 Move the cursor down to the bottom box and click once so you get a flashing line in the box. Now type a name, e.g. your own name, and then click on **Create** - the button only becomes active once you have entered a name. Now click on **Cancel** - that's the only way to close the dialogue box.

47 Now to set the basic bits. Click on the Pen tool, the one shaped like a pen nib, and it will open out. Click on the large **X**. A message box appears:

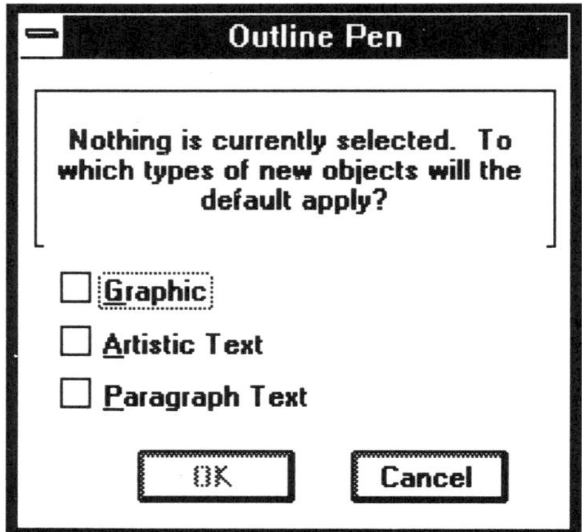

3.19 Outline message box

48 Click on **Artistic Text** and **Paragraph Text** and then on **OK**. What you have done is turn off any outline that might have been applied to text. In the normal course of events you don't want an outline on text.

49   Click on the **Pen** tool again and this time click on the **Nib** once it opens out.
You'll get the same message box as above but this time you want to apply the
outline to **Graphic**. Click on **OK** and you'll get a new dialogue box.

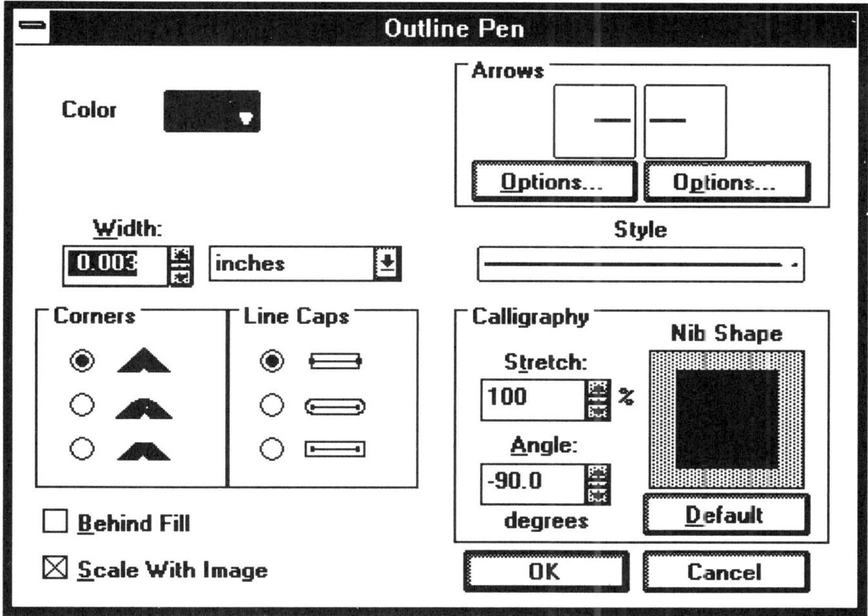

3.20 Outline Pen dialogue box

50   Here you can set the parameters for the outline that will be used for drawn
objects. The colour, the default for which is Black, can be changed by clicking
on the blank button. The palette will then appear and you simply click on the
colour of your choice. By default the line width is 0.003 inches. I usually change
this to 0.2 points. Why? Because a 0.2 point line is the thinnest line that can be
produced by a standard laser printer. It equates to a single dot at 300 dpi.

51   The one thing that you do want to do is turn off **Scale With Image**. If you leave
it on then the lines will get thicker or thinner as you enlarge or shrink an object.
I prefer to adjust the line thicknesses manually when I do this.

52   Click on **OK** to close the dialogue box once you have made the changes you want.

53   Click on the **Fill** tool, the final one in the toolbox that looks like a paint can, and it will open out. Click on the **X** and you will get a message box similar to the one in Fig 3.19. Check **Graphic** and then **OK**. That means that anything you draw from now on will not have a fill.

54   Open the **Fill** tool again but this time click on the circle wheel - the first icon on the top line. The Fill message box will appear. Click on **Artistic Text** and then on **OK** and a new dialogue box appears.

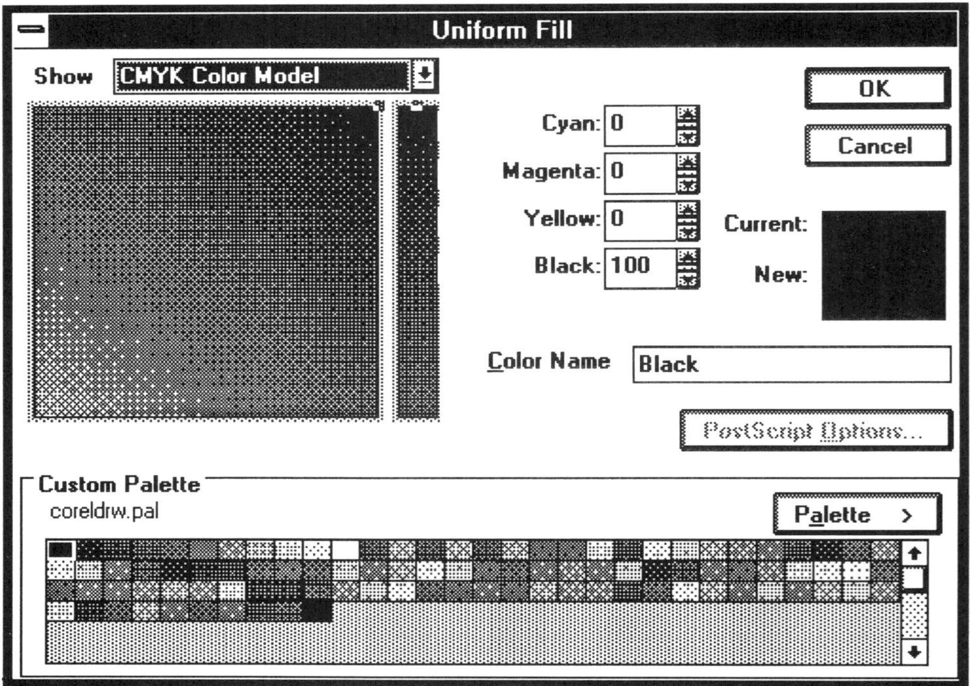

3.21 Uniform Fill dialogue box

55   Here you can set any colour you like for the Artistic text. But before you do that you need to load another palette. By default CorelDRAW loads the CORELDRW

palette which is a bit limited. Click on the button labelled **Palette** and a menu will appear. Click on **Open** and a dialogue box appears.

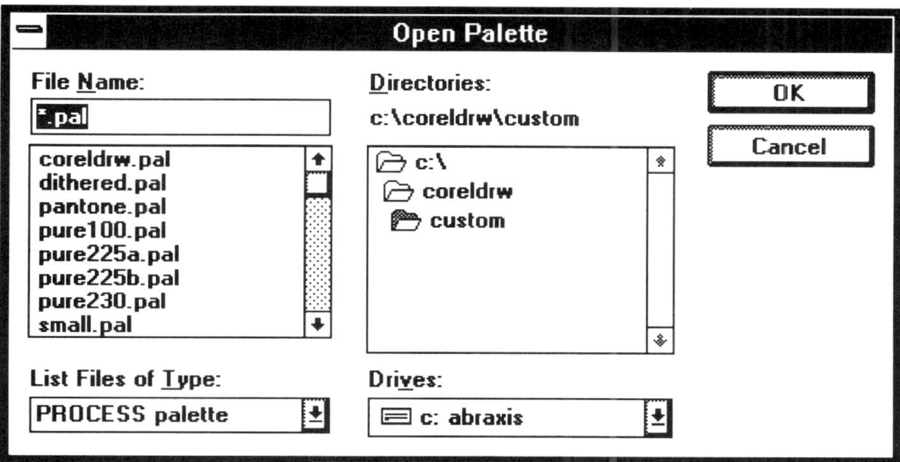

3.22 Open Palette dialogue box

56   Which palette you use is up to you but I use the DITHERED one because it has a wide range of colours and tones. Just double click on the one you want and you will go back to the first dialogue box.

57   Now you can select whichever colour you want for the artistic text. (In this case I'm going to leave it in black simply because so it will show up properly in the screen shots.)

58   Finally you want to set the colour for Paragraph text. Open the **Fill** tool again and click on **Black**. You'll get the same message box as before but this time you want only Paragraph Text selected. Click on **OK** and the cclour is assigned as the message box closes.

That's all the possible program customisation of CorelDRAW completed. You can amend things directly in the INI file but we'll come to that in the next chapter.

59   You now want to save what you have done. CorelDRAW will allow you to save a blank page. Press **Ctrl-S** and a dialogue box appears. Give the file the name

DEFAULT. You don't need to include an extension. Move the cursor down to the **Keywords** line and click once - the flashing cursor appears. Add whatever keywords you wish, e.g. Settings. Press **Tab** and the cursor will move down to the **Notes** area. Add whatever notes you wish.

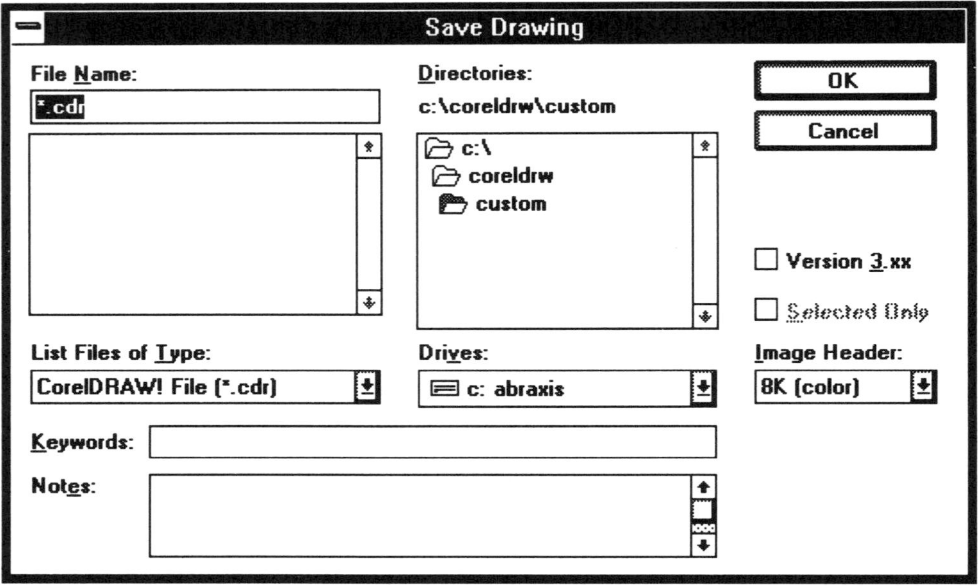

3.23 Save As dialogue box

60   As this is a blank page there is no point in it having a header. Click on the arrowhead on the **Image header** line. You'll get a drop down menu. Select **None**. (The image headers are the things that produce the thumbnails. They take up space and make the file larger.) Click on **OK** to save the file.

61   Finally, you should now close CorelDRAW. Do any of the following. **Alt-F4**, **Alt-F X**, **Alt-Space C** or double click on the **Control Box** at the extreme top left hand corner of the window.

4. CONFIGURATION

As well as setting parameters for CorelDRAW from directly within the program, you can manually edit the INI files directly. The easiest way to do this is to load the files into the Windows Notepad. In previous versions of CorelDRAW all of the configuration information was held in a single file, with CorelDRAW 4 this is not the case. There are a number of INI files and they all do different jobs as it were, either for different programs or for different aspects of the same program. You'll find that all the configuration files are now stored together in a sub-directory called **CONFIG** that subtends off the main CORELDRW directory. In this chapter we're going to look at the ones concerned mainly with CorelDRAW.

CORELAPP.INI

This file sets the basic parameters for CorelDRAW itself and the associated programs. The settings here will affect all the relevant parts of the entire suite of programs. It should look something like this:

```
[Config]
ProgramsDir=D:\COREL40\PROGRAMS
DataDir=D:\COREL40\PROGRAMS\DATA
CustomDir=D:\COREL40\CUSTOM
DrawDir=D:\COREL40\DRAW
ChartDir=D:\COREL40\CHART
ShowDir=D:\COREL40\SHOW
PhotoPaintDir=D:\COREL40\PHOTOPNT
MoveDir=D:\COREL40\MOVE
TraceDir=D:\COREL40\TRACE
MosaicDir=D:\COREL40\PROGRAMS
FontsDir=D:\COREL40\SYMBOLS
FiltersDir=D:\COREL40\PROGRAMS
```

The first few lines give the locations of the various directories for the various programs, filters, fonts, etc. In each case the destination lines should match the sub-directories in which you installed CorelDRAW.

CorelDRAW 4 - A Users Guide

FountainPresets=coreldrw.ffp

This line sets the basic preloaded parameters for the fountain fills in CorelDRAW, and other programs. You should not need to change this.

SpellLanguage=English
SpellDict=ienm9150.dat
HyphenateDict=hecrp301.dat
ThesaurusDict=com_thes.dis

These four lines give the information for the spelling checker and the thesaurus.

BigPalette=0
BigToolbox=0

If you are using a high resolution monitor, e.g. 1024 by 768, you may find that the toolbox and the palette are a bit small and difficult to use. By changing the values on these two lines to 1, i.e. on, instead of 0, i.e. off, the toolbox and/or the palette appear four times larger - each is twice as wide and twice as tall.

FontRasterizer=1

This controls the appearance of the display and printing of small font sizes. It is turned on by default and I have never needed to change it. With it turned on the fonts look better and cleaner.

3DLook=1

Determines whether or not the various dialogue boxes in CorelDRAW and the other programs appear in pseudo-3D. With the value set to 1, i.e. on, they do so. If you turn this off, i.e. change the value to 0, then the dialogue boxes, buttons, etc. will appear according to how you have them set in the Windows Control Panel, Colours.

TTFOptimization=1

Optimises the TrueType font display. I usually leave it alone because I don't use TrueType fonts anyway.

TextureMaxSize=257

Sets the maximum size for the appearance of text fills in pixels. Any texture beyond that size will simply be enlarged and thereby lose clarity.

[Registration]

The last two lines of the file give the registration details, i.e. your name and the serial number of the program.

CORELDRW.INI

This file controls CorelDRAW only and it looks something like this:

[Config]
AutoBackupDir=D:\COREL40\AUTOBACK

The first line gives the name of the directory that will be used for the auto backup facility in CorelDRAW. These files will have an extension of .ABK and they can be very useful - the problem is that they need disk space. The automatic backup is made according to the setting on the next line.

The backup files allow you to recover a file that has been lost, e.g. due to the program crashing, under certain circumstances. The ABK file is automatically wiped whenever you do a true Save, Save As, start a New file or close the program normally.

If you do lose a file for any reason do the following:

1   Log in to the AUTOBACK directory. Find the file you want. It will have the same name as your original file but its extension is .ABK.

2   Rename the file to [filename].CDR.

3   The file can now be opened in CorelDRAW.

Never, but never, load the ABK file directly into CorelDRAW or you lose the backup and another cannot be created due to MS-DOS file naming rules.

AutoBackupMins=10

Sets the time interval, in minutes, for the auto backup. By default it is set to 10 minutes. You may wish to change this. You can set the figure to be anything in the range 1 to 99. If you set it to 0 then you turn off the autobackup facility completely.

CalligraphicClipboard=1

Determines how any calligraphic pen outlines are treated in the Windows Clipboard when you use Copy and Paste and for some vector export filters. With the command turned on, i.e. 1, which it is by default any calligraphic outline is retained. If you turn the command off then the calligraphic effect is lost and all you will have is a standard line. Some vector export filters will retain the calligraphic line regardless of the setting here.

CMYKPalette=D:\COREL40\CUSTOM\DITHERED.PAL

Sets the default palette that you are using. The line is updated automatically whenever you reset the palette in CorelDRAW.

INKPalette=CORELDRW.IPL

Sets the spot colour palette that you last used in CorelDRAW. The entry is updated whenever you change it in CorelDRAW. The file shown above is the default and it is the Pantone Spot Colour one.

DelayToDrawWhileMoving=500

Determines how long you must be moving an object before it begins to redraw. If you move an object quickly then all you get is a bounding box. If you move it slowly then the object itself may appear according to the value set here. The delay is in milliseconds and you can use the range 1 to 32,000.

MakeBackupWhenSave=1

This creates a true backup of your file when you save it a second or subsequent time. The original file is renamed to [filename].BAK and then the subsequent file is called [filename].CDR. The next time you save the file the same thing happens, the last one becomes the BAK and the latest becomes the CDR file. Don't forget that you need to allow enough disk space for this to operate properly.

MaxCharsToDrawDuringKern=25

This line allows you to set the number of characters that will appear, as dotted blue shapes, when you kern the text with the Node Edit tool. If the number of characters is less than or equal to the number specified then you will see the characters as you kern them. If it is higher then you won't. The default is 25 characters.

MaximizeCDraw=0

This is another line that is updated as you use CorelDRAW. Quite simply it determines whether or not CorelDRAW appears as a maximised window or not. It the value is 0 then it doesn't, if it is 1 then it does. The line will be updated whenever you close CorelDRAW so that the program window reappears in the same way as it did the last time you closed it.

ShowObjectsWhenMoving=0

As you move objects they can appear in wireframe mode - at least they will if the value on this line is 1. With complex objects it can be a nuisance having it on because the refresh rate is slowed down. Therefore, it is up to you whether you leave the default, i.e. off, or not.

TextOnClpMetafile=0

This lines specifies how text is treated by the Windows Clipboard. If the value is 1 then text is treated as curves, i.e. not text, and if the value is 0, which it is by default, then you cut and paste text itself.

TemplateDir=D:\COREL40\DRAW\TEMPLATE

Specifies the directory for the CorelDRAW template files. It is determined when you install the program in the first place but if you move the templates to elsewhere you will need to amend the line.

AutoReduceOnImport=0

Some filters will resize images as images are imported. If the value here is 1, i.e. turned on, then any image that is larger than the page size will be shrunk to fit on the page. If the value is 0, which it is by default, then the images come in at the 'real' size.

MinCharsToBreak=3

The number on this line is the minimum number of characters that CorelDRAW keeps at the end of a line of Paragraph Text when you edit the envelope of that text. A new line will be started if there are the number of characters specified or more. The default value is 3.

EditTextOnscreen=1

Allows you to edit text directly on screen if the value is 1, the default. If you set it to 0 then you get the text dialogue box instead of placing the text directly on screen.

FullScreenBmpThumbnail=0

This determines whether or not you see the actual bitmap on screen. If the value is 0, the default, then what you get is a thumbnail of the image which means that things appear faster. If you change the value to 1 then the actual image is used and that will slow down the screen redraw rate.

[bmpExport]

[epsExport]

[wmfExport]

These categories control how some of the export filters on CorelDRAW work. You should never need to change them.

[ObjectDataPreferences]

Sets various parameters for the Object Data database. Again you don't need to do anything to these lines.

[LastUsed]

Under this heading there will be a list of the last four files that you used in CorelDRAW.

[DimensLabelFormat]

Gives the parameters of the Dimensioning labelling. It will be reset if you change the settings in CorelDRAW itself.

[ObjectDataFieldNames]

Gives the default settings for the Object Data Field Names. Again they will be reset automatically when you change them in CorelDRAW.

CORELFLT.INI

This file controls the various filters for all the programs in the CorelDRAW 4 suite. You should never need to change any of the lines in this file. It will look something like this:

[ImportFilters]

Gives the various names, filter name, the name that is displayed in the Import dialogue box, the extension and the kind of output that will result. You should never change any of these lines.

[ExportFilters]

As with the Import filters above. Again don't change any of the lines.

[CorelAIExport]

Specific information about the Adobe Illustrator filter.

[CorelBMPImport]

Specific information about the Bitmap filter.

[CorelDXFExport]

Specific information about the AutoCAD DXF filter.

[CorelHPGLPens]

[CorelHPGLColors]

[CorelHPGLExport]

These three lines are all to do with HPGL.

[ColorPath]

Sets the parameters for the colour in CorelDRAW and other programs.

[CorelTIFFExport]

Gives parameters for the TIF export.

[CorelFilterDirectories]

Gives information about the last three occasions when you made use of the filters. The lines here change constantly as you do things.

CORELFNT.INI

This file contains all the information about the CorelDRAW fonts. However, it is too large to load in the Windows Notepad, which has a maximum size limit of 16 Kb for files, so if you want to edit it you have to do so in something else. Having said that though, it is unlikely that you will ever need to amend it manually. Any line that starts with a semi-colon (;) is disabled. The main parts of the file look like this:

```
[Fonts]
GeographicSymbols=1 geograph.wfn
MusicalSymbols=1 musical.wfn
```

CorelDRAW 4 will allow you to use the original WFN font files from CorelDRAW 1 or 2 if you want to. If you do then you need to copy the files into the **\SYMBOLS** sub-directory and then add the details of them to the file under this section.

The name before the equals sign is the name that the font will have in CorelDRAW. The number after the equals sign gives the total weights of the font as follows:

1 is Normal
2 is Bold
4 is Italic
8 is Bold-Italic

To have multiple weights, and the font must be capable of doing so, you add the numbers together. Thus if you had a font that was capable of being used at all weights the value is 15, i.e. 1+2+4+8.

The final thing on the line is the name of the actual font file.

[Symbols]

This section gives the details of the Symbol Library files that are in WFN format. It doesn't include details of those symbols which are supplied as TrueType fonts. If you have any Symbol Library files that you created in previous versions of CorelDRAW you will need to copy the file to the **\SYMBOLS** sub-directory and then add the appropriate line to this section of the file.

113

CorelDRAW 4 - A Users Guide

[FontMapV20]

Maps fonts from CorelDRAW 2 for use with CorelDRAW 4. You should not need to change any of these lines.

[FontMapV30]

Maps fonts so that they can used. You should not need to change any of this.

[PSResidentFonts]

This section gives the comparative names for all the fonts for use with PostScript printers. Do NOT change any of this.

CORELPRN.INI

This file is concerned with printing from all CorelDRAW applications. It looks something like this:

[Config]
PSBitmapFontLimit=8

The first line sets the parameters for printing on PostScript printers. Essentially it changes the way some fonts are printed by using bitmaps instead of actual fonts - but only at small point sizes. Such bitmap renditions look better and print faster but they consume more memory. The only fonts that will be treated in this way are the ones that are not resident in the printer. The Line actually sets the number of different fonts that can be treated in this way. The default value is 8 but you can use anything in the range 0 to 255.

PSBitmapFontSizeThreshold=75

This line sets the threshold at which the bitmap rendition will take place. The size is in pixels and it corresponds to 18 points at 300 dpi. In other words 72 points is 300 dots, therefore 75 dots is 18 points.

PSComplexityThreshold=1500

This line specifies when an object is considered to be complex by CorelDRAW. The value is the number of segments that make up the object and if an object contains more than that then you will see a message in the print message box saying "Complex Image". However, complex fills, e.g. PostScript patterns, fountain fills, textures, etc., can cause the printer to exceed the complexity threshold anyway.

If that happens you will get Limit Check error on the printer. To try and avoid the problem you can increase the value here, in the range 20 to 20,000. If you do so then you should increase it in multiples of 500 until you get the result you want. If you increase the value too far you may find that you lose definition.

PSOverprintBlackLimit=95

Has to do with PostScript printing again.

WarnBadOrientation=1

This line causes you to get the message box about the paper orientation being different to the screen page orientation. If the value is 1 then you get the message, if the value is 0 then you don't. It's worth leaving it on. Remember that some Windows programs will not change the paper orientation back automatically so you should check it when you run subsequent applications.

[PSDrivers]

This section sets the various drivers that will be used by the program. You don't need to change any of it.

[ColorPath]

Sets the path and information for the Colour operation.

[300dpi]
[3386dpi]

Sets the output parameters for colour separations. There is a huge section of these with different frequencies for different output types and resolutions. Again you shouldn't need to change these.

There are other INI files, one each of CorelCHART, CorelMOSAIC, CorelMOVE, CorelPHOTO-PAINT and CorelSHOW. There isn't room to cover them all here and as the programs are only briefly looked at in this book, we'll leave them until the next book.

5. Basic actions

The time has come the Walrus said to start doing things with CorelDRAW itself - to paraphrase the Rev. Dodgson. The program is now fully configured, either directly or by manually modifying the INI files. This chapter is concerned with doing simple (ish) shapes and along the way it will cover polygonal shapes, colours, bitmaps, fills, PostScript pattern, grouping, combining and welding. Because it covers such a lot, I have broken the whole thing down into sections, each of which is a self-contained exercise with its own product. It is not necessary that you do them all but because later exercises build on these foundations of these you might like to at least glance at them all.

5.1 Basic Shapes

Just a quickie to get you started.

1   Is the Grid turned on? If it is then the Status Bar, which is just under the Menu Bar, will say **Snap to Grid**. If the words are not there then press **Ctrl-Y** to turn it on.

2   Select the Rectangle tool - the icon bearing a square in the toolbox, i.e. the fifth one down. When you move the cursor onto the page you'll have a small crosshair.

3   Click anywhere on the page and then drag the cursor down and to the right. A construction box appears. Watch the Status Bar because it tells you how big the shape is. Draw a rectangle that is 70 mms wide and 150 mms tall. To anchor the final point of the rectangle just release the mouse button. Now look at the Status Bar.

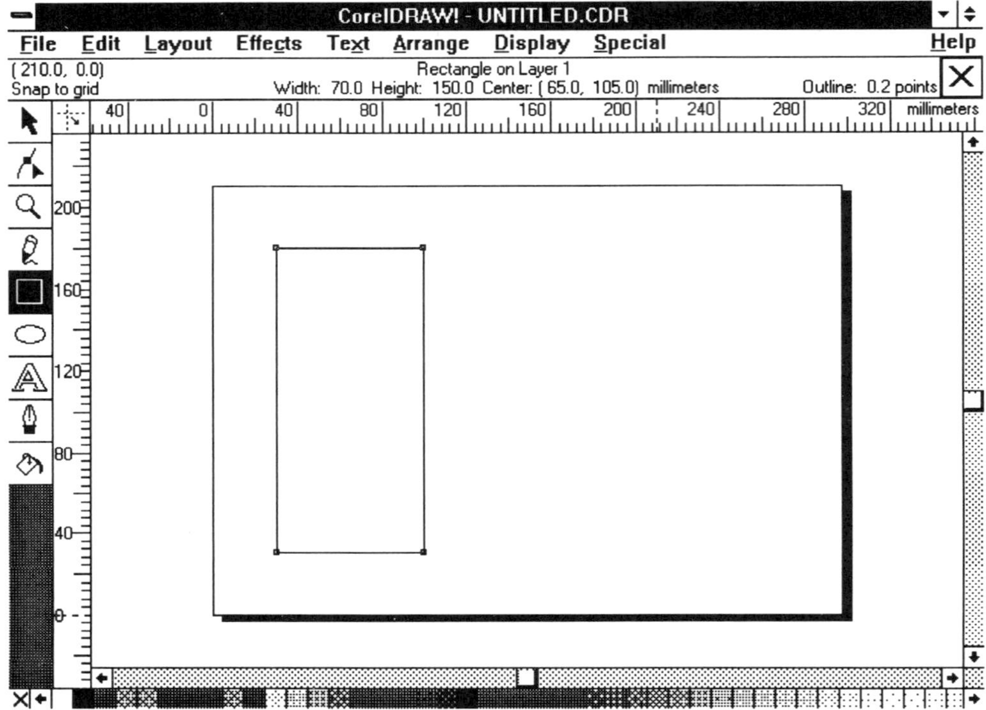

5.01 Rectangle

STATUS BAR

On the left hand side there are two numbers enclosed in brackets. These give you the current position of the cursor. Move the cursor slightly and the numbers will change.

Immediately below them should be the words **Snap to Grid**. That tells you that this function is turned on. You should note that **Snap to Guidelines** is also turned on but the Status Bar doesn't tell you so.

In the middle of the Status Bar are the words **Rectangle on Layer 1**, i.e. it is the **Object Definition**. CorelDRAW will allow you to have multiple layers but at this stage you only have three; Layer 1 - the one you are drawing on, Guides - which

118

contains guidelines but you haven't placed any yet, and Grid - which is a fixed layer. By the way squares are also called rectangles.

Beneath the object definition it says **Width: 70.0 Height: 150.0 Centre (xxx.x, xxx.x) millimetres**. This gives you the size of the object and the position of the centre of that object - you'll have numbers not x's.

At the right hand side of the Status Bar should be a little square with a large X in it. The icon tells you the colour of the object's outline, because it appears in that colour, and its fill - X means none. If the shape had a fill then the icon would be that colour. The words **Outline: 0.2 points** beside the icon simply tell you the thickness of the outline.

___

4 Move the cursor down to the palette at the bottom of the screen and click on any colour with the left hand mouse button. Click on a different one with the right hand button. Now look at the Status Bar again.

  The icon on the right has changed. It should be outlined in whatever colour you selected with the right hand button and the words **Fill: Colour** appear beside it. It won't actually say Colour - instead it gives you the colour name that you selected with the left hand mouse button.

5 Change the line thickness. Click on the **Nib** shaped tool, which is the Outline, and it will open out.

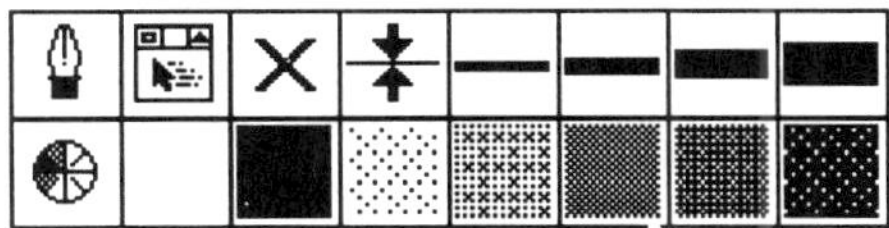

5.02 Outline tools

The first tool gives you access to the Outline dialogue box. The second opens the Outline roll-up. The third one gives you No Outline. Click on it and the outline vanishes and the Status Bar now says **Outline: None**.

6   There are two ways to put the outline back. Either you can open the Outline tool again and click on a line width or you can simply click on a colour in the palette with the right hand mouse button. If you do the latter then the outline will appear in that colour at 0.2 points - because that is the default line width.

7   Change the rectangle back to its original definition. The quick way is to click on Black in the palette with the right mouse button and click on the X in the palette with the left mouse button. You might also be able to do it by pressing **Alt-Backspace** (the keyboard shortcut for Undo) a number of times but it depends on how many actions you have done since you first drew the rectangle.

8   Open the **Outline** tool again and click on the roll-up icon, the second one along on the top line. The **Pen roll-up** will appear somewhere on the page. Click on its own **Control Box**, in the top left hand corner of the roll-up, and when the menu appears click on **Arrange**. The roll-up will move to the top left hand side of the open window and roll-up. Click on the arrowhead of the roll-up and it unfurls again.

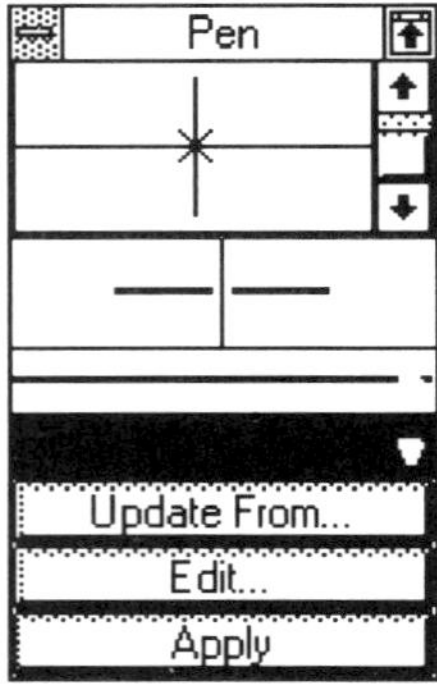

5.03 Pen Roll-up

Pen Roll-Up

The roll-up is divided into five parts:

The top part, which currently bears a thin lines with a vertical line and a diagonal cross on it is the **Line Thickness**. At present the thickness is 0.2 points. If you click on the up arrowhead to the right of it the line will get thicker in increments of 0.5 points. If you click on the down arrowhead then the line gets thinner, again in 0.5 point increments. If you try to make the line thinner when you have the 0.2 line showing then you will get an X, in other words no thickness.

Below the line thickness are two boxes side by side. These are the **Arrowhead** boxes. Using these you can apply an arrowhead to any open line. Because you currently have a rectangle on screen they will not do anything. (You can apparently set an arrowhead but it won't appear.)

Beneath that is the **Line Type** box. If you click on it, it will reveal a drop down menu containing lots of line types. CorelDRAW comes complete with 16 pre-defined line types. Note that all of them are single line types - CorelDRAW will not allow you to have double lines because they are so easy to draw that they would be redundant.

Underneath that is the **Line Colour**. Click on this and it will open out to give you a palette. The colours are the same ones that are displayed along the bottom of the screen.

The final part of the roll-up contains three buttons labelled **Update From**, which allows you to update the roll-up from another object; **Edit**, which opens the outline dialogue box; and **Apply**, which applies the roll-up contents to the selected shape(s).

---

9   Draw a square with dimensions of 100 mms. To do so you use the same tool as you did for the rectangle but you hold down **Ctrl** as you drag the mouse. This constrains the tool so that it only produces squares.

10   Hit the **Spacebar**. That will take you back to the Pointer tool. (It's useful to remember that. You can hit the Spacebar to switch between the current tool and the last one you were using.) The object handles, a series of 8 little black squares, appear around the square.

11   In the Pen roll-up change the line thickness to 5.0 points by clicking on the up arrowhead. Change the colour to Blue. Now click on the button labelled **Apply** and the square will have an outline of that thickness. Check the Status Bar.

12   Click on the button labelled **Update From** in the roll-up. The cursor will change shape and become a thick arrow bearing the word **From?**. Click on the original rectangle and the roll-up changes back to the original settings. Do it again and click on the square and the roll adopts the characteristics of the squares outline. This button can be extremely useful especially if you want to apply an outline from one shape to another.

13   Click on **Edit** and the Outline Pen dialogue box appears. This gives you much greater control over the outline, for example you can set the line thickness to any size rather than just the half point increments.

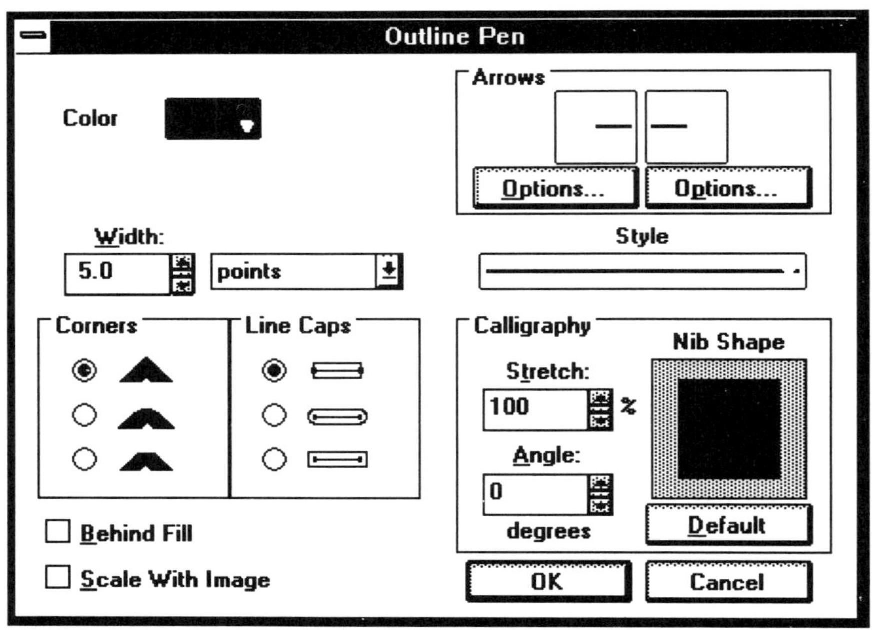

5.04 Outline Pen dialogue box

14   Change the outline of the square so that it matches that of the rectangle. Roll-up the roll-up by clicking on the upward pointing arrow on the roll-up's title bar.

15   Select the **Ellipse tool,** the one below the rectangle tool, that bears an oval. Draw an ellipse that is 170 mms wide and 50 mms high. Press **Ctrl-A** and the Align dialogue box appears.

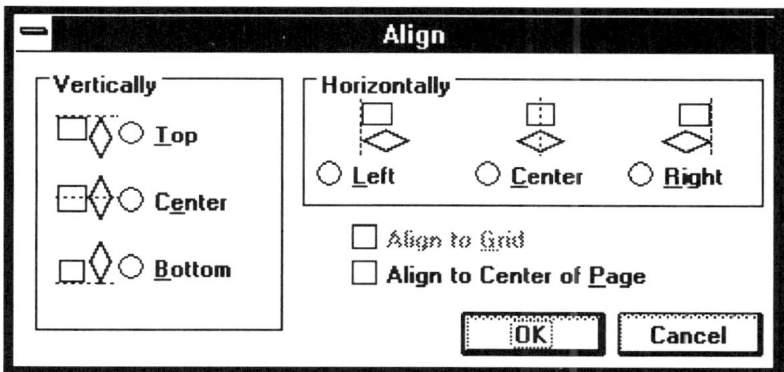

5.05 Align dialogue box

16   You can use this box to align two objects around a common point but for now we'll use it just to put the ellipse in the centre of the page. Click on **Align to Centre of Page** and then on **OK.** The dialogue box closes and the ellipse moves.

17   You can fill the ellipse and change its outline in the same way that you did for the rectangle.

18   Now draw a circle, 100 mms in diameter. Use the ellipse tool but hold down **Ctrl** which constrains the tool to producing circles.

19   We want to align the square and the circle together. Press the **Spacebar** and the handles appear around the circle. Hold down **Shift** and click on the square. The Status Bar should say **2 objects selected on Layer 1.** Now press **Ctrl-A** to bring up the Align dialogue box again.

20   There is a quick way to align two things together. Click on **Align to Centre of Page** - twice. Notice that the Centre commands in both the Vertical and Horizontal boxes are selected. Click on **OK** and the shapes will fit together.

ALIGN

When you align things together they will align themselves to the last object that was selected. So because you selected the square last the circle will move to overlay that. If you had selected the circle last then the square would have moved.

21   As you have both the square and circle still selected let's combine them. Press **Ctrl-L** and the objects will be combined into a single object. (Note: This keyboard shortcut has changed from CorelDRAW 3.0.) Look at the Status Bar and it now says **Curve on Layer I**.

22   Fill the resulting shape with a colour. You should find that the area between the square and circle fills but the central part of the shape, where the circle was, doesn't. The reason that it doesn't is because it is a hole.

5.06 Circle and square combined

COMBINED OBJECTS

When you combine objects you will get a hole wherever an even number of objects, e.g. 2, 4, 6, 8, etc., overlap. Where the number of objects is odd numbered, e.g. 3, 5, 7, etc., the shape will fill with colour because it is solid.

23 Now to align the ellipse with the rectangle. Select both shapes by dragging a bounding box around them - it appears as a dotted line rectangle. To do this you need the Pointer tool selected. Click anywhere on the page beyond the rectangle and then drag the cursor across the page so that you get the ellipse inside the bounding box that appears. Once you have both objects within the bounding box let go of the mouse button. Be careful that you don't include the circle/square shape. Check the Status Bar once you let the mouse button go. It should say **2 Objects selected on Layer I**.

24 You're going to align these two slightly differently. Press **Ctrl-A** to open the dialogue box. Try all the different combinations of alignments to see what happens. You'll have to open the dialogue box each time.

25 However, I want the ellipse to have the same orientation as the rectangle. You cannot do that using align, you have to rotate the ellipse first. Click on the page to deselect everything.

26 Now click on the ellipse and the normal handles appear. Click on it again and the handles change. What you now have are the **Rotational handles**.

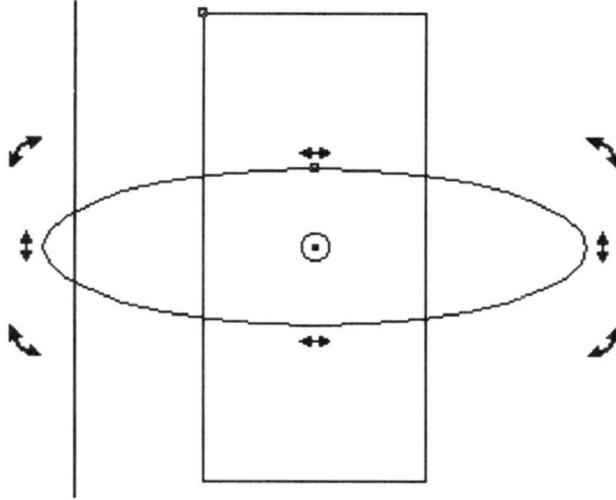

5.07 Rotational handles

CorelDRAW 4 - A Users Guide

There are actually two types of handles here:

The first type, which appear at the corners of the object, are the actual **Rotational Handles**. These allow you to rotate the object around the centre of rotation.

The second type, which appear in the middle above, below and to either side of the object are the **Skew Handles**. These will allow you to deform a shape by bending it up or down or side to side.

The little circle with the dot in it in the middle of the shape is the **Centre of Rotation**. This can be moved to anywhere on the available area and when you rotate or skew the object the rotation or skewing occurs around this point.

When you rotate or skew objects you can do so in increments, set in the Preferences dialogue box, by holding down **Ctrl** as you do so. You can also rotate or skew multiple objects if you have selected them.

27   Move the cursor to the rotation handle at the top right hand corner of the ellipse. When it is correctly in position it will become a small crosshair. Click and hold the mouse button and drag it around. The ellipse will stay where it is but you get a rectangular construction box that rotates as you move the mouse. Once you release the button the ellipse will redraw itself within the construction box at whatever position you left it in.

28   Press **Alt-Backspace** to return the ellipse to the original position. Now hold down **Ctrl** as you drag the handle - the same one as before. This time the construction box seems to jump around. That's because it is constrained to 15 degrees - it can only move in 15 degree increments around the centre of rotation. Watch the Status Bar as you move the ellipse. When it says **Angle: 90.0 degrees** let go of the button.

29   Now select the rectangle as well as the ellipse, i.e. hold down **Shift** and click on the rectangle, and then press **Ctrl-L** to combine them. Fill the resulting shape with Black. You should find that you have something like this:

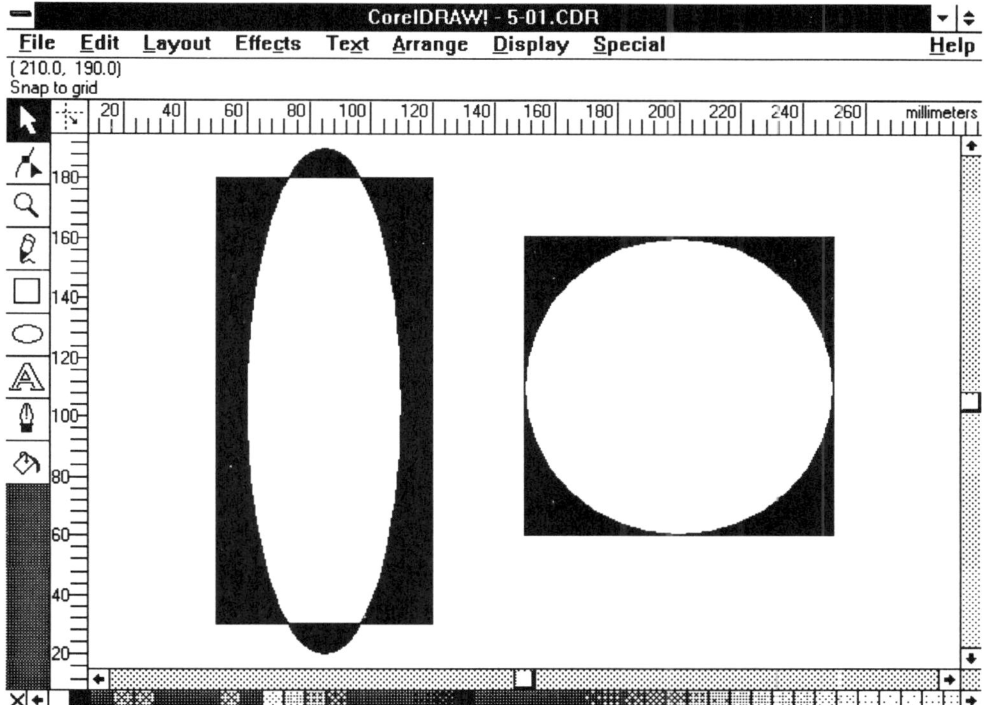

5.08 Shapes combined

30   If you now pick up the square/circle shape and drag it over the rectangle/
     ellipse you will be able to see the latter through the former. If you select both
     objects, align them to the centre of the page and then combine them both
     together you get more holes.

31   With the object selected, press the **Plus key** on the Numeric Keypad. The
     screen will flicker but otherwise apparently not change. It has though because
     it has just duplicated the object. Press **Alt-F8** and the Rotation dialogue box
     appears.

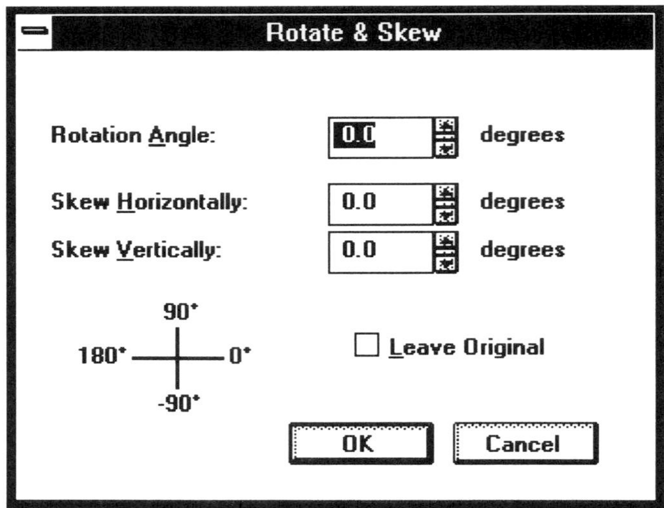

5.09 Rotation dialogue box

ROTATION DIALOGUE BOX

The dialogue box allows you to rotate objects exceedingly precisely, allowing for the fact that CorelDRAW doesn't use floating point math. You can enter any value into the **Rotational Angle** box, in increments of tenths of a degree. You can also use the dialogue box to skew objects precisely - but you cannot do both at the same time.

32   Change the Rotational Angle to **90 degrees** and then click on **OK**. Now you can see both objects. Select them both and combine them again. You should end up with this:

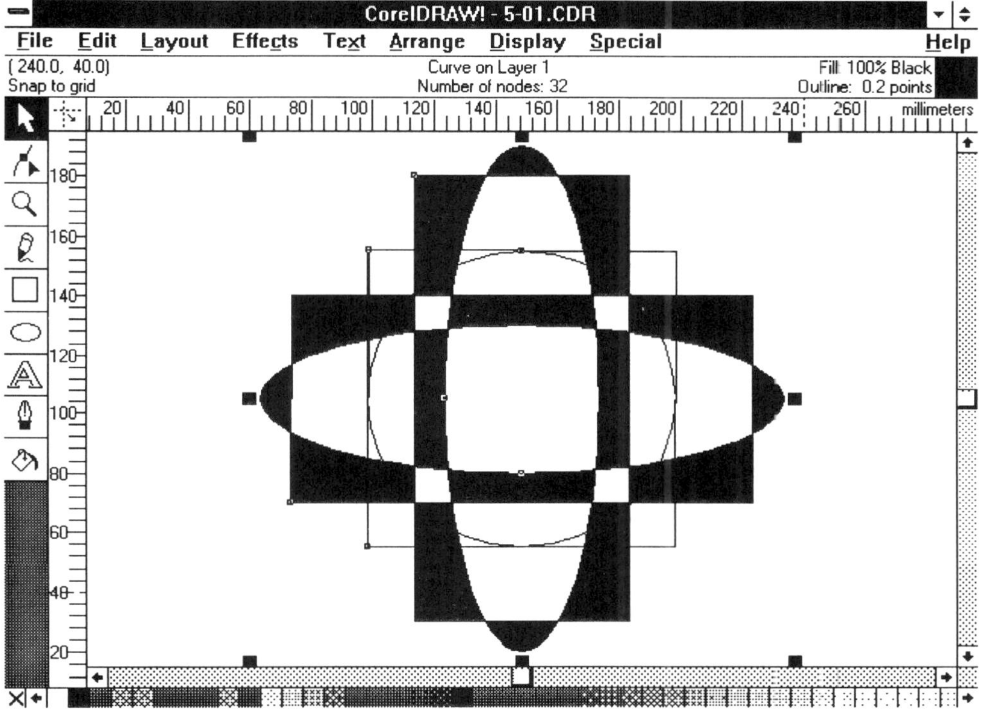

5.10 Finished shape?

33 Why is the square/circle not filled in? It has to do with the number of objects overlaying each other. Press **Ctrl-K** - the keyboard shortcut for **Break Apart**. You'll get lots of shapes all filled with black.

34 Click on the **X** in the palette with the left hand mouse button to remove the fill from all the shapes. Select one of the squares and then press **Del** to delete it. Then select one of the circles and delete that.

35 Now drag a bounding box around the remaining shapes and combine them again. Fill the resulting shape with black and it now appears correctly.

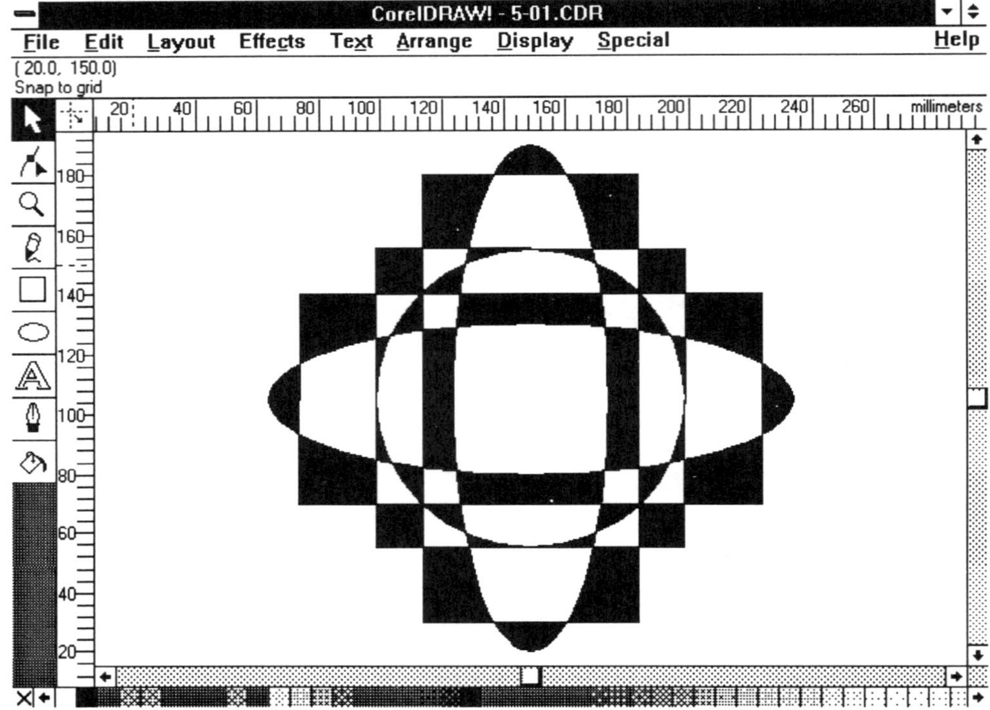

5.11 Finished shape

36   Save the file. Press **Ctrl-S** and the **Save As** dialogue box appears. Give the file the name 5-01 because you'll need it later.

SAVE AS DIALOGUE BOX

The Save As dialogue box, which will also appear whenever you save a file for the first time, allows you to define the saved file.

The first thing is **Filename**. You may use any combination of eight characters, bearing in mind the MS-DOS restrictions of filenames. There is no need to add an extension as all standard CorelDRAW files automatically have an extension of .CDR.

The central part of the dialogue box allows you to select a target directory to place the file in. It is always worth not putting the files into any of the CorelDRAW directories or sub-directories. You should use another directory that is unconnected with CorelDRAW in case you have to reinstall the program for some reason.

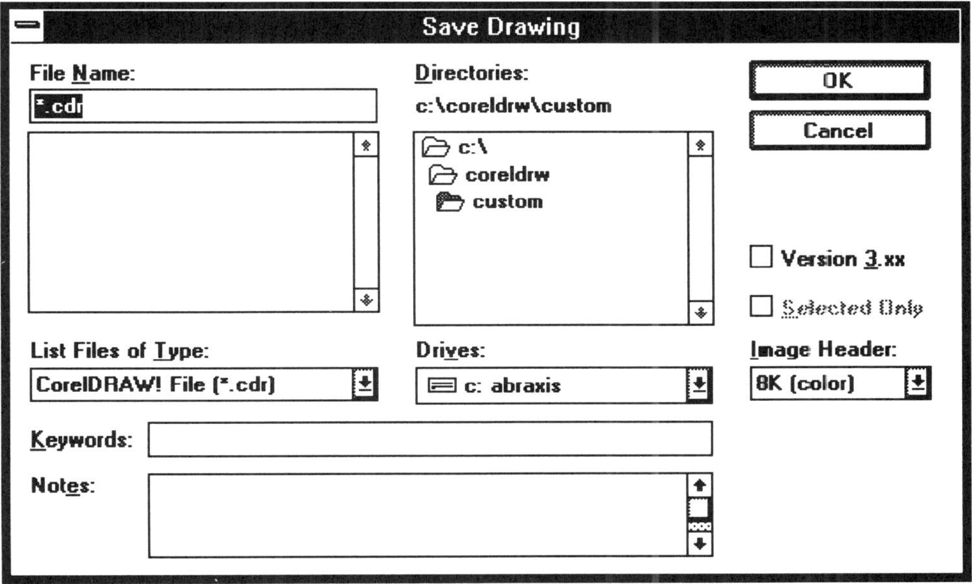

Beneath the directories box is a line labelled **Drives**. This allows you to change drive. Just click on the arrowhead and a menu will drop down listing all the drives on your system. By the way, you should not try to save a file directly to a floppy disk. Always save to a hard disk and then copy it to a floppy later if you need to. The reason is that saving produces a temp file on the target directory that may be too large to fit on a floppy.

To the left of the drive line it says **List Files of Type**. If you click on the arrowhead you'll get a menu that lists the kinds of files that you can save from CorelDRAW. They are standard CorelDRAW files with an extension of .CDR, Pattern files with an extension of .PAT and Template files with extensions of .CDT. When you select one of these types that extension is automatically added to the file.

Keywords are things used primarily by Mosaic but you can also have CorelDRAW search for files with specific keywords when you want to load a particular file - provided you can remember the keyword of course. You can have a number of keywords if you wish, just separate each one with a comma.

Notes are for your reference only. You can include anything you wish here.

Version 3.xx allows you to save the file from CorelDRAW 4 in CorelDRAW 3.0 format. The file formats are slightly different so that you cannot load a version 4 file into version 3 but you can do the reverse.

Selected Only causes the command to reduce the size of the file to contain only the information about the selected objects instead of the entire page(s) and all the contents. If you have only a small image then it is worth using this as it will greatly reduce the file size. You must have the object selected before activating the dialogue box.

Image Header refers to the thumbnails that appear in the Open dialogue box. There are five types of header, the sizes in kilobytes are actual and it means that the file will increase by those amounts:

> **None** which means just that, there will be no thumbnail of the image.

> **1K Mono** is the smallest header. It is monochrome and contains just enough information to see the thumbnail.

> **2K Mono** contains more information and will give a better defined thumbnail.

> **4K Colour** is the minimum colour definition.

> **8K Colour** is the most information header but is does add considerably to the file size.

You can set any or all of the possibilities in the dialogue box. Click on **OK** to close it and save the file in accordance with what you set.

5.2 POLYGONS

CorelDRAW doesn't possess a tool for drawing polygons as such, what it does have is a pencil tool that will allow you to create any sized or shaped polygon that you want.

1   Start a new page by pressing **Ctrl-N**. Or you could open the **File** menu and then click on **New**. You should be using an A4 landscape page.

2   A simple one first. Draw a triangle. Select the **Pencil** tool, the one above the rectangle tool. On the page click once to anchor one end of the line. Move the cursor and then click again. You'll get a line.

3   You can also draw squiggly lines. Click on the page and hold down the button. Move the cursor quickly and randomly all over the place. You'll get a squiggly line. Try signing your signature.

DRAWING LINES

CorelDRAW allows you to draw lines in three different ways.

Firstly, you can draw squiggles by clicking where you want the line to start. Then, while still holding down the mouse button, just move the cursor. Let go of the button when you have the squiggle you want.

Secondly, you can draw 'straight' lines by clicking once where you want the line to begin and then moving the mouse to where you want the line to end and then clicking again.

Thirdly you can draw constrained lines. Click once to anchor the line end, hold down **Ctrl** and then move the cursor. The position of the end of the line will be constrained to multiples of the Constrain Angle you set in the Preferences dialogue box. Click a second time to place the end of the line.

4   You're going to draw a five pointed star. You could try to do it freehand but you can use the constrain capabilities of CorelDRAW to make it much easier. Firstly, with the grid turned on, draw circle that is 180 mms in diameter. Align it to the centre of the page.

5   Now turn the grid off by pressing **Ctrl-Y**. Next you need a single guideline that lies in the middle of the page. Open the **Layout** menu and click on **Guidelines Setup**. A dialogue box appears:

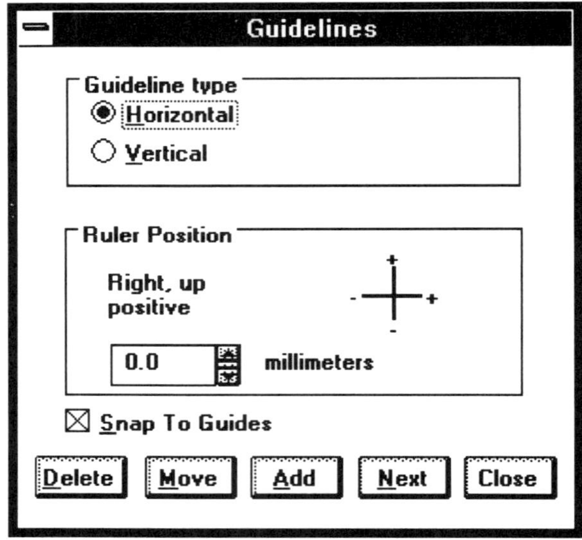

5.13 Guidelines setup dialogue box

6   Click on **Vertical**, change the ruler position to **148.5** and then click on **Add**. The dialogue box closes and you now have a vertical guide, shown as a blue dashed line, on the page.

7   Press **Ctrl-J** to bring up the **Preferences** dialogue box. Change the Constrain Angle to **72** degrees.

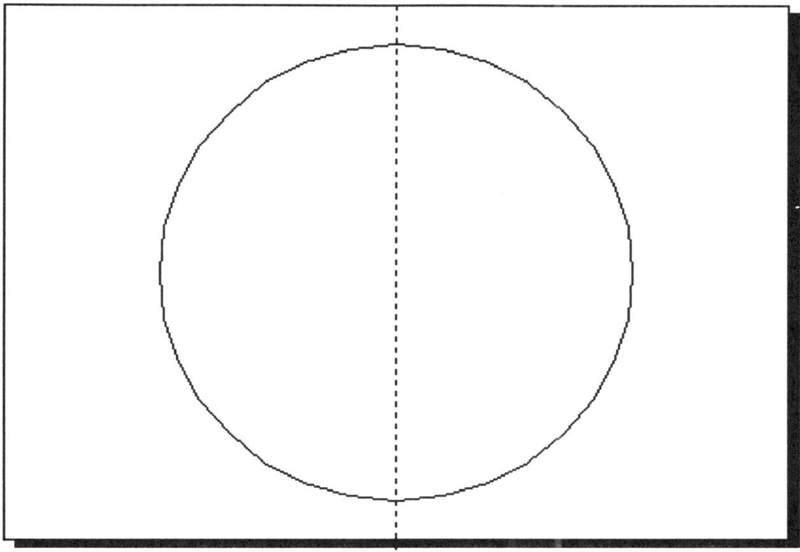

5.14 Guide in place

8   Now you can draw the shape. It's a little fiddly so press **F4** before you start. That will magnify the circle as much as possible so that it fills the available window space.

9   Select the **Pencil** tool. Move the cursor to the top of the circle where the guideline bisects it. Click once to anchor the end of the line. Now hold down **Ctrl** and move the mouse - slowly. You'll find that the line should appear in the right hand half of the circle, if you try it to the left it goes at a funny angle. Move the cursor down until it lies over the circle and then double click. It's very important that you double click because you are anchoring the end of the first line and beginning the second one all at the same time.

10   Still holding down **Ctrl**, move the cursor up and to the left. When you get to the edge of the circle double click again. Then move the cursor directly right - you'll get a straight line, and double click again when you get to the right hand side of the circle. Double click once more.

11   Move the cursor down and to the left. Double click when it is over the edge of the circle again. Then move the cursor back to the starting position and click once. That will join the final line to the original one. You should end up with something like this:

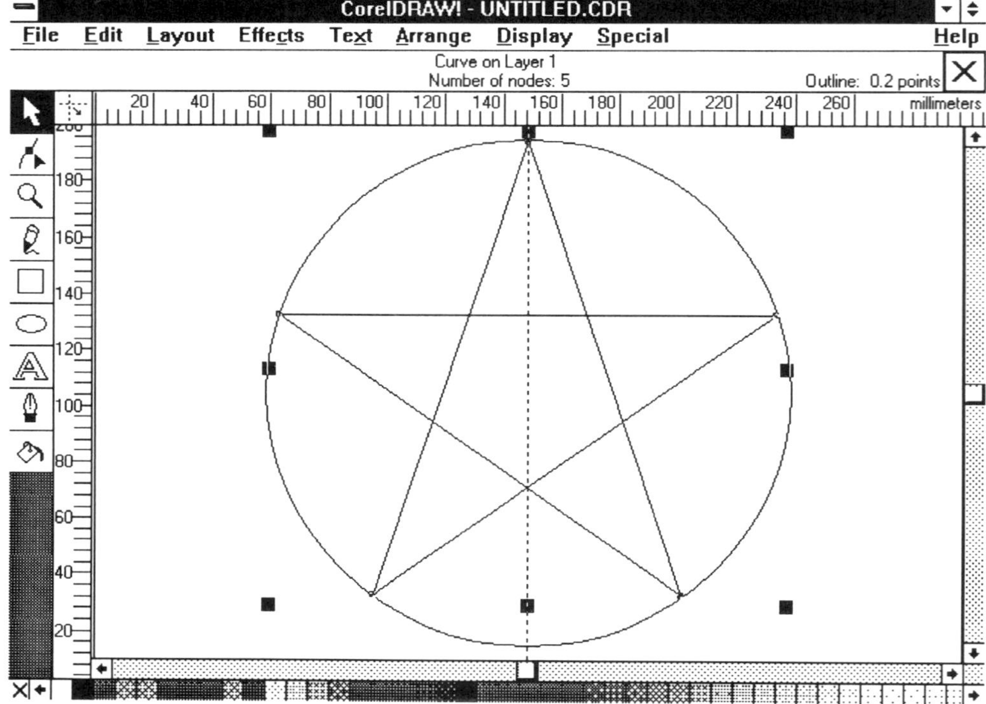

5.15 Star shape

12   Save the file and call it 5-02 because you'll want it in Chapter 7 when we'll turn it into a Celtic knot work pattern.

13   If you fill the shape with colour now you'll find that the points are filled but the centre remains empty. The centre is a hole in the same way that combined objects are. If you combine the star and circle the pattern changes - you'll get the points as holes and everything else filled.

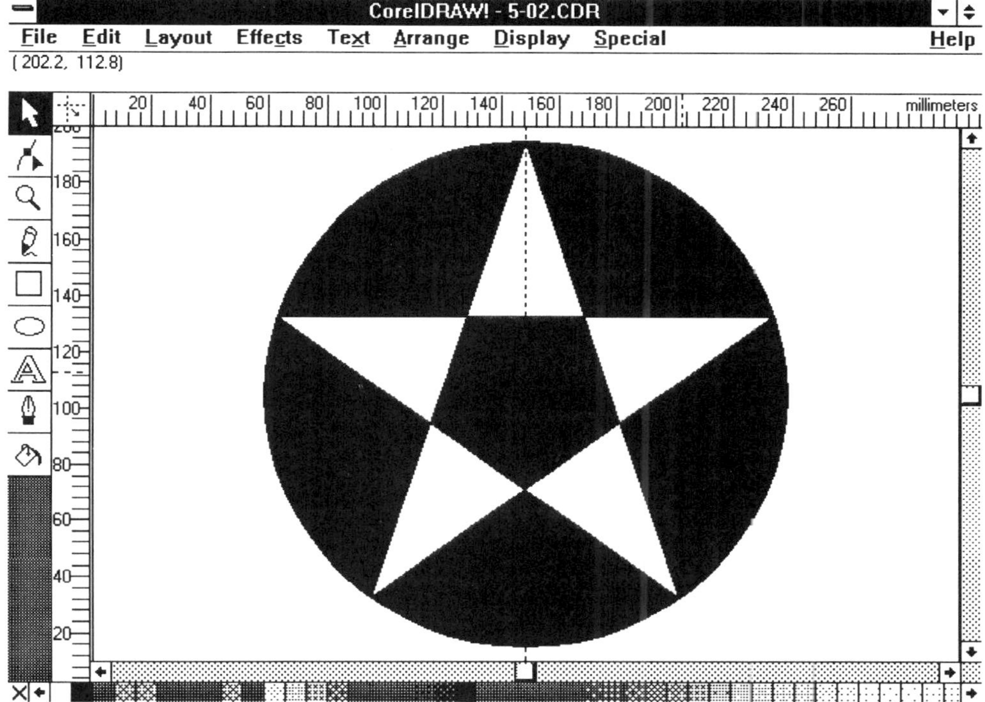

5.16 Filled shape

CONSTRAINED DRAWING

Using the constrain angle to draw polygons is very useful. By setting the angle to give you either complete angles or divisions of the complete angle allows you to draw very precisely. Try drawing nonagons, i.e. nine sided figures, or some other non-standard polygon. The trick is to place a circle first so that it is the diameter of the finished shape. Equally it helps to have a single guideline that gives you the start and end point of the shape. Remember though that the constrain angle you set will become the new default until you change it. The angle can be changed at any time by simply activating the Preferences dialogue box.

5.3 COLOURS

CorelDRAW allows you to use either Process or Spot colours. The former are based on the RGB (Red, Green, Blue) or CMYK (Cyan, Magenta, Yellow, Black) system. The latter are Pantone colours. You cannot mix two type of colour in one document. You have to select one or the other.

1   Start a new page by pressing **Ctrl-N**. Make sure that you don't overwrite the 5-02 file in the process. When you get a message box telling you that the file has changed click on **No**.

2   Draw a square, any size you like but about 100 mms would be good. Align it to the centre of the page.

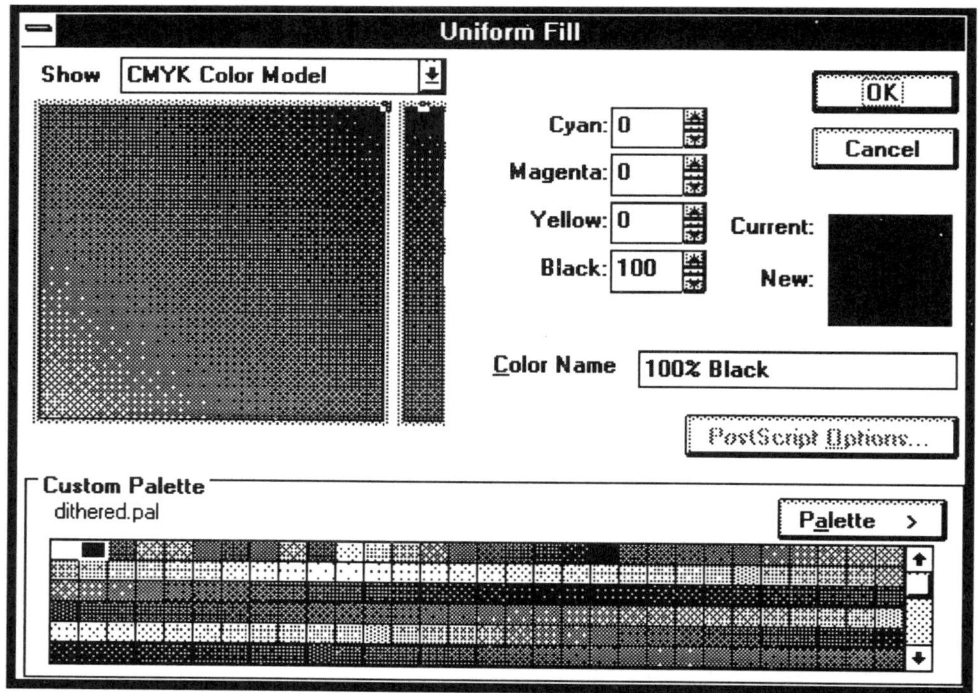

5.17 Uniform Fill dialogue box

3   Open the **Fill** tool and click on the wheel icon, the first one on the top row.
     You'll get a dialogue box.

4   The dialogue box is set to show Process Colours, i.e. the CMYK ones. If you
     click on the arrowhead at the end of the model line you get a menu that allows
     you to change to different colour models. In CorelDRAW 4 you can have
     Pantone Spot or Pantone Process Colours - just to make life a bit more
     confusing. Select **Pantone Spot Colours**. The dialogue box changes and you'll
     get a new command line that says **Show Colour Names**. Click on this and the
     Pantone names appear instead of the palette.

5   Click on any name and then on **OK** or just double click on the colour name. The
     dialogue box closes and your square will be filled with the selected colour.
     Take a look at the Status Bar and it will tell you what colour is being used.

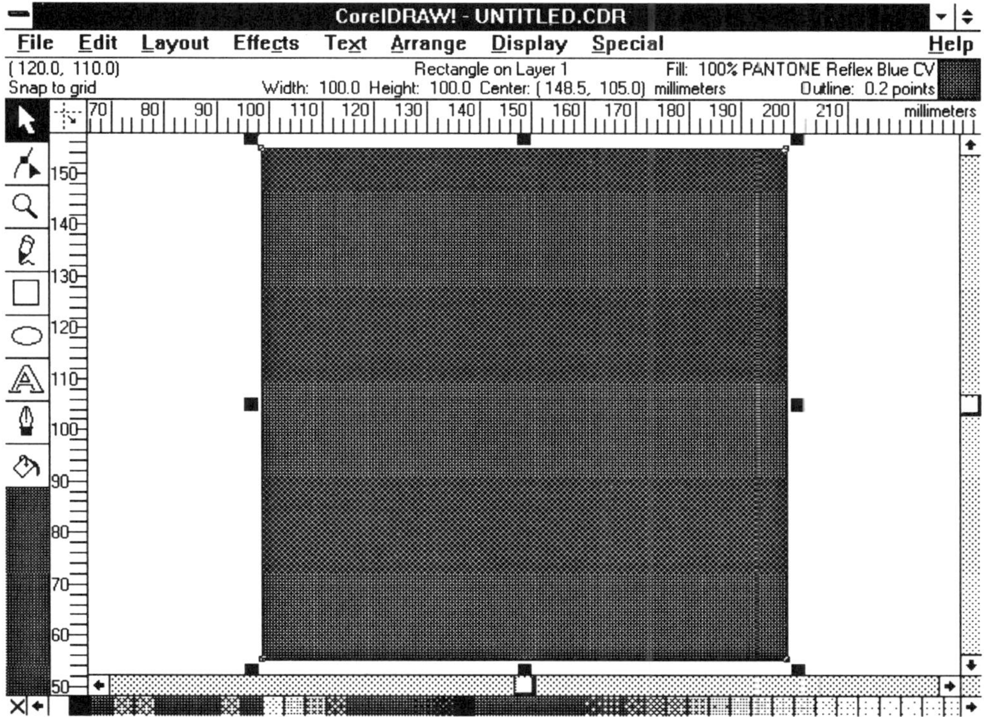

5.18 Pantone filled square

The Physics of Colour

You can skip this section entirely if you wish because it is concerned with the physics of colour, i.e. how it is produced; the psychology of colour, i.e. how human beings perceive colours; and the physiology of colour, i.e. how the human visual system interprets colour.

Colour is a function of light. The colour spectrum forms a very small part of the total electro-magnetic radiation that we experience every day. The Sun pumps out a huge range of radiation, everything from radio waves to microwaves to X-rays, all the time. We can actually only see a very small part of this - the colour spectrum.

The spectrum was 'discovered' by Isaac Newton in the 17th. century when he played a beam of sunlight through a prism and got the now familiar rainbow effect. What happened was that the light was refracted by the prism and split into its component parts. A rainbow appears in the sky for exactly the same reason, the raindrops refract the light to produce the spectrum.

The normal human eye can see colours ranging from 360 nanometers, the violet end of the spectrum, through to about 700 nanometres, the red end. By the way, there are said to be seven colours (Red, Orange, Yellow, Green, Blue, Indigo and Violet) in the rainbow because Newton was also an alchemist. At the time there were seven known planets and so Newton decided that there had to be seven colours, one per planet.

That's fine as far as light emitting objects, like the sun or a light bulb are concerned, but what happens with non-emitting objects? When the light hits an object, that object absorbs the majority of the spectrum but reflects back certain parts of it. The bits that are reflected are the colours that you see. So an honeydew melon appears yellow because that is the colour that is reflected back, the others are absorbed.

By the way, that's why the majority of supermarkets use incandescent light bulbs. These give out a full spectrum of light and so they emphasise 'natural' colours. Fluorescent lights on the other hand give out mainly the blue end of the spectrum and 'natural' colours appear darker and less natural. Perceived colour is a subjective phenomena. That means that the colour you see as red, for example, may not be identical to the colour I see. We both agree that a colour is red because of our upbringing but there is no guarantee that we are seeing the same thing.

5.4 FOUNTAINS

1   Start a new page by pressing **Ctrl-N**.

2   Draw a square, any size you like but about 100 mms would be good. Align it to the centre of the page.

3   Click on the Fill tool, the one that looks like a paint can and it opens up.

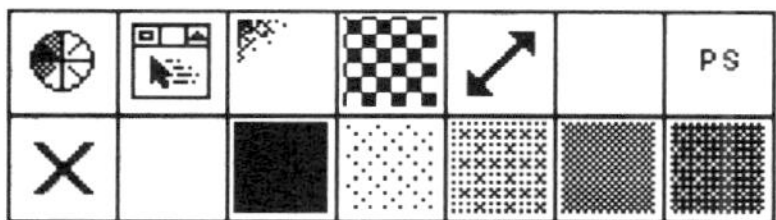

5.19 Fill icons

FILL OPTIONS

The Fill tool gives you access to a number of fills and seven preset colour options.

> The first icon which looks like a rainbow wheel, on the top row will activate the Fill dialogue box.

> The second icon, bearing the roll-up icon, brings up the Fill roll-up. The roll-up contains some of the functions of the fill tool.

> The third, containing a blended pattern, will activate the Fountain Fill dialogue box.

> The fourth, containing a checkerboard pattern, allows you access to the Bitmap or 2-Colour fill patterns.

> The fifth, with a large double-headed arrow in it, gives you access to the Vector or Full Colour patterns.

> The sixth is new. This allows you to use the Bitmap Textures.

The final icon on the top row, bearing the letters PS, allows you to use the PostScript patterns.

The icons along the bottom allow you to fill an object with preset densities of black. They are, in order, No fill, 100% black, 10% Black, 30% Black, 50% Black and 70% Black.

You can also use the palette along the bottom of the screen to fill any object with colour. Just click with the left mouse button on a colour once you have selected the object. You can page through the palette using the arrows at either end of it, and if you click on these with the right mouse button they will scroll so that the last one becomes the first.

---

4   Click on any of the bottom seven buttons. The square will fill as the tool closes. That's okay but it would be better if you could have all the tool options available all the time. You can't quite do that but you can have most of them.

5   Open the **Fill** tool again and click on the **Roll-Up** button. The roll-up will appear on screen. The roll-up allows you to use Fountain fills, Bitmap, Vector and Texture fill patterns.

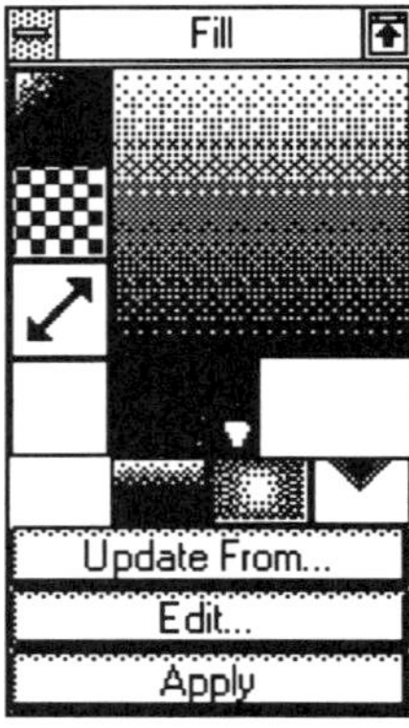

5.20 Fill Roll-up

6   Open the roll-up **Control Box**, in the top left hand corner, and click on **Arrange**. The roll-up will move to the top left of the window. Roll it down again.

7   By default the roll-up shows the Black to White Linear Fountain Fill. Click on **Apply** and the square, which should still be selected, will fill.

8   The fountain fill may be slightly banded. If you want to see how it really is press **Ctrl-J** to open the Preferences dialogue box. Click on **Display** and change the Fountain Stripes to 256. Then close the dialogue box. This will show the stripes properly but the display will be much slower. I suggest that you change the stripes back to 25.

9   Let's change the colours. The roll-up shows a representation of the fill and below that there are two buttons, one is black and other is white. Click on the Black one and the palette will appear. Click on any colour you like.

10   Now click on the White button, again the palette appears. Select another colour. (If you select the same colour then you don't get a fountain fill for obvious reasons.) The representation of the fill appears in the large square above the buttons. Click on **Apply** to fill the square with the new fill.

FOUNTAIN FILLS

CorelDRAW 4 now allows you three types of fountain fills:

Linear which is a straight blend from the bottom to the top, or vice versa. You select the first colour and then the second. The program then creates a blend from the one to the other. The effects can be very subtle depending on the starting colours.

Radial blends the two colours from the centre of a circular area to the outside.

The third type, which is new to CorelDRAW 4, is **Conical**. This blends the colours so that the first colour is at the bottom and the second is at the top. The colours then blend sideways around and into each other.

11   Beneath the colour buttons are three more buttons in a row. The first is for Linear fills, the second for Radial fills and the third is for Conical fills. Try them all by clicking on one of them and then clicking on **Apply** each time.

12   But you can do even more with fountain fills in CorelDRAW 4. With any fountain fill in use, click on Edit in the roll-up. A dialogue box appears:

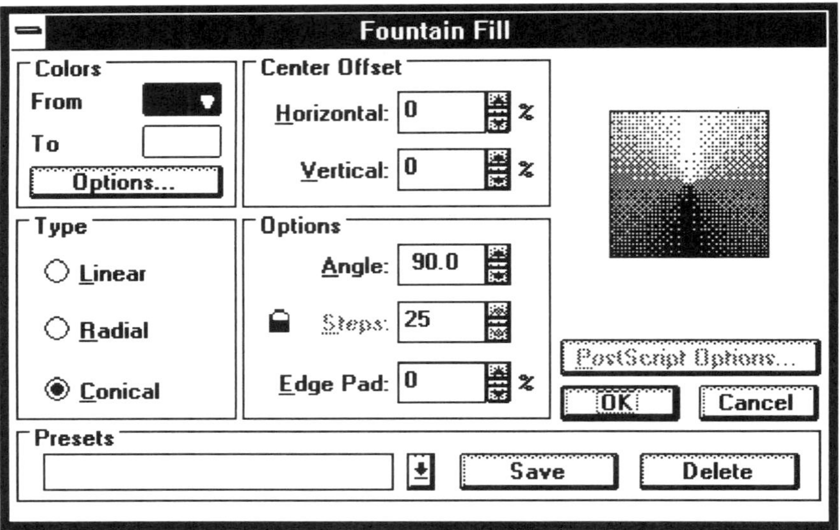

5.21 Fountain Fill Edit dialogue box

13   Click on the **Options** button and you will find that you can now have three types of blend including a Rainbow fountain fill. (You cannot use Black or White as the starting colours for this by the way.)

14   Click on **Rainbow**. On the right hand side there is now a rainbow wheel. You can change the start and end colours by clicking on the colour buttons as before. The rainbow wheel itself will now have a line on it. If one of the colours you have selected is white then you get a spiral line from the centre to the second colour. If you are using two colours then you get a circular line running from one to the other. If you are using the same colour for both the start and end then you get a full rainbow.

15   Set the colours whatever way you want and then click on **OK** to go back to the first dialogue box. Click on **OK** again to go back to the roll-up.

16   Click on **Apply** to fill the square with the new fountain fill.

HOW WE SEE COLOUR

Forget about RGB and CMYK for a minute, the human eye sees colour in terms of Hue, Saturation and Brightness. Hue is the basic bit, it gives you the actual colour. Thus red is a hue as are blue and yellow. Saturation is a measure of how dense the colour is, i.e. how much of a particular colour is present in what you see. Pink and red contain the same hue but the latter is more saturated. Brightness is a measure of how much light and dark there is in the colour.

That's the way you see colour but it can be affected by a range of other things. For example draw two rectangles in CorelDRAW, each half the size of the page and lay them side by side. Fill one with black and the other with white. Now draw two circles, both filled with red, and align each one in the centre of one of the rectangles.

On screen the circle against the black background appears brighter. That's because the monitor compensates for the colour and increases the saturation of the red. Also the circle against the black background appears larger. But if you print them out to a colour printer they will be reversed and the circle on the white is brighter.

In your retina there are two types of detector cells. One type is called cones and the others is rods. Cones detect colour and there are roughly 6 million of them. They are clustered near the centre of the retina. The cones can only work if there is sufficient light for them because they contain light-sensitive chemicals called Photopigments. Each cone has to be one of three types that detects either Red, Green or Blue. Now the odd thing is that of the total 65% detect red, 33% detect green and the remaining 2% detect blue.

When the light, as interpreted by the cones, passes down the optic nerve a certain amount of basic processing of that information is carried out by the optic nerve itself. No-one is quite sure how this works and until recently it was assumed that all processing was done in the brain. The result is that the process are analysed into opponent colours. That means that the colour information is interpreted in terms of how much red, green or blue it contains.

145

Because there are different types of colour interpretation it affects the types of colours you can see. For example you cannot see reddish green or bluish yellow because it involves two different receptors. Instead you can only see cross-combinations of colours so you can see reddish yellow and bluish green for example.

The trouble with the cones is that they can be saturated with light very quickly and when that happens they become fatigued and stop functioning. Look at a pure colour for a couple of seconds, try not to move your eyes, and the colour will gradually leech away and become grey.

One other thing, the colours of things affect our perception of distance. Red will tend to appear to be in front of blue for example. It's because the lens in your eye is not colour corrected and so it can only focus a single colour at any one time on to the retina. Okay so it skips from colour to colour very fast but the principle holds true. Equally because there are more red detector cones than blue one, you get more red and therefore it appears to be in front of the blue.

Talking about the lens. The lens absorbs some light in the process of transmitting it to the retina. It absorbs about twice as much blue light as any other colour. That's why blue appears to be a restful colour. You eye doesn't have to work very hard to see blue and so it's less work intensive. Because you can see more red your eye works harder and that involves all kinds of glandular activity, including the production of adrenaline, which is why red is an exciting colour.

Back to the rods. There are over 120 million of these in the average human eye and they are concentrated around the periphery of the retina. Rods can only see shades of grey but they are sensitive to movement, which the cones don't handle too well. That's why if something moves at the edge of your vision you can see it - the rods detect the movement.

The rods function best in very dim light, there has to be a minimum amount for them to work at all, but they are very good at detecting a wide range of grey in that light. That's why if you wake up in the middle of the night you can see enough to orientate yourself in space.

It used to be thought that the rods and cones acted independently but this is now known to be incorrect. They function together most of the time. The rods detect the edges of the colour objects and your eye skips around the edge all the time - if it didn't then the colour would wash out - to bring the colour into focus on the retina.

A quick word about colour blindness. There are very, very few people who are actually colour blind, i.e. unable to detect any colour at all. The majority of people who are described as colour blind are actually colour insensitive. Their cones lack some of the photopigments. The most common type is called Dichomatism, or Red / Green colour blindness, and it means that the cones lack the red or green photopigment. The red or green part of an image becomes grey instead of coloured. There are three different recognised varieties of Dichomatism depending on how much of the photopigments is missing.

One last thing. Colour experience is dictated by the culture you grew up in. So for West Europeans red is seen as a danger colour but in China it is the bridal colour. Blue is seen as a restful, calming colour in the West whereas in the East it is rarely used. We use yellow as a cautionary colour but in Brunei it is reserved for Royalty and in the East in general it is a funeral colour. Europeans tend to use bright, pure colours whereas in the East pastel hues are more usual. So if you are doing international things be aware of what colours mean for your target audience.

5.5 Bitmap Patterns

The Fill roll-up also allows you to use three types of pattern. In this section we're going to concentrate on the first two - Bitmap or 2-Colour and Vector or Full Colour.

1   You should still have your square on screen.

2   In the roll-up click on the Checkerboard pattern icon. The representation square will change to show you a circle with a quarter circle in each corner. Notice that there is a new button labelled **Tile**. Click on **Apply** and the square will be filled with this pattern.

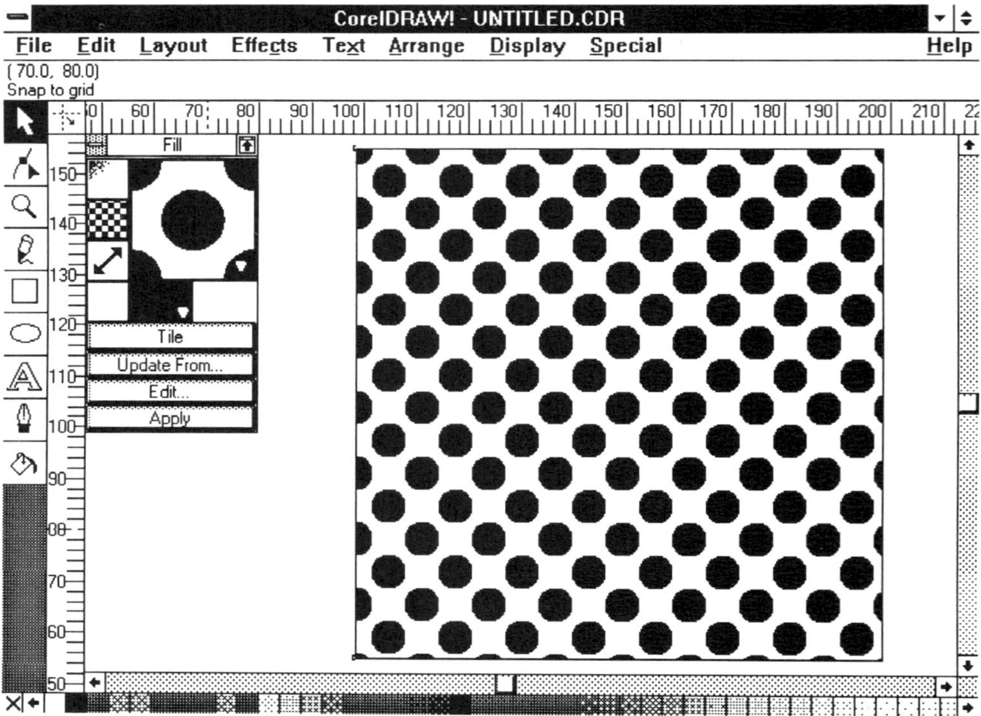

5.22 Bitmap pattern

148

3   Click on the button labelled **Tile** and you'll get two small squares appearing in the filled square. Press **F4** to make the square larger and they will be easier to see. These tiling squares allow you to change the size and position of the tiles that make up the bitmap pattern. The left hand one controls the size of the tile while the right one controls the position of the second and subsequent tiles.

4   Move the cursor to the tiny square that overlays where the two tile squares join. Now drag this out to make the tiles bigger. Because you have the grid turned on the tiles will jump around a bit. Make the tiles whatever size you want and then click on **Apply**. The pattern will change completely.

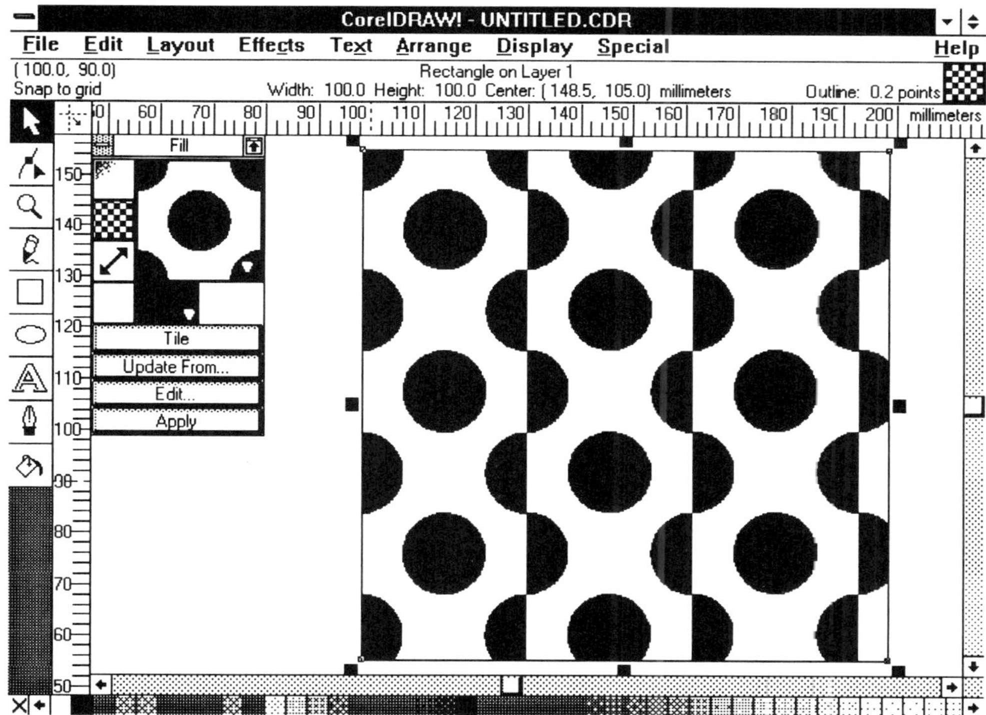

5.23 Tiled pattern

5   Now try to make the pattern go back to what it was by retiling it. A tip: If you hold down **Ctrl** as you tile the pattern it will only allow you to tile in multiples of the original pattern size - and it overrides the grid in the process.

6   Now move the cursor into the right hand tile. You can drag this around the left hand tile but not remove it from it. Move it so that it is about half way down the size tile. Click on **Apply**. You should get something like this:

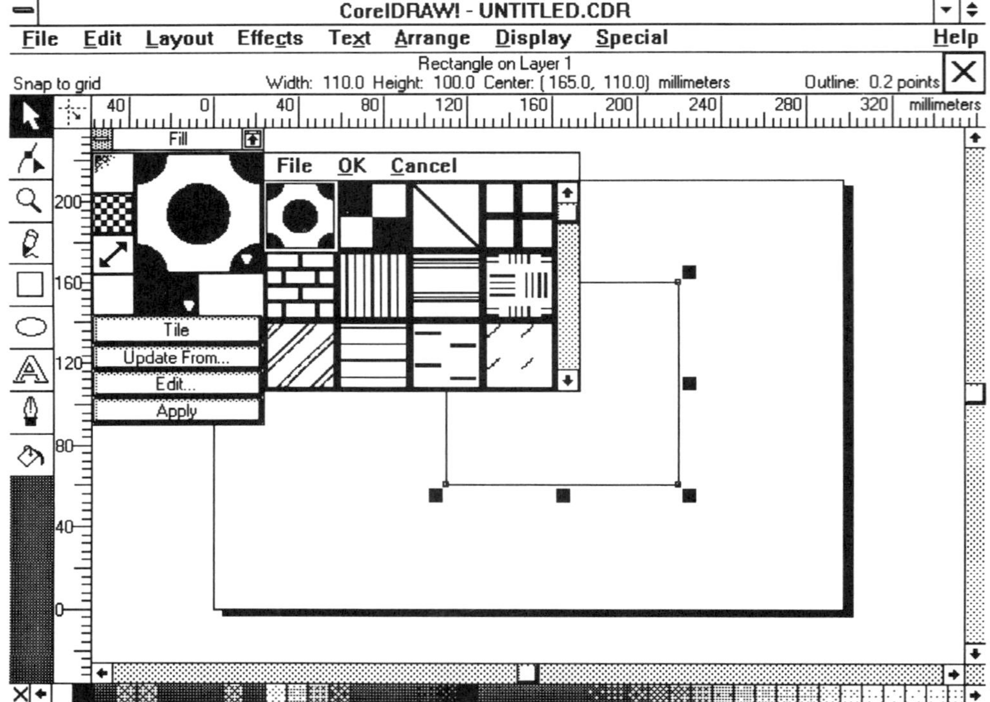

5.24 Possible patterns

7   Try using different patterns. If you click on the pattern representation you will get a menu bearing all the available patterns. To select one of them just double click on the one you want. Try different tiling effects.

5.6 Vector Patterns

As well as allowing you to use bitmap patterns, CorelDRAW will also allow you to use full colour, vector patterns. You can actually create these within CorelDRAW itself and then apply them to any object.

1   In the roll-up click on the icon with the diagonal arrow. The roll-up will bear a diagonal line - because no pattern is loaded. Click on the pattern representation area and it will open out to show you the first twelve patterns. To see more click on the scroll bar.

2   To select a pattern simply double click on it and it will appear in the representation area. Now click on **Apply** to fill your square.

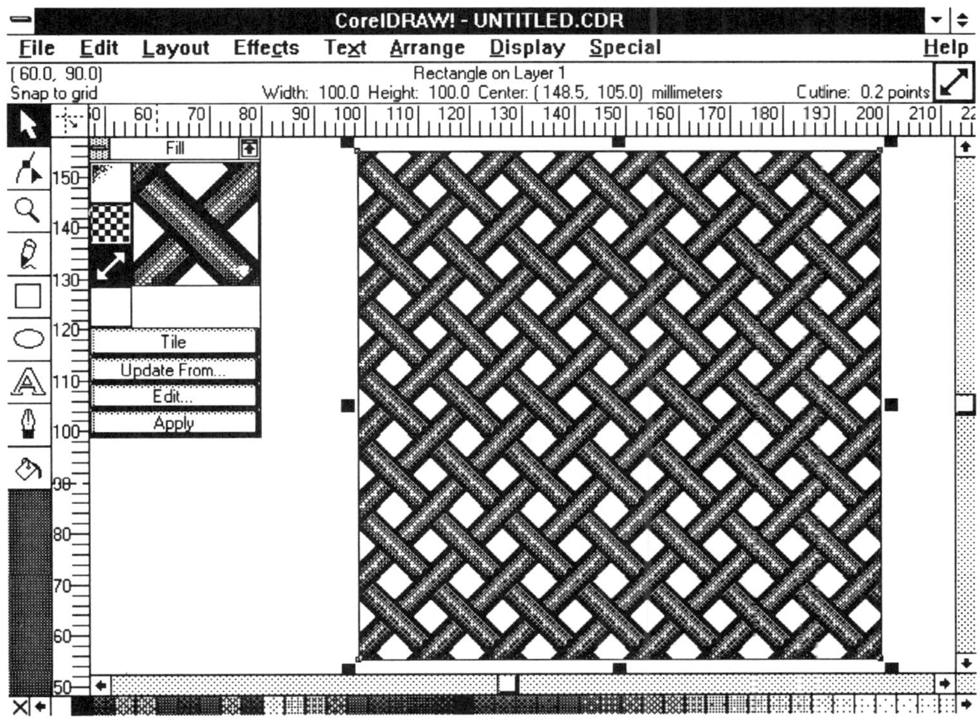

5.25 Pattern applied

3   As with the bitmap patterns you can tile a vector - in exactly the same way.

4   Click on **Edit** and a dialogue box appears:

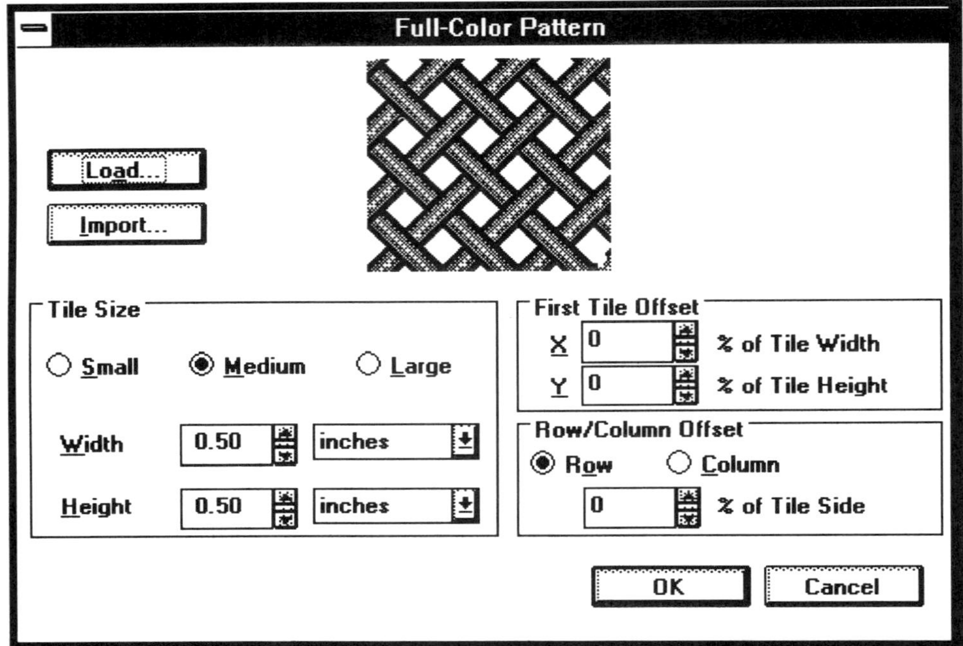

5.26 Edit pattern dialogue box

5   The dialogue box allows you better control of the pattern size and tiling than the roll-up does. Notice that there are three pre-determined **Tile Sizes**; Small, Medium and Large. By default CorelDRAW will always use the Medium size, the actual size will depend on the pattern. You can change the size to whatever you wish simply by overwriting the values.

6   **First Tile Offset** allows you to reposition the edge of the first tile. Normally any tile is placed so the left hand edge of it aligns with the left hand edge of the object being filled. This is fine if you are doing simple shapes, like squares, but when it comes to more complex objects you need much greater control of the positioning. This option gives you that control.

7   **Row/Column Offset** is the equivalent of moving the right hand tile after clicking on Tile in the roll-up except that you can now do it with percentages and apply it to either the row or column.

8   Play with the settings and try them out. Click on **OK** to close the dialogue box. The click on **Apply** to change the pattern in the square. You won't see the changes until you do so.

5.7 TEXTURES

CorelDRAW 4 gives you a new fill feature called Bitmap textures. The program comes complete with a wide variety of patterns all of which you can customise in thousands of ways. However, because they are generated bitmaps they can take a long time to produce and display. They work best for small areas rather than for large backgrounds.

1   In the roll-up click on the **Textures** icon, the one below the vector patterns. The roll-up will change.

5.27 Textures in roll-up

2   The textures come defined as Styles and if you click on the arrowhead beside where it says Sky 2 Colours, you'll get a drop down menu giving you the various preset patterns. Select one of them by clicking on it.

3   Now click on **Apply** in the roll-up. Depending on which pattern you selected you may have a long wait before the pattern appears. (You'll have to excuse the illustration quality. The textures are all full colour and they do not render well in monochrome unfortunately.)

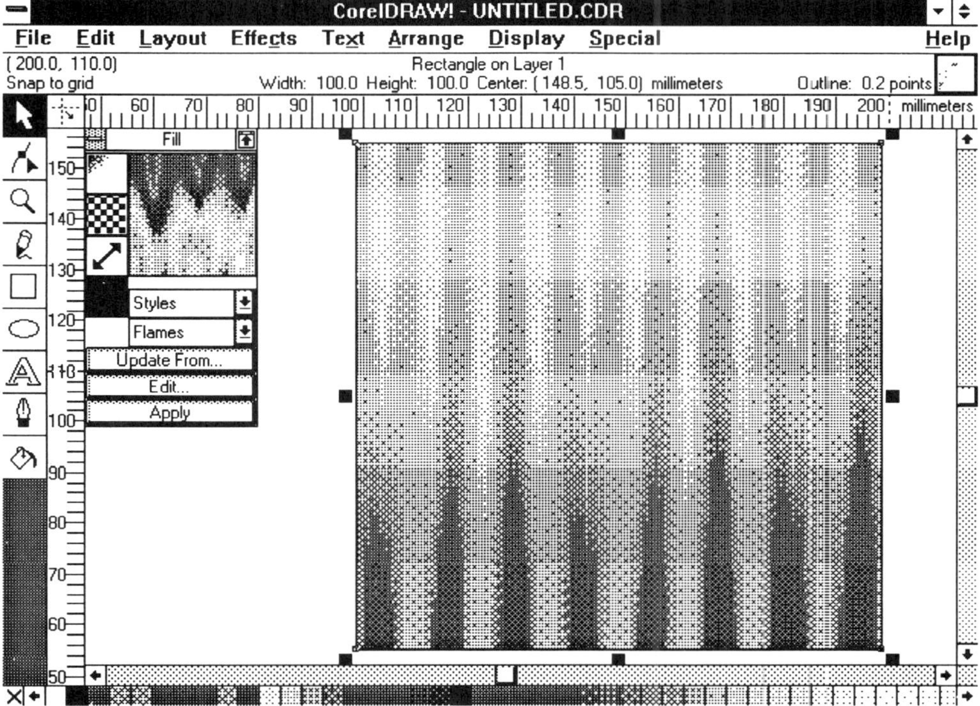

5.28 Flames pattern

4   Click on **Edit** and you'll get the dialogue box. This is different to the previous one.

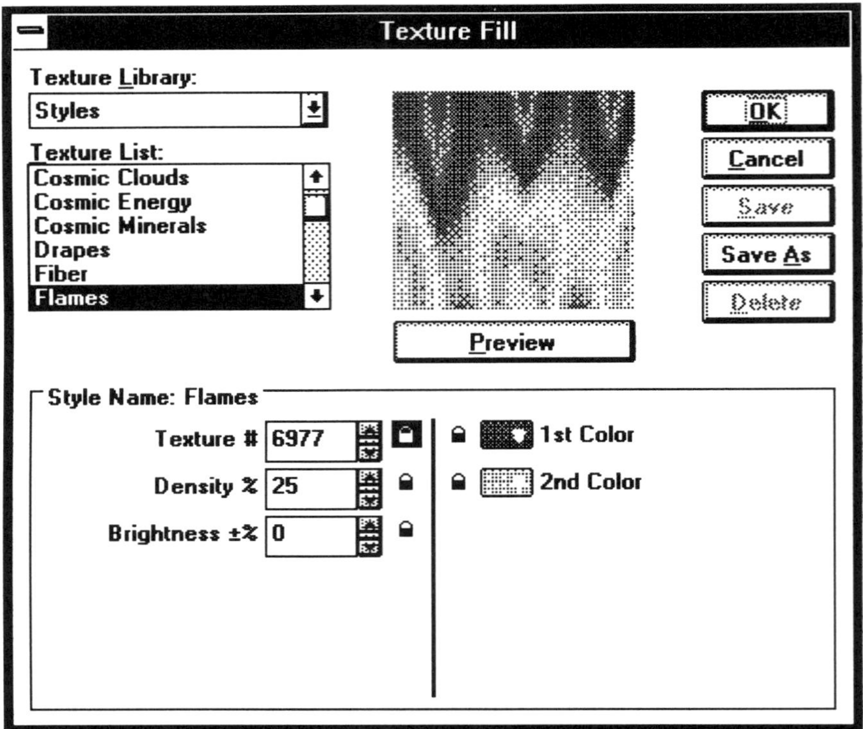

5.29 Texture Edit dialogue box

5   In the top left hand corner is a line saying **Texture Library**. The textures can be stored in conglomerate files called libraries. As the program is shipped there is only one library - Styles. If you click on the arrowhead beside the word you get a drop-down menu that contains only this name.

6   Beneath that is the **Texture List**. This gives you the names of all the textures within the selected library. The version I currently have contains 44 textures. You can scroll through them with the scroll bar. Be warned some are much more complex than others. Click on a pattern name and watch the bottom of the box. Depending on which pattern you select, the contents of this will change.

7   There are, theoretically, millions of possible patterns. Select the Flame texture. In the lower left hand side of the dialogue box you will then get three lines, Texture, Density and Brightness. On the right hand side you'll have First Colour and Second Colour. If you now click on the button labelled **Preview** the pattern will change and the Texture number changes.

8   You can play around with the pattern choices for ages because you can also select the texture numbers one by one. Try pattern number **2073**. You can change the colours to whatever you wish. Then click on **OK**.

9   The dialogue box closes and you go back to the main CorelDRAW window. The fill roll-up now contains the pattern you have just selected. Click on **Apply** to fill the square. Be warned, it takes a reasonably long time.

10   Play with the patterns. (I was going to include some screen shots here but they will not render decently in monochrome.) Some of them are truly beautiful but they can take a measurable amount of time to display.

5.8 PostScript Patterns

The final fill type that CorelDRAW gives you is PostScript patterns. These cannot be accessed from the roll-up though - you have to use the Fill tool. If you don't have a PostScript printer then you cannot use these.

1 Empty your square by clicking on the **X** in the lower left hand corner of the screen, at the end of the palette, with the left mouse button. Click on the **Fill** tool and when it opens out click on the icon labelled **PS**. A dialogue box appears.

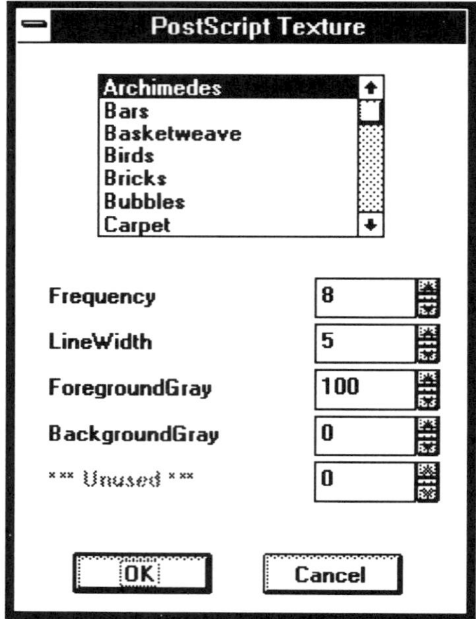

5.30 PostScript dialogue box

3 You cannot see the PostScript patterns until they are printed because they are actually PostScript code. Instead the dialogue box lists the names of the patterns. Click on any one of them and then on **OK**. The dialogue box closes and your square is now filled with lots of PS signs. If you look at the Status Bar it will tell you which pattern is being used.

5.9 CREATING PATTERNS

CorelDRAW allows you to turn just about anything into a pattern. There isn't room here to cover all the available ways of creating bitmap patterns so we'll just cover the basics.

1   You want to load the 5-01 file that you created earlier. Press **Ctrl-O** and a dialogue box appears:

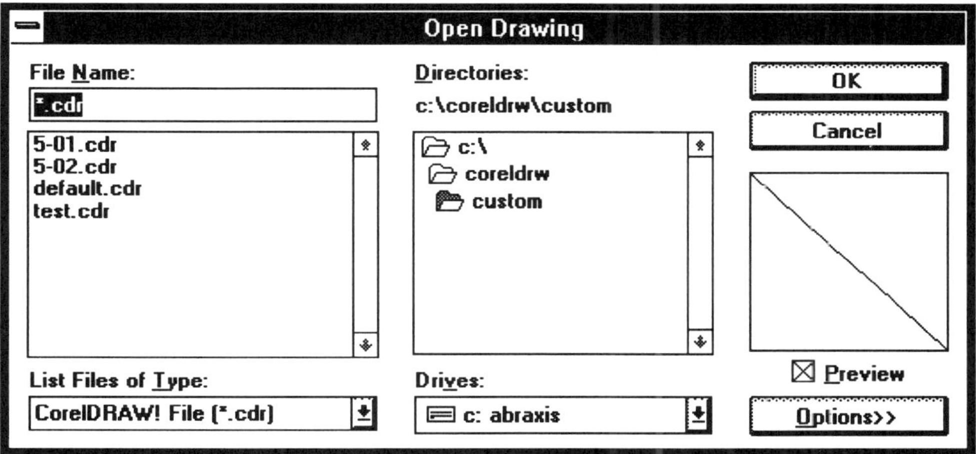

5.31 Open dialogue box

LOADING FILES

CorelDRAW will allow you to load three different types of files:

Those with an extension of .CDR, i.e. the standard CorelDRAW format files.

Those with an extension of .PAT, i.e. CorelDRAW patterns.

Those with an extension of .CDT, i.e. CorelDRAW templates.

You have to select which file type you want. Once you do so the list of files bearing that extension will be displayed in the large box on he left.

You can log into other directories using the Directories box in the middle, and change drives using the Drive line below that. If you click on Options the box opens up:

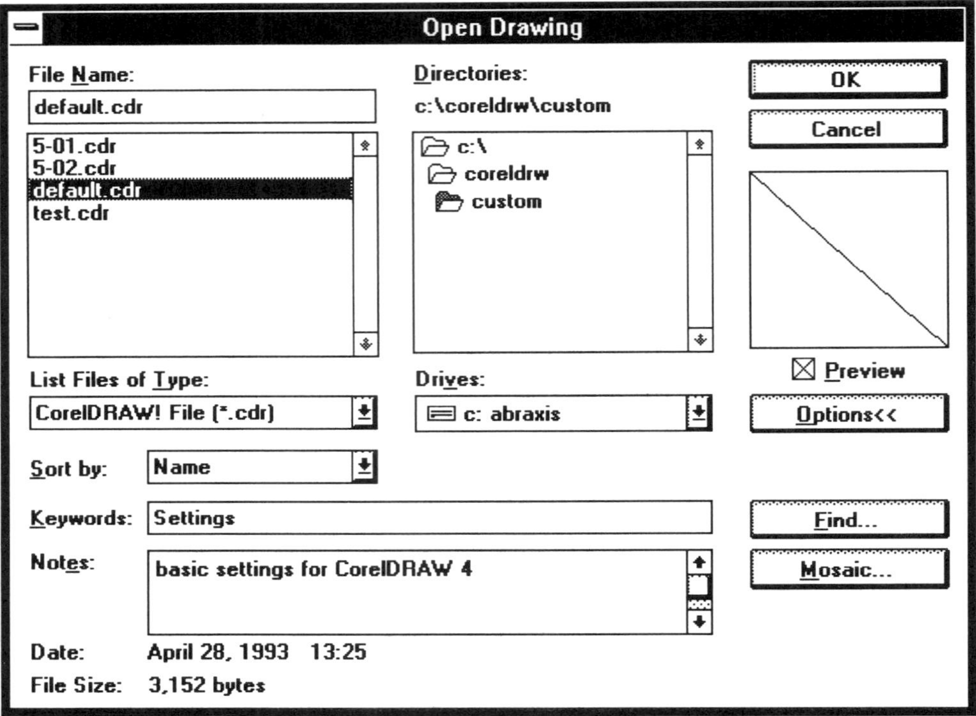

5.32 Options for loading

If you now click on a filename you will be shown the keywords, notes, the date of creation and the file size of the selected file. At the same time the Preview box, on the right hand side, will display the thumbnail of the image if one exists.

You can use the options button labelled **Find** to source files on the basis of the keywords. Clicking on the one labelled **Mosaic** will run the Mosaic program for you.

2   Double click on the file named **5-01.CDR** and it will be loaded. Turn the grid off (if it is on) by pressing **Ctrl-Y**.

3   Press **F4** to make the image fill the screen. (F4 makes whatever is in the file fit on the screen by magnifying or shrinking things as appropriate.)

4   Click on the image to select it so that the handles appear around it.

5   Open the **Special** menu and click on **Create Pattern**. A dialogue box appears:

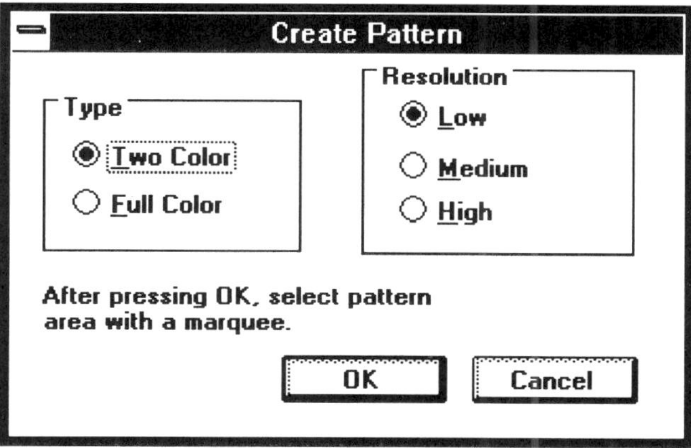

5.33 Create Pattern dialogue box

6   You're going to create the two different types of pattern. Firstly the bitmap pattern, which is what the dialogue box defaults to. Change it to **Medium Resolution** and then click on **OK**.

7   You now get two large crosshairs. This is the Marquee selection. Move the cursor to the centre of the upper left hand handle. Click once and then drag a bounding box to the centre of the lower right hand handle. Once you let go of the mouse you'll get a message box asking if you want to create a pattern with the selected area. Press **Enter** or click on **OK**.

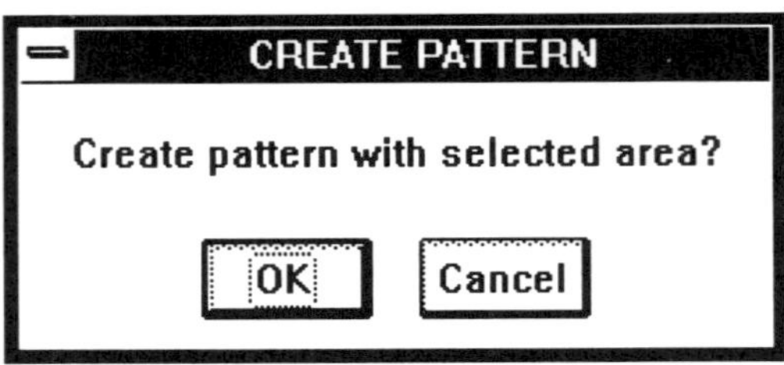

5.34 Create Pattern message box

8   The hourglass cursor will appear and spin as the pattern is added to the bitmap patterns already in existence.

9   Open the **Special** menu again and click on **Create Pattern**. This time click on Full Colour pattern type. The options on the right hand side of the box will now be greyed out. Click on **OK**.

10   You'll get the marquee selection cursor again. Move the cursor to the centre of the upper left hand handle. Click once and then drag a bounding box to the centre of the lower right hand handle. Once you let go of the mouse you'll get a message box asking if you want to create a pattern with the selected area. Press **Enter** or click on **OK**.

11   You now get a dialogue box similar to the standard Save As one, except that this one saves patterns. Give the file a name, e.g. 5-01, and then click on **OK**.

12   Start a new page by pressing **Ctrl-N**. Draw a 100 mms square. Open the Fill tool and click on the roll-up icon.

13   Click on the Checkerboard pattern. Then click on the pattern representation area. A drop down menu appears. The new pattern will be at the end of the available patterns so scroll down until you find it and then double click on it.

14   Click on **Apply** in the roll-up and there's the square filled with the new pattern.

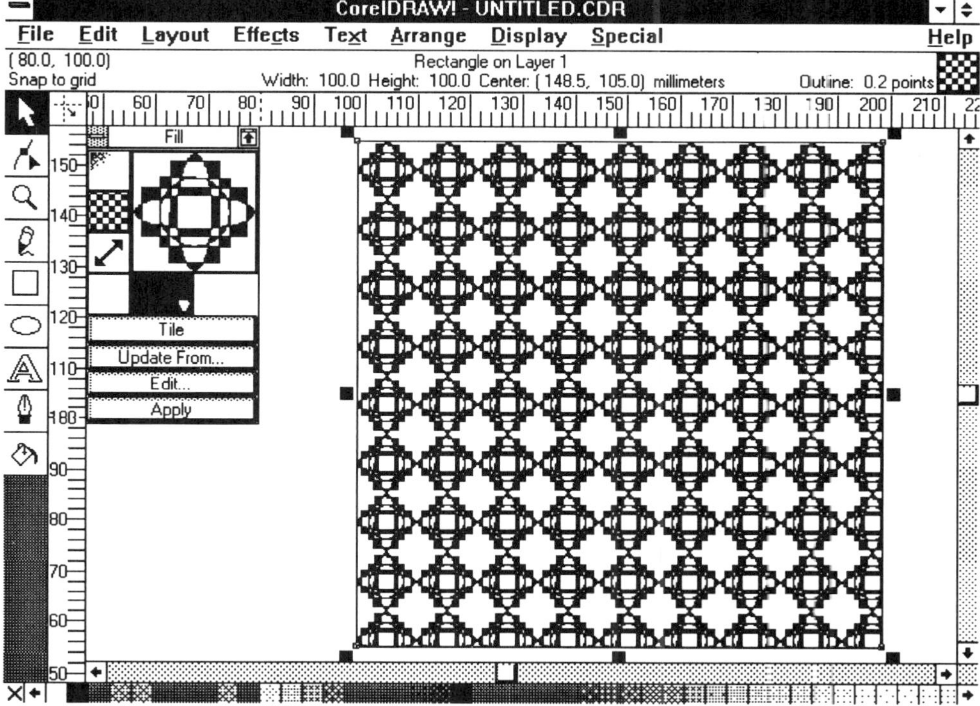

5.35 Bitmap pattern applied

15   Now for the full colour one. Click on the vector pattern icon, the one with the diagonal arrow. Then on the pattern representation area again. Scroll down through the patterns until you find you pattern - it won't necessarily be at the end. Double click on it.

16   Click on **Apply** in the roll-up to fill the square.

163

CORELDRAW 4 - A USERS GUIDE

PATTERNS

Vector patterns are generally better than bitmap ones especially if you are using shapes other than squares or rectangles. Why? Because they are fully scaleable and resizing them will result in little or no distortion.

A bitmap on the other hand is intended to be used at a fixed size and so resizing or reshaping it will lead to various amounts of distortion.

If you are creating bitmap patterns there is no point in using colour because CorelDRAW allows you to colour the foreground and background colour individually once you have applied the fill.

With vector patterns on the other hand you can use colours in the image as much as you wish.

However you should be wary of creating patterns that are too complex because they will result in very large file sizes.

6. TEXT

CorelDRAW allows you to use three different kinds of text - Artistic, which is intended for single lines like banners; Paragraph, which allows lots of text: until this version it limited you to roughly 4,000 characters; and Symbols, which are little images. With the advent of CorelDRAW 4 the text handling capabilities of the program have been enormously enhanced, it's almost as if they combined CorelDRAW and PageMaker into a single package. You can now have multiple pages, up to a maximum of 999, with linked text, automatic text flow, wrap around and what-have-you. There isn't room in this book to do more than just glance at the new text capabilities - that would almost require a book all by itself - but we will examine all the possibilities briefly.

There is a major point to bear in mind when using text and that is the amount of resources you have available on your system. Text handling is expensive in terms of resources, memory and display capabilities - especially if you have a high number of undo levels. Remember that the more fonts you have installed the less resources you have available overall and that will adversely affect text handling. Just because you have a squillion fonts there is no need to have them all loaded all the time. Be selective, install the fonts you use all the time and limit yourself to half a dozen or so. Remember the classic design rules.

If you need to load additional fonts for a particular purpose, install them, use them and then remove them once you've finished. That will keep your resources at a high level and you'll have less problems.

CorelDRAW 4 comes with 750 fonts, on the CD-ROM, but that doesn't mean that you should have them all loaded. In fact if you do you'll probably not be able to do anything because your resources will drop through the floor. Equally you'll use up disk space at a phenomenal rate. The average TrueType font needs 50 to 60 Kb of disk space so if you have 750 installed, let alone loaded, you will need somewhere between 37.5 Mb and 45 Mb! Do you have that much space free? And even if you do, do you want to use it for storing fonts that you might only use once in a blue moon? Far better to leave the fonts on the CD-ROM and take them off only when you need them.

6.1 Artistic Text

CorelDRAW has always had artistic text. It is limited to approximately 250 characters. However, this is an average. The actual number of characters you can have depends on the font you are using and the number of nodes that these entail multiplied by the number of characters. So if you use a very flowery, curly or artistic font you can, for obvious reasons, use less characters. If you use a very formal straight line, blocky font then you should get more characters.

1   Start a new page. Press **F8** to select the **Text** tool or just click on it. Move the cursor on to the page and click once. Now type some text, e.g. The quick brown fox jumps over the lazy dog. (This phrase uses all the letters of the alphabet.) The text will appear in whatever typeface and font you set as the default for Artistic Text.

2   Click on the **Pointer** tool. When you are using any of the text modes you cannot press the **Spacebar** to go back to the last tool - because it gives you a space instead.

3   Align the text to the centre of the page with **Ctrl-A**.

4   With the text selected, press **Ctrl-T**. A dialogue box appears.

TEXT DIALOGUE BOX

The text dialogue box gives you total control of the text and allows you to set everything from the typeface to the size to the alignment.

The major area of the dialogue box shows the text string. It will be shown in the system font which makes it nice and easy to read.

On the left hand side is a box labelled **Fonts**. This lists all the fonts that you have installed on your system, both the Abode Type 1 fonts and the TrueType ones, in alphabetical order. You can select any font by scrolling through the list and then clicking on the typeface name. (Tip: A quick way to scroll though the list is to click on any name and then press the initial letter of the typeface you want to use. The list will scroll to the first font beginning with that letter.)

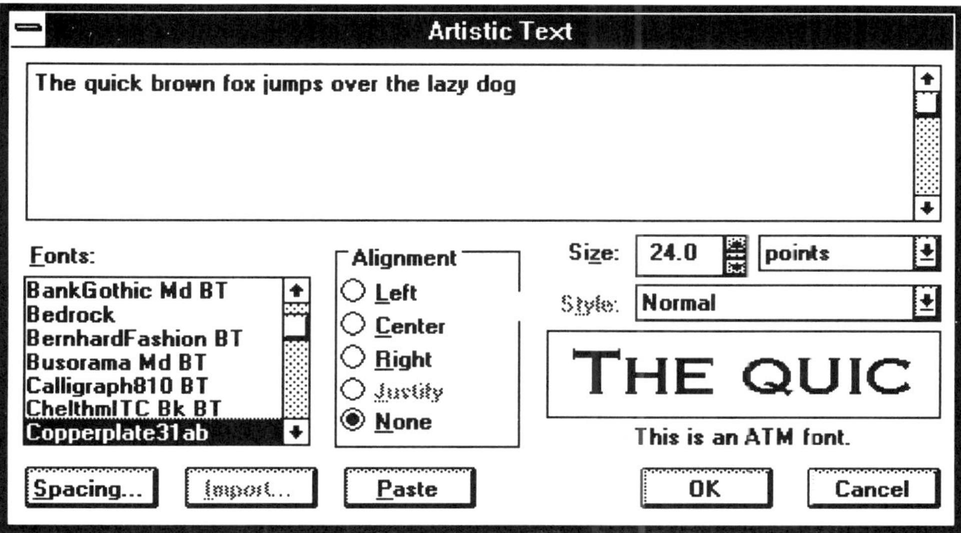

6.01 Text dialogue box

In the middle of the dialogue box is a box labelled **Alignment**. By default this always says None. You can change it to be any of the following:

>**Left**, which causes the text string to appear to the right of wherever you clicked.

>**Centre**, which centres the text around where you clicked.

>**Right**, which causes the text string to appear to the left of wherever you clicked.

>**None** allows you to reposition any of the characters, using the Node Edit tool, within the text string without affecting all the others.

On the right hand side is a line labelled **Size**. You can apply any size you wish to text, using any form of measurement. Just set the measurement system you want to use and then adjust the size.

Below that is a line labelled **Style**. This refers to the type of font you have selected. Some fonts have only a single possibility, e.g. normal or bold, in which case this line will be greyed out. If it isn't then you can change the printing effect to use one of the others. Some fonts have a whole host of capabilities.

Beneath that there is a large rectangular area that shows you what the first few characters of the text string will look like in the selected font. Below this box it also tells you the kind of font you are using, e.g. Adobe Type 1 or TrueType.

---

5   Set the font to CopprplGoth BT - which is a version of Copperplate - and change the size to 72 Point. You can simply overwrite the size rather than having to use the arrows. Then click on **OK**. The text string will now be too long to fit on the page.

6   You can edit it in two ways. Either go back to the text dialogue box and put a carriage return in after the word brown and another after the word over, or select the Text tool again, click just after brown and then press **Enter** then move the cursor to just after over and press **Enter** again. Realign the text to the centre of the page and you should have something like this:

6.02 Text on page

7   There is another way to edit text and that's with the Text roll-up. Press **Ctrl-F2** to bring this up. It will appear somewhere on the page. Open its Control Box and click on **Arrange**. It will move to the top right hand corner of the window and roll-up will close up. Roll it down again.

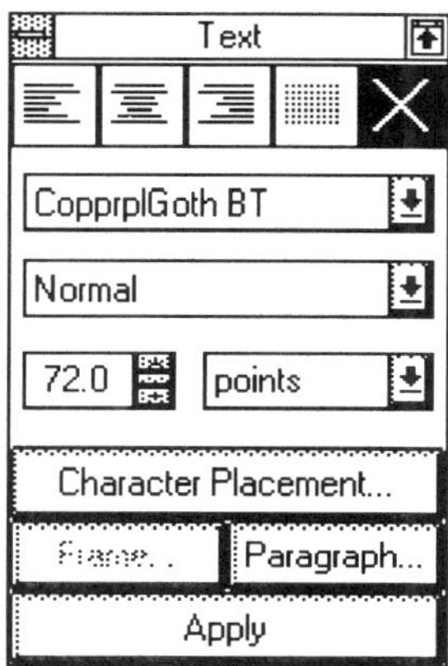

6.03 Text roll-up

8   Make sure the text is selected and then click on the arrowhead beside the typeface name in the roll-up. As you do and as you click on other typeface names so a box appears similar to the one in the dialogue box that shows what the text will look like.

9   The top of the roll-up contains five boxes or icons. The end one bearing a large X, is currently selected. These are the justification settings. Click on the second from the left, which is centre justify.

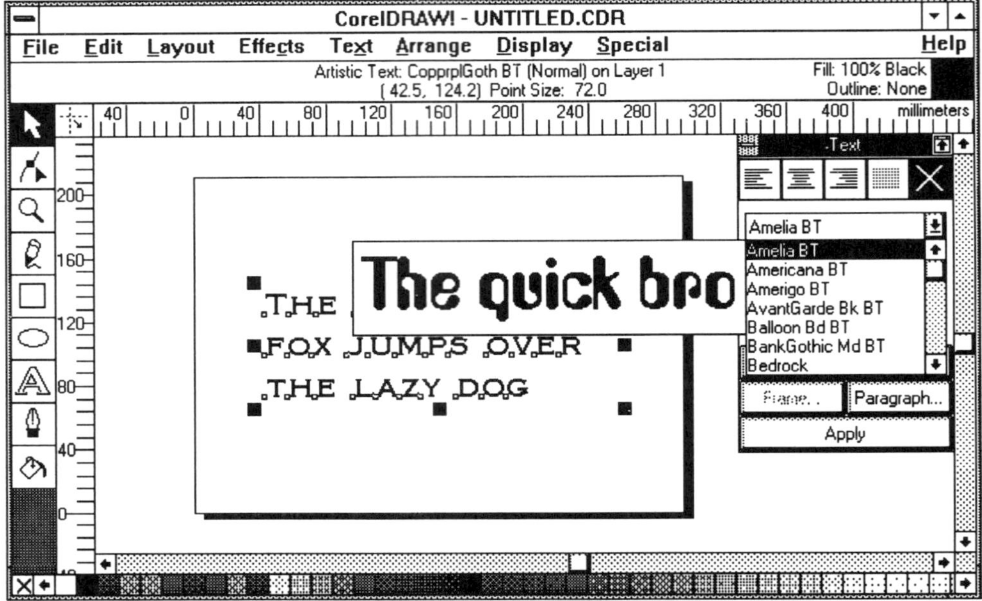

6.04 Selecting typefaces

10   Change the size to 84 points and then click on **Apply**. The text will shift on the page so you will have to align it to the centre of the page again. You should end up with something like this:

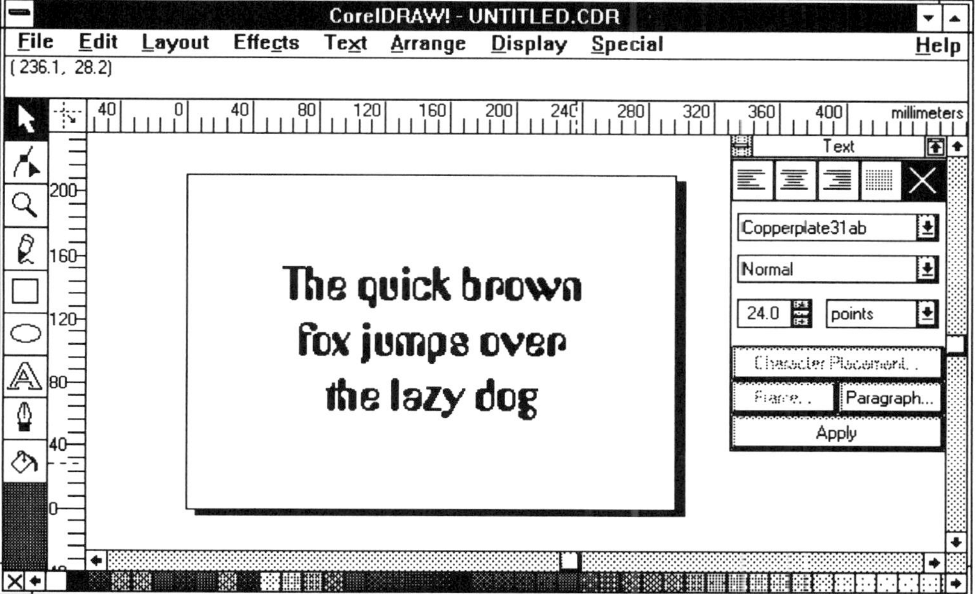

6.05 Text changed

11   Notice that the roll-up goes back to showing the default settings that you set for Artistic Text. Play with the roll-up until you are comfortable with it.

12   If you click on the button labelled Paragraph you will get a new dialogue box.

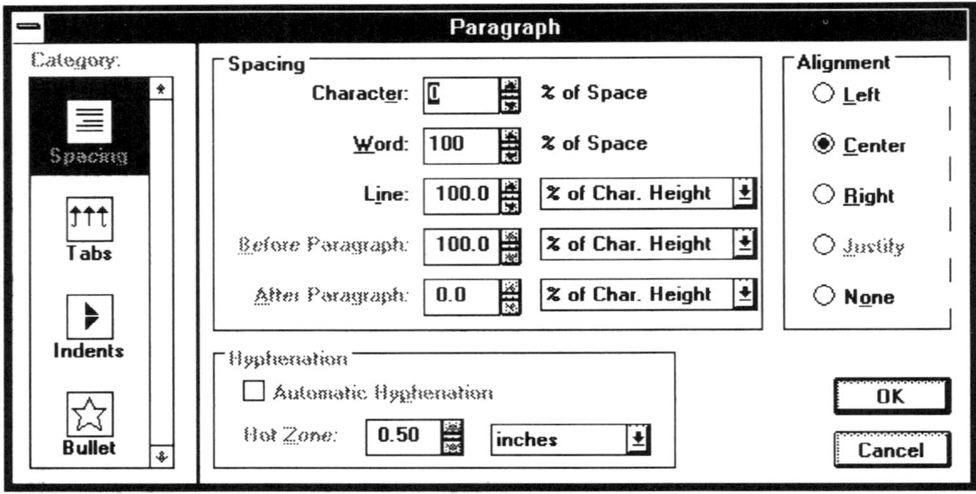

6.06 Paragraph dialogue box

13   The dialogue box will allow you to change the spacing for the text string and that's all. Because you are using artistic text you cannot change anything else. Try different spacing values. You have to click on **OK** to close the dialogue box and then click on **Apply** in the roll-up to see the changes. Be warned, CorelDRAW doesn't apply line spacing the same way as any other program.

14   Save the file, and call it 6-01, because you'll need it for the next chapter.

6.2 PARAGRAPH TEXT

In previous versions of CorelDRAW you were limited to a maximum of 4,000 characters for paragraph text. This is no longer the case in CorelDRAW 4. You are now limited to the number of pages but the more pages you use the more resources you will use up.

1   Start a new page. Make it A4 portrait rather than landscape.

2   There are two ways to use Paragraph text. The first is by typing it directly, which we'll do here, and the other is by importing it, which we'll do in the next section.

3   Click on the text tool and hold the mouse button down. In a few seconds you'll get a pop-out set of icons. You want the second one that looks like a rectangle with lines in it. Click on it and the text tool changes to show it. This is the Paragraph Text tool.

4   Move the cursor on to the page and click once. A paragraph box appears. You can also create a sized paragraph box by clicking and then dragging with the tool. Now type some text.

5   Press **Ctrl-T** to bring up the Paragraph Text dialogue box. Notice that this is identical to the artistic text one except that you can now also have Justified alignment.

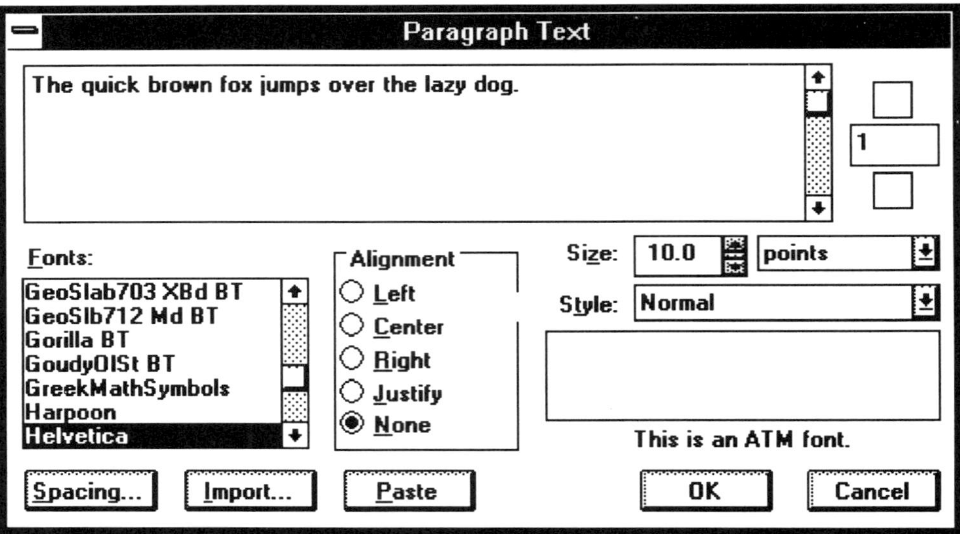

6.07 Paragraph Text dialogue box

6   Click on **Cancel** or press **Esc** to close the dialogue box. Click on the **Pointer** tool. You'll get the normal handles appearing around the paragraph box plus two special ones. These look like unfilled squares and there is one in the middle of the top and bottom lines. Drag the bottom one about half way up the page.

7   Notice that the text is not really visible, that's because it is greeked to make the display faster. If you zoom in on the paragraph box then it will eventually become visible.

8   Open the text roll-up. You'll find that it now bears whatever the defaults are that you set for paragraph text. Click on the fourth justification icon, the one that bears a number of equally sized lines, which is fully justified. Then click on **Apply**. The text in the paragraph will be justified for you.

9   Click on the button labelled **Frame** and a dialogue box appears. This allows you to set the number of columns for the paragraph. Change the number of **Columns** to 3 and the **Gutter Width**, which is the gap between the columns, to 10 millimetres. Click on **OK** to close the dialogue box. Then click on **Apply** in the roll-up to change the actual paragraph.

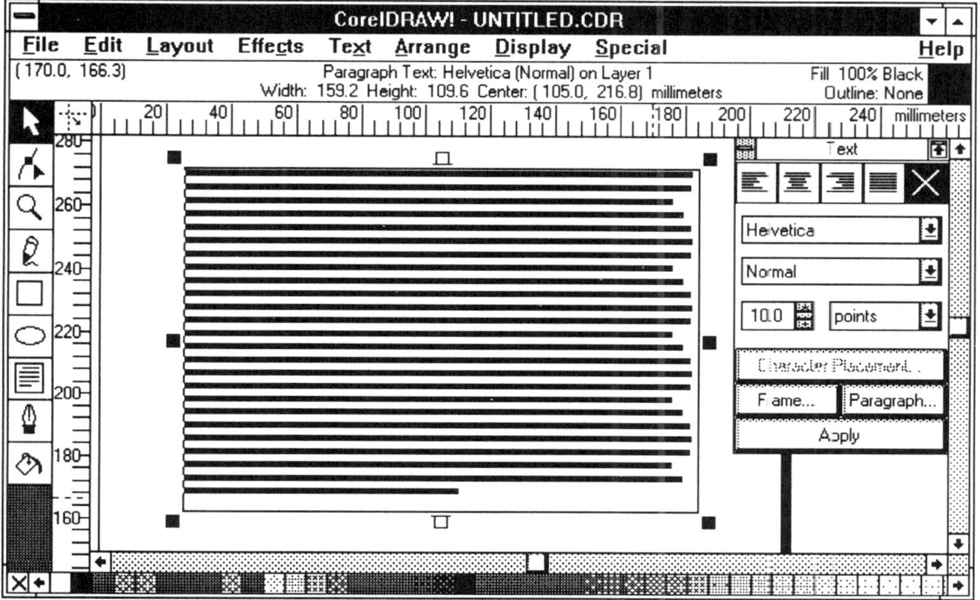

6.08 Paragraph handles

6.09 Frame dialogue box

10   Click on the button labelled **Paragraph** to get the dialogue box. Notice it is different this time because everything is available to you now.

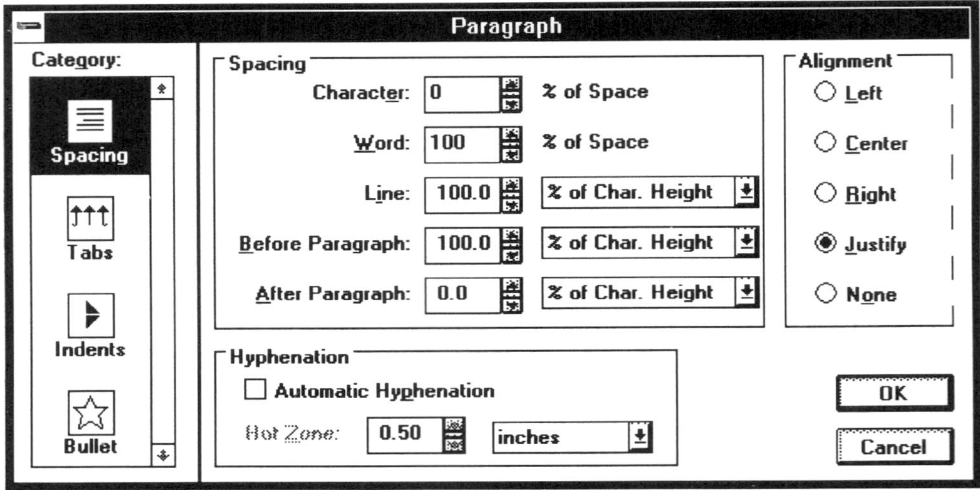

6.10 Paragraph dialogue box

PARAGRAPH DIALOGUE BOX

The paragraph dialogue box allows you to set a wide range of parameters for any given block of text. On the left hand side the dialogue box contains four icons, Spacing, Tabs, Indents and Bullets.

> **Spacing**, which is shown by default, allows you to adjust the various spaces that are used by characters and lines of text. The spacing attributes are based on the text plus a certain amount of white space around the text.

> > **Character spacing** defines the space between the characters. The actual amount of space for each character depends on the font being used. The value is set in terms of a percentage of an Em space. An Em is a square that is equal in width to the height of the character in points. Thus you can have a 12 point Em space, i.e. a square that is twelve points tall and 12 points wide.

> > **Word spacing** defines the space that words, i.e. a string of text characters between two spaces, occupies. Again the space is determined as percentages of *an Em*.

Line spacing defines the space occupied by a line of text. The value here is set in terms of percentages of the largest overall character height or you can set it in terms of points. The important thing to realise is that the spacing at 100% takes account of the largest character in the text string plus an allowance for the amount of white space above and below the character. (White space is just that - space that is blank.)

Before Paragraph spacing is the amount of space allowed before the first line of the paragraph. In CorelDRAW 4 you can define this in terms of percentages of the largest character height or in points, as with Line spacing. This is a bit unusual because normally you would define this in millimetres, points or lines.

After Paragraph spacing is the same as the above but it applies after the paragraph. Again it's a bit odd and will take some getting used to.

Hyphenation is just that. Do you want the program to automatically hyphenate words or not? If you do then set a Hot Zone value and any word that can be cut to fit on two lines and which intrudes into this space will be hyphenated. Personally I always prefer to hyphenate manually so I leave it turned off.

Alignment allows you to set the justification for the paragraph.

Clicking on the **Tabs** icon will change the dialogue box.

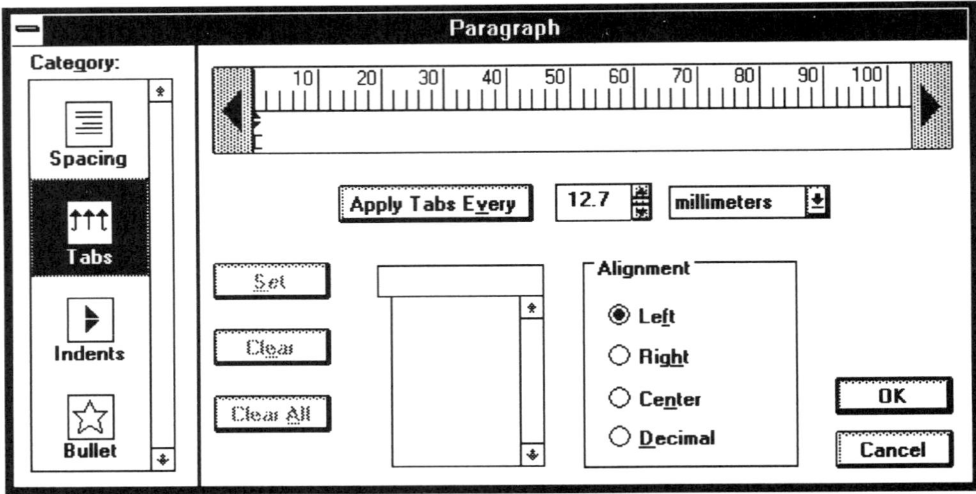

6.11 Tabs dialogue box

By default the program is set to produce tabs every half inch which it translates into 12.7 millimetres. You can overwrite this with any other value. For example, I set it to every 10 millimetres. Click on **Apply Tab Every** to set the tabs.

You can also set tabs by entering a value on the line beside Set, then clicking on the kind of tab you want before clicking on **Set**.

> **Left aligned tabs** will cause the first character of the tabbed string to align itself to the right of the designated tab.

> **Right aligned tabs** cause the last character of the tabbed string to align itself to the left of the designated tab.

> **Centre aligned tabs** causes the entire tabbed text string to align itself around the designated tab.

> **Decimal tabs** are used for numbers. They allow you to align the decimal points in numbers to produce neat columns of figures.

You can clear any individual tab by clicking on the one you want to remove and then clicking on **Clear**.

To remove all the tabs click on **Clear All**.

Clicking on **Indents** will change the dialogue box yet again.

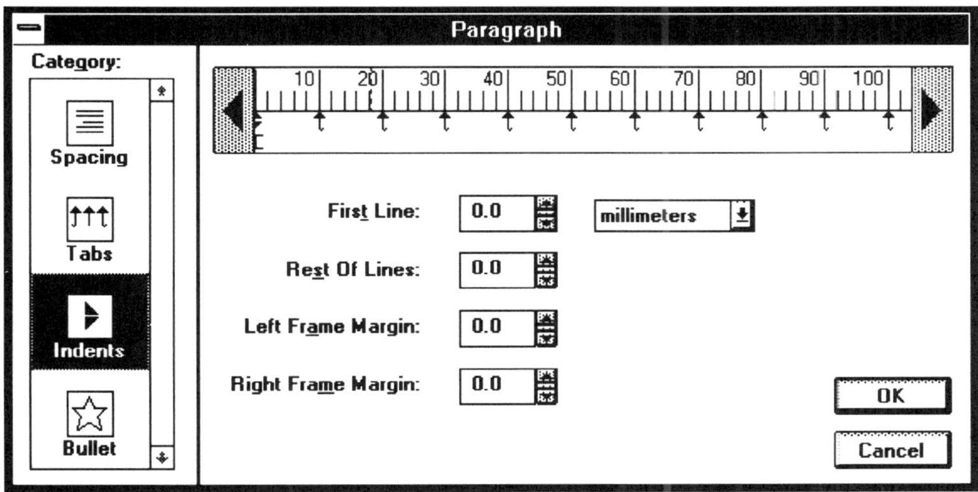

6.12 Indent dialogue box

This dialogue box allows you to set indentations for the paragraph. You can have an indent for:

The **First Line** which will indent just the first line of the paragraph so that it is moved in from the left hand edge of the text frame.

The **Rest of Lines** which indents all the lines except the first one. So you can have hanging indents if you specify an indentation here that exceeds that of the first line.

The **Left Frame Margin** indents the entire paragraph from the left hand edge of the frame.

The **Right Hand Margin** does the opposite of the above and indents the entire right hand side of the paragraph.

Note that setting left frame margin will also change first line and rest of lines automatically.

Click on **Bullet** and the dialogue box changes again:

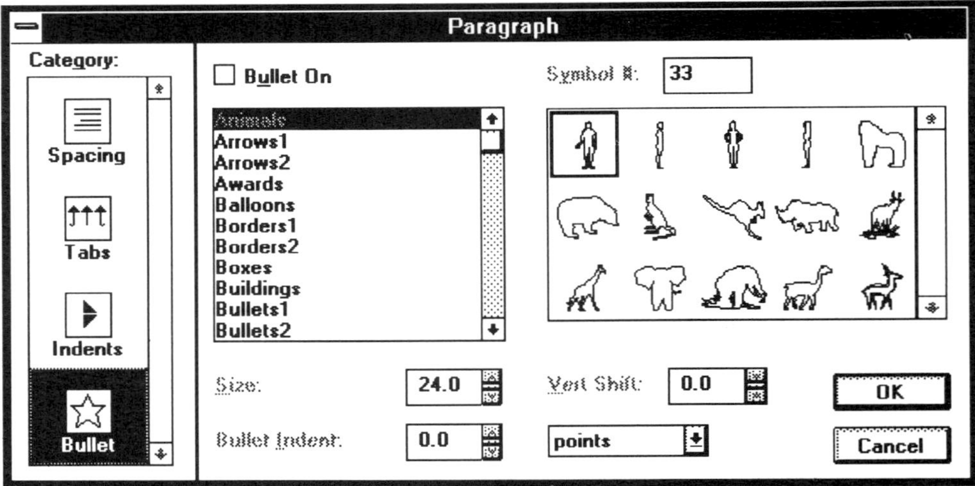

6.13 Bullet dialogue box

By default the **Bullet On** command is turned off so you can't do anything with this dialogue box. Click on the command to turn it on and the dialogue box becomes active.

CorelDRAW 4 allows you to use any of the 4,000 plus symbols as a bullet. Select the symbol library you want to use by scrolling through the list. As you do so the symbols on the right hand side of the box will change. Click on whichever symbol you want to use.

The **Size** of the bullet needs to be set. You can either overwrite it or use the arrowheads to increase or decrease it. You may find that you need to make the bullet symbol smaller than the actual text.

Bullet Indent specifies the amount of space between the bullet itself and the left hand edge of the text frame.

Vertical Shift is useful because it allows you to effectively superscript or subscript the actual bullet. You can also change the measurement used for this.

Note that if you change the measurement for the bullet indent it also changes for the size, so it is worth setting the size in points first and then changing the measurement for the indent.

Once you've made changes click on **OK** to close the dialogue box and go back to the roll-up. You then have to click on Apply to employ the changes you have just made.

11   Make some changes to the dialogue box and then apply them. Because you have the whole block of paragraph text selected the changes will apply to everything.

12   You can also make specific paragraph changes. Select the **Paragraph Text** tool and click on a paragraph within the text frame. Now click on Paragraph in the roll-up. This time the changes you make will only apply to the paragraph you have clicked on.

Play with the paragraph capabilities of the programs until you are comfortable with them and you understand what each bit does.

6.3 IMPORTING TEXT

As well as typing text directly onto the page, CorelDRAW 4 will allow you to import text directly. Because it now has DTP capabilities and multiple pages this feature is impressive. You can now import files directly from any of the following:

Ami Pro Versions 2.0 or 3.0
Lotus 123 for Windows plus MS-DOS Versions 1A, 2.0 or 3.0
MacWrite II Versions 1.0 or 1.1
Microsoft Excel Versions 3.0 or 4.0
Microsoft Word for Mac Versions 4.0 and 5.0
Microsoft Word for Windows Versions 1.x and 2.x
Microsoft Word Versions 5.0 and 5.5
WordPerfect for Windows plus MS-DOS Versions 5.0 and 5.1

plus Microsoft Rich Text Format and any pure ASCII file.

1   Either clear the page or start a new one.

2   Open the **File** menu and click on **Import** or just press **Alt-F I**. The import dialogue box appears:

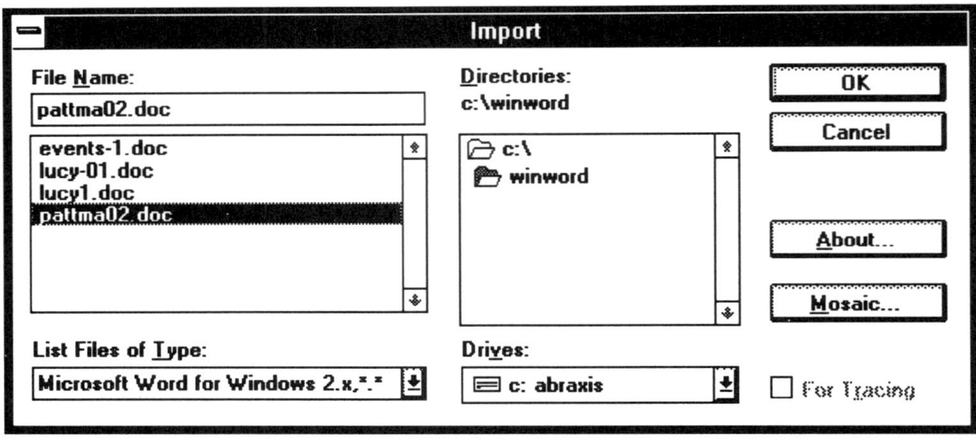

6.14 Import dialogue box

3   Change the **File Type** to one that you have a word processed document in. Select the file and click on **OK**. You'll get an importing message box as the file is loaded.

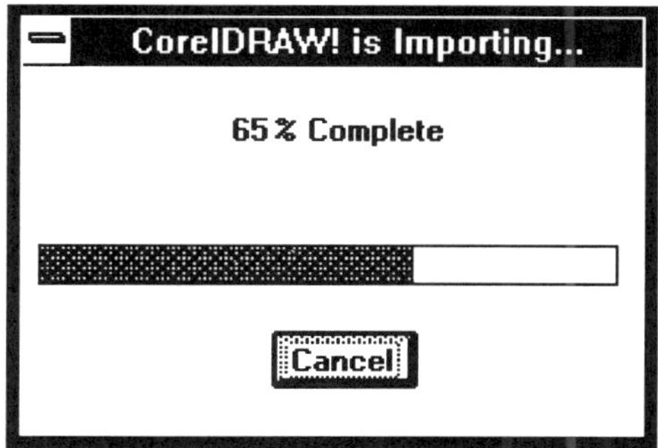

6.15 Import message box

4   The hourglass will appear and turn as the file is formatted for CorelDRAW and eventually you will get the file on the page. CorelDRAW adds a the frame and as many pages as necessary. You should end up with something like Figure 6.16 overleaf.

5   Notice that there is an extra indicator at the left hand edge of the horizontal scroll bar. This tells you what page you are currently looking at and how many pages there are in the document. CorelDRAW 4 allows you to have a maximum of 999 pages. To move to the next page either click on the arrowhead in the indicator or just press **Pg Dn**. Pressing **Pg Up** will take you back a page.

6   Notice also that the frame handle, the unfilled square, at the bottom of the frame on page 1 now has a plus sign in it. That informs you that the text continues to another page and/or frame. On page 2 the frame at the top will bear a plus sign in the same way.

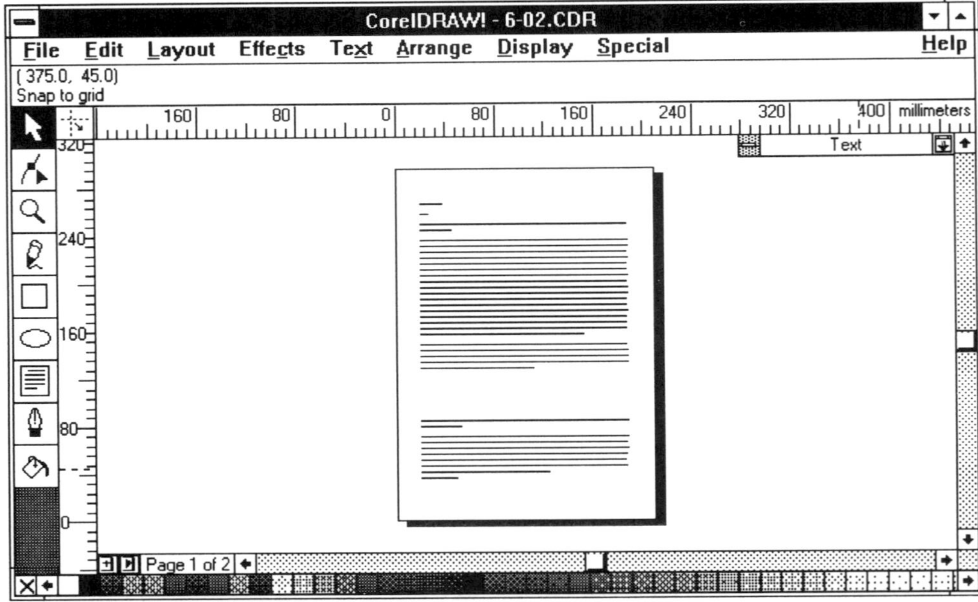

6.16 File imported

7   Now play with changing the text and paragraph dialogue box on the file you have imported until you are comfortable with it.

8   Try changing the number of columns. Select page 1. In the text roll-up click on **Frame**. In the dialogue box that appears change the number of columns to 3 and the gutter width to 10 mms. Click on **OK**. Then click on **Apply**.

9   Now go to page 2. Notice that this frame is still single column. The change you made in the last step applied only to the selected frame. If you want this frame to match the one on the previous page you have to reset the frame parameters. The maximum number of columns you can have, by the way, is eight.

6.4 Spell checking

CorelDRAW 4 includes a full spell checker which is licensed from Houghton Mifflin, the same company who do the one for Word for Windows. Unfortunately you cannot use the dictionary from one program with another - at least not yet. The spell checker in CorelDRAW is very easy to use.

1   With the **Pointer** tool, select the text in the frame. Open the **Text** menu and click on **Spell Checker**. A dialogue box appears.

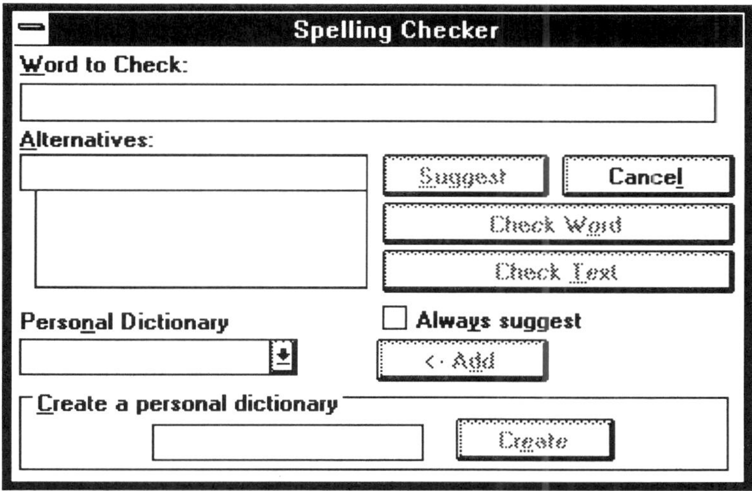

6.18 Spell checker dialogue box

2   Before you begin you should create a personal dictionary if you have not already done so. Move the cursor to the line that says **Create a personal dictionary** and click once so that the flashing cursor appears. Type a name, e.g. yours, and then click on **Create** which will become active once you've typed something.

3   Next, click on **Always Suggest**. This means that the spell checker will always try to find words that it thinks are correct rather than you having to do so.

4   Now click on **Check Text**. The process begins and the dialogue box changes. When the spell checker finds a word it doesn't recognise it will do this:

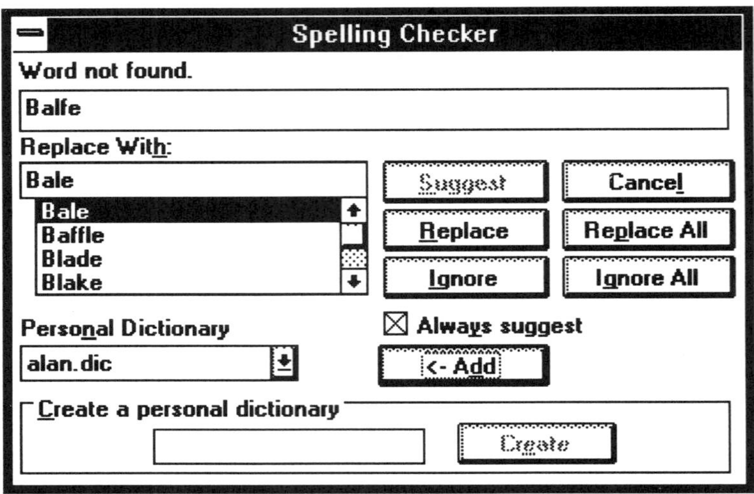

6.19 Word not found

5   You now have a choice of replacing the unknown word with one of the alternatives, which you can do by simply double clicking on the word you want to use instead. Alternatively you can click on the new word once and then click on **Replace**. Clicking on **Replace All** will change every occurrence of the unknown word with the replacement throughout the document without you having to do anything.

6   If you want to leave the word alone click on **Ignore**. If you want the word to be used because it is correct, e.g. a proper name, then you can click on **Add** which will add the word to the personal dictionary. If you do so then you get a message box telling you that the word has been added. Click on **OK** and the checking continues.

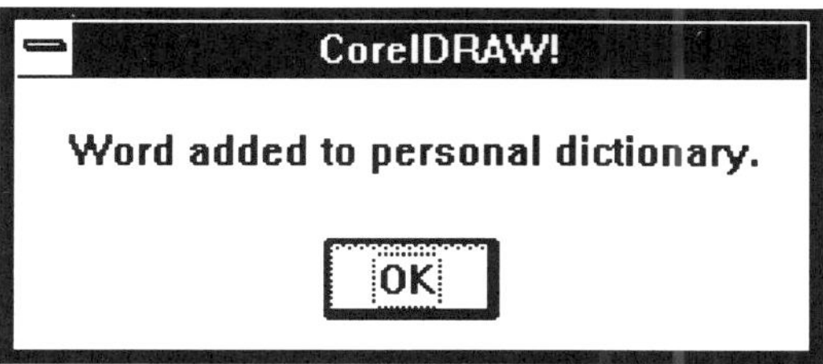

6.20 Word added

7   Occasionally the dictionary will find a word that it doesn't recognise but for which it can find no alternatives. If that happens then you get another message box telling you so.

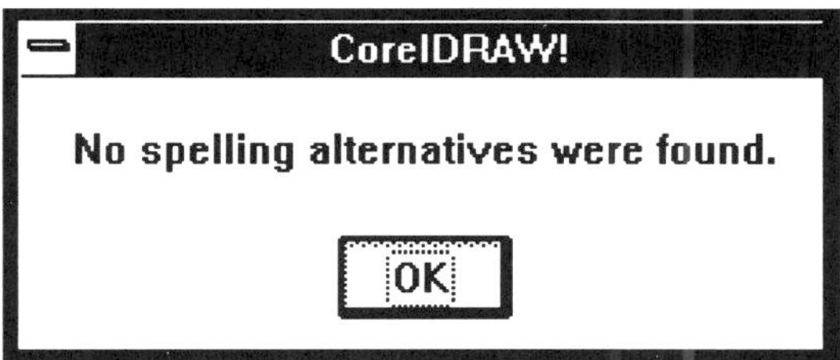

6.21 No alternatives

8   You can then add or ignore the word. Alternatively you may want to overwrite the offending word with a correct spelling. (Spell checkers are not omnipotent.) This is likely to happen if you have run two words together for example. To do so simply highlight the word on the **Replace with** line and then type the correct spelling. Then click on **Replace** and the process continues.

9   Once the checking is finished you'll get a message box telling you so. Click on **OK** and the process if finally completed.

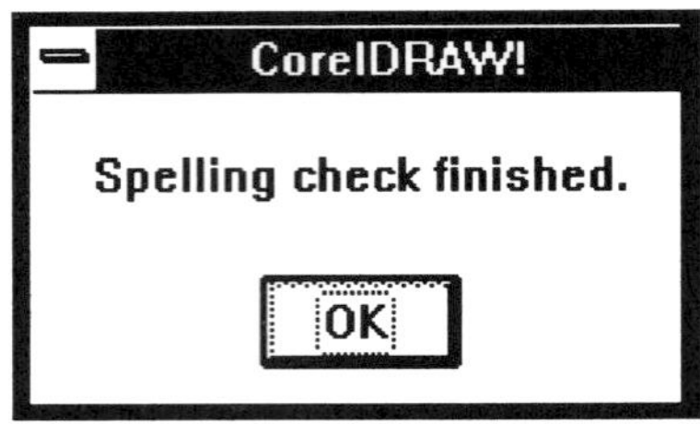

6.22 Spell check finished

It has to be said that the spell checker in CorelDRAW is one of the best I have ever come across. It's far simpler than the one in PageMaker for example.

6.5 THESAURUS

As well as the spell checker CorelDRAW includes a very good thesaurus.

1   Type some text on the page, e.g. the quick brown fox string, or you can use a word from an existing paragraph. The thesaurus works with both artistic and paragraph text and it applies to single words only.

2   With the text tool, highlight a single word, e.g. jumps. Open the **Text** menu and click on **Thesaurus**. You'll get a large dialogue box.

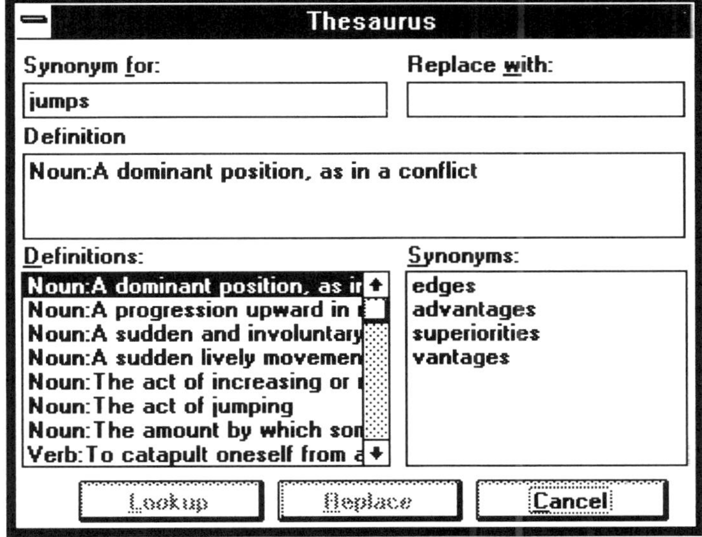

6.23 Thesaurus dialogue box

3   This dialogue box and the thesaurus itself is phenomenal. It's far, far better than any other thesaurus in any other program. On the left hand side it lists the available definitions of the selected word, giving nouns, verbs and what-have-you and a definition of each. On the left is a list of synonyms.

4   Move the highlight down to '**Noun: A sudden lively movement**' and the left hand box will give you a choice of four words. To use one of these you can either highlight it and click on **Replace** or simply double click on the word you want to use.

That's all there is too it. See how many different ways you can change the text string - it's fun.

6.6 FIND AND REPLACE

CorelDRAW also gives you extensive find and replace facilities as you would expect.

1   You're going to need a paragraph of text, e.g. the one you were using earlier. The paragraph I'm using has the quick brown fox repeated a large number of times.

2   Select the **Paragraph Text** tool and click in a paragraph. Open the **Text** menu and click on **Find**. A dialogue box appears:

6.24 Find dialogue box

3   Type the word you want to find. If you click on **Match Case** then the finder only finds words that are exact matches for what you've typed. Click on **Find Next** and the program will work its way through the text to find a match. Once it does so it will highlight the word. If it reaches the end of the text without finding the target text you'll get a message box.

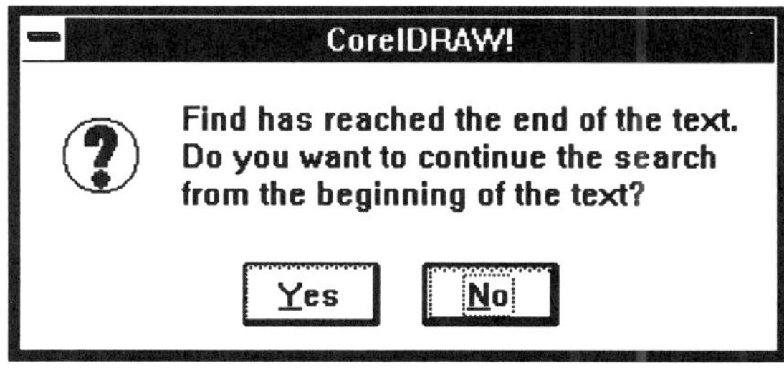

6.25 Reached end of text

4   If the word is not found at all you'll get a message box telling you show.

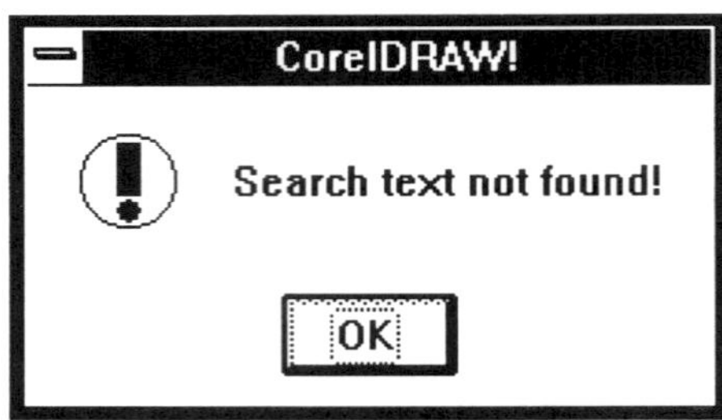

6.26 String not found

5   As well as the find facility, CorelDRAW provides you with a replacement option. Click in the text so that the cursor is within it and then open the **Text** menu and click on **Replace**. A dialogue box pops up.

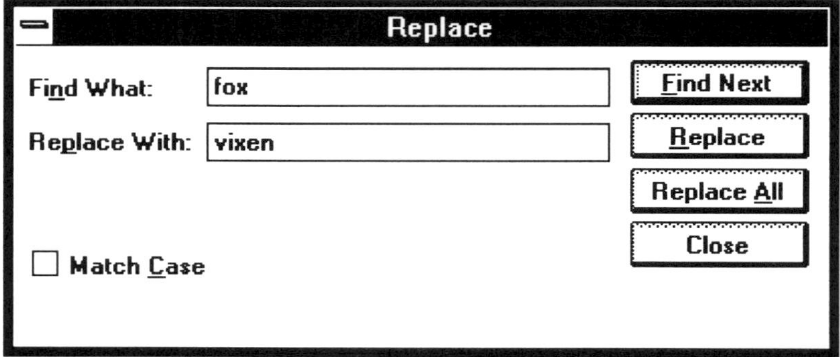

6.27 Replace dialogue box

6   Type the word you want replaced on the top line and what you want it replaced with on the second line. Click on **Match Case** if necessary. You then have two options, you can either **Find** the next occurrence and **Replace** it when it is found or you can simply **Replace All**.

7   The program then goes through the text replacing the word as requested. You can also use the dialogue box to replace strings or words with a single word

or vice versa. Once the search has been completed you get a message box telling you that it has reached the end of the document. Click on **Yes** to redo it or **No** to close the dialogue box.

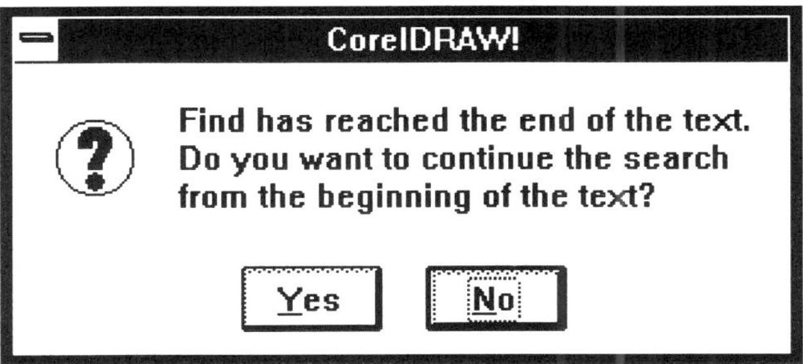

6.28 Finished? dialogue box

6.7 Symbols

As well as using pure text, CorelDRAW allows you to use symbols. These are all stored in libraries, they are actually WFN files, which you'll find in the Symbols sub-directory. CorelDRAW 4 comes complete with over 4,000 symbols.

The symbols are automatically given the default fill and outline attributes that you set for graphics. It is important to realise that the Symbols are not text - they are graphic objects - but they are accessed from the text tool.

1   Start a new page, set it to A4 Landscape.

2   Click on the **Text** tool and hold down the mouse button until the extra icons appear. You want the end one, the one that bears a star. Click on this and the **Symbol** roll-up will appear. You can resize the roll-up by the way by dragging the sides, top and bottom outwards or inwards - even to the extent where it covers the entire window.

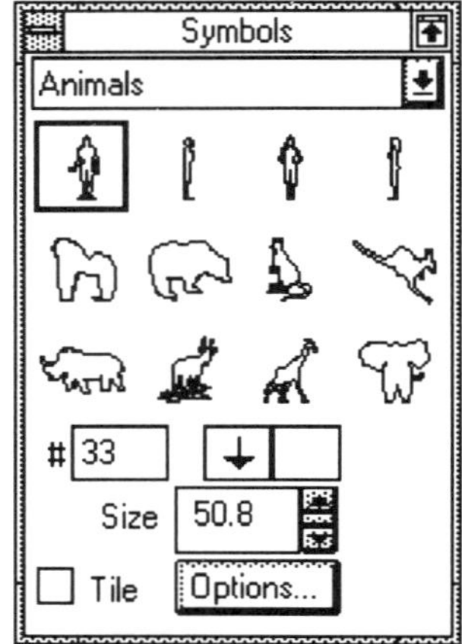

6.29 Symbol roll-up

3   To place a symbol on the page, first set the size that you want to use. The size is set in whatever measurement system you are using for the grid and rulers - in the illustration above it's in millimetres. You can use the arrows to increase or decrease the size or you can simply overwrite it.

4   Now click on a symbol and drag it on to the page. Release the mouse button and it will appear on the page in the size you set. As it does so it will also be outlined and filled.

5   You can also have symbols tile themselves automatically so they cover the entire page. Click on the **Options** button and a dialogue box appears.

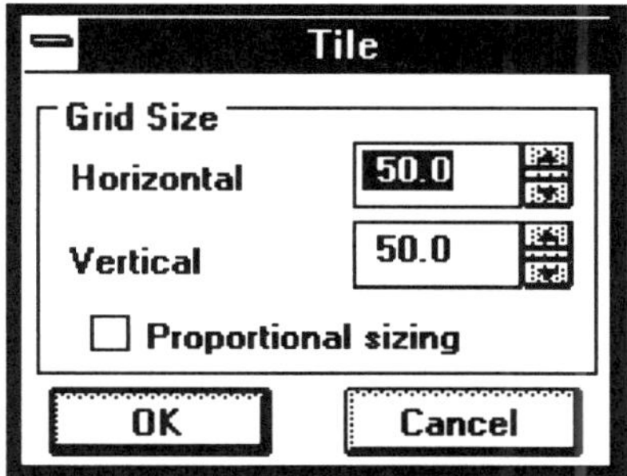

6.30 Symbols options

6   The dialogue box allows you to set the size of the tiles that the symbols will occupy. In general you have to guess at the size because it depends on the symbol. If you are using a tall thin symbol then you need narrow tiles rather than using a wide fat one. If you click on **Proportional sizing** then you get square tiles. Roughly speaking you will need to allow about 5 mms extra for the tile.

7   At the top of the roll-up is a line giving you the name of the selected library. It defaults to Animals. Change this to **Stars I**. Set the size to 25 mms. In the options dialogue box set the tile size to 30 mms square.

8   Click on the second star shape on the top line and drag it onto the page. Release the mouse button and you'll get a grid of stars, 8 across by five down. They'll be filled with whatever colour you set for a graphic.

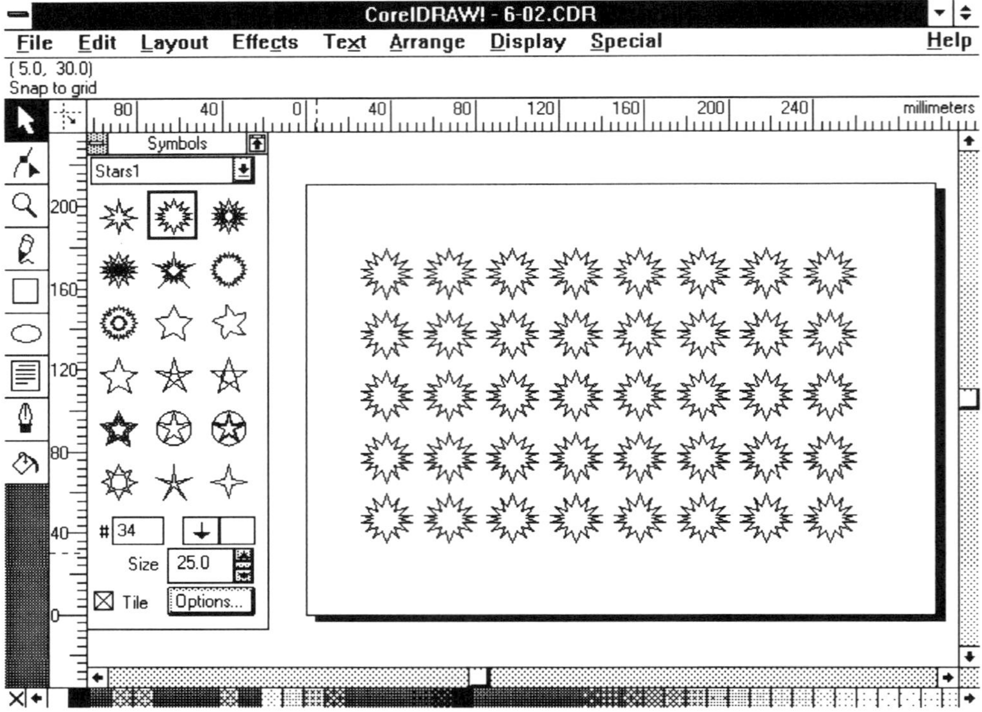

6.31 Stars tiled

9   Try different shapes and different tile sizes. You can delete the entire collection of tiles by deleting the first one. Look at the Status Bar and it will say Control Curve on Layer 1 for the first star, the others say Clone Curve on Layer 1. (We'll get to clones later.) If you place a symbol without using tile then the Status Bar just says Curve on Layer 1.

10   If you resize the control curve then all the clones will also resize automatically. You don't get any more or any less, they just resize. Whenever you place a tiled symbol the program will automatically leave an unadjustable margin around the tiled area.

6.8 FILLED TEXT

Because text is an object that CorelDRAW recognises you can apply any fill to it.
However, if you start using complicated fills then you have to be aware that you need
lots of resources available.

1   Clear the page. Select the **Text** tool either by clicking on it or by pressing **F8**.
Type to word '**Corel**' press **Enter** and the type '**DRAW**'. Align it to the centre
of the page. Press **F4** so that the words fill the screen. The words will have
whatever fill and outline attributes you set as a default.

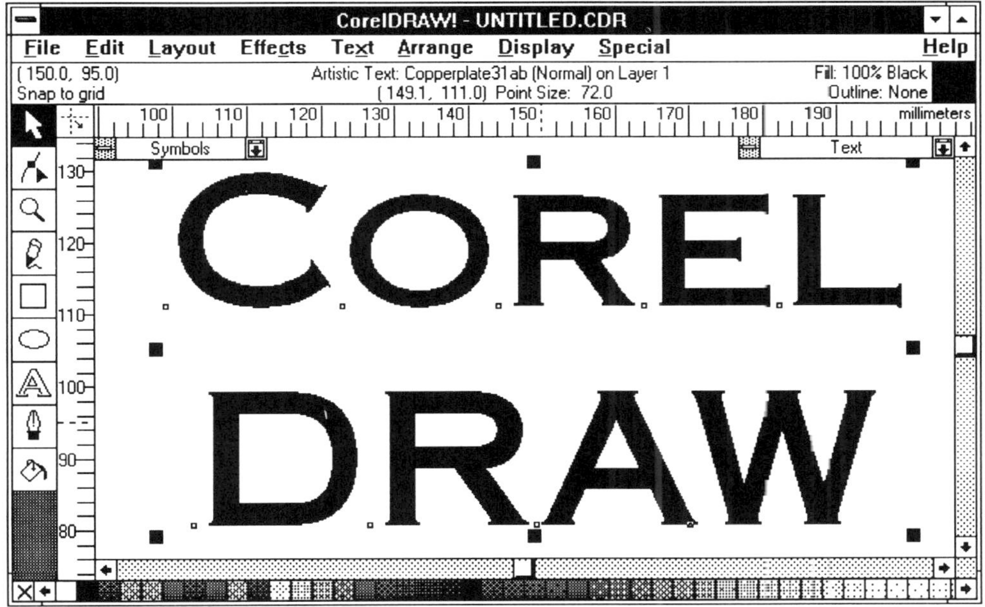

6.32 Words ready

2   Click with the left mouse button on any colour in the palette along the bottom
of the screen. The text fills with the selected colour.

3   Click on the X in the palette with the left mouse button and then on Black with
the right hand one. You'll get outlined text.

197

4   Open the **Pen** tool and click on a line thickness and the text will fatten. You can also make invisible text by the way by giving it no outline and no fill. Why you would want to though is anyone's guess.

5   Open the **Fill** tool and bring up the fill roll-up.

6   By default the roll-up contains a black to white Linear fountain fill. Click on Apply and the text is filled accordingly.

7   Try changing to the one of the bitmap fills. You can get some very odd effects. Try the vector fills too.

8   Now try the textures. These can take a long time to appear so be patient. However, in most cases the wait is well worth it because you can produce really dynamic and vibrant text.

9   You can also fill text with the PostScript patterns if you wish. Open the Fill tool and click on the PS icon. Select the pattern you want to use and the text will be filled. You cannot, unfortunately, see the results until you print it though.

7. Nodes

Because CorelDRAW uses Bezier curves for all objects you can edit the control points, called Nodes, that produce the lines making up the object.

There are different kinds of nodes for different purposes:

Cusp nodes which allow a line to turn sharply.

Smooth nodes which cause the line to have a different curve either side of the node.

Symmetrical nodes which causes the line to have the same curvature either side of the node.

As well as that rectangles and ellipses have different kinds of nodes.

7.1 Regular shape nodes

1   Start a new page. Draw a square 100 mms to a side.

2   Select the **Node Edit** tool either by clicking on it or by pressing **F10**. You won't have the handles around the square, instead you'll have four little squares, one at each corner. (Actually they are four paired sets.)

3   Move the cursor on to one of the nodes and then drag it sideways. Notice that all four nodes move by the same amount. The corners become rounded. Keep dragging, slowly. There is a limit to how far you can drag it - eventually the square becomes a circle. It's not a real circle though - just a deformed square. You can make ellipses in the same way by using rectangles.

That's all you can do with the nodes on squares and rectangles. If you have the grid turned on then the nodes can only move from grid point to grid point.

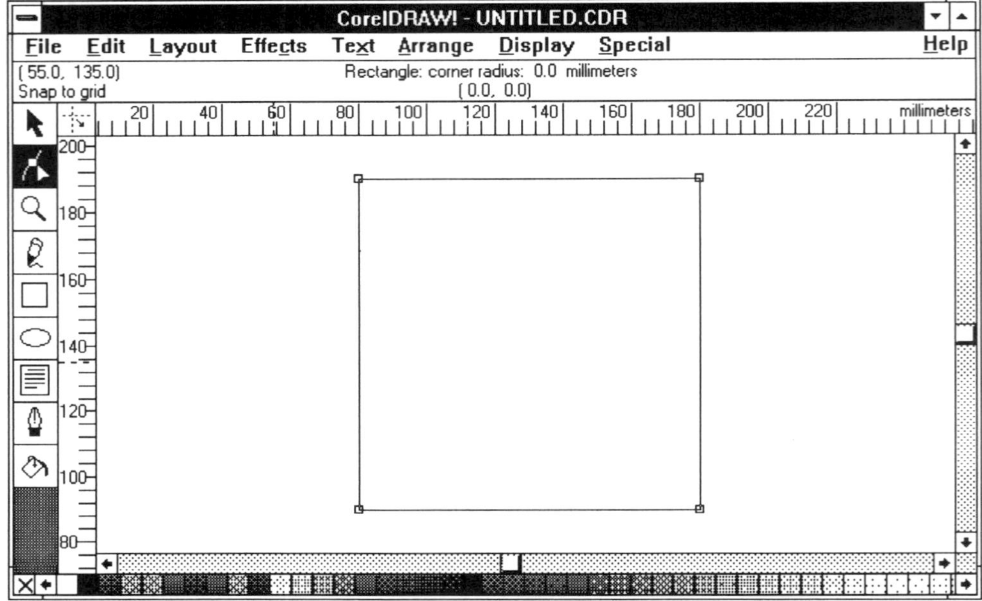

7.01 Square with nodes

4   Move the shape off the page and then draw a 100 mms circle. Select the **Node Edit** tool again. This time you have a single node only. (Actually it's a paired set.)

5   Click on the node and drag it sideways - actually it can only move around the circumference of the circle. If you drag it from inside the circle then you get a pie slice, if you drag it from outside then you get an arc.

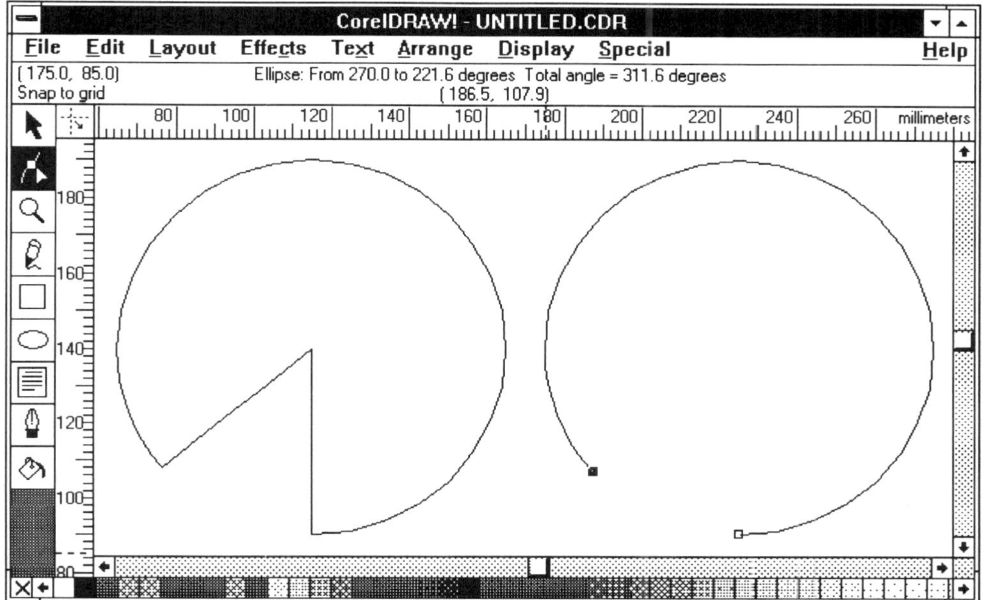

7.02 Circle nodes

6   If you hold down **Ctrl** as you drag the node then it will be constrained to whatever incremental angle you have set in the Preferences dialogue box.

That's all you can do with ellipse or circles nodes.

7.2 CURVE NODES

To do anything really dynamic with the nodes you need to be using curves rather than formal shapes. You can change any regular shape into a curve by pressing Ctrl-Q - the Convert to Curves command which is in the Arrange menu.

1   Select the square you originally created. Put the nodes back to where they should be, i.e. one at each corner.

2   Press **Ctrl-Q** to convert it to curves. Watch the Status Bar and it will change from saying **Rectangle on Layer I** to **Curve on Layer I** and beneath that it will say **Number of Nodes: 4**.

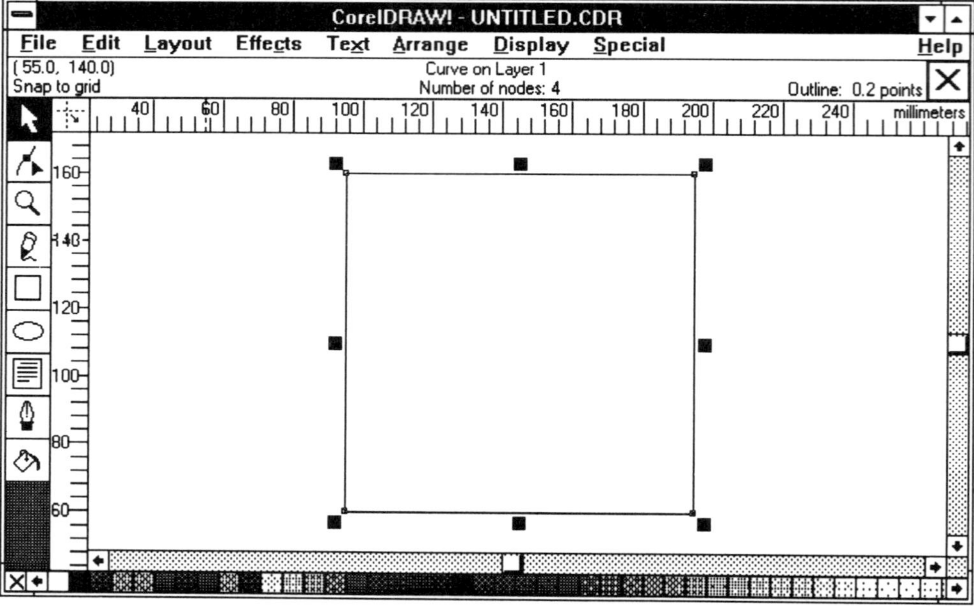

7.03 Converted square

3   Now select the **Node Edit** tool again. You'll get four nodes again but one of them is much larger - this is the First Node. Try moving any of the nodes around. If you have the grid turned on the nodes jumps from grid point to grid

point. As you move the node the shape of the object, which is no longer a square remember, will change.

4   You can move two nodes at the same time if you have them selected. To select multiple nodes either drag a bounding box around them or hold down **Shift** as you click on the ones you want. The selected nodes will then move in unison.

5   Select the circle and convert that to curves too. That will also have four nodes, one at each of the compass points, one of which will be the first node. These behave slightly differently. Click on one of them and you'll get this:

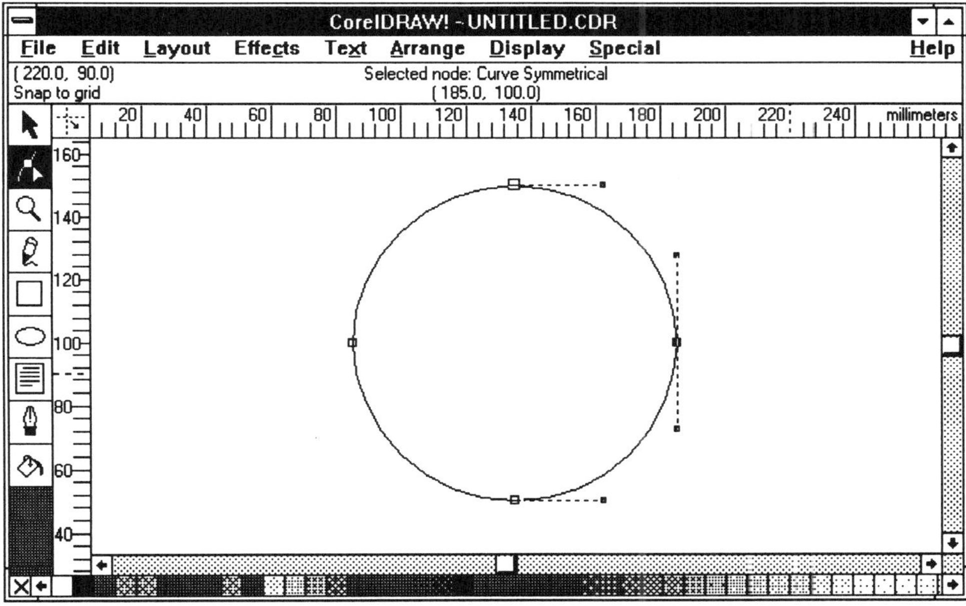

7.04 Nodal circle

6   The point is that each node is a Symmetrical one. You can move the node itself or you can move those little squares at the end of the dotted lines. Moving the latter will change the line completely. Play with them and see what you can do. Making a knot pattern is relatively easy. Just transpose each node control point.

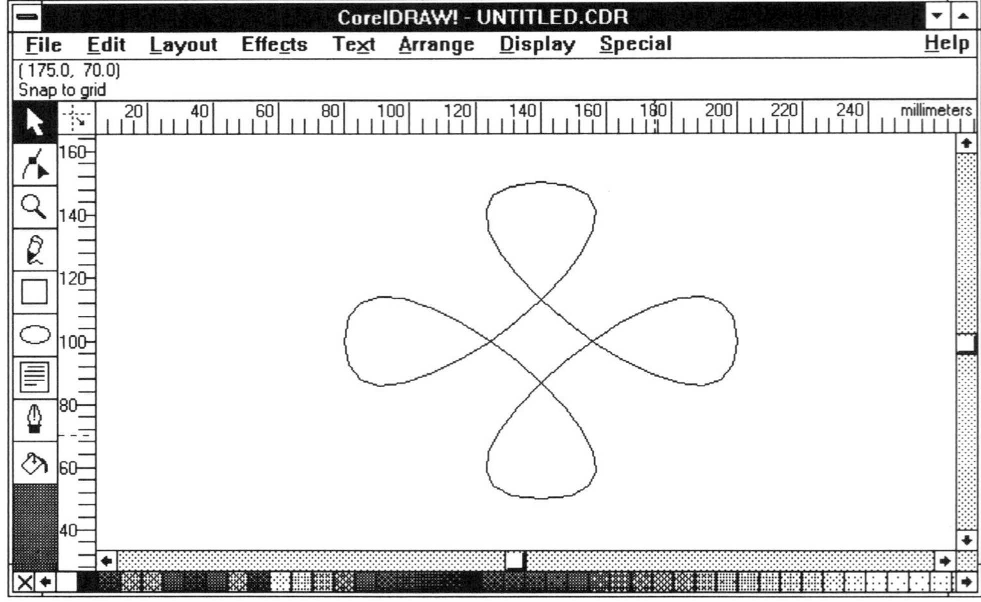

7.05 Knot pattern

7   Once an object has been node edited it can then be treated as any other object, e.g. you can rotate, skew, move, duplicate, combine it or do whatever you want. Equally they can be filled or outlined however you wish.

Be warned - you can spend hours playing with the node effects on simple shapes, like the converted squares and circles.

7.3 NODE EDITING

For this one you're going to need the 5-02 file you created earlier.

1   Load the file. The star shape is okay but it can be made much more interesting by duplicating and interleaving it to make a kind of Celtic Knotwork pattern. However, it takes time and a good eye. (It took me three hours to do this the first time!)

2   Turn the grid off. Place two guidelines, a horizontal one at 105 mms and a vertical one at 148.5 mms - assuming you're using A4 Landscape. (Tip: A quick way to add precise guidelines is to place one anywhere and then double click on it. You'll get the Guidelines Setup dialogue box.)

3   What you have to do is break the star but before you do so you need to add some nodes. To make this easy to follow, let's call the points on the star A to E going clockwise from the top. Select the **Node Edit** tool and then zoom in to where the line from A to D crosses the line from E to B. Click as close to that point as you can but make sure you're on the A to D line. You'll get a small black circle. Double click and the Node roll-up appears.

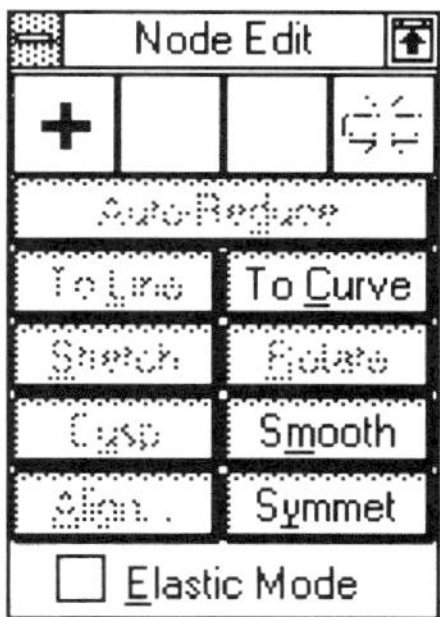

7.06 Node roll-up

4   Click on the **Plus icon** or you can just press **Plus** on the numeric keypad. You'll get a new node where you clicked. Now click on the broken link icon in the roll-up - the one at the extreme right. This breaks the line at the node point you

added. (You can break the line directly but it's more accurate to add the node
first and then break it.)

5   Zoom out and then zoom in to where the line from A to C crosses the line from
B to D. Double click near where the lines cross and then add another node.
Break these apart by clicking on the broken link icon again. You should now
have something like this:

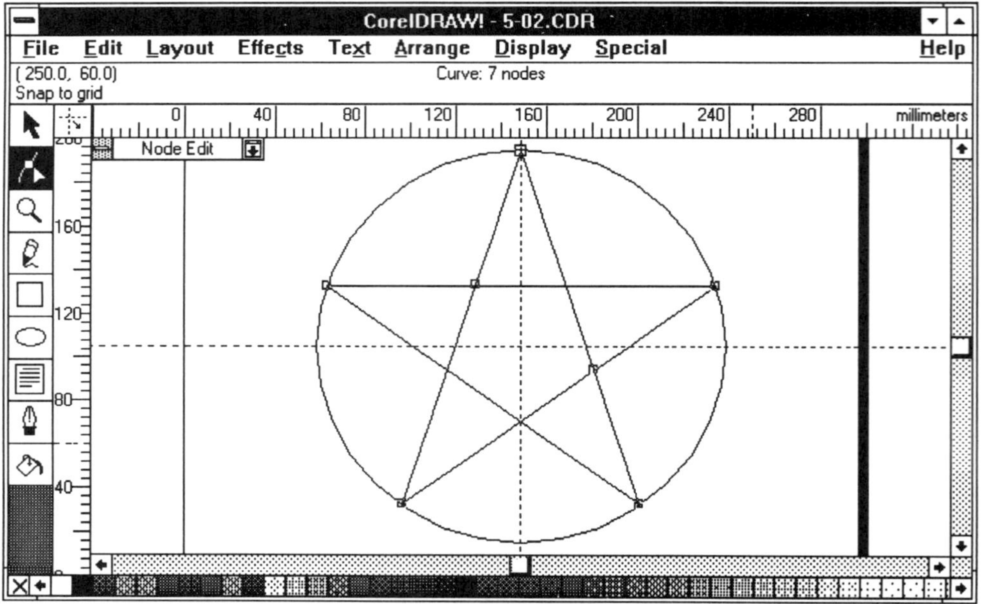

7.07 Nodes added

6   You now have a single shape that's made of two sub-paths. Switch back to the
Pointer tool by pressing the **Spacebar**. Press **Ctrl-K** to break the two objects
apart. Click on the page to deselect everything. Then click on the star shape at
either C or D. Press **Del** to remove the lines. You've now got an open triangle
with one line longer than the other.

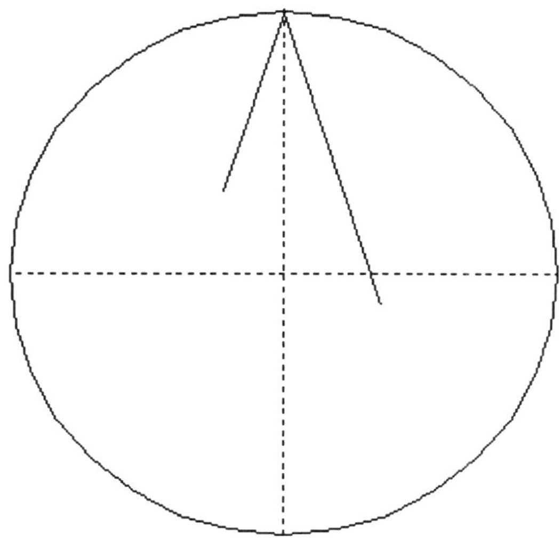

7.08 Line by itself

7   Open the Preferences dialogue box - **Ctrl-J** - and set the Constrain angle to **72 degrees**. Close the dialogue box. Click on the lines twice and you'll get the rotational handles. Move the Centre of Rotation to where the guidelines cross.

8   Press the **Plus** key on the numeric keypad to duplicate the lines. Then hold down **Ctrl** and drag one of the corner handles downwards. You now have two sets of triangular lines. Duplicate the second line and rotate that. Repeat that again and again until you have five sets of lines. They will look like the original star shape when you've finished.

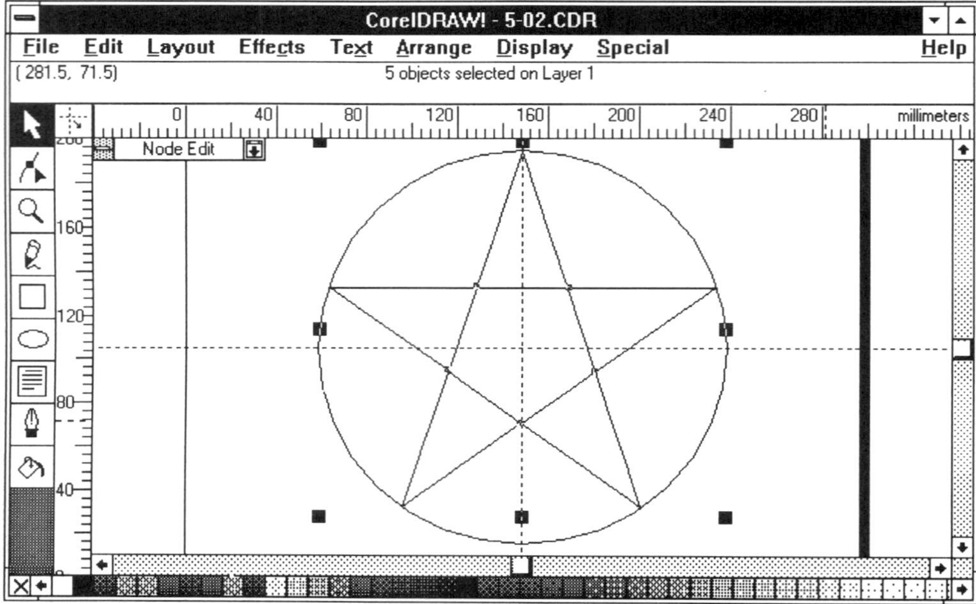

7.09 Lines duplicated and rotated

9   Select all the lines. The quick way is to press **Alt-E A**, which is the shortcut for select all, and then deselect the circle. Now give the lines a 16 Point outline - that's the penultimate preset line thickness in the Pen Tool.

10   Now for the fiddley bit. It helps doing this if you make each line a different colour. (I don't have that advantage because I'm doing this in monochrome.) Select the **Node Edit** tool again. Zoom in, as far as you possibly can, to where the lines cross, like this:

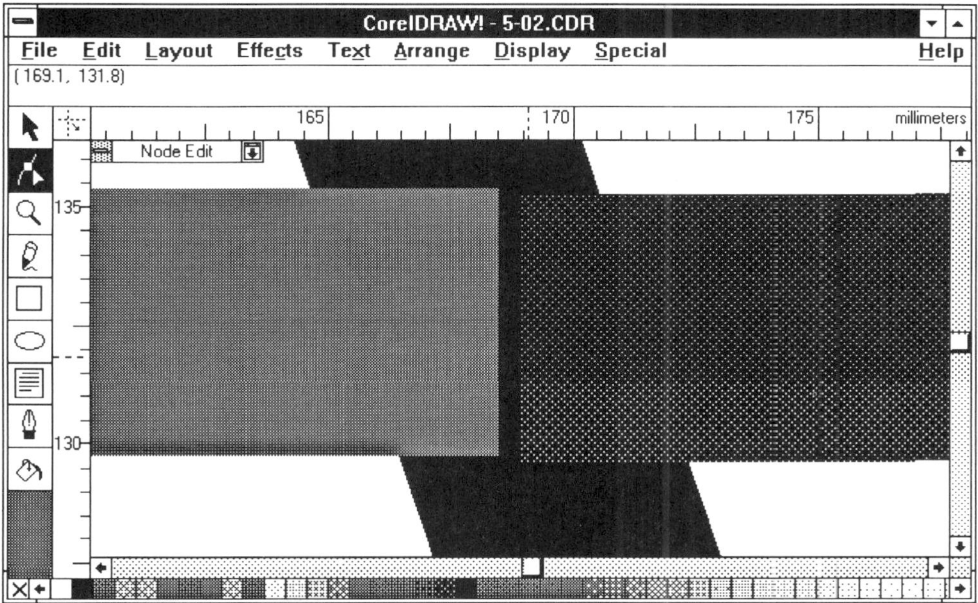

7.10 Lines crossing

11   What you have to do is move the nodes of the lines that cross the diagonal line so that the end of the line moves fractionally to one side it. In other words, the lines on the left and the right in the illustration have to be moved slightly sideways. If you hold down **Ctrl** as you move the nodes they are easier to control. You're not going to get it perfect, because the program won't let you, and so you'll always have a slight overlap. Don't worry about it too much.

12   Then move the line endings on all the other lines where they cross a straight line.

13   Now, for each line in turn, duplicate it. Change the line width to 8 points and make it white. Fill the circle with another colour. You should end up with something like this.

7.11 Interlaced star

It's extremely difficult to make the interlaced star correctly. You can fiddle around with it for hours. It gets easier if you add extra nodes and do it with extra lines. However, in the end you can always rely on the fact that the human eye will happily fill in what it thinks is necessary to make the star look the way you want.

7.4 NODES AND TEXT

All text also has nodes but they behave in a slightly different way again. By the way any text can be converted to curves in the same way that the circle and square were. However, if you do change it to curves then it becomes a graphic and is no longer text, i.e. you cannot edit it with the text tool.

1   Start a new page. We'll do an old trick and recreate the CorelDRAW logo. Type the word **CORELDRAW!** on the page - just like that. It doesn't matter what typeface or size you use. Then press **F4** to make it fill the screen.

7.12 Word on screen

2   Select the **Node Edit** tool. Each letter will now have a single node - at the lower left hand corner. Drag a bounding box around the first five letters so that you 'capture' their nodes.

3   Double click on any of the selected nodes and you'll get the Character Attributes dialogue box. Change the typeface to **Times Roman** or the CorelDRAW equivalent. Change the Style to **Bold-Italic** and then click on **OK**. The other thing you have to change is the Size. It wants to be two thirds of the size of the remaining characters, e.g. if you used 24 point text originally you need to reduce the size to 18 points.

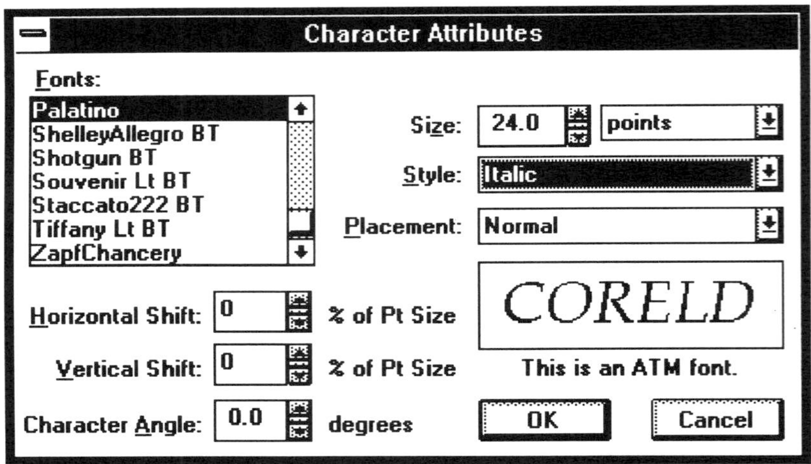

7.13 Character Attributes

4   Drag a bounding box around the remaining characters to select their nodes. Double click on one of them and then set the typeface to Freestyle Italic or the CorelDRAW equivalent. You should now have something like figure 7.14.

5   It still doesn't look right. That's because the first five letters need to be moved closer together and the remaining characters need to be outlined. Double click on the node of the letter C. In the Horizontal Shift line you want a value of **20%** of point size. Click on **OK** and the letter moves to the right.

6   Select the letter R and move that -10%, the letter E -15% and finally the letter L -20%. That places the first five letters correctly.

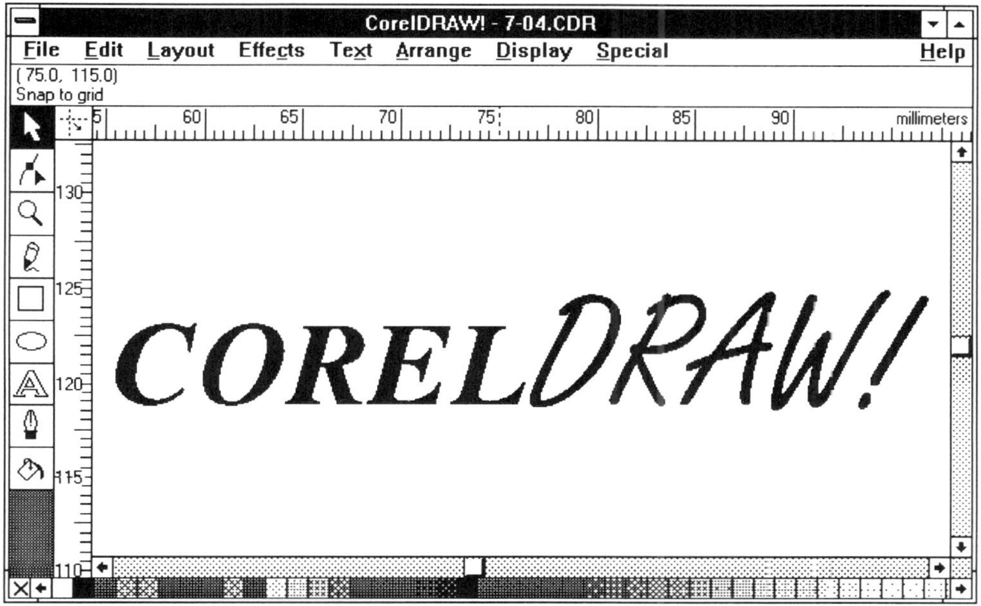

7.14 Text changed

7   Select the final five characters, open the **Pen** tool and activate the **Outline** dialogue box, or you could just press **F12**. Change the outline to 1 point and then close the dialogue box.

8   Now with the final five characters still selected, drag them to the left. To do so, just click in any of the selected nodes and then drag the characters. Hold down Shift as you do so and the letters won't move off the baseline.

9   Finally they need to be moved up slightly. Double click on a node to get the **Characters Attribute** dialogue box again. You need to set a positive value for the **Vertical Shift**. Because I used 24 point text, a 3% shift was correct. Try it for yourself - you'll have to do this bit by eye. Finally you should end up with this:

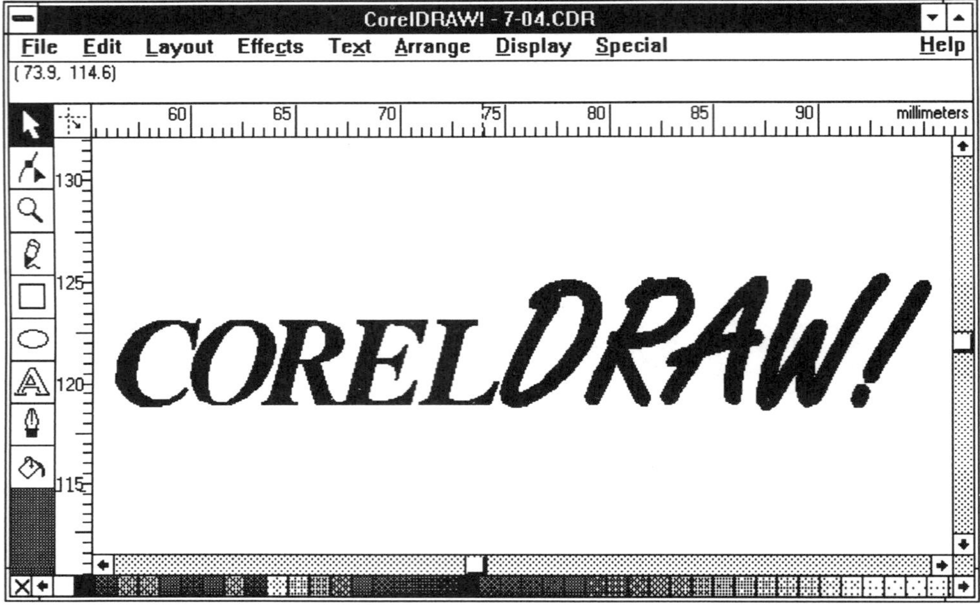

7.15 CorelDRAW logo

You can use the Node Edit tool to change any character, the position of any character or the outline and fill of any character. The possibilities are limited only by your imagination!

7.5 BITMAPS AND NODES

You can use the node edit tool with bitmaps. In this case it allows you to crop the graphic.

1   Start a new page. Open the **File** menu and click on Import - or just press **Alt-F I**. In the dialogue box change the File Type to TIFF 5.0 Bitmap. Log on to the CLIPART\TIFS sub-directory and you'll find some files.

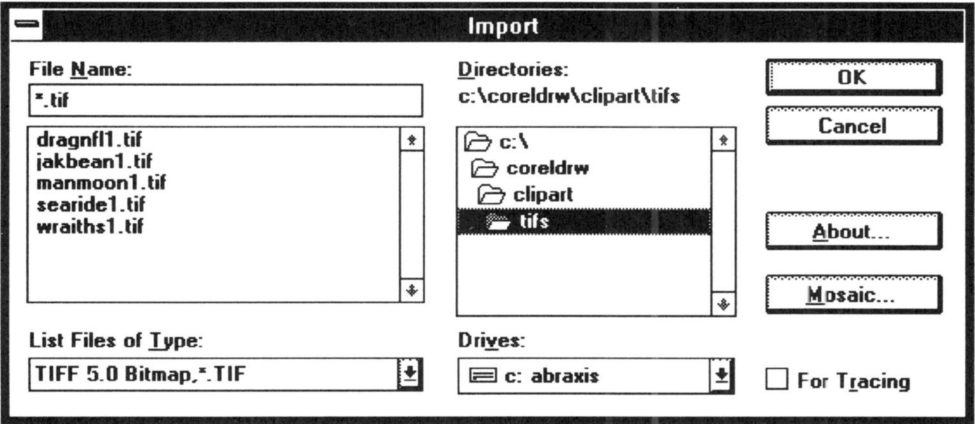

7.16 Import dialogue box

2   Double click on any of the files that you fancy. (At this stage I don't know what clip-art will be shipping with CorelDRAW 4.) The import bar graph will appear as the file is loaded. Press **F4** to make the file fill the screen.

3   Select the **Node Edit** tool and click on the image to select it. Look at the Status Bar. It now says "**Bitmap: Crop left 0%, Right 0%, Bottom 0%, Top 0%**". Notice that as well as the normal handles there are also four smaller ones, one at each corner. These smaller handles simply mark the edge of the image.

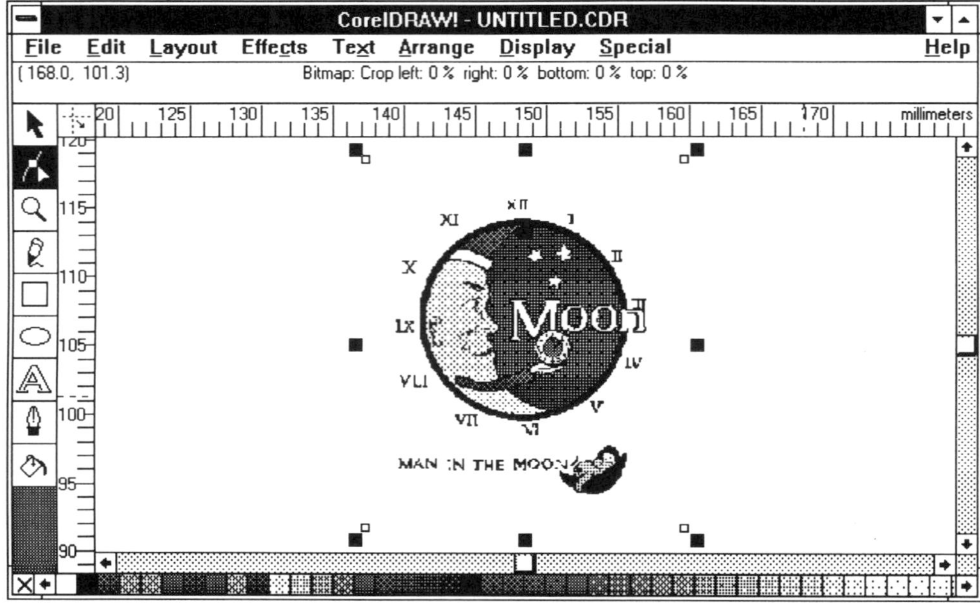

7.17 Image imported

4   To crop the image just drag one of the handles. You cannot drag the handles
     outwards at this stage because the image is already fully sized. As you move
     the handles so the Status Bar will tell you the amount by which you have
     cropped the image.

8. PRINTING

The entire printing process from CorelDRAW 4 has been completed rewritten and improved. All the programs in the suite now use the same basic dialogue box with the same options.

People often ask what is the best printer to use with CorelDRAW. That's a bit like asking how long is a piece of string? There is no hard and fast answer. To get the best from CorelDRAW you need to use a PostScript printer, it's not essential but it will work better and it gives you more capabilities. At the very least you need a laser printer. Personally, I use a Star Laser Printer 4, which is a PostScript compatible printer, all the time and it has never given me any problems. It will print anything I throw at it from CorelDRAW without any hassle. The printer has 2 Mb of RAM, the minimum necessary for running PostScript, and that's all. It will accept any ATM fonts, or TrueType for that matter. It has a standard resolution cf 300 dpi.

The CRC for this book, by the way, will be printed out on a Star Laser Printer 5 which has just been launched and which Star have kindly loaned to me for a while. This gives a resolution of 600 by 300 dpi and is one of the few printers I know of that has full True Image capability as well as PostScript. With a price of under £1,000 it is well within everyone's reach.

One thing that you have to be aware of, regardless of which printer you use, is the resolution that the printer is capable off. The majority of laser printers will give you a resolution of 300 dpi. That in turn means that the thinnest line they can produce is 0.25 points. There are seventy two points to an inch, so 1 point is (300/72) which needs 4.16 dots. Seeing as you cannot have partial dots it means that 1 point is 4 dots. Therefore a single dot must be one quarter of one point.

If you use 600 dpi then a 1 point line is (600/72) which is 8.33 dots, round it down and you get 8 dots to a point. Therefore the thinnest line possible, i.e. one dot, is 0.125 points.

If you output to an image setter, e.g. with 2400 dpi, then the thinnest line possible is exceedingly thin, less than a thirtieth of a point. You should be aware than all graphics programs, not just CorelDRAW, are capable of producing a hairline. In CorelDRAW you set the line thickness to 0.01 points to achieve this. With a setting like this, the printer will produce the thinnest line it is capable of - regardless of the resolution. So, producing a hairline on a standard laser will give you a 0.25 point line because that's the thinnest line possible. If you then print the same file on an image setter then the same line will almost invisible.

Equally, an image setting will give you much better graduations for fountain fills than a standard laser can produce - simply because of the resolution. However, outputting to an image setter is very expensive, around £5 to £7 per A4 page, which is beyond the purse of most of us. So we're going to concentrate on using ordinary PostScript printers here.

1   Open the interleaved star file that you produced earlier. Open the **File** menu and click on **Print Setup**. This will bring up a dialogue box.

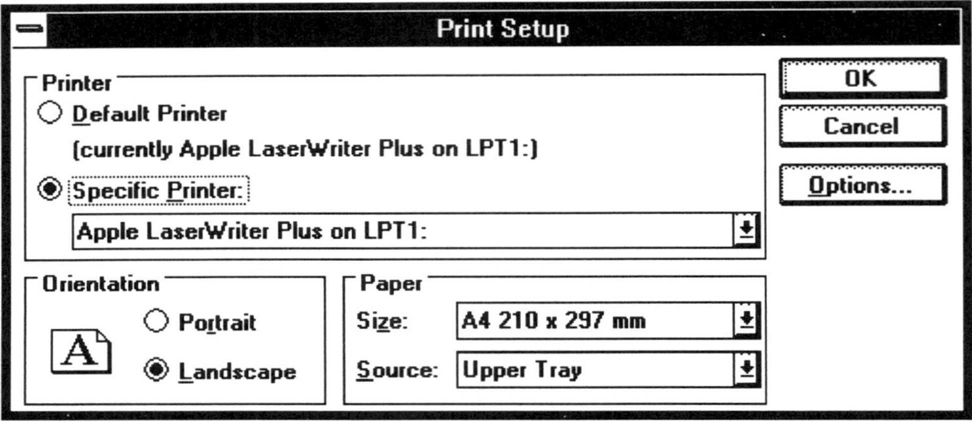

8.01 Printer Setup dialogue box

2   In the dialogue box you can select any of the printers that you have installed on your system. The top line gives the default printer and below that is a line labelled **Specific Printer**. If you click on the arrowhead at the end of this line you'll get a drop down menu of all the printers installed on your system.

By the way, the latest PostScript printer driver for Windows, at the time of writing, is Version 3.55. If you have an earlier version then you should ring Microsoft and ask them for the later one. It is a free upgrade available for the asking.

3   Once you have selected a printer, click on **OK** to close the dialogue box. It is not worth going into the **Options** for the printer because CorelDRAW doesn't use them, instead it uses it's own. (The reason is historical and it's too complex to go into here.)

4   Now press **Ctrl-P** to activate the print command. If you have the printer set incorrectly, e.g. for Portrait when you're using a Landscape page or vice versa, then you'll get a message box asking if the program should adjust the print itself.

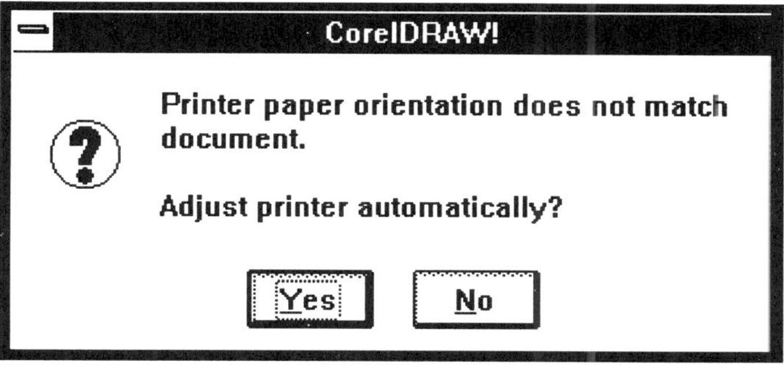

8.02 Adjust printer

5   Click on **Yes** to have it do so. (Be warned, some other programs won't recognise that the printer orientation is changed so if you use them you'll have to change it back later.) You'll then get the actual print dialogue box.

6   Just click on **OK** to print the file.

Print dialogue box

The print dialogue box is now so interactive and comprehensive that it needs full description.

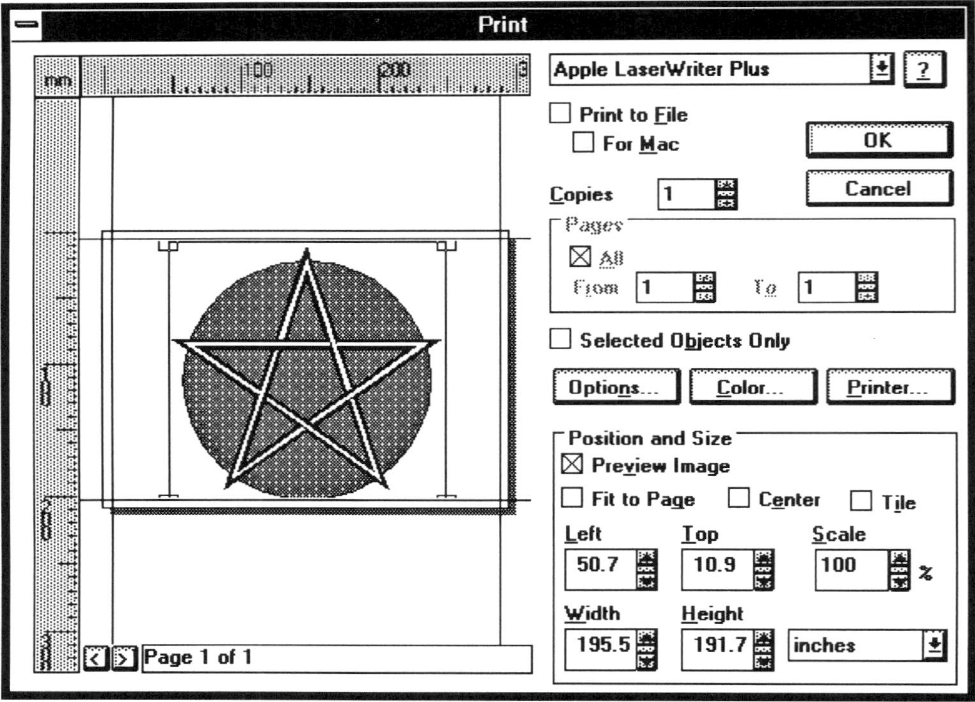

8.03 Print dialogue box

On the left hand side is a representation of the page bearing the graphic - in full colour. This shows what the page will look like when it is printed. You can resize the image on this preview screen to scale it although it is easier to use the scaling options. If you resize the image here it doesn't affect the actual image in CorelDRAW, just the print option.

Where there are handles at the corners of the image on the preview is where the crop marks will be printed - if you select them. Note that you cannot have crop marks on an A4 page if you have an A4 image. The crop marks take up about 2.5 mms square so any image that needs them must have at least that much margin on the page.

In the bottom left hand corner are two opposing arrows. These allow you to scroll through the pages of a multiple page document to select pages to print. It will tell you which page you are looking at as you do so.

The Rulers around the edge of the dialogue box are for reference only. They will be shown in whatever measurement system you have set in the box at the lower right hand side of the dialogue box.

It is the right hand side of the dialogue box that is the most complex. It contains a multitude of buttons that activate second level dialogue boxes, plus a range of commands. Most of these you will never need to use but they are there in case you do.

At the top of the right hand side of the box, it gives you the printer name. Beside this is a question mark. If you click on this you'll be given more information about your printer than you probably want. Some of it is handy, like the actual minimum size of the margins, but most of it is beyond me. (Half of the things in the dialogue box I've never even heard of!) Click on **OK** to close the dialogue box.

Below that is a command labelled **Print to File**. This allows you to produce a PRN file that is needed by some bureaux to output on to an image setter. If you use this then you don't actually print the file, instead you get a disk file.

Below that again is another command called **For Mac**. Again this is intended only for use when you are outputting via a bureau that use Apple rather than PC machines. (Appendix 3 gives a list of some bureaux that can output CorelDRAW files in a variety of ways directly for those who need them.)

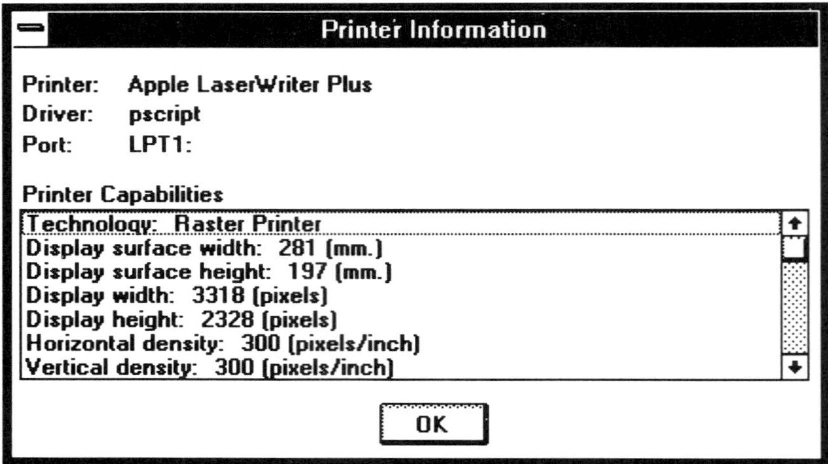

8.04 Printer capabilities

Beneath that is a line labelled **Copies**. You can have anything up to 9,999 copies if you wish! Just click on the arrowheads to increase or decrease the numbers - or you can simply overwrite them.

Below that is an area that is only active if you are using a multiple page document, labelled **Pages**. In here you can set the number of pages to be printed, either All, which is the default, or you can set a From and To page.

Under that is a line labelled **Selected Objects Only**. That means exactly what it says. It is only active provided you have any object selected. If so then you have the option of printing just that object rather than everything.

Below that are three buttons, we'll come to them in a minute.

In the bottom right hand corner of the box is a single section labelled **Position and Size** containing a number of options. Any change you make here affects the printed output only - it does not affect the actual image in CorelDRAW.

Preview Image affects the left hand side of the dialogue box. If it is turned on, which it is by default, then you get to see the image on the page. With complex images, especially ones using complex fills, it is worth turning it off. When it is off all you get is a bounding box being displayed in the preview area.

Fit to Page will take the image and change it so that it fits within the available margins. In other words the image is scaled as much as necessary in order to fit. The command works both ways, either it will expand a small image or reduce a large one.

Centre moves the image so that it sits in the mathematically correct middle of the page.

Tile allows you to print images that are larger than the page size at full size by using additional pages.

Left and **Top** allow you to adjust the position of the image on the page. You can either move the image in the preview or use these boxes to position the image. When you change the value in one box the other will change automatically to maintain the image's aspect ratio.

Scale allows you to increase or decrease the size of the image. Values of less than 100% reduce the image, values higher than that increase it. Be warned, if you scale files containing bitmaps the quality of these will suffer as a result.

Width and **Height** give you the size of the image itself. The values here will change as you scale the image itself. When you change the value in one box the other will change automatically to maintain the image's aspect ratio.

Clicking on **Options** will bring up another dialogue box.

8.05 Options dialogue box

Set Flatness To determines the number of segments that PostScript printers will use to draw curves and ellipses. The default value is 1 which gives true curves. Increasing the value will create curves that look like polygons, decreasing it makes the curves smoother.

Auto Increase Flatness will automatically increase the flatness, to a maximum of 10, for you until the image prints. If the image still cannot print once the maximum is reached then CorelDRAW ignores it and goes on to the next image.

Screen sets the frequency for the halftone screen used when printing. Default is the screen used by the particular printer that you are using. Alternatively you can change it to one of the existing values.

Fountain Stripes is the number of stripes used for fountain fills. All fountain stripes have a tendency to band somewhat, depending on the printer. Changing the value here allows you to increase or decease the banding effect. If you have changed the number of stripes in the Fountain Fill Edit dialogue box then that will override any setting you make here. In this way you can produce different effects for different objects.

Print Negative creates a reversed image, i.e. black as white and vice versa. Colours will be transposed to their complimentary opposites.

Emulsion Down is intended for image setters for when you want the image to be produced emulsion side down.

All Fonts Resident can speed up printing text files tremendously. However, you can only use it if you limit yourself to those fonts that are resident in your printer or which have previously been down-loaded.

Print as Separations will give you a different page for each colour. Again it applies mainly to image setters and for litho-printing in full colour where you have to produce separate plates for each colour.

The area labelled **References** contains a number of commands, most of which only become active when you are doing colour separations.

Crop Marks however can be printed on any file but remember you can only have crop marks if the page size in CorelDRAW is smaller than the sheet of paper you are printing.

Registration Marks only applies to colour separations. There are special marks used to align the various colour plates properly.

Calibration Bar prints strips of colour or grey scales. It's used as a reference only.

Desitometer Scale is similar to the above. It's used to gauge the accuracy of the printed output.

File Information will print the file name, the screen frequency, the date and time of the file. You need to allow room for this information. If you use **Within Page** then the data should be printed on the page itself.

Clicking on **Colour** will bring up another dialogue box.

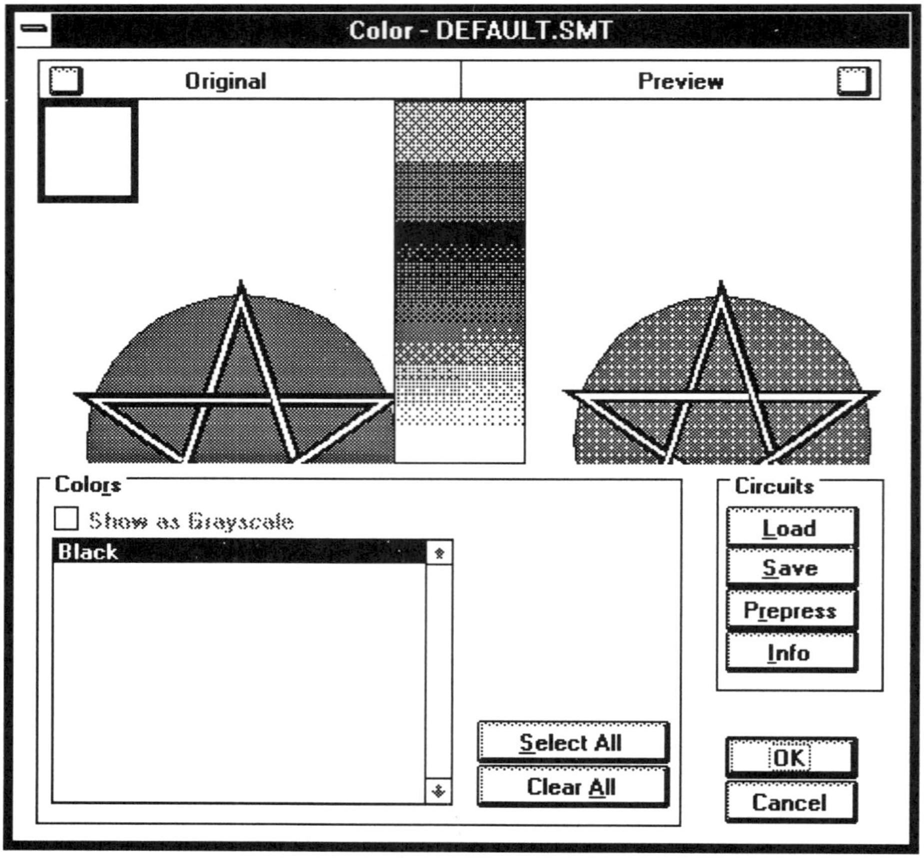

8.06 Colour dialogue box I

The dialogue box is used to calibrate colours, an area that we don't have room to go into here. The usage of this dialogue box and the secondary boxes it contains are outside the scope of this book. For standard laser printers you are unlikely to need to use it.

Clicking on **Printer** brings up the dialogue box that you should be familiar with from Windows Control Panel, Printer Setup.

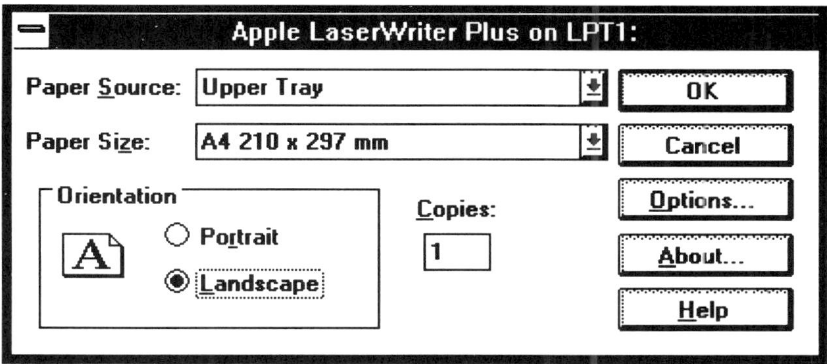

8.07 Printer dialogue box

The dialogue box allows you to adjust certain features of the printer setup. Don't bother with options within this dialogue box because CorelDRAW doesn't access that information.

Once you have the various parameters for the print, clicking on **OK** will begin the process. As the image is being sent to the printer you will get a message box and an indication of how far the process has been completed. Once the message box vanishes you are free to continue doing things in CorelDRAW itself.

PRINTING PROBLEMS

This section deals with the major printer problems that you may experience - it is not comprehensive nor definitive. The problems and the solutions that follow are the most common ones.

WHEN YOU PRINT YOU ONLY GET A PARTIAL PRINT, I.E. SOME OF THE IMAGE IS MISSING.

This is usually caused by lack of memory in the printer. It's printing as much as it can with the resources it has available. Sometimes you will get a second page with the missing elements on that. The solution is to make sure that the printer has enough on-board RAM.

WHEN PRINTING IN COLOUR, THE PRINTED COLOURS DON'T MATCH THE SCREEN COLOURS.

They never will simply because the means of producing the colours are totally different and, essentially, incompatible. The printed page contains reflective colours while the monitor uses projected colours. The worst offendr is likely to be blue and its derivatives. Printing the correct shades of blue is extremely difficult. Some printer manufacturers use software to try to colour match screen and page - with varying degrees of success - but none of them are perfect.

PROBLEMS PRINTING TO A POSTSCRIPT PRINTER.

Make sure you are using the latest PostScript driver. Run Windows Control Panel, click on Printers then Setup and finally About. You'll get a message box telling you which version you are using. The latest version, at the time of writing, is 3.55. Unfortunately Windows itself still ships with version 3.5. You can get a free upgrade directly from Microsoft by asking for it.

YOU CREATED A PATTERN USING TEXT BUT WHEN YOU TRY TO PRINT ANYTHING USING THAT PATTERN YOU GET AN ERROR MESSAGE.

There is a problem using text in vector patterns. The way round it is to convert the text to curves and then create the pattern.

YOU TRY TO PRINT TrueType FONTS BUT YOU DON'T GET THEM.

This can be caused by a wide range of things. Before you do anything else, try removing the fonts from the Windows Control Panel, then delete the FOT files from the \WINDOWS\SYSTEM directory, then Add the fonts again in the Control Panel. That should solve most problems.

Another thing to check is the way that the fonts are downloaded. In Windows Control Panel, click on Printers, Setup, Options, Advanced and you'll get a dialogue box telling you how the fonts are being downloaded. Usually you have a choice of Adobe Type 1 (which is why I use ATM fonts in the first place) or Bitmap (Type 3). You should use the first option if you have a PostScript printer and the second if not.

PRINTING TAKES A LONG TIME AND YOU KEEP GETTING A TIMEOUT MESSAGE.

Change the TransmissionRetryTimeout setting in the WIN.INI file to 995. That should cure the problem.

USING A HP IV CAUSES PROBLEMS.

There are a number of known problems using a HP LaserJet IV. Most of these are solved by getting hold of the latest printer drivers and using them. Contact HP Technical Support.

THE PROGRAM CRASHES WHEN PRINTING.

This is probably caused by lack of TMP file space. A Windows temp file must go into contiguous space. Use a disk defragmenter, e.g. Norton Speed Disk, PC

CorelDRAW 4 - A Users Guide

Tools Compress or MS-DOS 6 Defrag, to tidy up your disk. You need to do this daily! The first time you run it the process will take a long time but it gets faster the more often you do it.

Whenever you get a program crash you should close the offending program, close Windows, remove all the TMP files off your hard disk and then reboot the computer completely.

General troubleshooting.

If you are having problems printing there are some steps that you should go through to try and eliminate the problems.

1   Check the printer driver you are using. Most manufacturers produce their own printer drivers for specific machines. In order to get the latest driver you have to call the manufacturer direct - they are not sent out regardless.

2   If you are using PostScript then make sure you are using the latest Windows PostScript driver, Version 3.55 or later.

3   If text won't print, save you file (so you have a backup copy - make sure you don't overwrite it with the converted file) then convert the text to curves and try printing that. If the problem persists then you probably need more RAM in the printer.

4   If you get banded fountain fills it is probably due to the printer resolution. Try increasing the number of stripes but there may be nothing you can do about it.

5   If you get blank borders when using PostScript patterns, it is probably due to a limitation of the pattern rendering. There is little you can do about it other than using masks. Some patterns cause the problem more than others.

If you are still having problems call Corel Technical Support.

9. LAYERS

Everything you do in CorelDRAW sits on layers, but you have layers within layers. The program allows you to have as many layers as you wish - or as you have resources for - and you can name them, set various parameters for them and what-have-you. However, each layer can contain a number of objects and these effectively stack on top of each other - even though they are on different parts of the page.

9.1 STACKS

Objects are stacked within CorelDRAW in the order that you create them in, the latest image being place at the top of the stack each time.

1   Start a new page. Draw a rectangle in the lower left hand corner of the page, a circle in the upper right hand corner, a squiggle in the top right and put some text in the bottom right, like this:

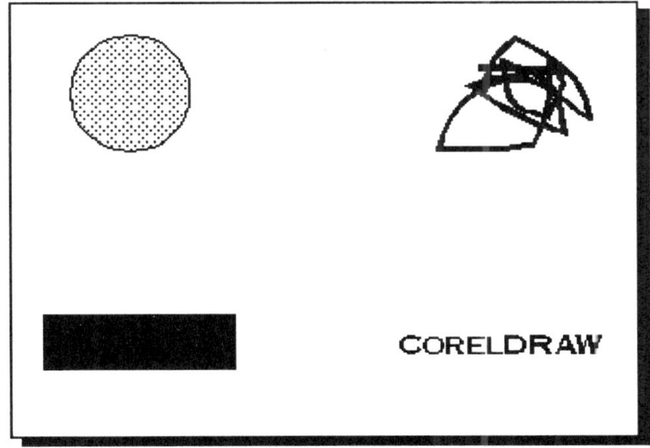

9.01 Four objects

2   Select all the objects and then Align them to the centre of the page. The rectangle is at the bottom of the stack, because you drew it first, and the the whole lot to the centre of the page. You'll get this:

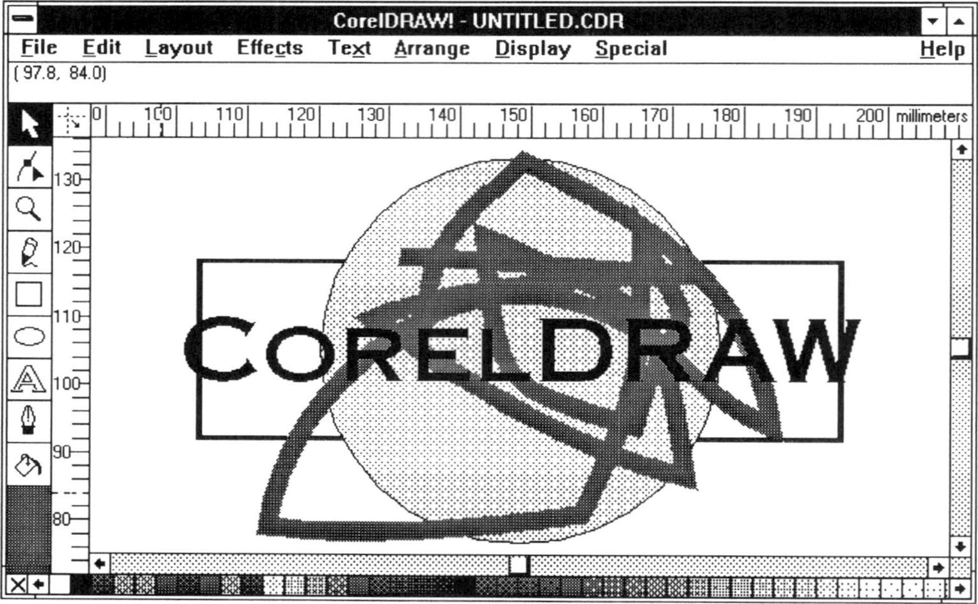

9.02 Aligned objects

3   You can change the relative positions of the objects within the stack using the keys or you can use the commands in the Arrange menu - the former is much quicker. Select the text. Press **Shift-PgDn**. The text should vanish behind the rectangle because you have now moved it to the bottom of the stack. Press **Shift-PgUp** and it comes back to the top.

4   Press **Ctrl-PgDn** and the text moves behind the squiggle but stays above the circle. You have moved the text down one level of the stack. Press the keys again and it moves behind the circle, do it a third time and the text moves behind the rectangle.

5   Press **Ctrl-PgUp** and the text moves back up one level. Repeat to keep changing the relative position.

6   You can move objects up and down through the stack even when they are not stacked on top of each other. Move the objects apart again just by dragging them so that they no longer overlap. Now draw a large square that almost fills the page and which overlaps all the existing objects. Fill it with a fountain fill. Fill the rectangle and the circle with different fountain fills.

7   The square is now the top object. You can prove it by pressing **Ctrl-W** - the keyboard shortcut for **Window Refresh**. (You used fountain fills because they take time to display.) The objects will be redrawn in the order that they lie in the stack.

8   Play with the stack changing options until you are comfortable with them.

9.2 LAYERS

As well as using the stack positioning you can also use the layers themselves to place things in different orders. The layers really come into their own when you are doing complex images. For example, I have a map that contains over 2,000 objects spread across 25 layers. The image is very complex but by using stacks I can edit only certain parts of it and have the others display quickly.

1   Press **Ctrl-F3** to activate the **Layers** roll-up. Arrange it and it will move to the top left hand side of the screen. Roll it down again. Layer 1 will be highlighted because that's the default.

9.03 Layers roll-up

LAYERS ROLL-UP

The roll-up contains the names of all the layers currently in use plus three special additional ones:

Layer 1 is the normal default layer. You can edit and modify this as necessary.

Desktop is a special layer that is used mainly for multiple page documents. Anything placed on to this layer is available to all the pages of such a document, whereas everything else is for the individual pages only. By putting something on the Desktop layer you can then copy it to any other page.

Guides is the layer used for the guidelines. You can place objects on this layer and use them as guides if you wish. This layer is not necessarily active across multiple pages.

Grid is normally the bottom layer. It contains the grid settings. This layer is active across multiple pages.

---

2   You can change the positions of any layer in the roll-up simply by dragging them up and down in the roll-up itself. For example, in Figure 9.03 all the layers are backwards. I changed by clicking on a layer, holding down the mouse button and then dragging them into a new order. It now reads Layer 1, Desktop, Guides and Grid in that order. Do the same thing.

3   Click on the large triangular arrow at the top of the roll-up and you'll get a drop down menu. Click on **New** and you'll get a dialogue box.

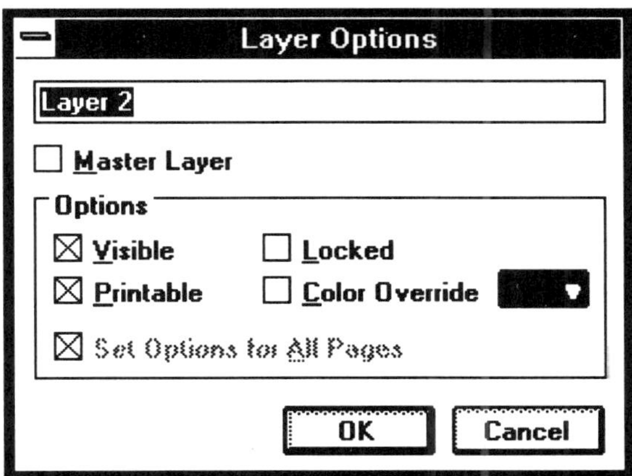

9.04 New layer options

CorelDRAW 4 - A Users Guide

The dialogue box allows you to set a number of options for the new layer, you also get the same dialogue box when editing a layer.

The top line contains the name of the layer. You can call a layer anything you wish, including using spaces. By default the name will always be Layer x, where x is the next number after the existing layer number. In this case it is Layer 2 because we already have Layer 1. If you had renamed layer 1 then this layer would be layer 1.

Master Layer is an option that applies to multiple page documents. With this option turned on, which it is by default, anything placed on the layer is available to all the pages of the document. If you turn the command off then the layer is available only to the page it is set for.

The first main option is **Visible** and that's what it means. If a layer is visible then you can see what it contains. Once you turn it off it's as if the layer wasn't there. This command is extremely useful when dealing with complex multiple layer files.

Printable means that the contents of the layer will print and it is on by default for most layers. If you turn it off then you can see the contents of the layer on screen but they won't appear on the printed page. Guides and grid for example are not normally printable.

Locked has the effect of freezing the images on the layer so that you cannot change any of the objects or add extra ones. Again it is very useful for complex images. By default it is turned off.

Colour Override is a really nice option. What it does is make all the objects on the layer appear in wireframe mode, i.e. without any fill, in the colour you set. All the others layers appear in normal colour. To set a colour override colour just click on the colour button and then pick a colour from the palette. Using this option will greatly speed up the display of complex images. The layer objects still print and display in full screen preview mode correctly - provided the layer is printable.

Set for All Pages applies to Master layers particularly. Turn it off if you are using these.

On the Grid and Guides layers only you also get a button labelled **Setup**. This will bring up the associated dialogue box.

---

4   Give the layer a name, e.g. Square, and set it to Visible and Printable only. Click on **OK**. Move the layer to the top of layers list in the roll-up.

5   Now select the large square. The Status Bar says Rectangle on Layer 1. Click on the broad arrow in the roll-up and then click on **Move To**. You'll get a wide arrow shaped cursor bearing the word To?

6   Click on the new layer name you have just created. The Status Bar now says Rectangle on Square.

7   Edit the layer, which you can do by either clicking on the broad arrowhead to get the menu or you can just double click on the layer name. You'll get the dialogue box. Click on **Colour Override** and change the colour to Yellow. Close the dialogue box.

8   You'll now get all the objects on Layer 1 appearing as normal but the large square is shown in outline, in yellow, only.

LAYERS MENU

The drop down menu that appears when you click on the large arrow head contains six commands:

New allows you to create a new layer using the dialogue box already mentioned.

Edit, which can also be accessed by double clicking on a layer name, brings up the same dialogue box but for the highlighted layer.

Delete removes a layer and all it contains. Note, you used to get a message box asking you to confirm this in CorelDRAW 3 but you don't in version 4.

Move To allows you to move items from one layer to another - provided Multilayer is active. You must have at least one object selected for this command to be active. You can move an individual object or multiple objects depending on what you have selected.

Copy To is similar to the above but it copies rather than moves objects.

Multilayer, which is turned on by default, allows you to use the Move to and Copy to commands. It also means that you can click on any object on any layer. If you turn the command off then you cannot use the layer move and copy commands and to select any object you must have the corresponding layer selected in the roll-up.

---

9   You can resize the roll-up if you wish or need to, e.g. because of long names, by simply dragging the edges of it around.

10   You can also move the positions of layers and their contents by dragging them up or down within the roll-up. Click on the Square layer and drag it below the Layer 1 layer. The screen redraws and gives you the square first.

Layers are really useful when you have complex images with multiple fills that you need to work on. By locking and colour overriding some layers the whole graphic refreshes faster.

10. ENVELOPES

Every object you create in CorelDRAW, regardless of what it is, exists within an envelope. You can then distort that envelope to produce unusual effects. This is a nice simple exercise, albeit an old one, that shows the Edit Envelope facility to advantage.

1   You want six 50 mms diameter circles. The quickest way is to draw one and then duplicate it to get the others. Scatter them around the page so they are not touching each other.

2   Next you want the six letters B, U, B, B, L, E, each as a separate text string. Make the text Eklektic, 120 Point Bold. Place one letter in each circle. They don't have to be exactly in the centre of the circles, in fact they will be better if each letter is slightly off centre. You should end up with something like this:

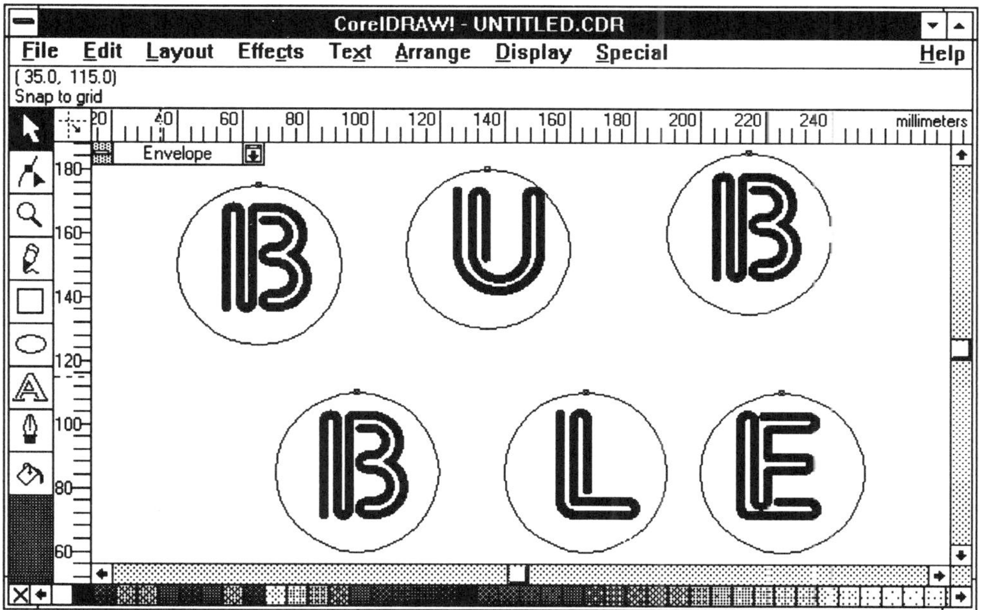

10.01 Letters and Circles

3   Save the file at this point, call it Bubble, because each step will add complexity and you don't want to have to redo it completely if anything goes wrong.

4   Zoom in to one of the circle and letter combinations. If you use **F2** you can magnify just the two elements that you want. Select the letter and then open the **Effects** menu. Click on **Envelope roll-up**.

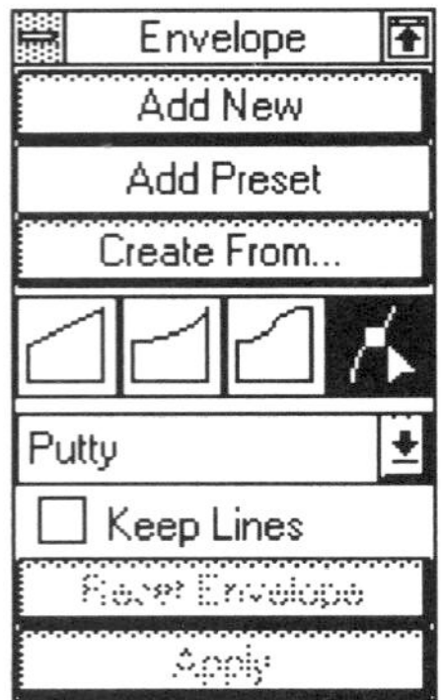

10.02 Envelope roll-up

ENVELOPE ROLL-UP

The roll-up gives you a number of commands and options:

Add New adds another envelope to the existing one. On occasion you may want to edit an envelope to distort the object and the add another envelope so you can distort that. The only exception is paragraph text, adding a new envelope to that will simply replace the existing one.

Add Preset will display a number of predefined envelopes for you. Just click on one of these to select it and it will be used. This is handy because it saves you having to edit the envelope yourself.

Create From allows you to create a new envelope shape from an existing one. The object in question must be a single curve one, i.e. you cannot use rectangles, squares, circles, ellipses or combined objects.

240

Next there are four possible button icons:

Straight Line envelope allows you to move the envelope handles in straight lines only.

Single Curve envelope will give the envelope a single smooth curve as you move the node point.

Double Curve envelope gives a double, S-shaped curve to the envelope as you move the node.

Freehand envelope allows you to edit the envelope in any way that you please. The nodes will have control points that affect the lines of the envelope.

Using the envelope editing function can be combined with the keys to produce certain effects.

Holding no key down will give you general movement as you would expect.

Hold down **Ctrl** as you edit the envelope and the node opposite the one you are moving will also move in the same direction and by the same increment.

Hold down **Shift** and the opposite node moves in the opposite direction to the node you are moving - by an equal amount.

Hold down both **Shift-Ctrl** and all four corners or sides of the envelope will move in opposite directions, again by the same increments.

Beneath the icons is a line bearing the word Putty - this is the **Mapping Node** control. Click on the arrowhead and you'll get a drop down menu with the extra modes:

Original will make the object bounding box match the envelope by aligning the corner handles of each. The side handles are mapped along the edge of the bounding box.

Putty maps the corner handles only and the other handles are ignored. This option gives you better control and radically distorted shapes.

Vertical will shape the object to fit the envelope overall but will then squash it vertically to make it fit.

Horizontal also stretches the object to make it fit the envelope but it will squash it horizontally.

Text is selected automatically, and the others are not available, when you are editing the envelope of paragraph text.

Keep Lines forces the program to keep using lines rather than curves when you edit the object envelope. Normally when you edit an envelope the program will convert straight lines to curves as you do so. You may not want this so click on this command to prevent it.

Reset Envelope will change everything back to what you had before you made any changes.

Apply applies the envelope to the selected object.

---

5   The letter must be selected. Click on **Add Preset** and then choose the circular envelope by clicking on that. You'll get what looks like a circular bounding box around and through the letter as in figure 10.03. This is the envelope.

6   Now gently move the nodes of the envelope to around the edge of the circle but stay just inside it. Make sure that the grid is turned off or this is almost impossible. Once you have all the nodes in place click on **Apply** in the roll-up and the letter will distort to fit the new envelope as opposite.

7   Try different **Mapping Modes** to see the different effects that are possible. I found that Putty gave the best results.

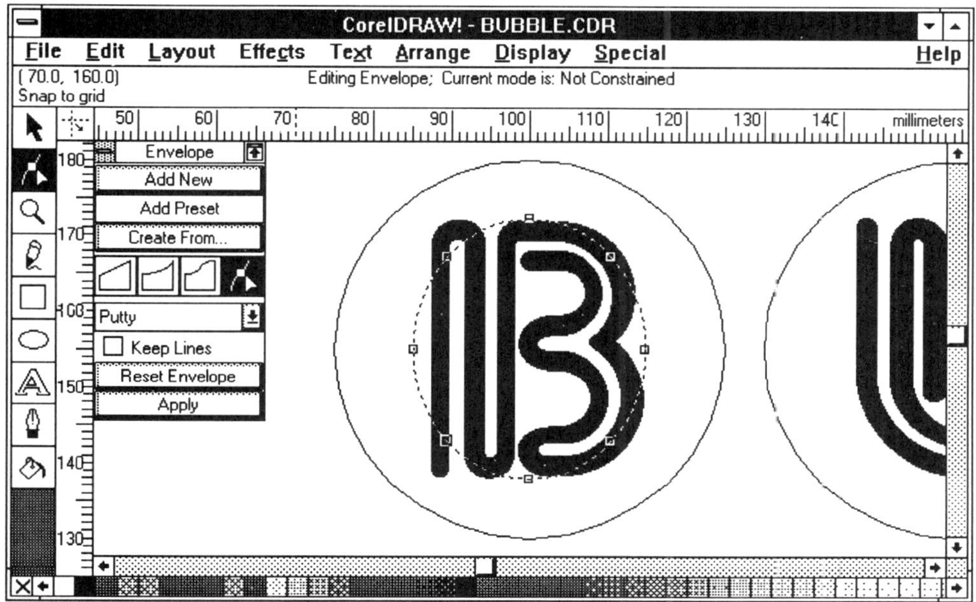

10.03 Envelope visible

10.04 Distorted letter

8   Once you've done one letter, do all the others in the same way. But don't make them all look the same, each letter should be distorted differently, but still basically making a round shape for each letter. Be warned you can fiddle around with this for ages.

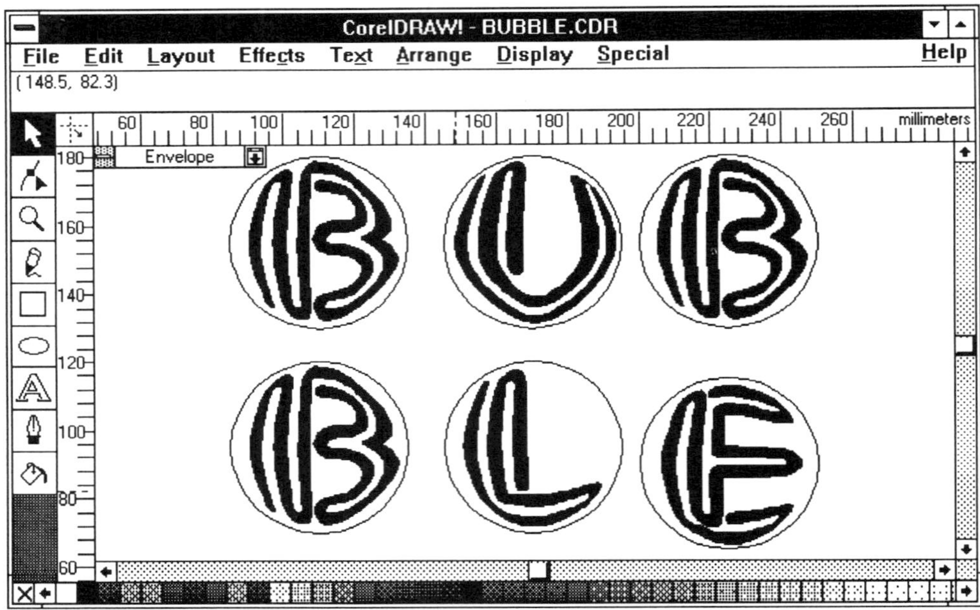

10.05 Distorted letters

9   Save the file again. Now draw a large ellipse, so it nearly fills the page, and place it in the middle of the page, using Align to Centre if necessary. We want this to be behind everything else so, with it selected, press **Shift-PgDn**.

10   Save the file. (As you start doing more and more complex things with CorelDRAW it is vital that you save the file constantly.) Arrange the letters and circles so that they fit into the ellipse. They have to be in the right order to spell Bubble but they should not be in a straight line. To move a pair of shapes, drag a bounding box around the circle and letter and you can then move them together. They can even overlap slightly. If they are too small or too large you can resize them as necessary. You can even rotate each pair slightly to get a better effect.

244

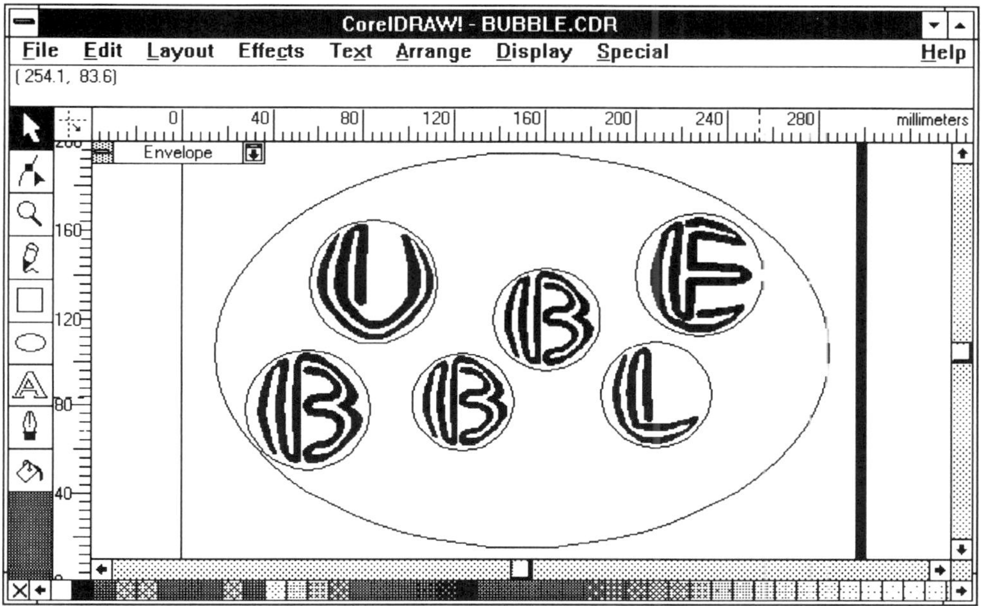

10.06 letters in ellipse

11   Save the file. That's stage one complete. You now want to add some more circles, little ones, around the letters but still within the ellipse. Make them different sizes but not too big. Scatter the circles around, they are supposed to be bubbles rising and bubbling within the ellipse.

12   Save the file again. Now add colour. Because I need to make an illustration of this I'm limited to using greyscales, and it doesn't look brilliant, but you should be able to use full colour. Each bubble bearing a letter wants to have a radial fountain fill. Use the roll-up and you can then move the centre of the fill to good effect. Make the letters prominent by using a different colour for each one.

13   Save the file. That's the basic thing finished. (The colour image looks much better than the illustration by the way.) To get to this point has taken me about an hour - but then I'm writing this and doing the exercise at the same time. You can now play around with it as you wish. Try different colours, change the angle of the radial fill and so on.

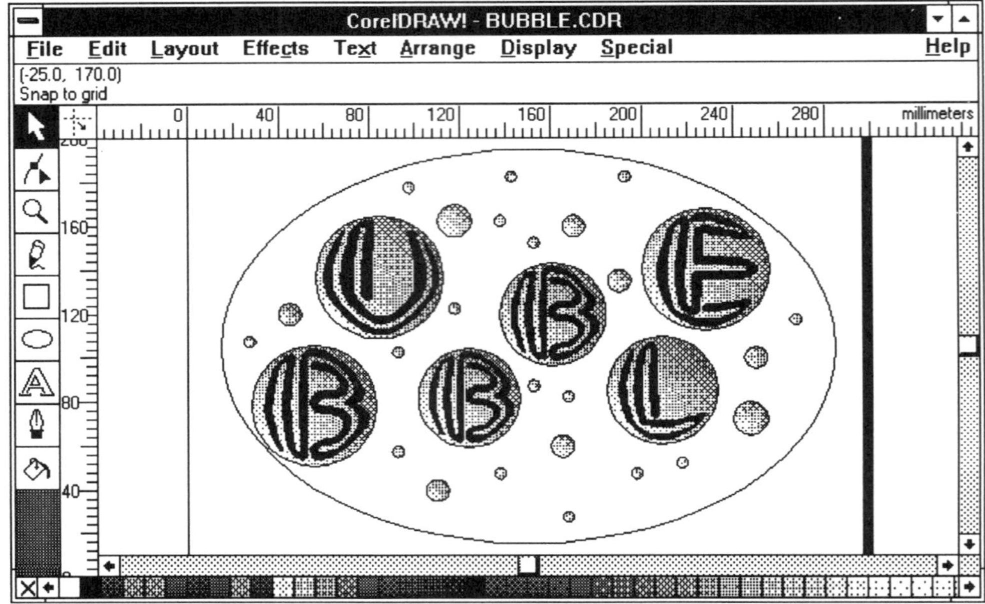

10.07 Finished image

I'll leave it to you to play with the other envelope features. You can produce dynamic and complex graphics using them. They can also be used to allow you to flow text around a graphic.

11. Text and Paths

One of the nice features of CorelDRAW is its ability to fit text to a path of any shape. You can only do this with Artistic text by the way, not with Paragraph text. The program gives you lots of control of how the text is applied, the way it looks, even how it flows along the path.

Simple paths

1   Start a new page. Put some text on the page, preferably in 72 point, that contains a couple of words, e.g. Alphabet Spaghetti. You want to use a font that has real upper and lower case characters and not one that uses small caps.

2   Draw a 100 mms circle and align it to the centre of the page. Select both the text and the circle and then press **Ctrl-F** to get the **Fit Text to Path** roll-up. Click on **Apply** to fit the text to the circle using the defaults.

5   In the centre of the roll-up there is a square containing a circle sub-divided by two diagonal lines. At the top of this are two letters, xy. This controls the position of the text around the shape. Click on it at 3 o'clock and then on **Apply**. The text should move round to the right hand side of the circle.

6   Try the other positions. Each time the text string remains the same length - it doesn't change in size - it simply moves around the circle.

7   Click on **Place on other side** and try the different placements. The text will now appear inside the circle rather than outside.

8   The text is still editable by the way. Click on the page to deselect both objects. Then click on just the text. The Status Bar will tell you that you have **Text on Path on Layer 1**. That's true and because it is linked to the path you cannot select it as normal. Instead you need to hold down **Ctrl** and then click on it. Now the Status Bar says **Artistic Text** and it is therefore editable. Press **Ctrl-T** to bring up the text dialogue box and change the text string to CorelDRAW Version 4.

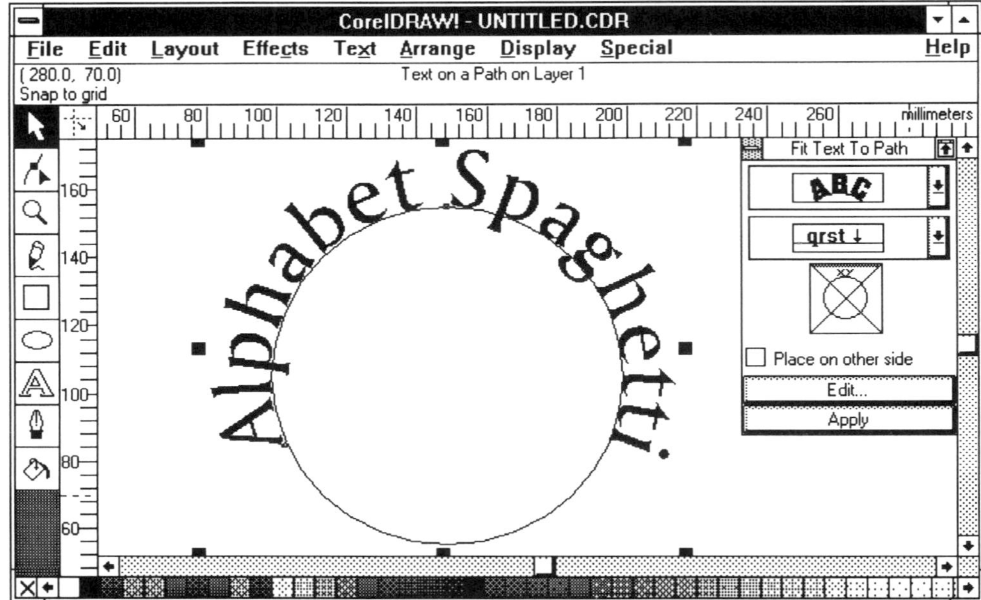

11.01 Fitted with defaults

9   The text will change and fit itself to the path. If you look at the roll-up though the commands are greyed out. You have to deselect the text and then click on it again to get the Text on Path before you can do anything else with it.

10   Save the file, call it T-PATH, because you'll need it later.

FIT TEXT TO PATH

All fitting of text to the path is controlled from the roll-up and therefore it seems simple, however you can fit text in a multitude of different ways and combine the commands of the roll-up in many different ways. The net result is that there are approximately 40 different ways of fitting text to the path.

The roll-up breaks down into five different areas:

The first is **Text Orientation**, shown by the letters ABC. This is the way that the text will be orientated once it is on the path. There are four possible methods:

Rotate Letters, the default, which does just that. The letters are rotated so that they follow the outline of the path.

Vertical Skew will skew the letters slightly on the vertical axis to give the impression that the characters are standing upright on the path. The actual skew amount depends on the shape of the path. This works best on semi-three dimensional looking shapes like ellipses. The image will have a definite depth to it.

Horizontal Skew does the same sort of thing as the above but the characters will be skewed horizontally slightly so that they look as if they are turning away from or towards you. Again the exact skew amount depends on the path. You can get some very weird effects using this option.

Centre Base effectively treats each letter as a distinct entity and it will align the baseline of each one to the path. Using this some of the characters will tend to run over the path because each one is aligning itself properly.

The next option, shown by the letters qrst followed by a downward pointing arrow, control the **Vertical Alignment** of the characters on the path. This contains five sub-options, the order of which may vary slightly:

The first, selected by default, is **Baseline**. This aligns the baseline of the text with the path itself.

The second is **Top** which causes the text to align the ascender height with the path. In other words it will generally include a certain amount of white space.

Third is **Bottom** which aligns the base of the descender, instead of the baseline of the text, with the path.

Next is **Centre** which places the text such that the middle of the characters, i.e. halfway between the ascender height and the descender depth, is what is aligned to the path.

There is also a fifth option called **Variable**. This allows you to move the text up and down away from the path but still following the shape of the path.

The next major option, which isn't in the illustration above because it applies to open paths and true curves, is **Horizontal Alignment** and it contains three sub-options:

Start, shown by the letters abc and a left pointing arrow, aligns the text with the start of the curve. The first node of a line is the starting point.

Centre, shown by the letters abc with an arrow either side of them, places the text on the centre of the path.

End, shown by abc preceded by a right pointing arrow, aligns the text with the end of the path, i.e. where the end node is.

Custom, which only becomes active if you move the text, allows you to position the characters along the path where you want them. You use the Node Edit tool to do so.

The alternative major option is **Quadrant Select**, which is only active for regular shapes like ellipses and rectangles. It has four possible sub-options, each designated by the letters xy in one quadrant, Top, Right, Bottom and Left.

The major option is **Place on other side**. This places the text on the other side of the path but it also reverses the path's starting and ending nodes.

Finally there is a button labelled **Edit**. Clicking on this brings up a dialogue box that allows you to specify exact values for the placement of the text both horizontally and vertically.

11   Select the **Pointer** tool and then click on the circle. Press **Ctrl-Q** to convert it to curves. Now click on the text and the roll-up will change to lose the quadrant box and give you the Horizontal Alignment line instead.

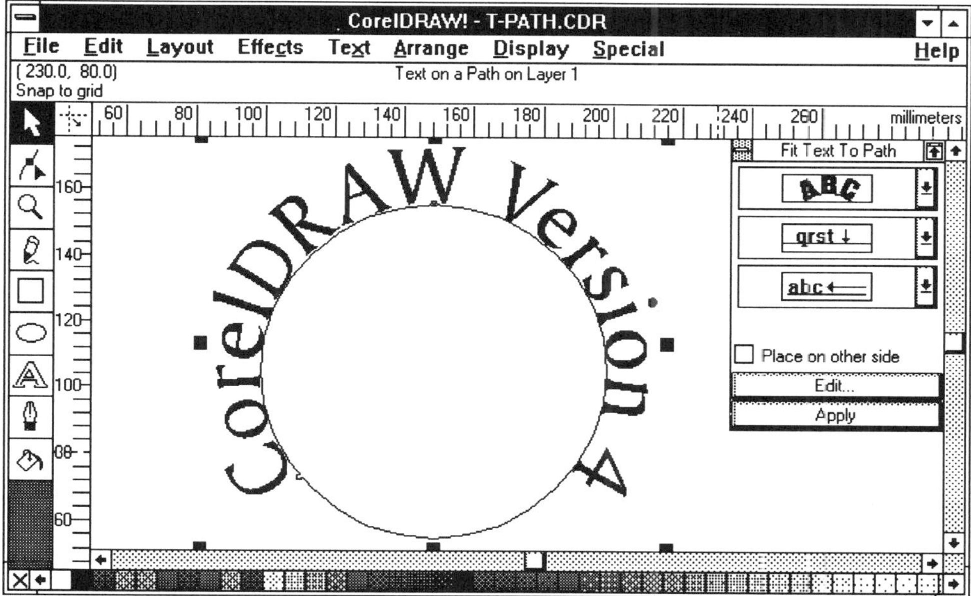

11.02 Using curve

12   Click on **Apply** and the text will move around the circle - because the starting node of the circle has a position and the text aligns to that. Click on the arrowhead in the horizontal alignment and select **Centre**, then click on **Apply** again. Try Right alignment.

13   You might find that the text won't run around the top of the circle. That's because of the way that you drew the circle, because that affects the position of the starting node of the converted circle. If you rotate the circle itself you can correct this.

14   Click on the arrowhead one the **Vertical alignment** line. Select **Custom**. You'll get what looks like nodes appearing on the text. Click on **Apply**.

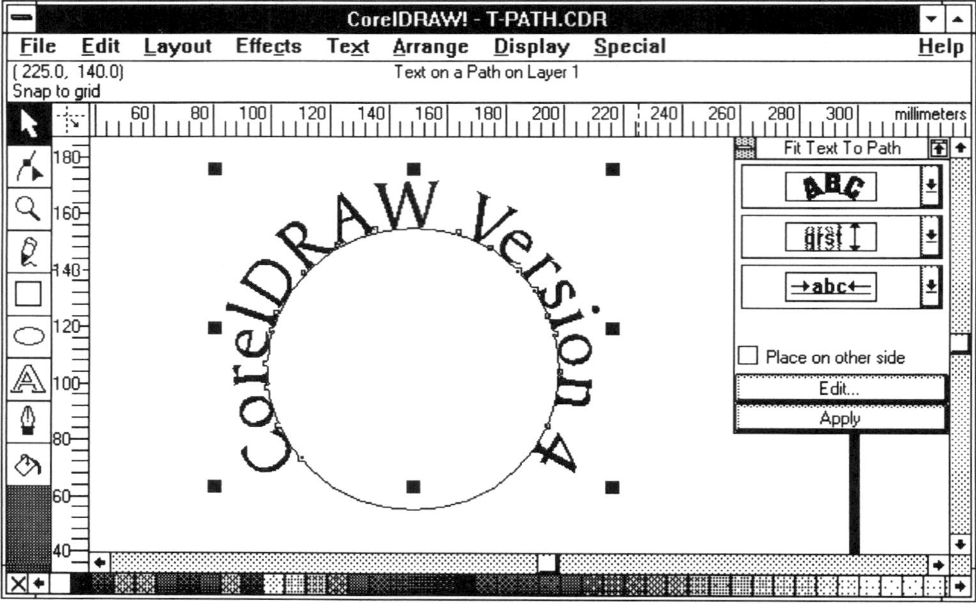

11.03 Custom alignment

15   This can be a bit tricky. Click on any letter and hold the mouse button down. Drag the cursor away from the curve. You'll get what looks like an arrow and a small curve growing away from the circle. That's the new path. Move it to where you want it and then release the mouse button. The text will reflow to fir the new path you have just set.

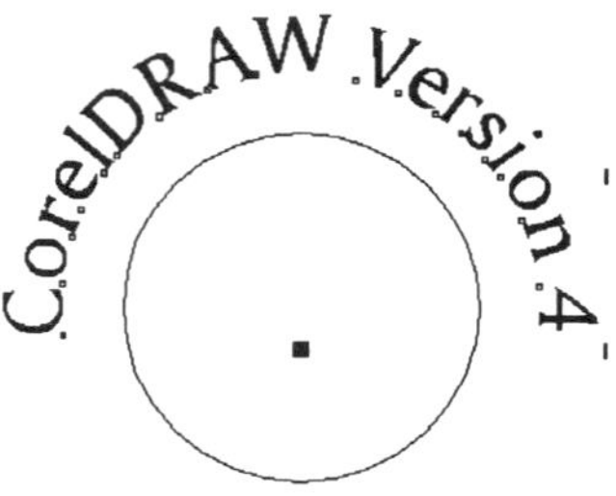

11.04 Text moved

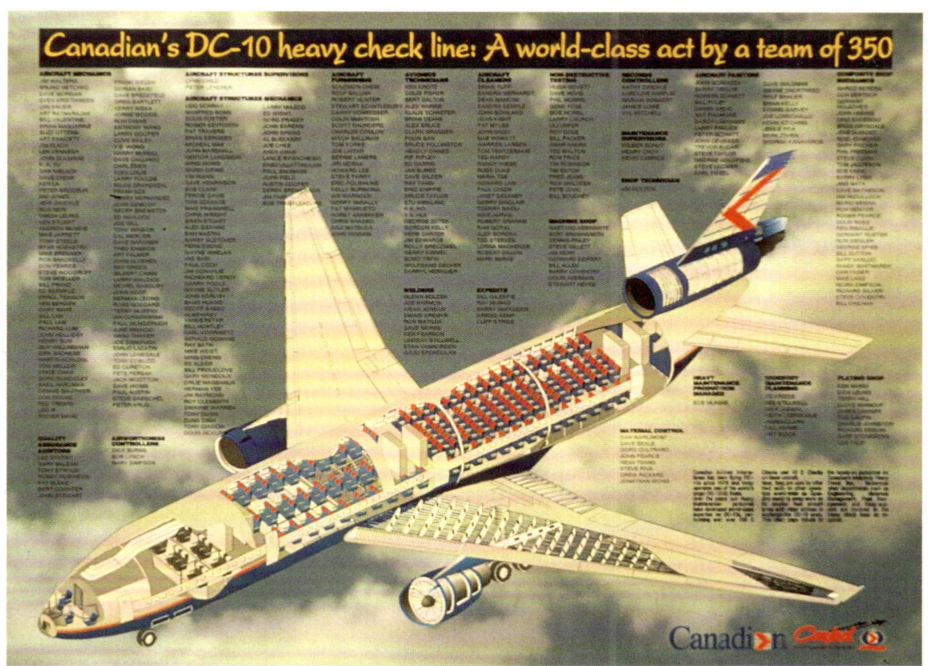

1 Winner, Technical Illustration – Steve Bain

2 Winner, Product Illustration – José Simancas

3 Winner, Page Layout and Design – Stephen Arscott

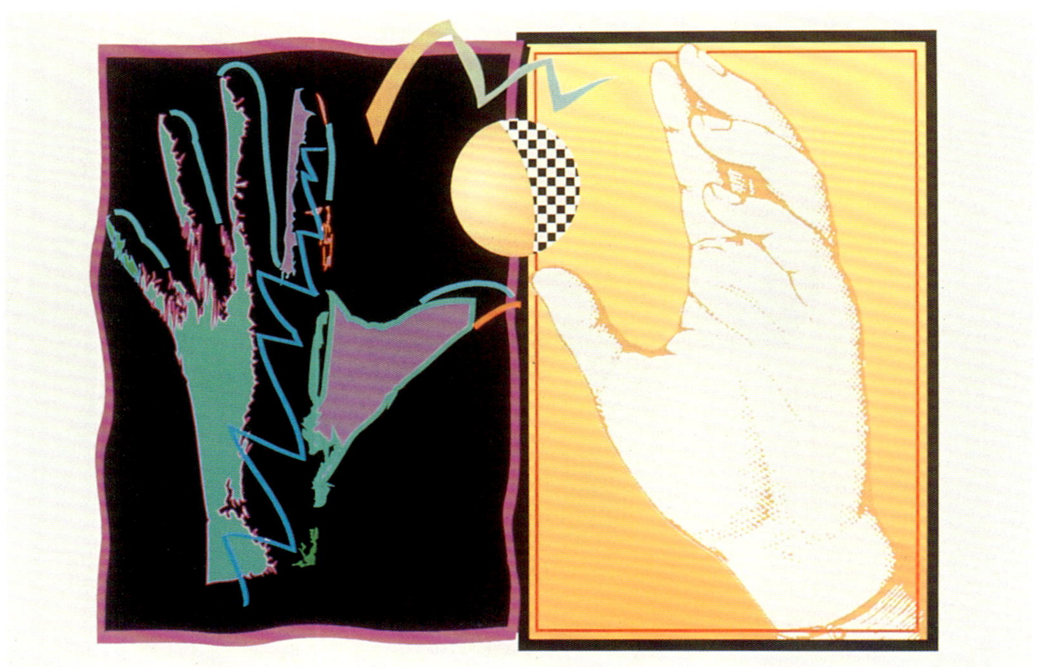

4 Winner, Corporate ID – Priester/Carter

5 Winner, Speciality – Ceri Lines

6 Winner, Corporate Illustration (February 1993) – R. Majziz

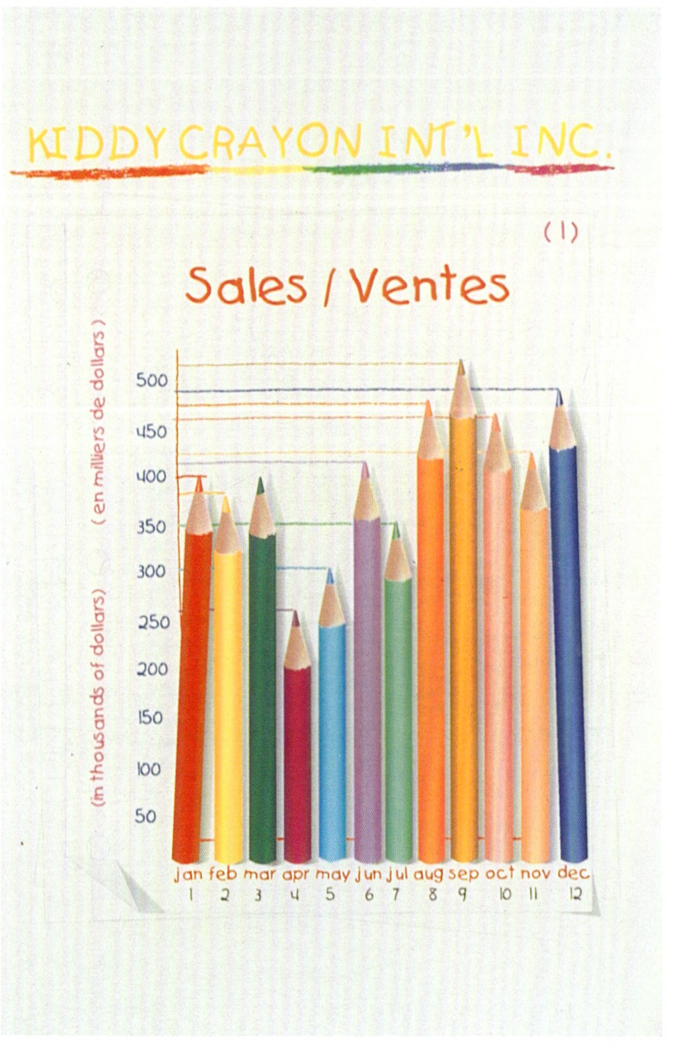

8 Winner, Charts & Graphs – Joe Donnelly

7 Winner, Environmental Illustration – Georgina Curry

16 Change the alignment back to baseline using the roll-up. Select the second option for **Text Orientation** and then click on **Apply**. You should get this:

11.05 Vertical skew orientation

17 Change the orientation to **Horizontal Skew** and you'll get this, notice the radical distortion of some letters:

11.07 Horizontal skew orientation

18   Finally change to **Baseline** and apply that to get this:

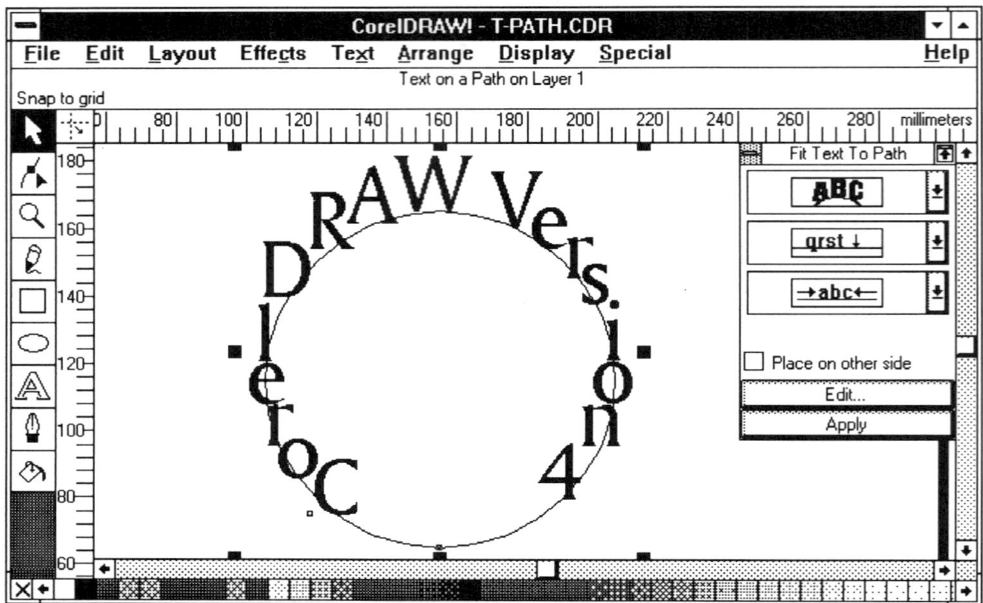

11.07 Baseline orientation

19   Play with the different possible settings, singly and in combination. You can
create some very odd effects. Try using lines and rectangles or changing the
text both in terms of font and size.

MULTIPLE PATHS

As well as applying text to simple paths, CorelDRAW will allow you to apply two or more text strings to the path - regardless of the path shape.

1   Clear the page. Draw a circle and then node edit it to produce a semi-circle. Convert it to curves when you are finished and align it to the centre of the page. You then want two strings of text, ideally in different fonts. You should end up with something like this:

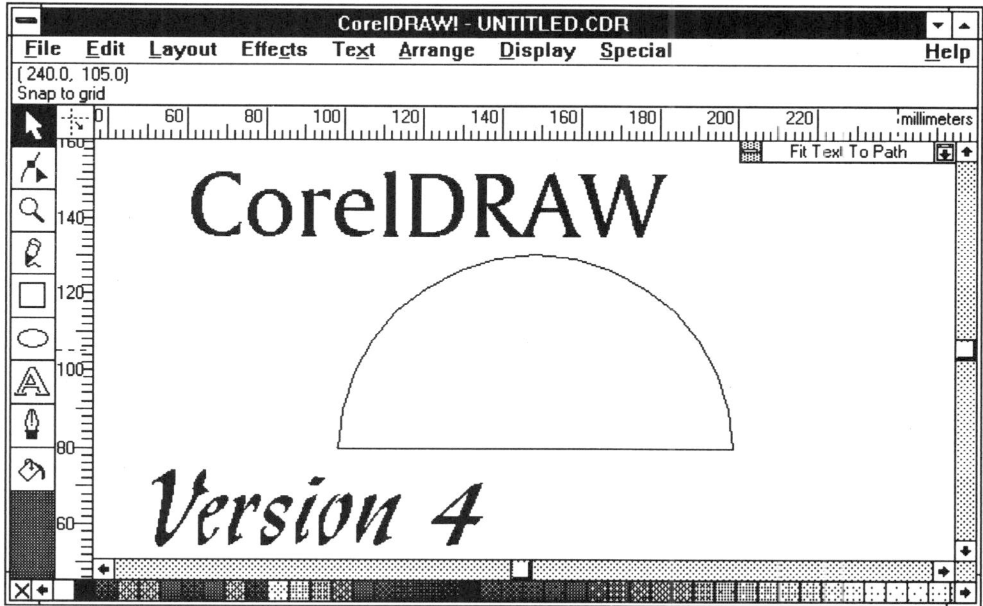

11.08 Text and semi-circle

2   Select the semi-circle and the first text string. Set the **Orientation** to Rotate, the **Vertical Alignment** to Baseline and the **Horizontal Alignment** to Centre. Click on **Apply**. The text should be running around the top of the semi-circle.

3   Select the text and then change the Vertical Alignment to **Custom**. Move the text about 10 mms away from the semi-circle.

4   Now select the second text string and the semi-circle. Set the **Vertical Alignment** to Top and the **Horizontal Alignment** to Centre. Click on **Apply**. The text should go inside the semi-circle.

5   Change the **Vertical Alignment** to Custom and move the text further inside the semi-circle. You should then end up with something like this:

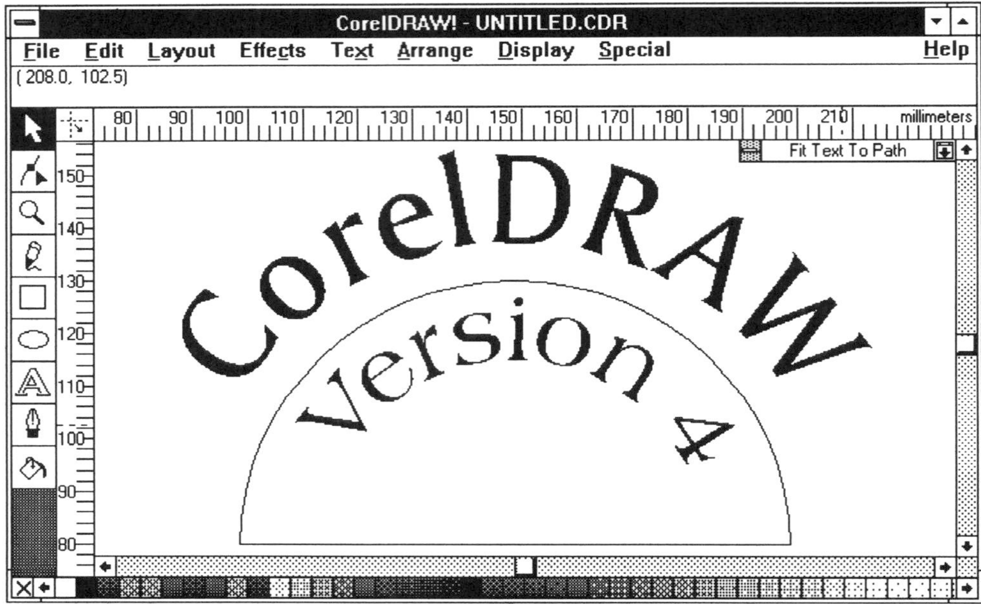

11.09 Two strings fitted

6   Now flip the semi-circle, using the Stretch and Mirror dialogue box, and watch what happens. Because the text and the shape are linked together dynamically, any change to the one will affect the other. Try changing the size of the text or the typeface. Try reducing the size of the semi-circle. Any change you make to one object will affect the whole.

7   You can change the text in other ways too. Select the **Node Edit** tool and then click on the inside text. You'll get the kerning handles. Move the right hand one to the right and the spacing between the letters will open up. Once you let the

mouse button go the text will reflow within the shape. Kern it too much and the text flows around the semi-circle too far.

8   You can also change the individual characters. Double click on any text node with the Node Edit tool and then change the font in the Text Attributes dialogue box. Again the text will reflow around the path to accommodate the changes.

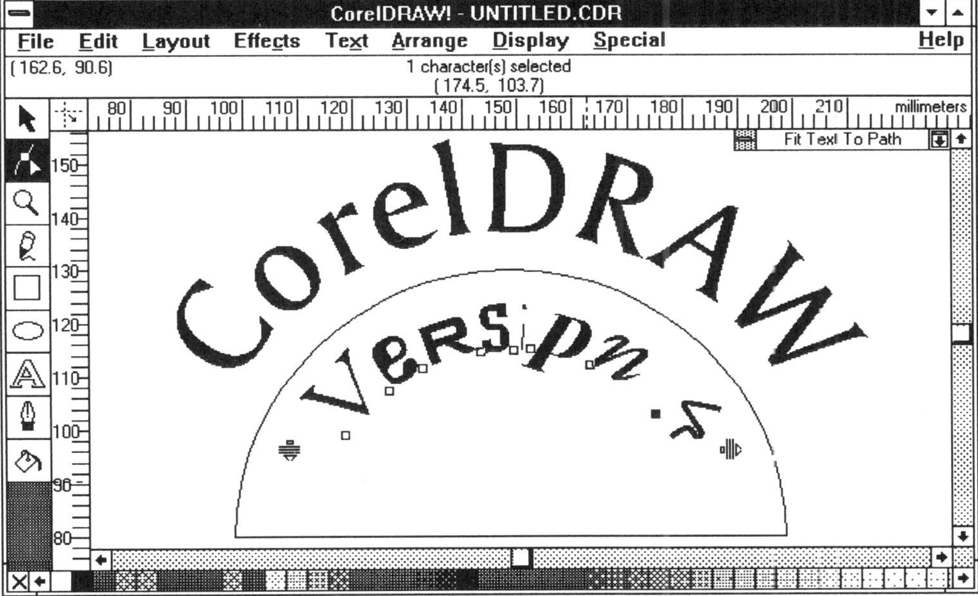

11.10 Text changed

9   Try Node editing the semi-circle to really make some odd effects.

12. PERSPECTIVE

CorelDRAW will allow you to have mathematically correct perspective - subject to the limitations of integer maths. You can add a perspective to anything, line, graphic or text.

1   Start a new page. Draw square and place it in the bottom left hand corner of the page.

2   Open the **Effects** menu and click on **Add Perspective**. The tool will change to the Node Edit one and the Status Bar will say "Editing Perspective Vanishing Points Very Far".

3   Drag one of the right hand corner handles up and to the right. Do it slowly and eventually a value will appear for the vanishing point on the Status Bar and you'll see an X appearing. The X is the vanishing point.

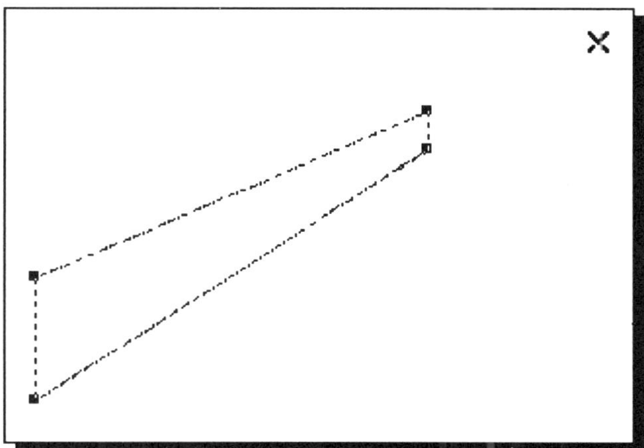

12.01 Vanishing point

4   Once it has appeared you can drag it around. There is a second vanishing point too. Drag the left hand handles and it will appear as before. Once you have it

in position change to the **Pointer** tool to fix the perspective in place. If you look at the square now you'll see that the nodes are in odd places because they have been moved due to your actions.

5   To get rid of a perspective change, open the **Effects** menu and click on **Clear Perspective**. The square will return to normal.

6   Move the square to the lower left hand corner of the page again. Now draw a circle within the square. Combine the two together with **Ctrl-L**. Fill the shape with a colour of your choice.

7   Now edit the perspective again so that the vanishing point is at the upper right hand corner of the page. You should have something like this:

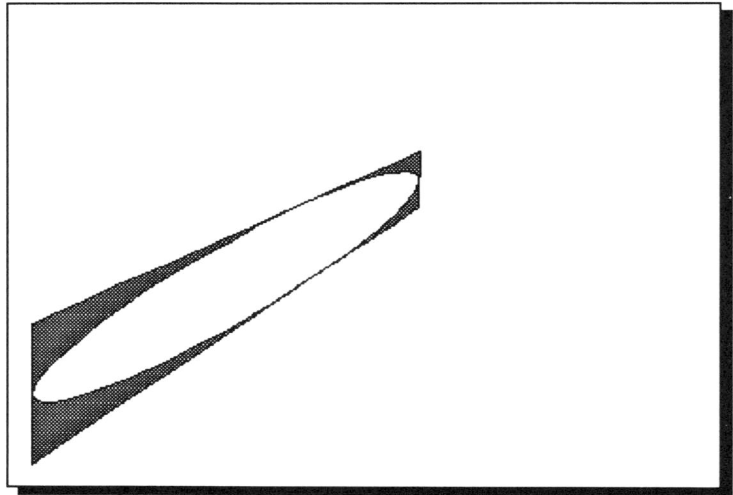

12.02 Combined perspective

8   Now add a short text string to the page. We want to apply the same perspective to that, so open the **Effects** menu again and click on **Copy Effect From**. A pop-out menu appears.

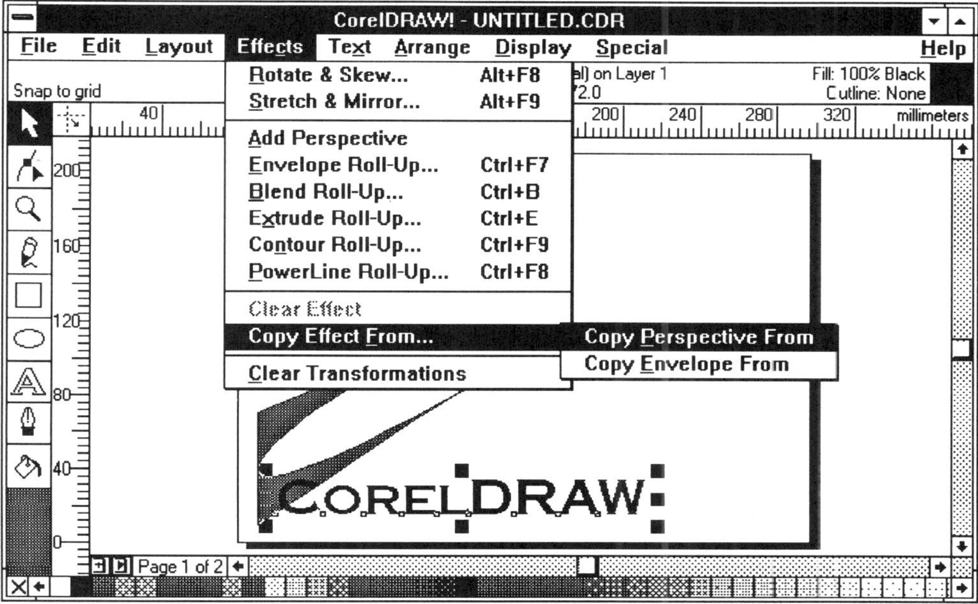

12.03 Copy effects from

9   Click on **Copy Perspective From**. The menu closes and the cursor becomes a wide horizontal arrow bearing the word From? Click on the transformed square and circle. The hourglass will appear and spin and then the text will be changed. The effect might be a little bit strange but the text now has the same perspective applied to as the square and circle combination.

10   Delete the text. Clear the perspective from the square and circle. Now type the letter **A** and make it large so that it fits within the circle. Align them together and then combine them.

11   Edit the perspective again and you should end up with something like this:

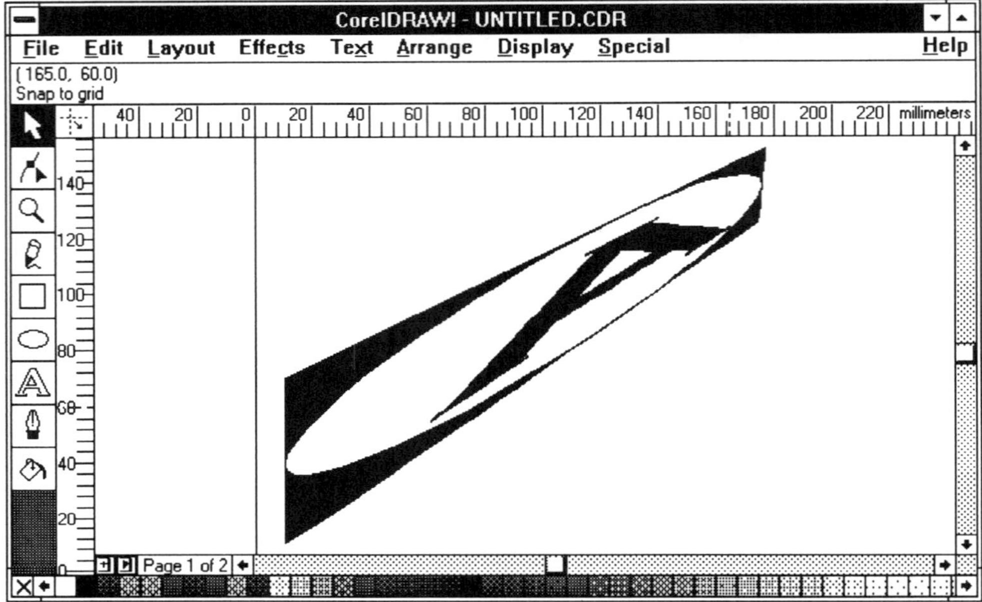

I2.04 All perspective

12   Play around with it and explore the command's capabilities. It is fairly easy to make a landscape style image using lots of rectangles.

13. EXTRUSIONS

CorelDRAW will allow you to extrude just about any kind of object you want. The extrusions can be in many different varieties including full perspective - which is why we did perspective first.

1   Clear the page. Draw a smallish empty square, say 50 mms to a side, and align it to the centre of the page. Press **Ctrl-E** and the **Extrude roll-up** appears.

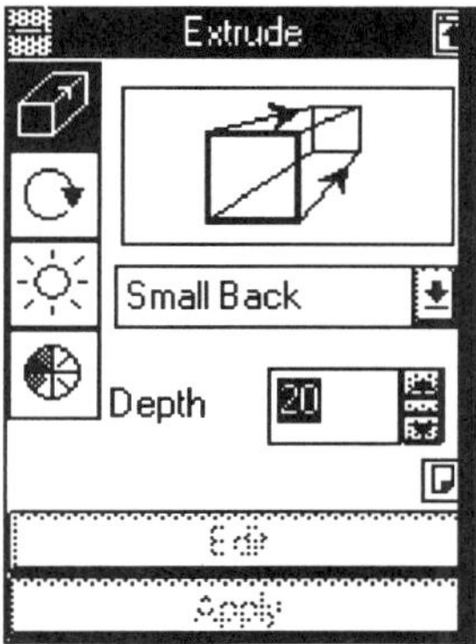

13.01 Extrude roll-up

2   In the middle of the square you have just drawn is a large X. This is the vanishing point of the extrusion. Click on **Apply** in the roll-up and the extrusion will be drawn.

3   Click on the page and you'll be able to see the extrusion properly.

4   Click on the extrusion again to select it. Now click on **Edit** in the roll-up. The X will appear again. Drag this to the top right hand corner of the page. As you do so construction lines for the extrusion will appear. Once you have the X where you want it, click on **Apply** and the actual extrusion is created.

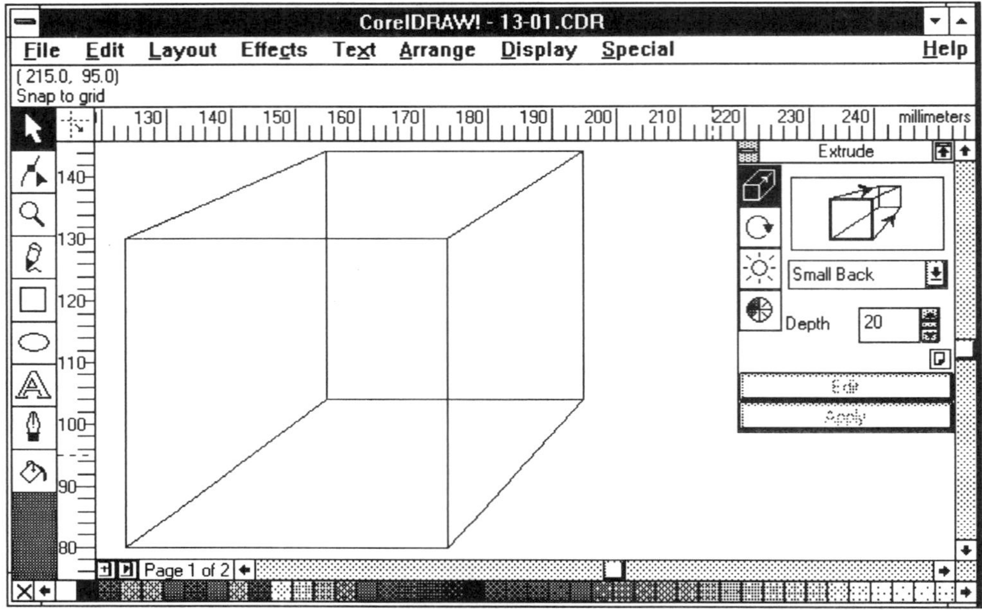

13.02 Extrusion created

5   What you currently have is a Small Back extrusion. This means that the extrusion is in perspective and runs from the square, which is front, backwards towards the vanishing point. Click on the arrowhead beside the words and a drop down menu will appear. Click on **Back Parallel** and then on **Apply**.

6   You now have the original square, wherever you positioned it, and a second square at the point where the vanishing point is. Connecting the two are a series of lines making a kind of square tunnel shape. Because the original square has no fill you can see all the lines. Fill the square with white and then you can only see the outside of the extrusion.

Extrude roll-up

The Extrude roll-up controls all the operations of the extrusion process in a single operation. You can set any part of the command process and apply it individually or collectively. The roll-up is divided into five sections:

Initially the roll-up displays the **Depth** option, i.e. the little window with the sample extrusion shown, because that icon is highlighted. Below this is a list box that drops down to reveal the different types of extrusions that are possible:

Small Back is a perspective extrusion that means that the original object is at the front and the extrusion moves away from you towards a smaller duplicate of the original.

Small Front does the opposite. The original object remains in position and the extrusion comes towards you, again with perspective, towards a smaller version of the original.

Big Back means that the extruded copy is larger than the original object and it is behind the original. Again it uses perspective.

Big Front is similar to the above but the extrusion comes in front of the original, again in perspective.

Back Parallel produces an extrusion without perspective, i.e. the extruded object is identical in size to the original, that leaves the original object in front of the extrusion.

Front Parallel does the same thing but leaves the original object behind the extrusion.

The line labelled **Depth** applies only to perspective extrusions. It is a percentage of how far the extrusion extends to the duplicate of the original. The maximum value you can have is 99%.

Beneath the depth line is a little icon that looks like a page with one corner turned up. Clicking on this will change the roll-up so that you can set the vanishing point of perspective extrusions directly.

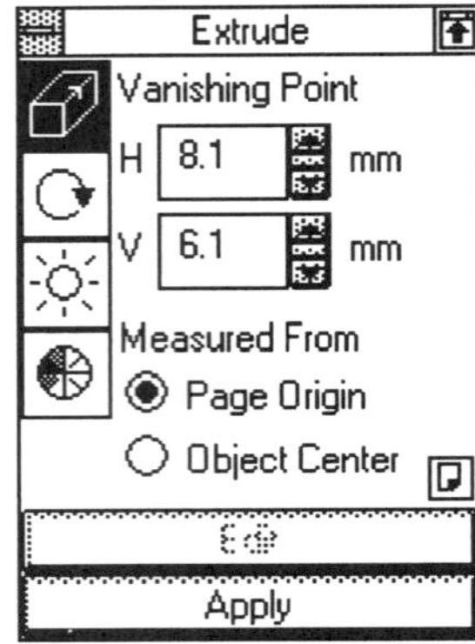

13.03 Setting vanishing point

Clicking on the second icon, the one bearing the circular arrow, will change the roll-up again to this:

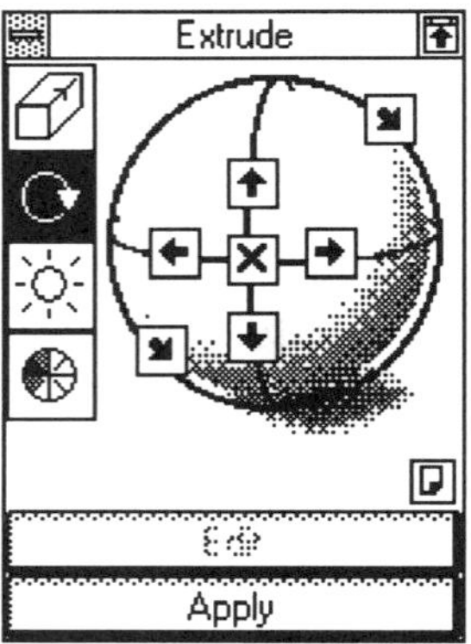

13.04 Rotation roll-up

This area of the roll-up controls the **Rotation** of the extrusion and the original object. Clicking on any of the arrows will rotate the extrusion in the direction you click on. The extrusion is dynamic so the whole thing moves.

Clicking on any of the four arrows pointing to the compass points in the centre of the ball will rotate the whole extrusion in that direction as if the extrusion had a centre point half way along it.

Clicking on either of the arrows around the outside of the ball will rotate clockwise or counter clockwise around the centre of the original object.

Clicking on the little page icon allows you to set the rotations numerically.

Click on the sunburst icon and you'll get the **Lighting** roll-up area.

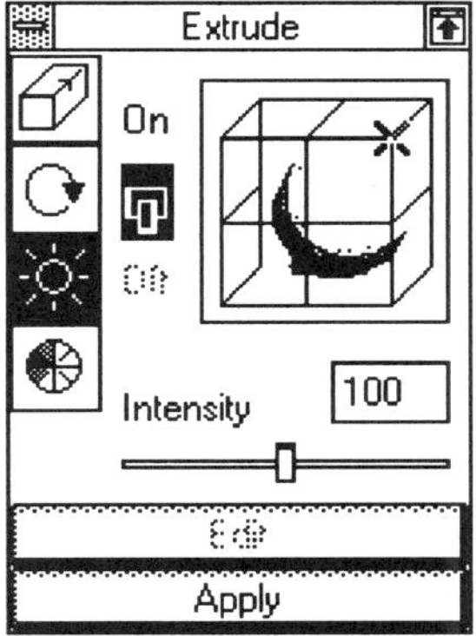

13.05 Lighting roll-up

This allows you to set where the light source is in relation to the extruded shape. The grid lines in the roll-up are the possible positions of the light. Turn it On, it is off by default, by clicking on the word and a sphere appears in the grid with an X at a junction of the grid lines The X marks the position of the light source relative to the extrusion.

With the lighting turned on any colours that were previously applied to the extrusion no longer apply as such. Instead they will be graduated, as if they were a fountain fill, according to the light source position. The only time that this doesn't work is if you place the light source at the mouth of a tunnel shape. The whole extrusion will turn black. The reason is that it is assumed that the originating object is filled with a colour and therefore no light can possibly get to the inside or the sides.

Intensity allows you to adjust how bright the light is. You have to drag the slider along the bar. By default it is set to 100% but you can change it in the range 0 to 200%.

The final icon button in the roll-up bears a rainbow wheel. This controls the Extrusion **Colours**.

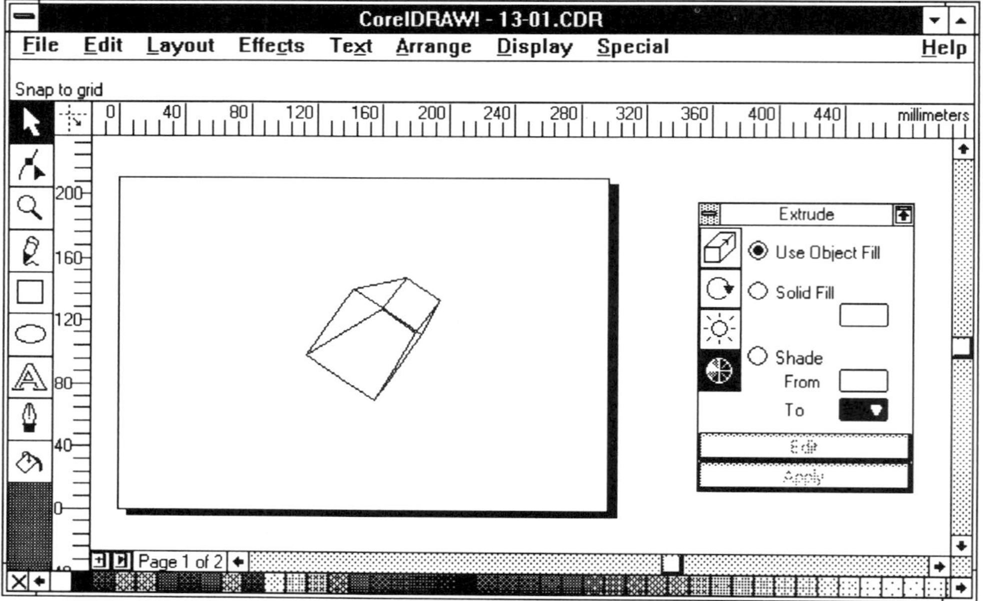

13.06 Extrude Colours

The top option is **Use Object Fill**. This will fill the extrusion with the same colour as the originating object. If the original object has no fill then the extrusion will also have none, i.e. you get a wire frame extrusion.

If you have filled the original object with a bitmap or vector fill then the extrusion will use the same thing but.... unfortunately the fill will not be distorted so that it extrudes properly. This is hardly surprising as the mathematics of doing so must be horrendous. The same thing applies if you use a fountain fill in the original object. Each side of the extrusion will be fountain filled but the fill is not distorted as you might expect. In fact you can get some odd but exciting fills in the extrusion doing this.

Use Solid Fill does just that. The extrusion, but not the originating shape, will be filled with whatever solid colour you select. Click on the button and a palette will open out that you can select a colour from.

Shade is similar to a fountain fill in many ways but should not be confused with it. To start with you can only have a straight line fill, even if you are using curved shapes. The colours you select, as using a solid fill, go from whichever object is on top to whichever is behind.

The final option available in the roll-up is **Edit**. This simply allows you to change the extrusion that already exists. You'll get the vanishing point appearing and the construction lines.

You can extrude any shape you wish, Artistic Text but not Paragraph text, and lines. You can create some very nice looking effects using extrude on simple lines and curves. Play with the roll-up and find out what it can do.

14. POWERLINES

This is a new feature in CorelDRAW 4 and it is intended primarily for those people who use a graphics tablet rather than a mouse. What it does is draw lines that have shape rather than just being lines of different thickness. For example, you can draw octopus legs in one go because the line can be thicker at one end than the other.

1   Clear the screen and then draw a straight line running from one side of the page to the other. Press **Ctrl-F8** to open the Powerline roll-up.

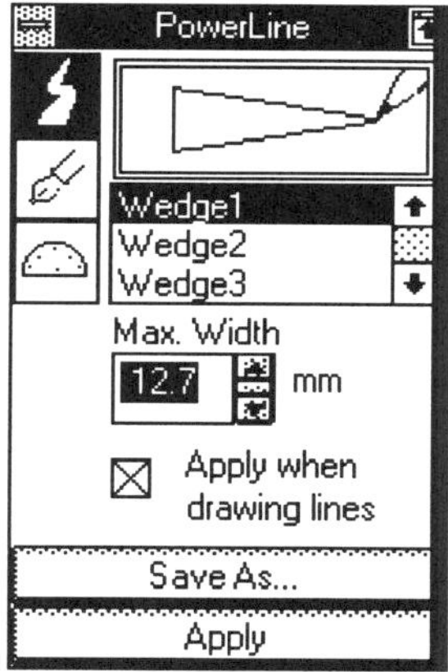

14.01 Powerline Roll-up

2   Click on **Apply** and you'll get a triangular line with the apex on the right hand side of the page. Because a powerline is an enclosed shape you can outline and fill it as if it were a normal object. You can use any kind of fill that you wish.

3   To make the line wider simply change the value under **Max. Width**. That will widen the left hand side of the line for you.

4   You can change the shape of the line itself by simply selecting another from the area that starts with Wedge 1. All told CorelDRAW 4 comes with a total of 23 pre-defined lines for you. Don't forget you have to **Apply** each change.

POWERLINE ROLL-UP

The roll-up contains three main elements:

Powerline Shape which is just that. By default the roll-up always shows Wedge 1 which is a triangular shape with the apex on the right. Below the representation of the line shape is a list box giving the names of the pre-defined shapes. To select any one of these just scroll through the list and click on the one you want.

Below that is a line labelled **Max. Width**. This sets the width of the widest part of the line, regardless of its shape.

Under that is a ticked box with the words **Apply when drawing lines**. This is turned on by default. I suggest you turn it off.

The second icon button controls the **Nib Shape**.

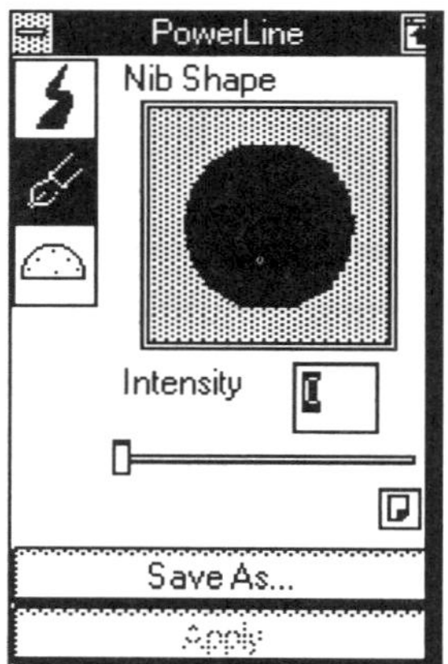

14.02 Nib shape

You can control the nib shape by clicking and dragging on the shape itself. Alternatively click on the turned page icon and the roll-up will allow you to enter the adjustments numerically.

272

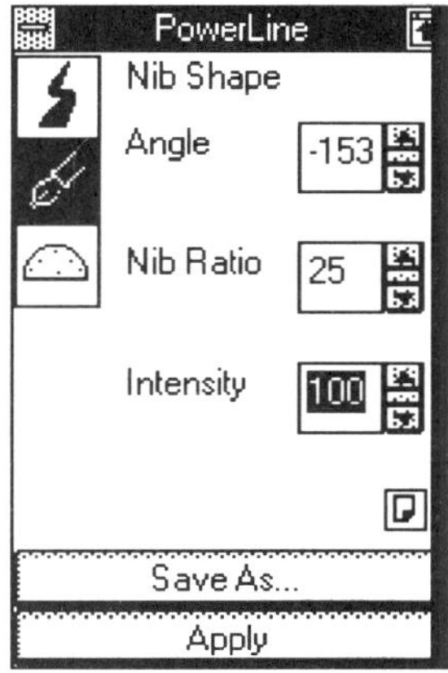

14.03 Nib shape numeric

The line labelled **Intensity** allows you to vary the thickness of the line along its entire length.

The third icon button contains a semi-circle. This controls the **Speed, Spread** and **Ink flow** for the line.

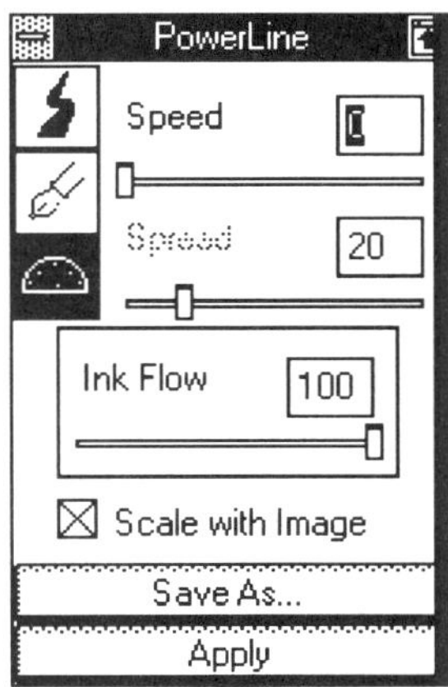

14.04 Speed control

Any increase in the **Speed** causes the line to widen appreciably at points where it changes direction.

Change the **Spread**, only when the speed is greater than 0, to control the smoothness of the line. The larger the value you set the smoother the line will be.

The **Ink Flow** controls the overall appearance of the line. With a value of 100, the default, the shape of the line extends from one end to the other. If you decrease the value then the line peters out before the end.

Scale with Image maintains the proportion of the powerline when you change the overall size of it.

There is also a button labelled **Save As**. Click on this and you'll get a dialogue box. You need to use this only if you have created a new powerline or if you want to delete any of the pre-defined ones.

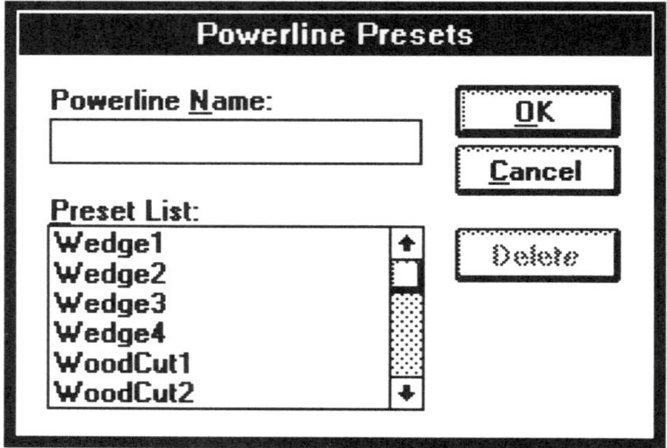

14.05 Save As dialogue box

The powerline features can be very useful but they do take some getting used to. The powerline itself is a complex object. If you take it and then open the Arrange menu and click on Separate you'll find that you have two objects. One is the original line that you drew and the other is a group of two objects. Ungroup this and you'll find

274

that you have two shapes that were the original powerline. Both contain a huge number of nodes.

Using powerlines is very resource intensive but if you have a system that has sufficient resources you can generate some nice, dynamic effects with them.

15. BLEND

The CorelDRAW blend feature is impressive to say the least and the use of it is literally limited only by your imagination. The command is accessed via a roll-up and you have total control of the number of intervening objects and their colour. You can blend simple objects, groups of objects and combined objects. The blend group is a dynamically linked set so that any changes to the start or end object will be reflected in the whole. You can even blend along a path.

1   Start a new page. I used A4 landscape as always. Make sure that the grid is turned on.

2   Draw a circle 15 mms in diameter. Fill it with white. Duplicate it using the Stretch and Mirror dialogue box (**Alt-F9**) with values of 300% for both axes and **Leave Original**. Move the duplicate 150 mms to the right.

3   Edit the envelope of the large circle using the second envelope option, i.e. single curve. Use **Shift** as you move the middle bottom handle upwards and swap the top and bottom handles over. Then use **Shift** again as you drag one of the middle side handles 10 mms away from the starting point. Click on **Apply** and you should end up with a knot like this.

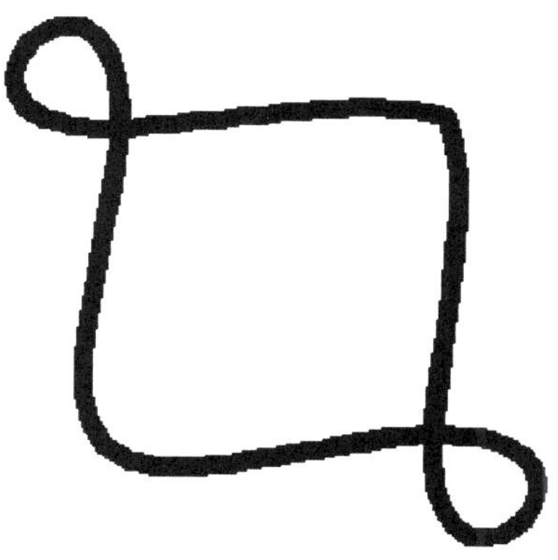

15.01 Knot

4   Drag a bounding box around both objects. Press **Ctrl-A** and in the dialogue box click on **Align to Centre of page** but then turn off **Vertically Centre**. Click on **OK** and the two objects are moved into the middle of the page but still separated. Select the knot and rotate it **-45** degrees.

5   Press **Ctrl-B** to bring up the Blend roll-up. **Arrange** it so that it moves to the top right hand corner of the page. Open it out again.

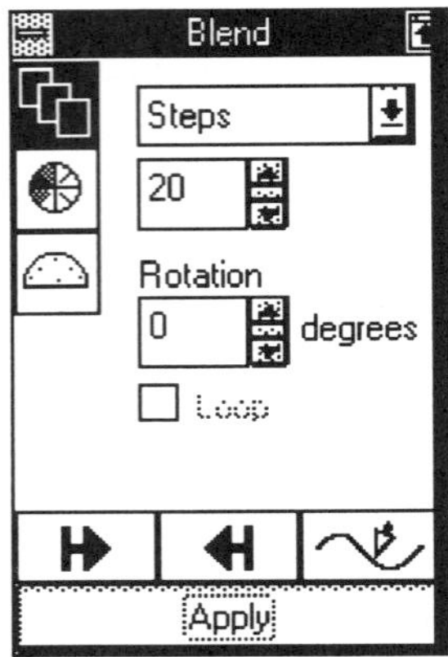

15.02 Blend Roll-up

6   In the roll-up increase the number of steps to **200** and change the Rotation value to **720** degrees. Click on **Loop**. Click on **Apply**. The hourglass will appear and spin and then you'll get something like this:

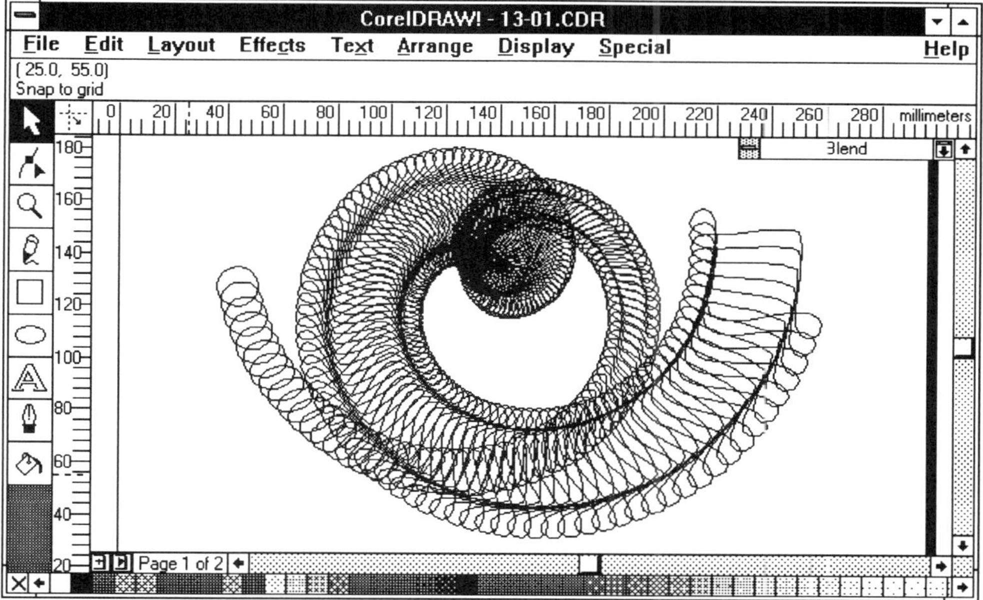

15.03 Ramshorn

7   The end of it looks a bit small. Click on the knot. Use **Ctrl-Q** and increase its size by 150% on both axes. There will be a slight delay but then the entire blend redraws as the size of the knot changes. Fill both the start and the end shapes with colour and you should get something rather pleasant.

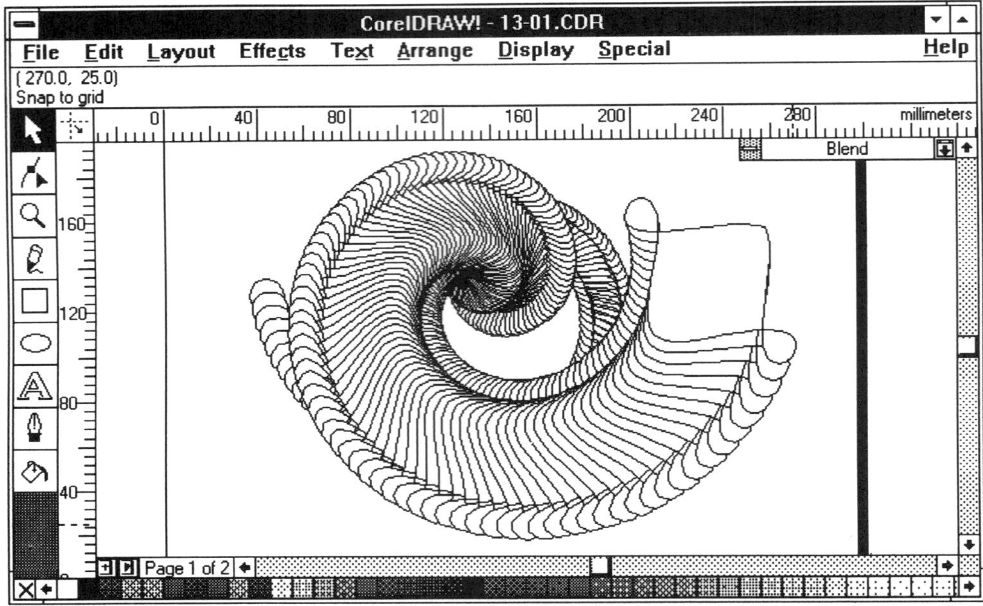

15.04 Ramshorn

A blend is a group of dynamically linked objects, that's why when you changed the size of the final knot the whole thing changed. Likewise if you change the colour of the knot then the entire blend will change too.

8   Click on the blend itself, not the final knot. Open the **Arrange menu** and click on **Separate**. The Status Bar will tell you that you have three objects selected. Click on the page to deselect everything and then click on the blend group again. Press **Del** to remove it.

9   Select the circle and the knot and then click on **Apply** in the roll-up - without using **Loop**. You get a sort of spiralled, unicorn's horn instead.

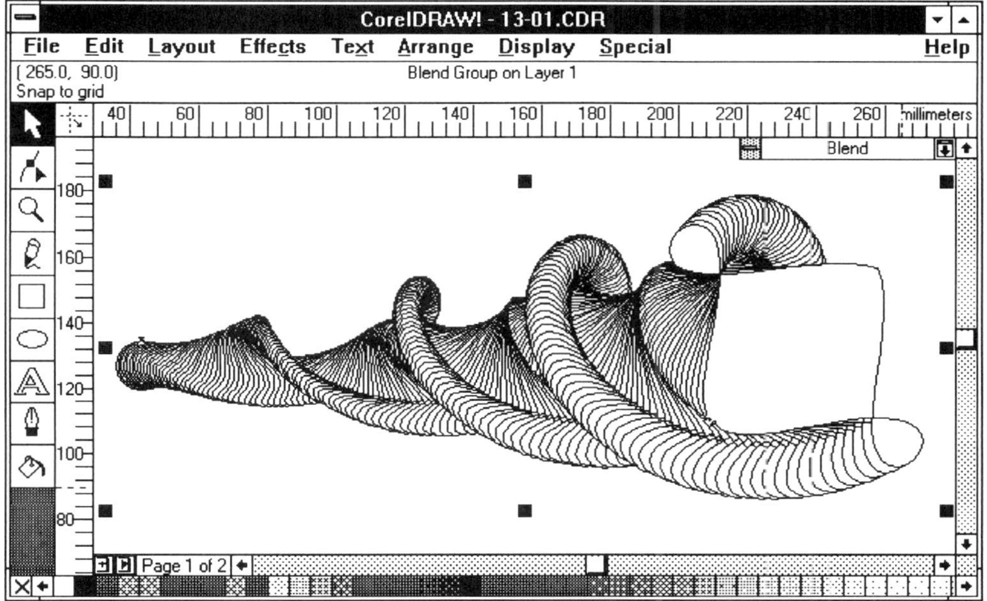

15.05 Unicorn Horn

The rotational angle in the roll-up causes the objects within the blend group to rotate about a common axis and this causes the spiral effect. A positive value causes the objects to rotate anti-clockwise, a negative value causes them to rotate clockwise.

10   Change the value in the roll-up to **-720** degrees and then click on **Apply**. The spiral reverses itself.

11   But suppose you want to be able to see the back of the spiral, i.e. you want it reversed not upside down. Go back to the original ram s horn. Open the **Arrange menu** and click on **Order**. In the menu that pops-out click on **Reverse Order**. That changes the way that the blend is drawn and so the whole thing is reversed.

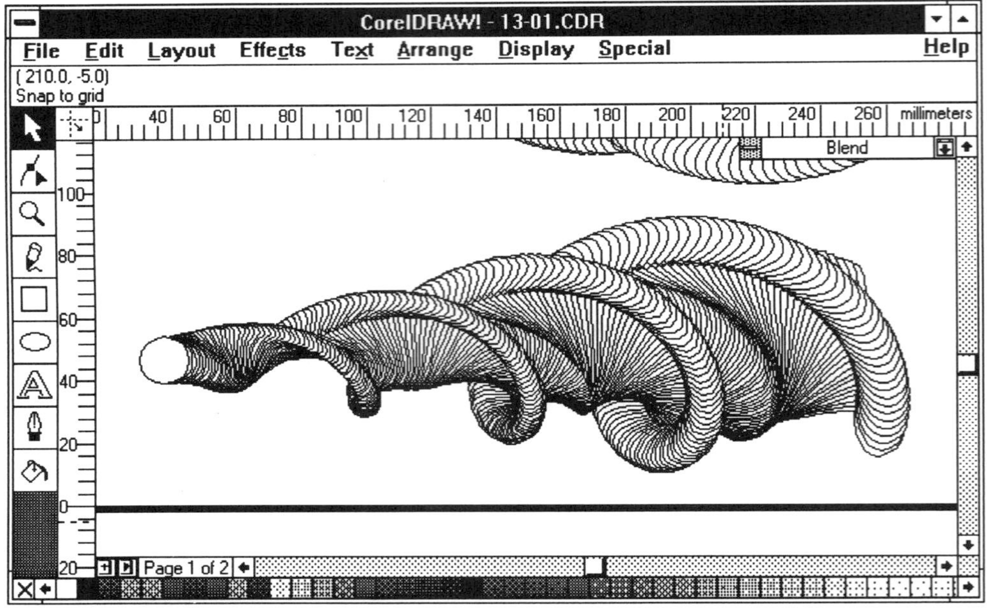

15.06 Reversed unicorn horn

12   Try using a very high value, like 1440 degrees. Then try a low value, e.g. 15 degrees. See what happens. Try it with Loop on or off.

Be warned - you can spend ages just playing with the values and producing beautiful shapes as a result. But it's lots of fun!

BLEND ROLL-UP

The roll-up contains all the commands, and their parameters, that you need for making blends as you would expect.

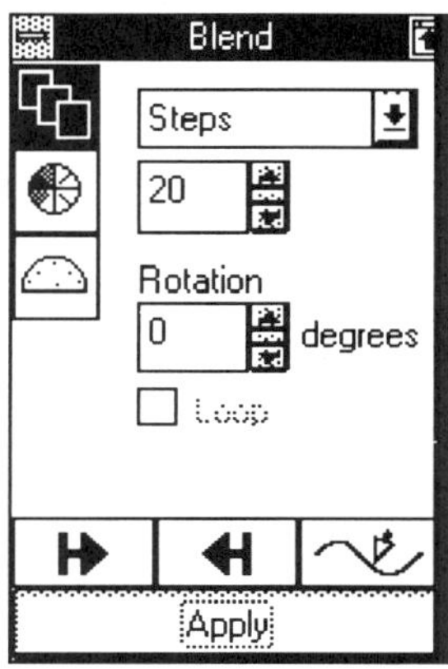

15.07 Blend roll-up

The first part of the roll-up is concerned with the number of steps and the rotation of the objects being blended.

Whenever you open the roll-up the defaults will appear as shown above. The arrow head at the end of the **Steps** line has no effect by the way! You can set the number of steps, i.e. intervening objects, to be anything from 1 to 999. The more steps there are the longer the blend will take to create, especially if you are creating spirals.

The **Rotation** angle causes the intervening objects within the blend to rotate about a common centre. With some shapes this will have no effect but with others it will have a very marked effect. You can set the angle to be anything from -1440 to 1440 degrees.

Loop only becomes active when you are using an angle greater or lesser than 0. With the command turned on the blend loops around.

The two arrows allow you to set the **Starting** and **Ending** object for the blend. These are only of use if you intend blending different objects. You cannot use them if you have only two objects. To reverse the blend you have to use the **Reverse Order** command of the Arrange menu.

The funny squiggle button is **Fit to Path**. This allows you to cause a blend to follow a definitive path that you have created, it can be a line, a curve or an object. When you are using a path the roll-up changes to bear the following:

> **Full Path** causes the blend to use the full extent of the path you have chosen. Normally the blend will flow along the path taking the shortest distance possible between the start object and the end object. By using this option you force the blend to use the full length of the path with the starting and ending objects occupying the same position and the blend objects running along the path.

> **Rotate All** causes all the objects within the blend group to rotate as they flow along the path.

Clicking on the **Rainbow Wheel** causes the roll-up to change again. Using this gives you control of the way that colours are used in the blend. You have to be using at least one colour, other than white or black, for this to be worth using.

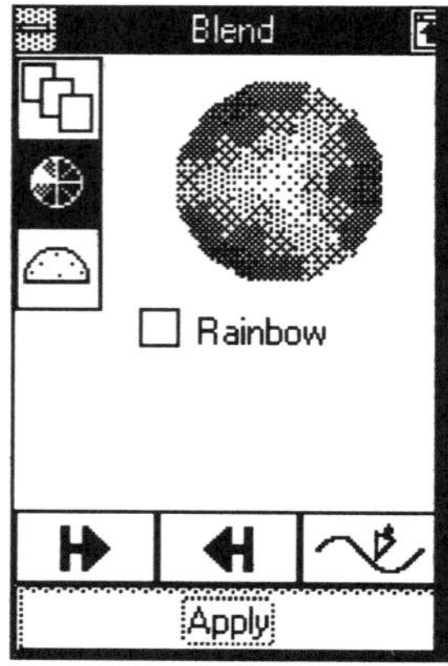

15.08 Colours

The large colour wheel will have a line running from the start colour to the end colour. If both objects are the same colour then it can't. Click on **Rainbow** and the roll-up changes again. You now have a long line running around the edge of the colour wheel and two buttons, one going clockwise and the other anti-clockwise.

Normally the blend will flow from colour to colour in a straight line, like a fountain fill. So if you had a yellow starting object and a blue ending object the intervening shapes would be variations of the amount of blue and yellow as they blend together. But by using the colour wheel you can cause the intervening shapes to use the colours of the wheel instead - in either direction. If you make both the start and end objects the same colour you can have a full rainbow for the intervening shapes. Be warned if you use a full rainbow and lots of steps then the blend can take ages to appear.

Clicking on the semi-circle brings up some changes to the roll-up:

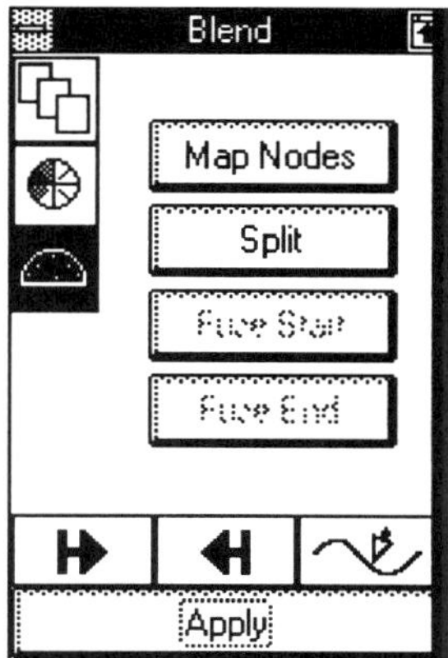

15.09 Map Nodes

Map Nodes changes the cursor to allow you to select a node on the two objects of which you want to map the nodes. Depending on which nodes you select you can create radically different blend results.

Split allows you to split an existing blend and then reblend to and from the object at that position.

Fuse Start or **Fuse End** only become active after you've split a blend. One or other of the commands will become available depending on the kind of split you did. What it does is get rid of the intervening object and go back to the original one.

16. POSTSCRIPT

CorelDRAW is intended for use with a PostScript printer. The use of the page description language affects everything within CorelDRAW from lines and fills through to filling objects with specified PostScript patterns.

The most basic effect that CorelDRAW can produce with PostScript is that of the PostScript Halftone Screens. These can be applied to both the outline and the fill of an object - but only if you are using Spot colours, i.e. the ones based on the Pantone colours. In both the Outline and the Uniform Fill dialogue boxes there is a button labelled **PostScript**. Clicking on this will bring up the following dialogue box, provided you are using spot colours:

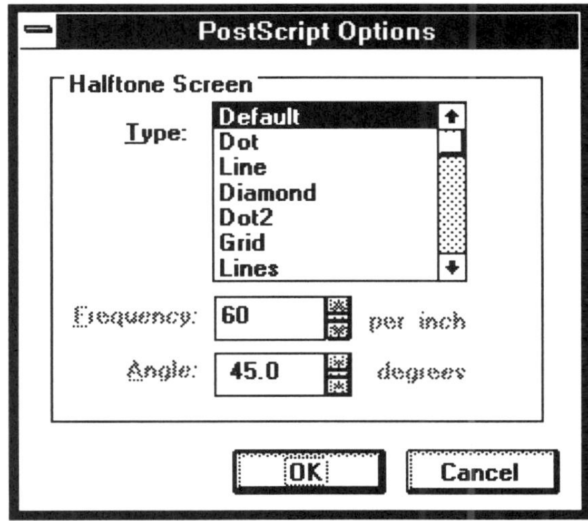

16.01 Pantone Halftone Screen

The list box contains the names of the eleven possible screens. The first of these is Default, i.e. that which is used by the printer itself. To select one of the others simply scroll through the list until you get to the one you want.

It is only when you select an alternative screen that the **Frequency** and **Angle** options become available: they are normally greyed out. Changing either of these can have a marked effect on your graphics but there is something that you must bear in mind. The frequency can be anything in the range 10 to 1000 and the angle can be anything from 0 to 360 degrees. A point to bear in mind is that if you are using 100% black then when you print the graphic, regardless of what frequency or angle you are using the object will be completely black. This is because the screen affects the colour within the object and black is black, grey on the other hand is a mixture of black and white and as the printing only affects the black areas you get a result.

On the following pages are examples of the halftone screens all using different frequencies. In each case the rectangle was first filled with Spot Black and then the tint was reduced to 30% before the screen frequency was changed. A word of warning: if you change from one colour type to another, e.g. Spot to process, then all frequency and angle changes will be lost. The examples are given only for the frequency range 10 to 60 because thereafter there is no real discernible difference on most standard PostScript laser printers.

Halftone Screen : Dot

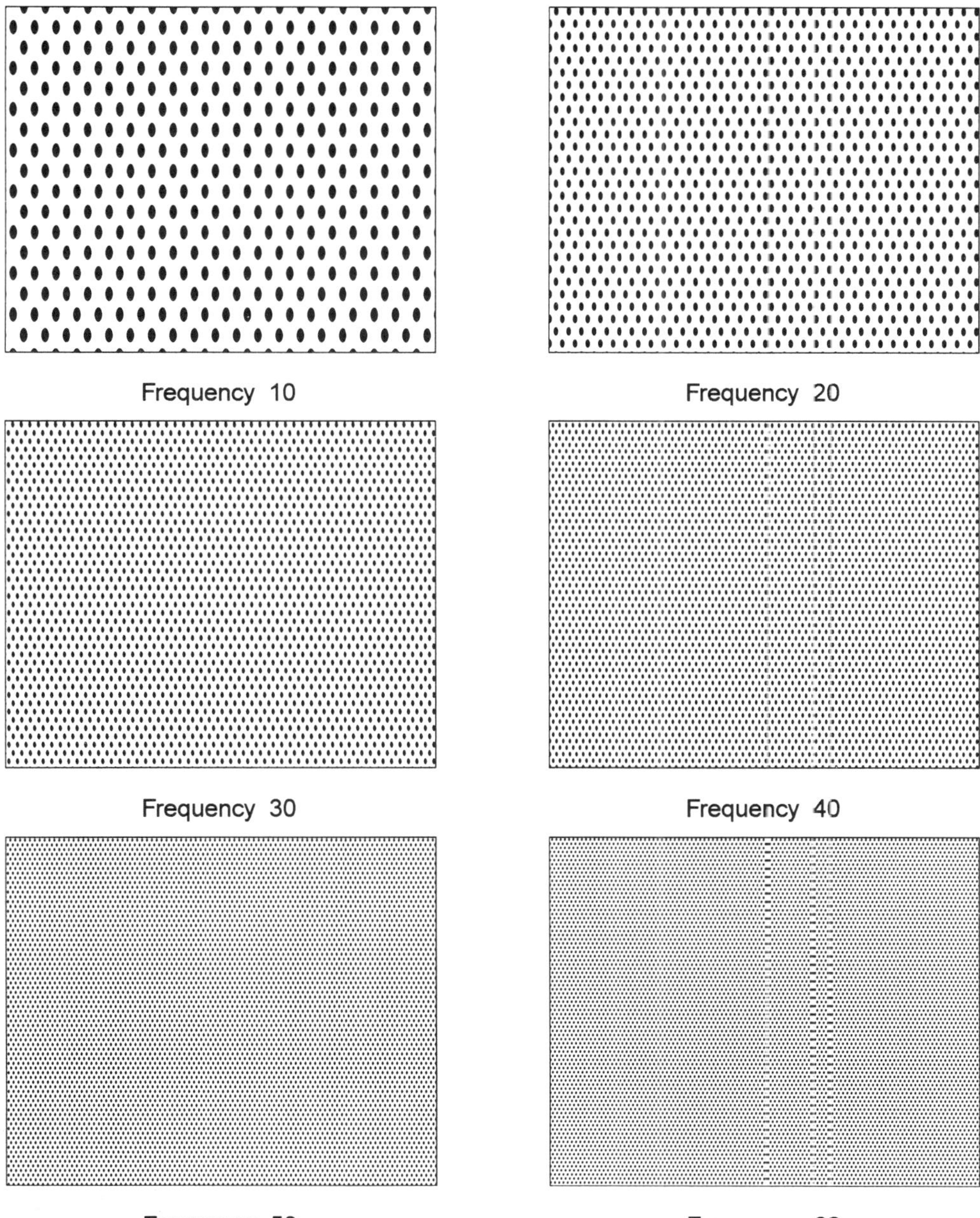

Frequency 10

Frequency 20

Frequency 30

Frequency 40

Frequency 50

Frequency 60

Halftone Screen : Line

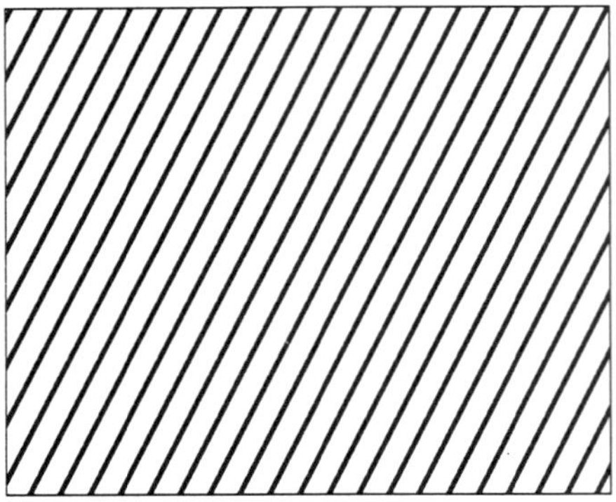

Frequency 10

Frequency 20

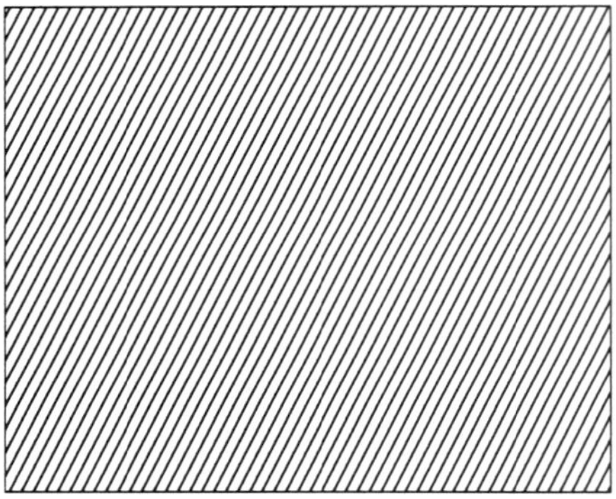

Frequency 30

Frequency 40

Frequency 50

Frequency 60

Halftone Screen : Diamond

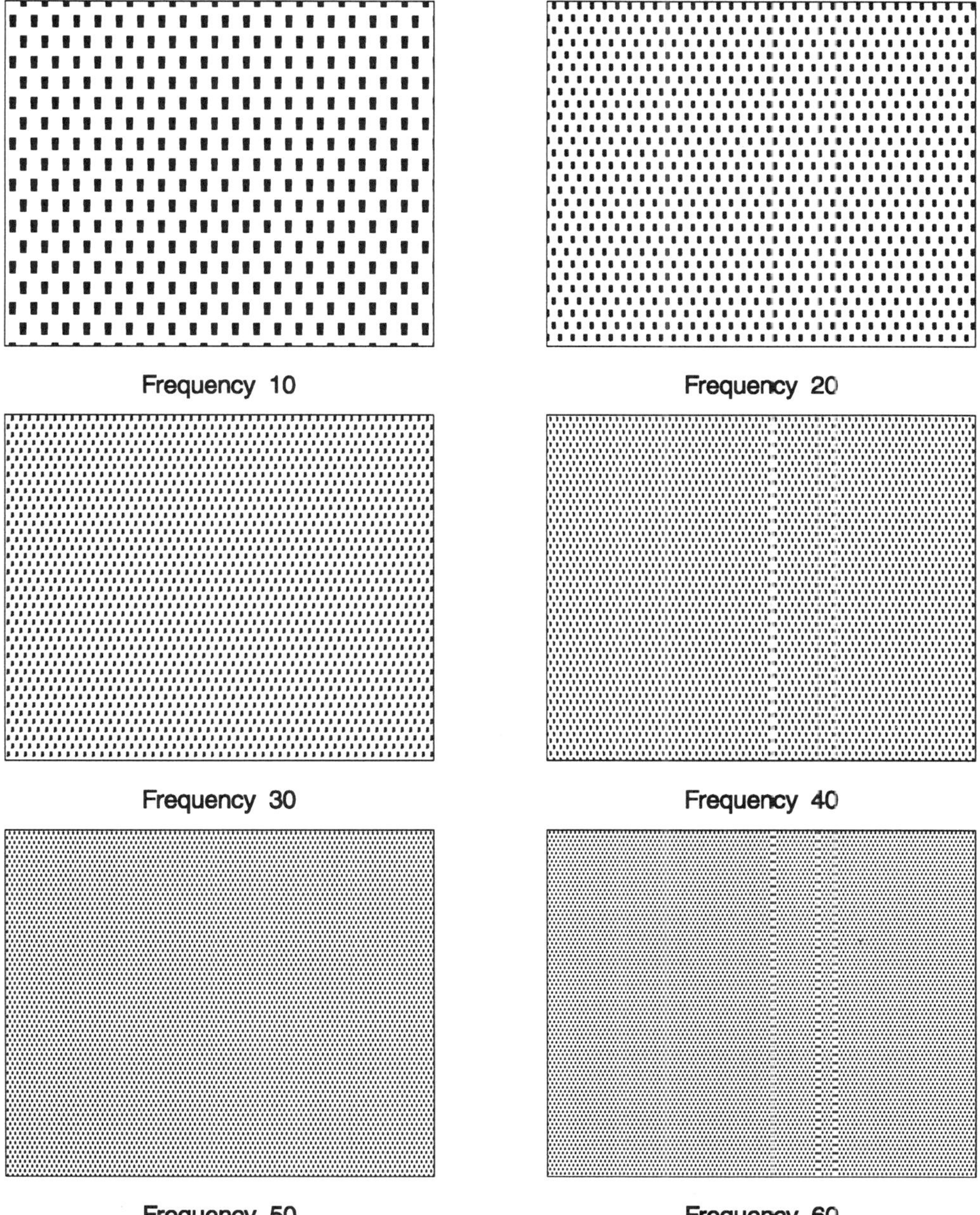

Frequency 10   Frequency 20

Frequency 30   Frequency 40

Frequency 50   Frequency 60

Halftone Screen : Dot2

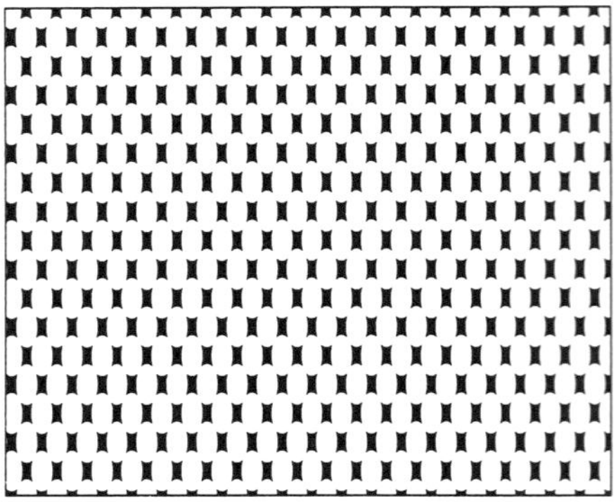

Frequency 10

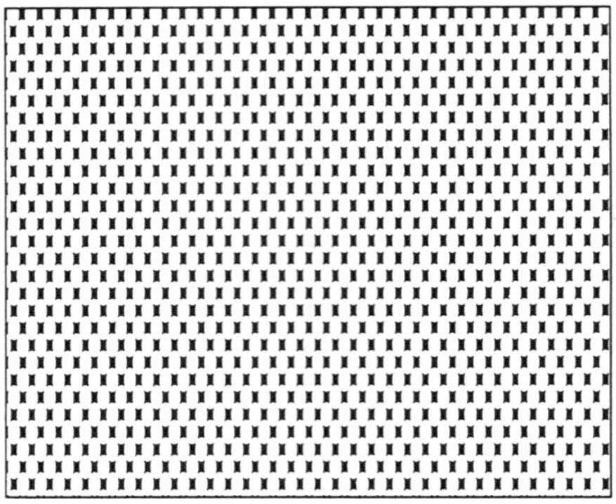

Frequency 20

Frequency 30

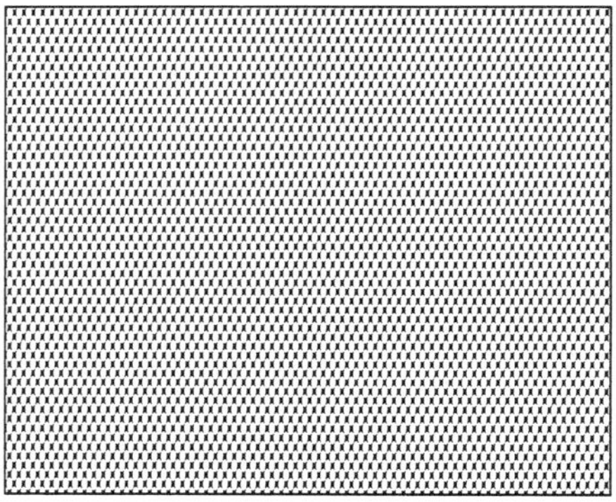

Frequency 40

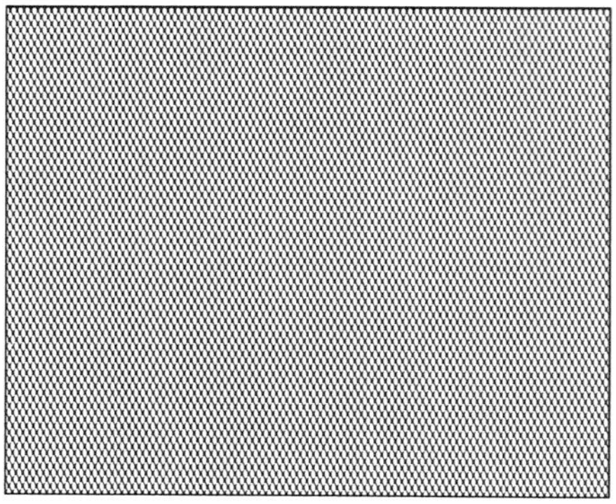

Frequency 50

Frequency 60

Halftone Screen : Grid

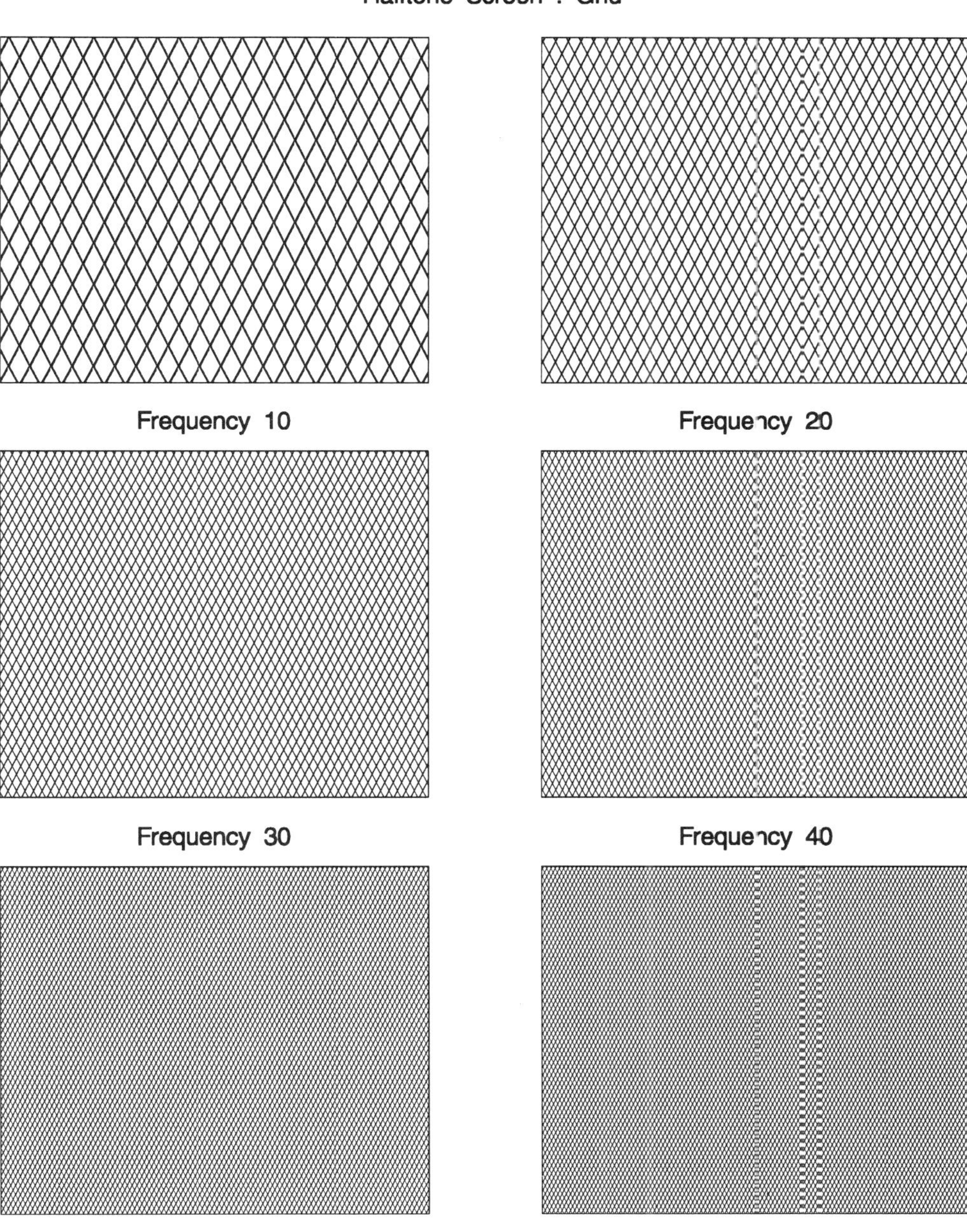

Halftone Screen : Lines

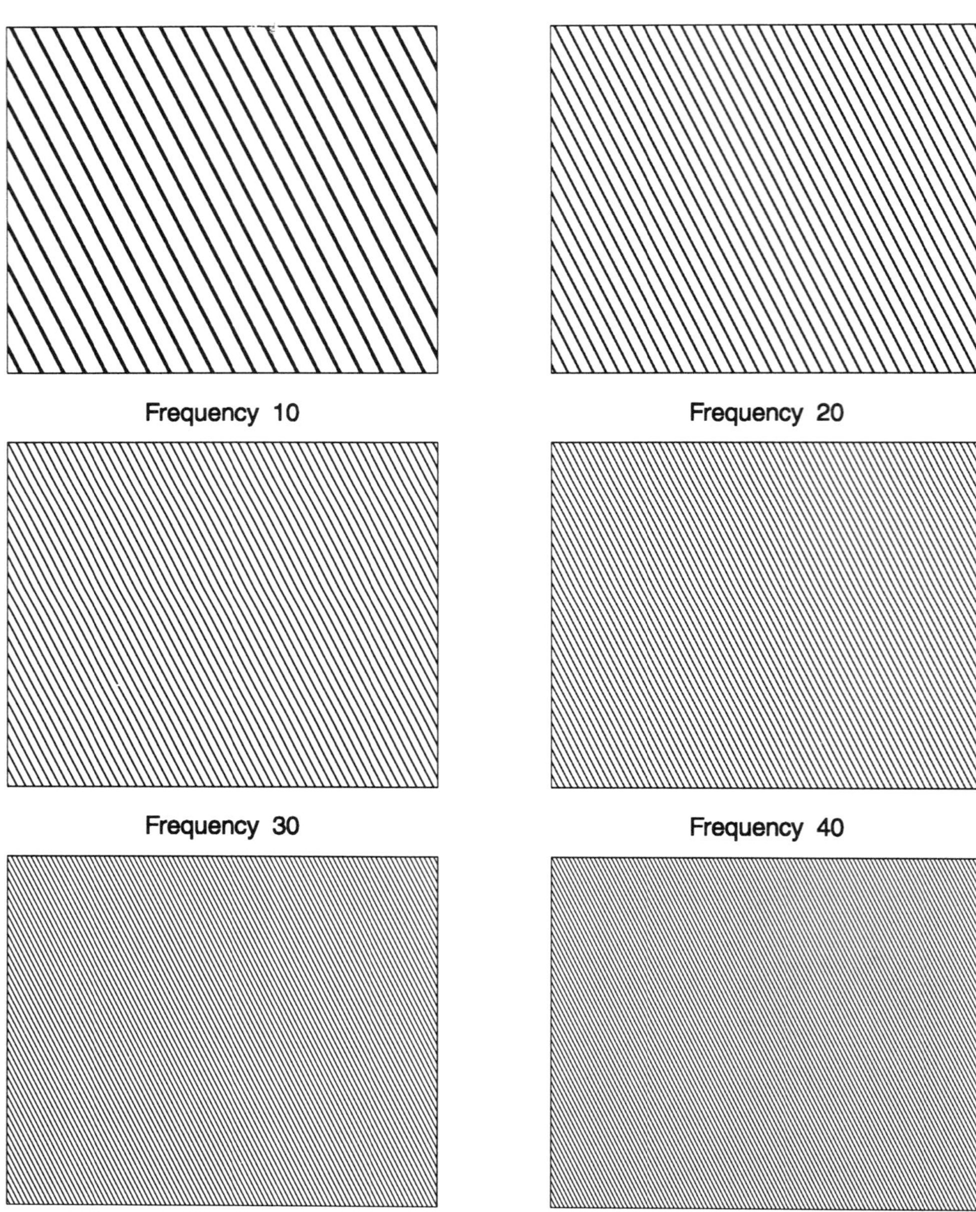

Frequency 10   Frequency 20

Frequency 30   Frequency 40

Frequency 50   Frequency 60

Halftone Screen : Microwaves

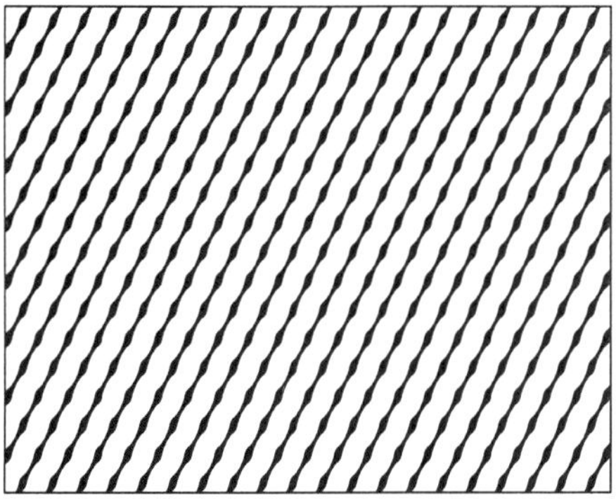

Frequency 10

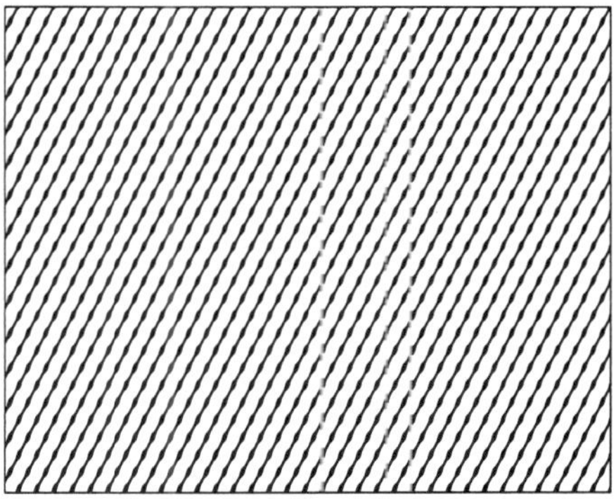

Frequency 20

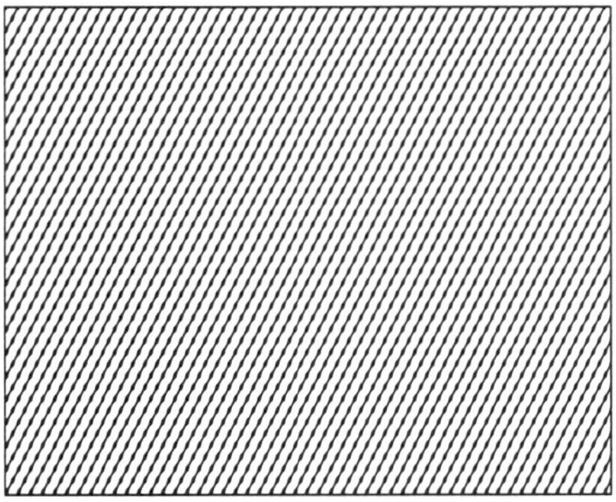

Frequency 30

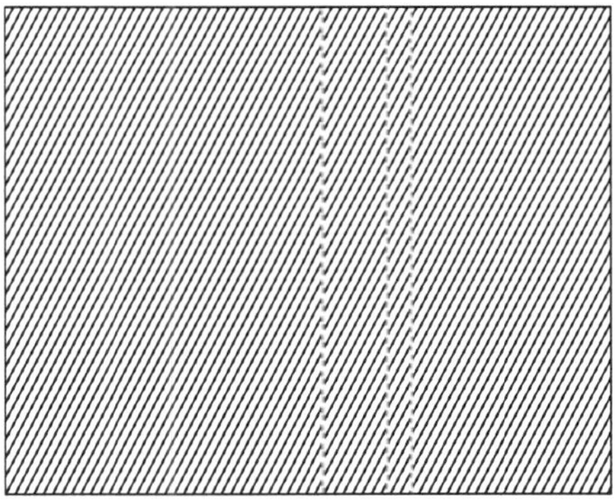

Frequency 40

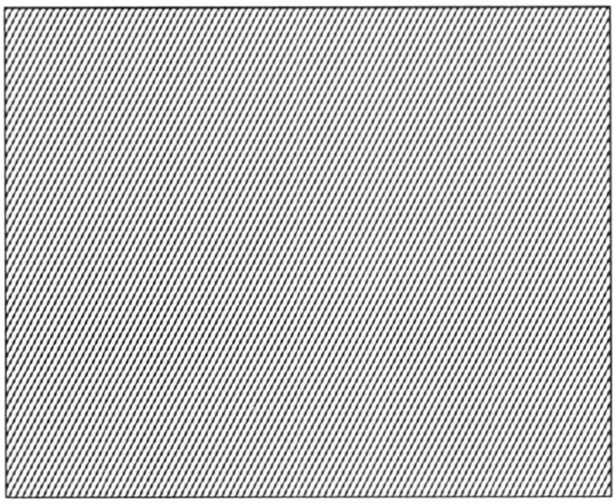

Frequency 50

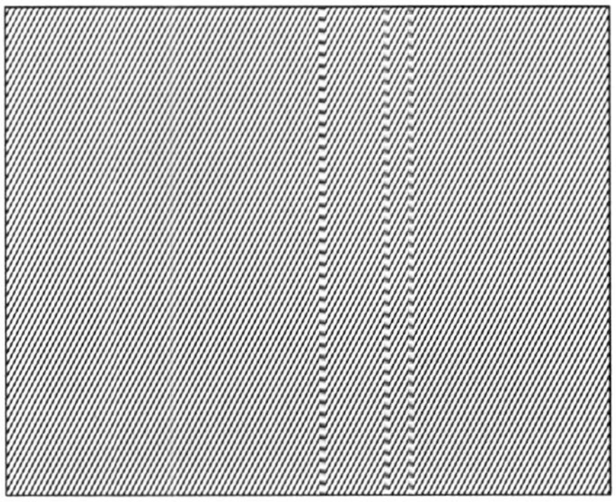

Frequency 60

Halftone Screen : Outer Circle Black

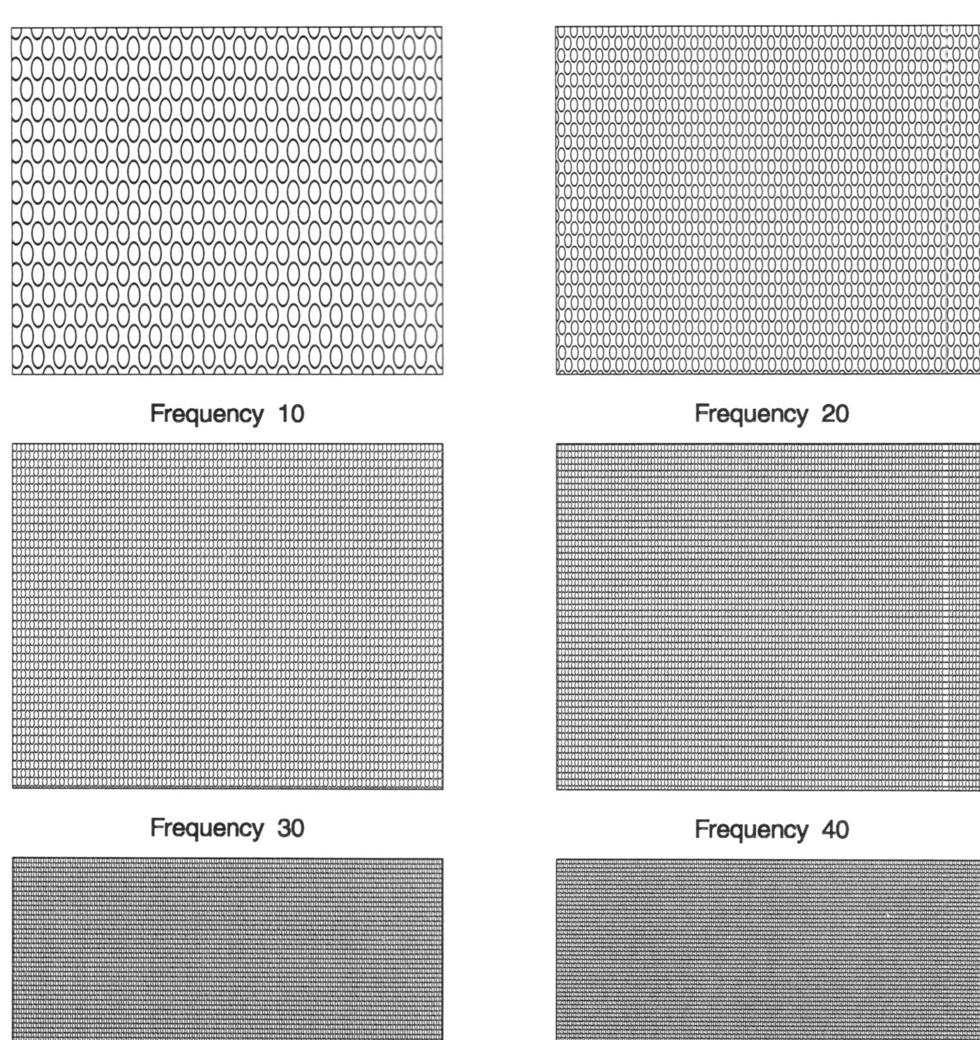

Frequency 10

Frequency 20

Frequency 30

Frequency 40

Frequency 50

Frequency 60

Halftone Screen : Outer Circle White

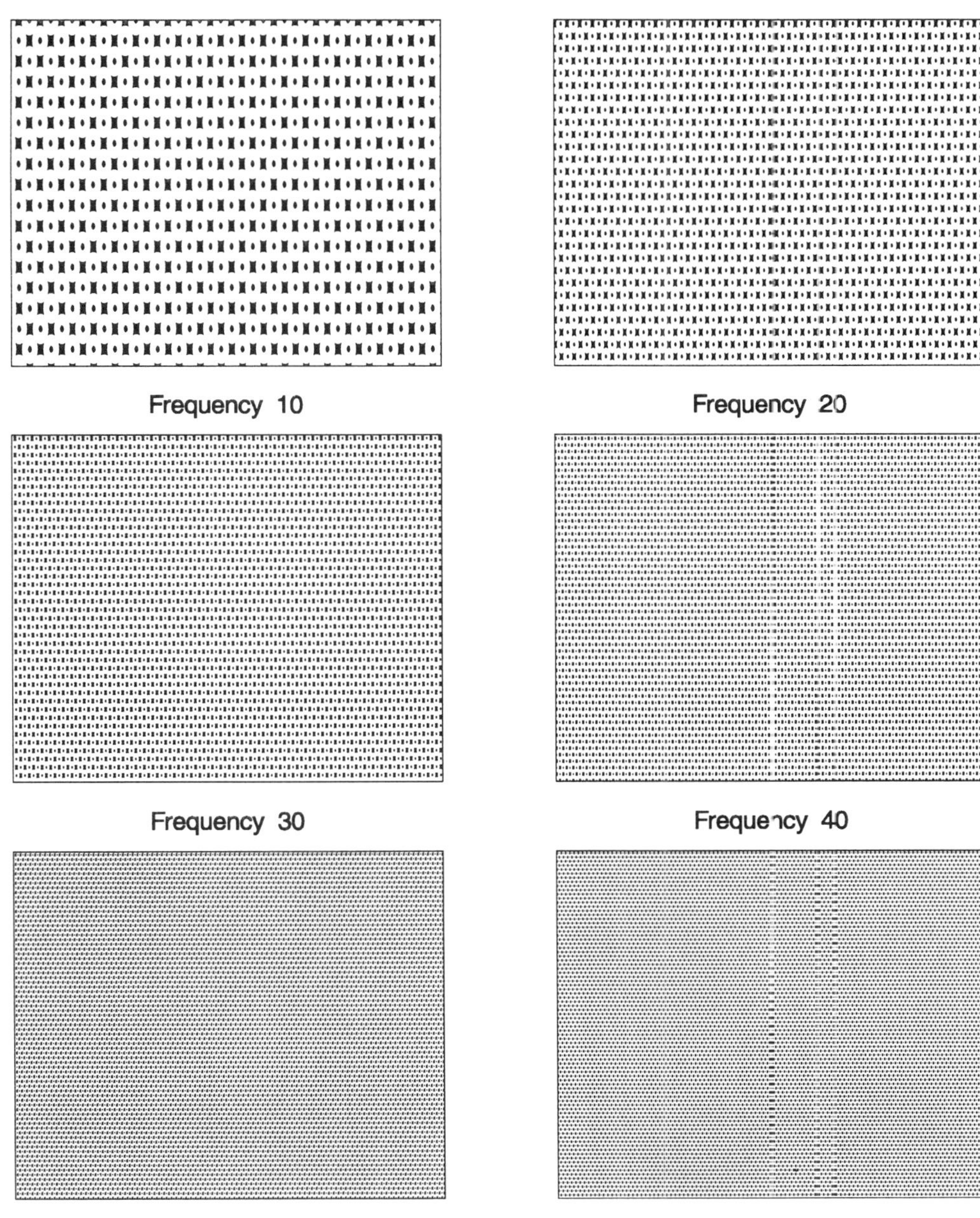

Halftone Screen : Star

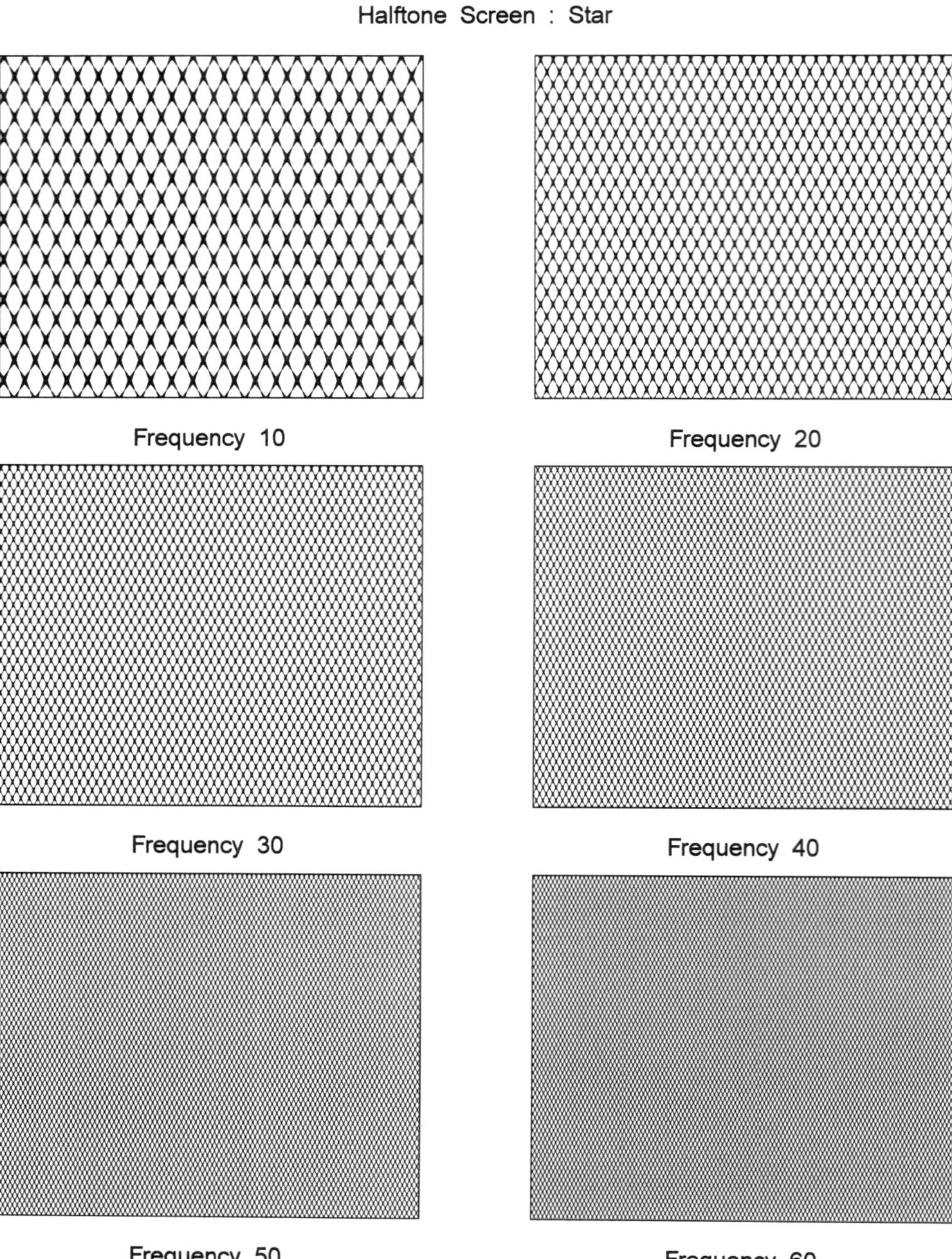

Frequency 10

Frequency 20

Frequency 30

Frequency 40

Frequency 50

Frequency 60

POSTSCRIPT FILLS

There is one other major thing that CorelDRAW will allow you to do with PostScript and that is to use the page description language and its program to create special fills. Fortunately the programmers at Corel Systems have already created a number of these for you and so you don't have to go out and learn PostScript before you can use them.

The PostScript Fills are found in the fill menu as the final button on the top row. When you click on the button the following dialogue box appears:

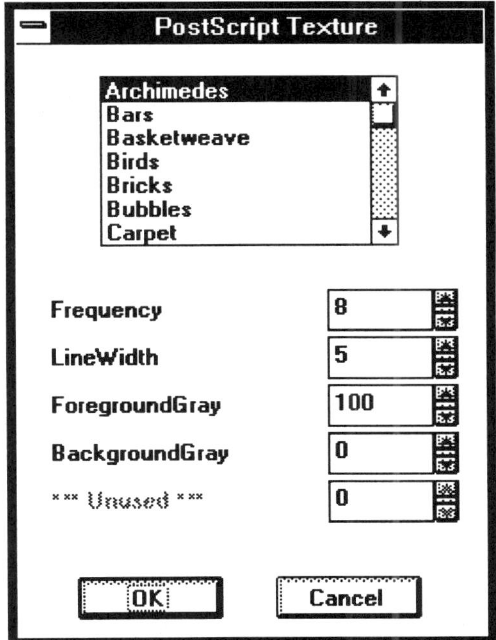

16.02 PostScript Fill dialogue box

The main part of the dialogue box is the list box which contains the names of the forty three patterns that are pre-programmed. The rest of the dialogue box will vary from fill type to fill type. For example, under Bars the categories are:

CorelDRAW 4 - A Users Guide

Width
Spacing
Maximum Grey
Minimum Grey

while under Cracks they become:

Number
MaxLength
MinLength
StepLength
LineWidth

I don't propose at this stage to examine each one of these in turn, I'll leave it to you to play with them and see what different effects you can produce. When you use a PostScript fill in an object, it will not be shown on the screen. Instead the object will be shown on the Preview screen as containing loads of PS's. You can only see the result when you print the file.

On the following pages are all the available fill patterns as their standard formats, i.e. without changing any of the defaults, because this book would be ten times as large as it is if I included all the possible changes. Even making a single change, e.g. changing the line width, can have a marked effect on the printed results.

I have purposely not changed the images in any way. The boxes are all the same size and they have had the different fills applied to them. In some boxes you will notice that there is a border between the fill and outline of box itself. That's the way they print on my printer. The odd thing is that the border only appears at certain sizes, make the boxes smaller or larger and they vanish.

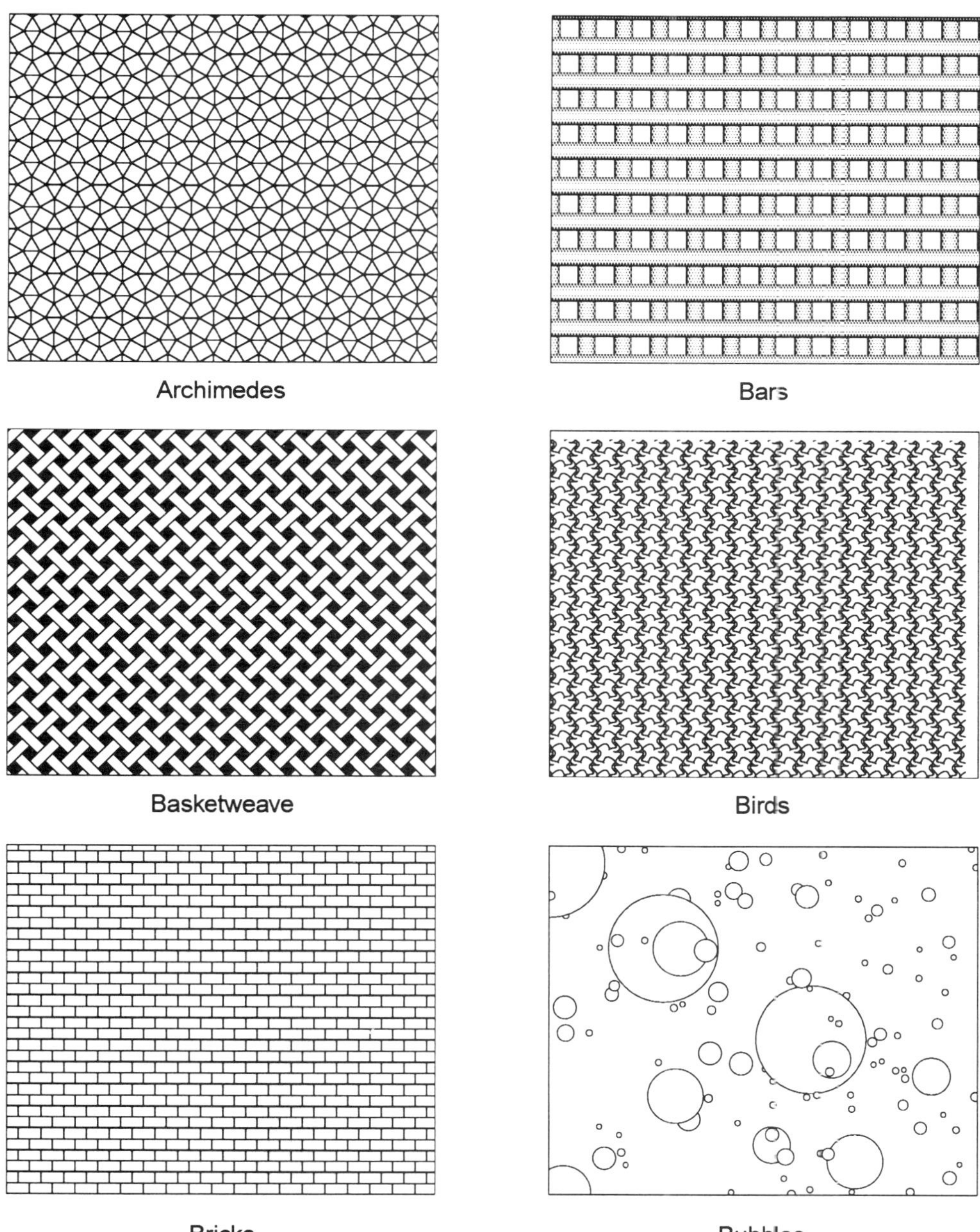

Archimedes

Bars

Basketweave

Birds

Bricks

Bubbles

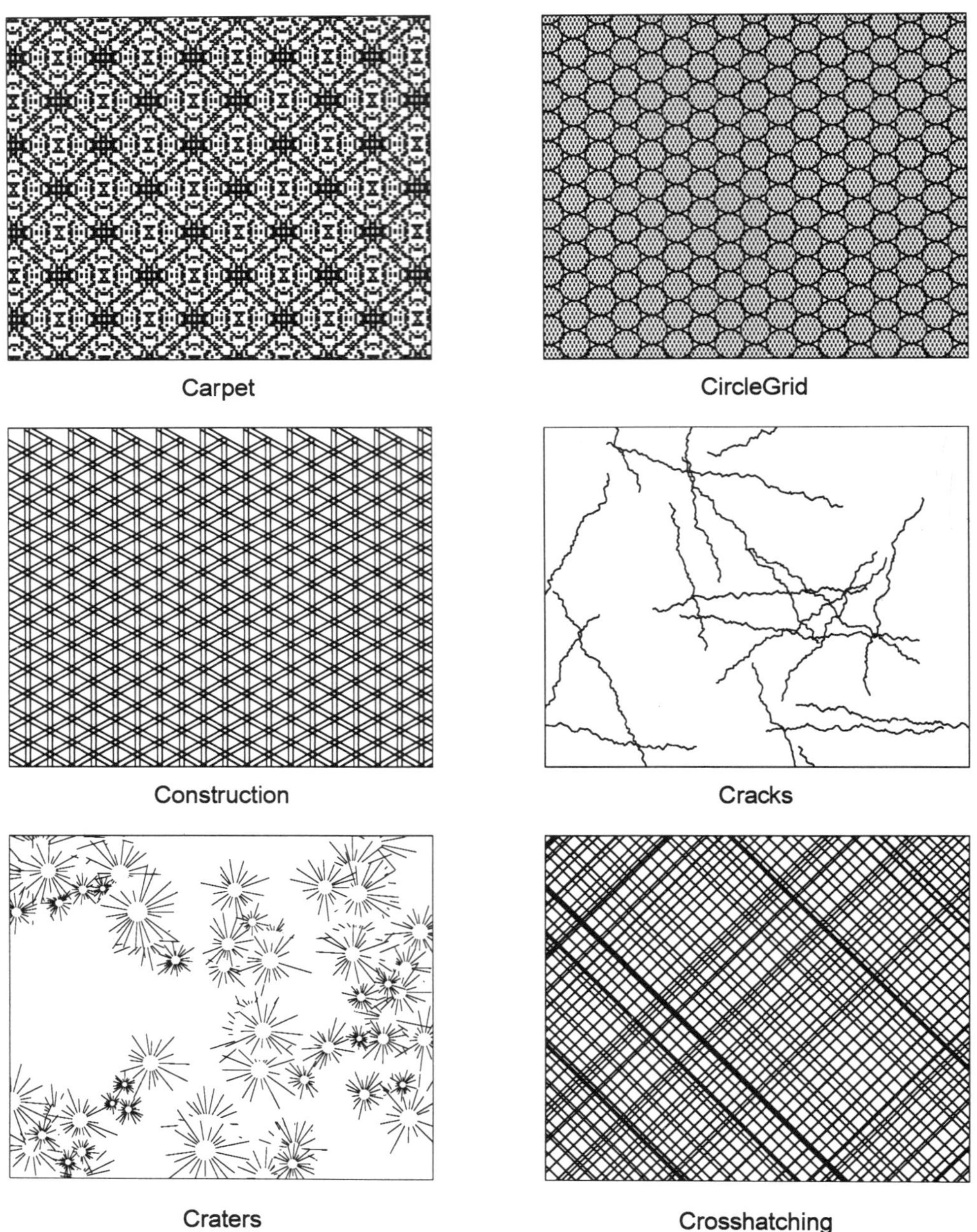

Carpet

CircleGrid

Construction

Cracks

Craters

Crosshatching

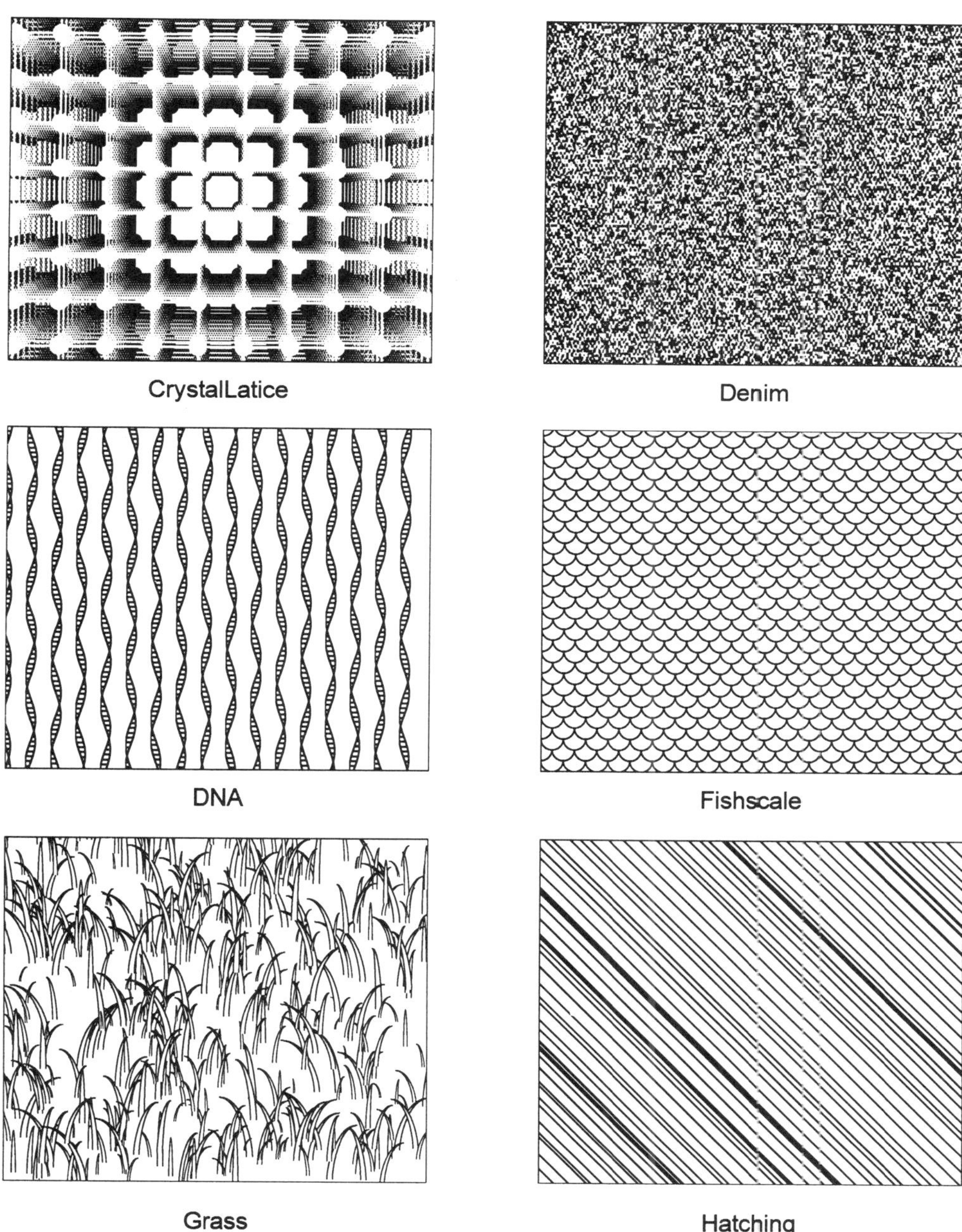

CrystalLatice

Denim

DNA

Fishscale

Grass

Hatching

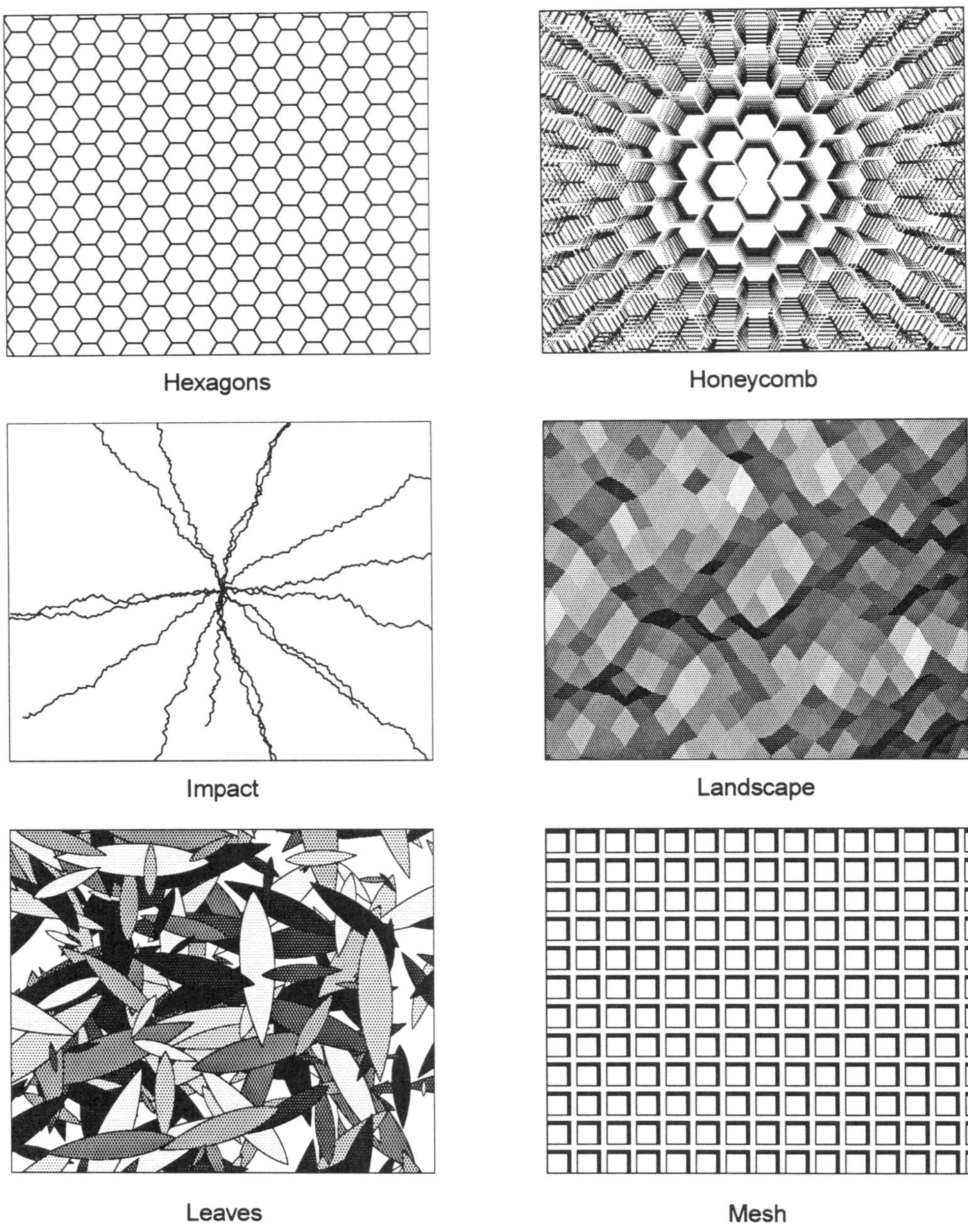

Hexagons

Honeycomb

Impact

Landscape

Leaves

Mesh

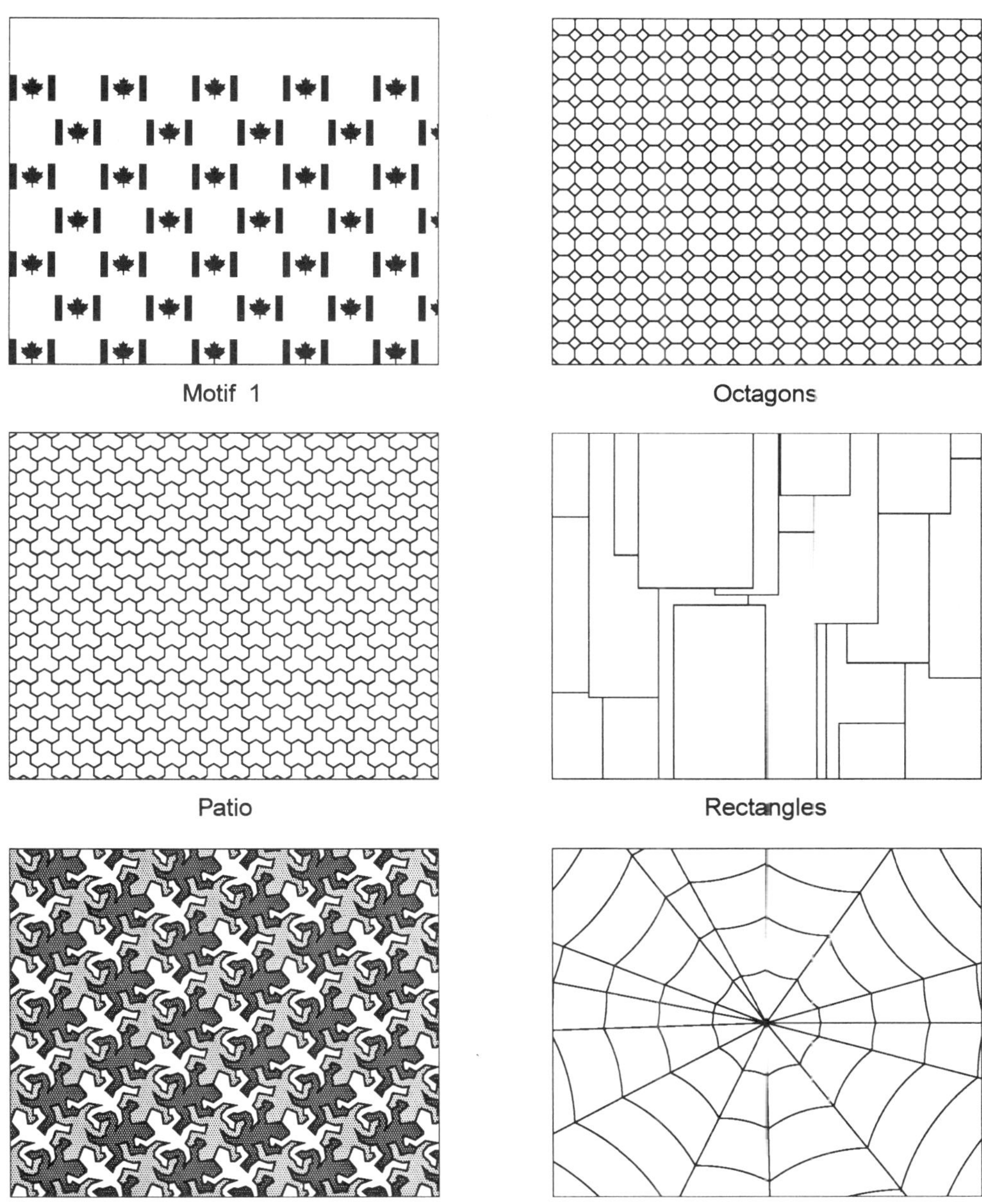

Motif 1

Octagons

Patio

Rectangles

Reptiles

SpiderWeb

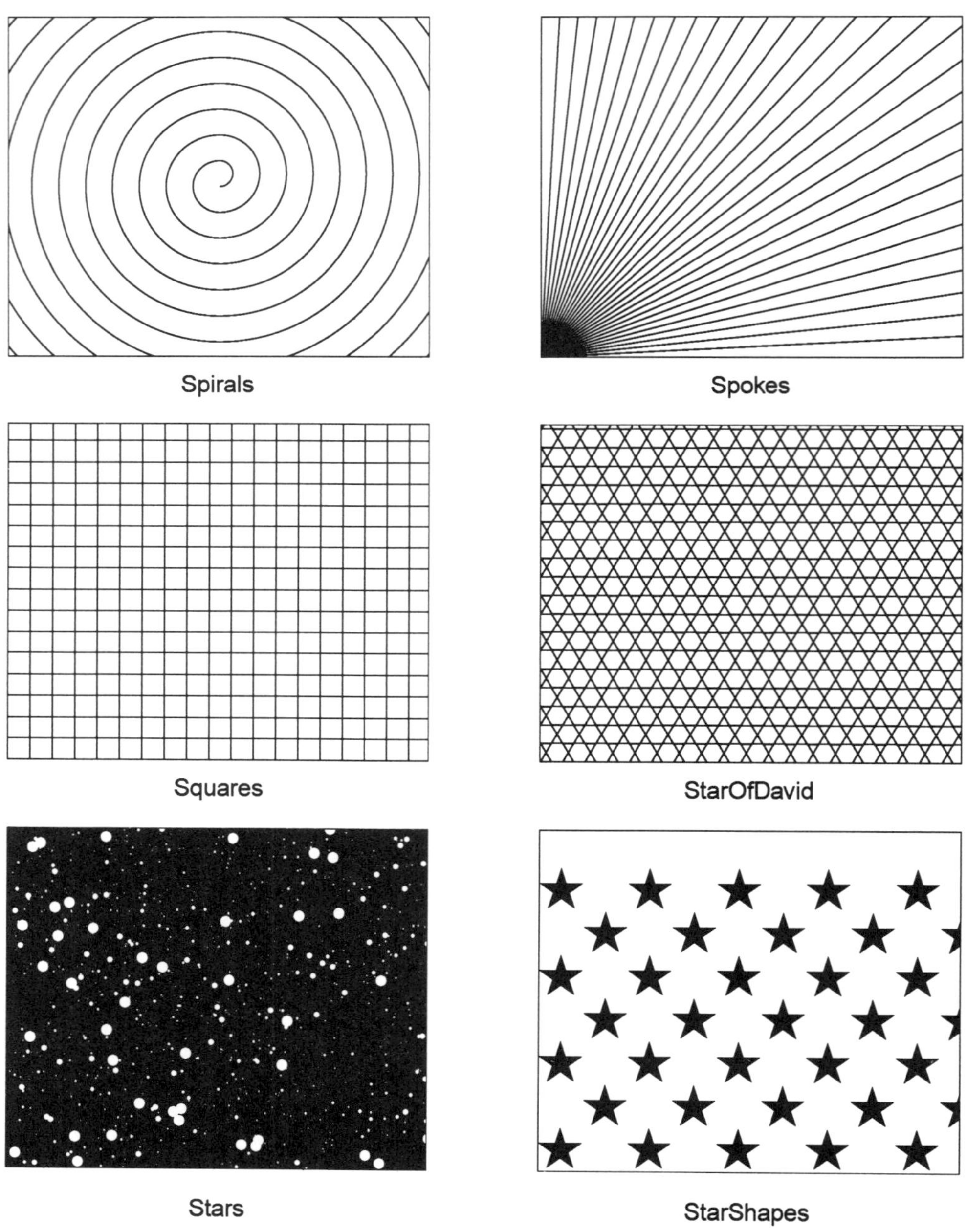

Spirals

Spokes

Squares

StarOfDavid

Stars

StarShapes

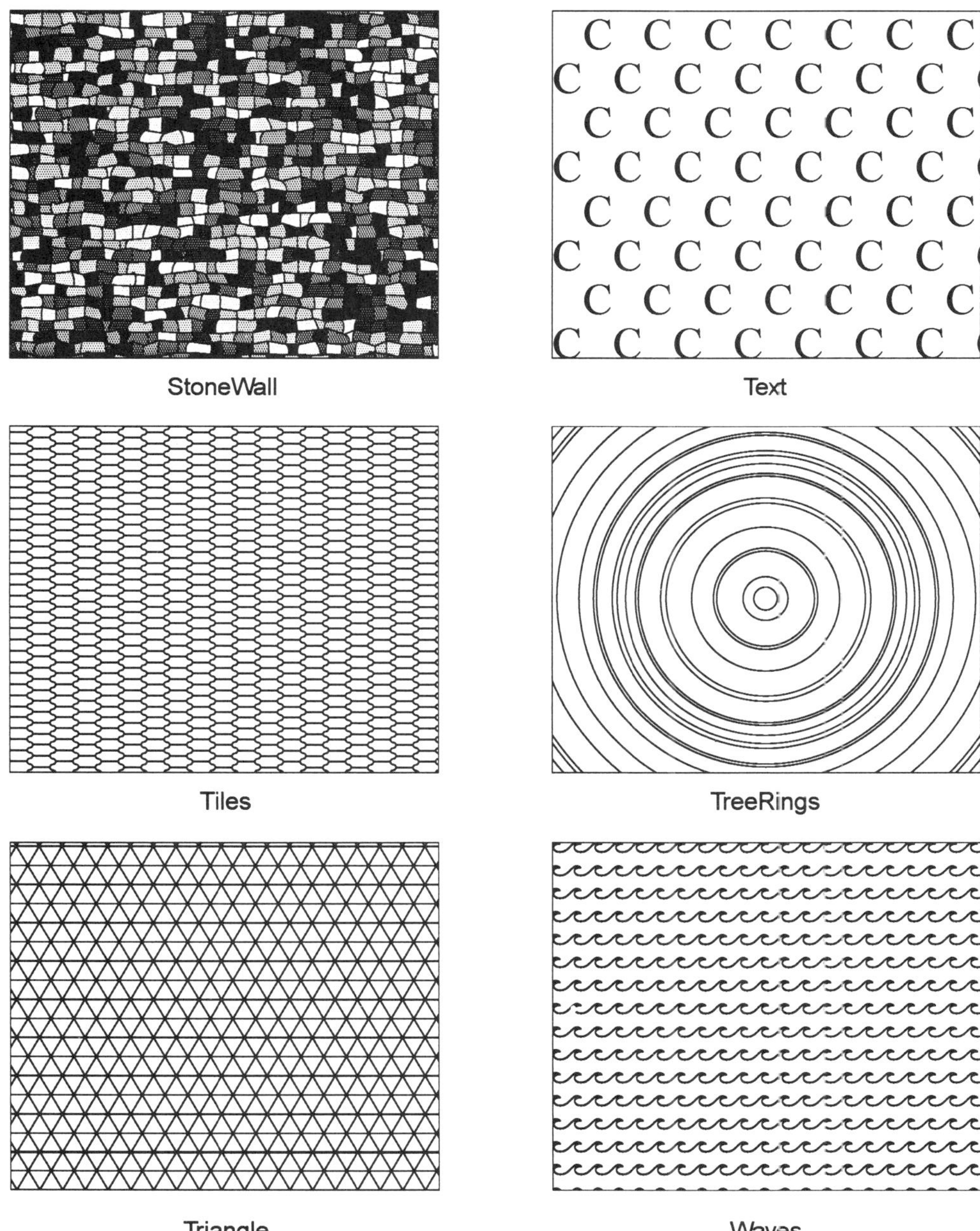

StoneWall

Text

Tiles

TreeRings

Triangle

Waves

17. Import & Export

The new version of CorelDRAW provides you with more import and export filters than ever before. As well as all the graphic file imports you would expect, the program can now import a huge range of word processed files - directly. All told there are a total of 36 possible import filters and 21 possible export filters.

Importing bitmaps

CorelDRAW 4 can import bitmap style graphics in a variety of different formats. My problem is that I don't know which bitmaps you have so we'll just have to use some of the samples that accompany Photo-Paint.

1   Start a new page, the size and orientation doesn't matter. Open the **File** menu and click on **Import** or just press **Alt-F I**. You'll get a dialogue box.

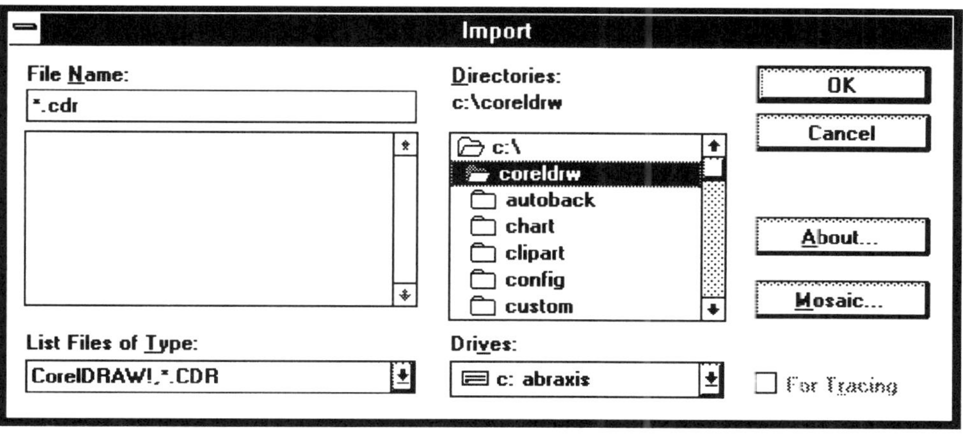

17.01 Import dialogue box

2   Change the **File Type** area to CorelPHOTO-PAINT!, *.PCX and then, in the **Directories** area of the box, log in to **\PHOTOPNT\CANVAS** directory. The large box on the right hand side will then display a range of files. You can pick any one of these.

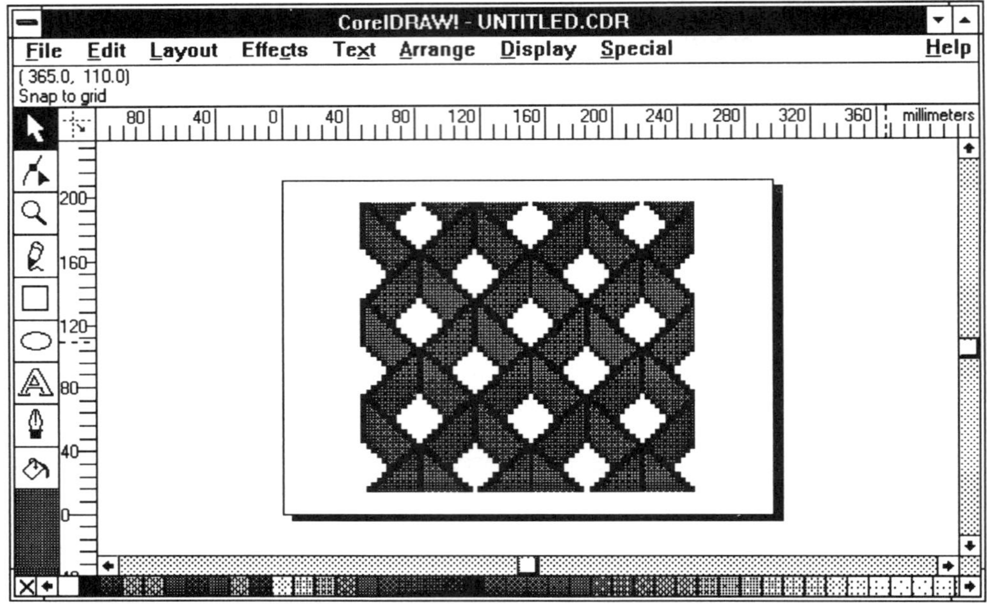

17.02 Bitmap imported

3   The file will be imported and centred on the page. Note that the bitmap will be resized so that it fits the page but it will retain its aspect ratio. The image in the illustration above is actually 66 pixels by 60 pixels and was scanned at 160 dpi - according to Photo-Paint - that means the image is actually 10.48 mms by 9.53 mms. Yet on the A4 Landscape page it becomes 202.1 mms by 183.7 mms. In other words it has been enlarged nearly twenty times over. Similarly, if you import an A3 image it will be reduced to fit on the page. In each case though the aspect ratio of the imported image is retained.

4   Once you have the image on screen you can do things with it. If you are using a colour bitmap then you cannot recolour it. If the image is monochrome then you can change the foreground and background colours only.

5   The image can also be rotated. In all previous versions of CorelDRAW, when you rotated a bitmap you got a grey box on screen instead of the image. But CorelDRAW 4 shows the rotated image properly.

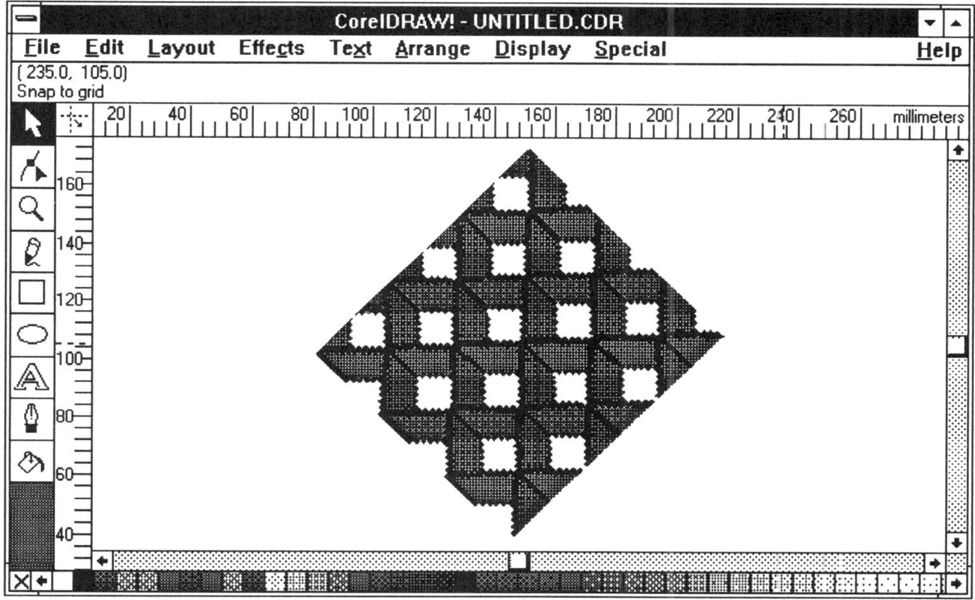

17.03 Rotated bitmap

6   You can node edit a bitmap to crop it, i.e. reduce the visible area, using the Node Edit tool.

IMPORT DIALOGUE BOX

The dialogue box is very similar to the Open or Save dialogue boxes and uses the same conventions.

On the left hand side is a large list box area, labelled **File Type**, that displays the filenames bearing the selected file type extension. The extension name on the top line changes automatically as you select a file type. To import one of the files just double click on the filename.

Below that is a line labelled **List Files of Type** followed by a single line bearing the name of the program, or a program, that can produce files of the type you want. You can only display one file type at a time. Click on the arrowhead to drop down the menu containing all the possible types.

In the centre of the dialogue box is a list box labelled **Directories**. You can use this area to log into any directory of the current drive. By the way, you are better off importing directly from the hard disk rather than from the floppy.

Below that is a line labelled **Drives**. This allows you to select any of the drives, floppy, hard, CD-ROM or Ramdrive, that you have on your system.

Clicking on the button labelled **About** will give you a message box bearing the version and revision number of the filter that you are currently using. When you select a file type, the correct filter is used automatically.

17.04 About message box

Clicking on the button labelled **Mosaic** will activate the CorelMOSAIC program so that you can pick the file to import visually rather than just on filename. See the chapter on Mosaic for details.

Finally, the lines **For Tracing** allows you to import and image and then trace it directly in CorelDRAW. The command is only active for bitmap files. If you want to trace an image in CorelDRAW then you need to turn the command on before you import the file.

TRACING BITMAPS

CorelDRAW 4 comes with a program called CorelTRACE which is the bitmap to vector converter par excellence. However, for simple images you can also trace them directly in CorelDRAW itself. The results won't be as good as using Trace but then they are not meant to be. You can trace any bitmap format file.

1   Clear the page. Run the Import dialogue box and find a simple monochrome file. (I'm using Shermy from the earlier CorelDRAW because it's a nice simple image.) In the dialogue box make sure you click on **For Tracing** before you load the file. Once the file is loaded notice that the Status Bar says For Tracing on the right hand side.

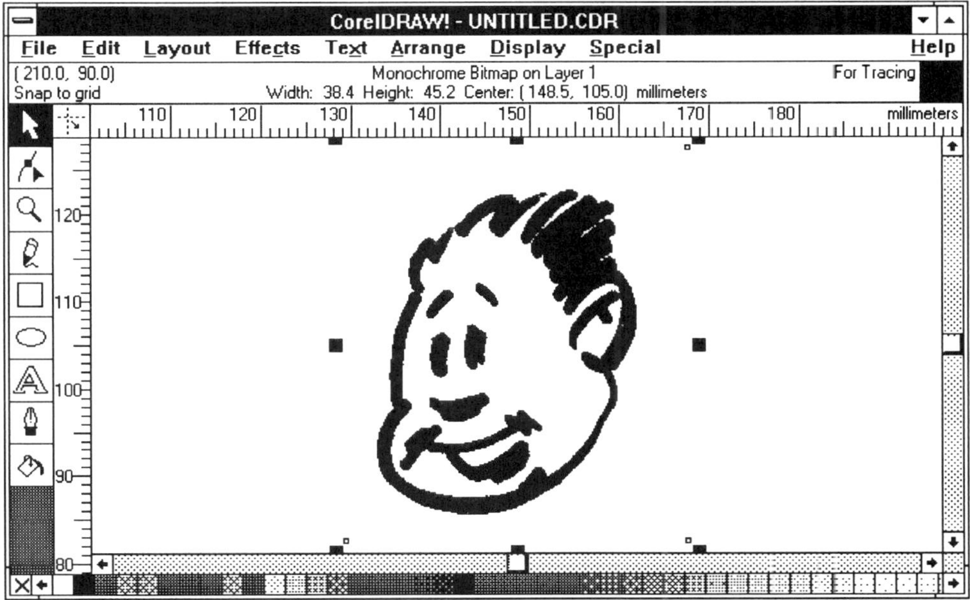

17.05 Shermy loaded

2   Select the Pencil tool, **F5**, and watch the cursor. The arm of the crosshair on the right hand side is longer than normal. That's the tracing point. Move the cursor close to the left hand side of the image and then click once. The hourglass will spin as the image is traced.

3   The trace function works by tracing areas of different colours along the boundary line between the areas. So you have to trace each part of the image bit by bit. It is easier to do if you switch the display to wireframe mode, **Shift-F9**, because then the bitmap appears as a grey shape but the trace line appears in black. (The rectangular box around the bitmap is the total bitmap area.)

17.06 Wireframe bitmap

4   Once you have traced each part of the image go back to the standard screen display by pressing **Shift-F9** again.

5   Select the **Pointer** tool and then drag the bitmap to one side. You should have something like this:

17.07 Original and Trace

6   If you now fill the traced image with black you will find that it is almost, but not totally, identical to the original bitmap. The difference is that you can now resize and reshape the traced image without losing any definition whereas the bitmap will lose clarity if you resize or reshape it.

Importing Vectors

As well as importing bitmaps, CorelDRAW will allow you to import a variety of vector format files. When you import a file all you get is the image itself, i.e. without the page definition. On the other hand if you were to open a file then the page size information comes with it. Again, I don't know what vector format files you have so we'll just use a CDR file.

1   Clear the page - just select everything and press **Del**.

2   Open the **Import** dialogue box, change the **File Type** to **CorelDRAW!, .CDR**, and log in to the directory that contains the Star you did earlier. Double click on the filename and the file will be imported.

3   Because you are importing a CDR file you don't get an import message box - the file just comes straight in.

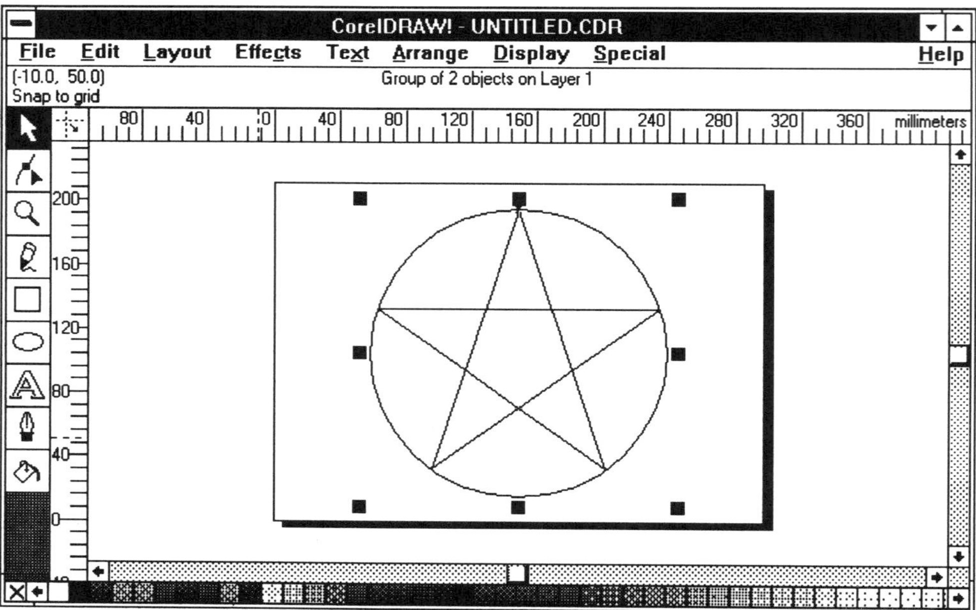

17.08 File imported

4   Notice that the object comes in as a group. In this case there are only two objects but you can have the situation where you get a group of 2 objects and when you ungroup them you find that you have further groups. The reason is that if a group contains groups then the latter are, as far as the program is concerned at this point, distinct elements. You may find that you have to ungroup a number of times to get the individual items.

IMPORTING TEXT

CorelDRAW 4 allows you to import text from a huge variety of word processors, both Windows and Mac based ones. You can now import fairly large files directly on to the page because CorelDRAW will add frames and pages as necessary.

1   Start a new page. You will then need to change the **Page Setup** to be **A4 Portrait**. In the same dialogue box change the **Display** to be **Facing Pages** with **Right First**. Click on **OK** and you'll get the page being displayed on the right of the screen.

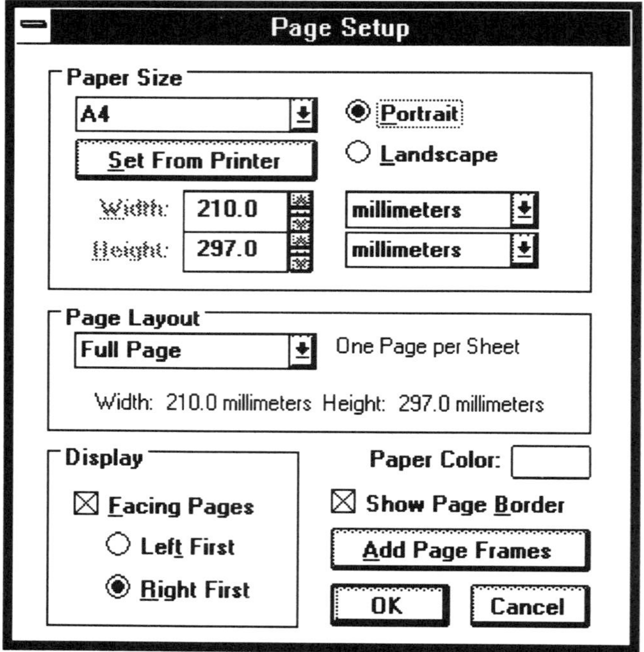

17.09 Page Setup dialogue box

2   Open the **File** menu and click on **File Import** or press **Alt-F I**. Change the **File Type** to whichever word processor you have installed and have documents for. Log into a directory containing files and double click on one of them. As

the file is being imported you'll get a message box telling you how far the process has progressed.

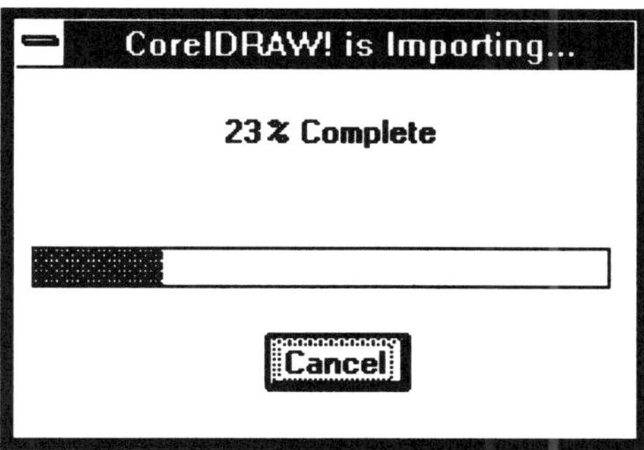

17.10 Message box

3   The hourglass will appear and spin as the file is assimilated into CorelDRAW - exactly how long it spins depends on the file length. Eventually it will vanish and you'll have text on the page.

4   You should find, if you brought in a large enough file, that the text goes beyond page 1. Press **PgDn** and you'll move to the next pair of pages. The link between the text frames is dynamic so that if you reduce the frame size on one page the text will reflow on the other.

5   Go back to the first page. Reduce the size of the frame by dragging the bottom handle halfway up the page. Notice once you have done so that the frame handle at the bottom contains a plus sign. This means that there is more text than is currently shown. It is actually linked to the frame on the next page.

6   To break the link between frames, select a frame with the Pointer tool and then open the **Arrange** menu and click on **Separate**. It works a bit oddly though. The text will be moved to the next frame and the current one will be blank and the link symbol, the plus sign, disappears.

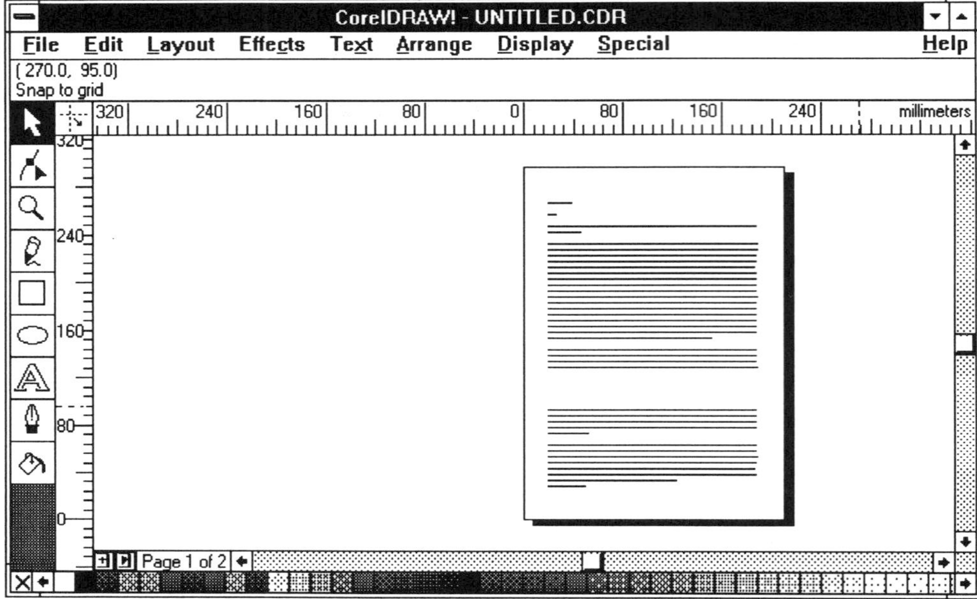

17.11 Text imported

7   You can also create new links. Move to the second page. The text frame will now have all the text from the first frame. Find a frame that doesn't have a plus sign in it. With the **Pointer** tool click on the frame handle. You'll get a funny looking cursor.

8   Move this to a blank area of the page and click once. A new text frame will appear bearing the additional text. This will have the link symbol in the top handle and the original frame now has the plus sign in the bottom handle.

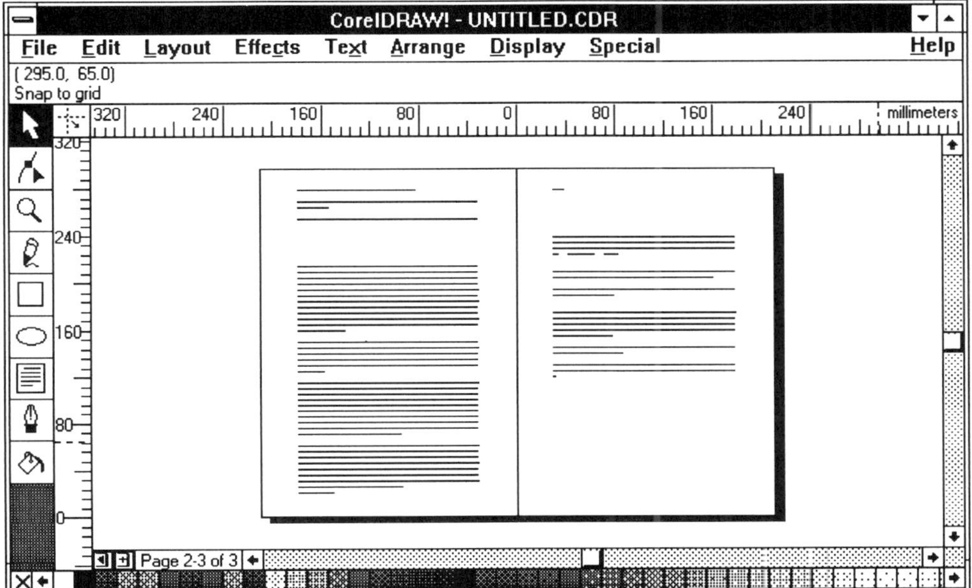

17.12 Two frames

TEXT IMPORT LIMITATIONS

CorelDRAW will import your text directly on to the page but the text comes in as pure ANSI text with the default Paragraph text style applied to it. (See Chapter 19 about Styles.) In other words, if you have created a document in Word for Windows and used different fonts, sizes and headings these are not brought into CorelDRAW. You have to change the text manually. In addition CorelDRAW cannot handle any of the following in the text it is importing:

> Headers, footers, footnotes and endnotes.
> Underlining of any kind.
> Embedded graphics.
> Columns
> Tables
> Macros

Any of the above will simply be ignored as the file is imported.

Equally if you are importing foreign language text you may find that some characters are wrong because of the code page support. Where CorelDRAW cannot find a matching character for foreign language characters you will get an underscore character instead.

When you import text, CorelDRAW will try to maintain the size of the text even if that means that the text frames extend beyond the size of the on-screen page. This means that you may have to resize the text frames in order to make them fit.

All in all the text importation facilities in CorelDRAW 4 are fairly good but you should not expect them to be on a par with say PageMaker, Ventura or Word for Windows. After all CorelDRAW is primarily a graphics program not a DTP one and you cannot expect the same facilities and capabilities as you would get in a full DTP program, any more than you would expect a DTP program to produce graphics of the quality that CorelDRAW can produce.

BITMAP EXPORT

You can only export images that are on the currently shown page of a multiple page document. As well as providing you with lots of ways of getting images into CorelDRAW, the program also gives you a huge number of ways of getting the images out. A tip: before you export the file, in any format, you should save the file to your hard disk in the standard .CDR format.

1   You need to have something on the page - you can only export if you have an image to use. Draw a simple shape or put a symbol on the page. Then open the **File** menu and click on **Export**. You'll get a dialogue box.

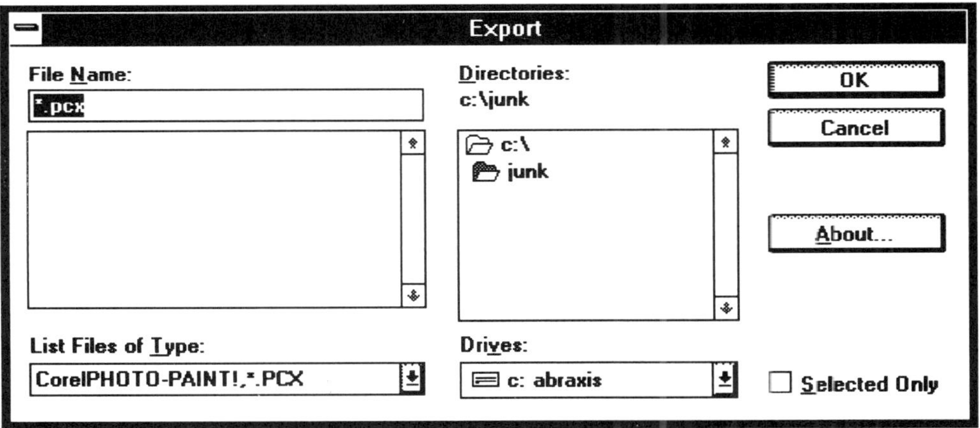

17.13 Export dialogue box

2   The dialogue box looks identical to the Import one because it is. The only difference is that this one is used to save in different formats whereas the other is used to load different formats. You should be aware that there are more import filters than export ones. By default the dialogue box selects PCX export. Click on the arrowhead at the end of the file type line and a drop down menu appears bearing all the possible exports.

3   Select the one you want to use. Highlight the asterisk on the **File Name** line and type the filename you want to use. You don't need to add an extension because that is added automatically depending on the type of export you are using.

4   Set the path to the directory that you want the exported file to be in and then click on **OK**. If you have selected a bitmap export, i.e. BMP, GIF, PCX, TGA or TIF, you will get another dialogue box.

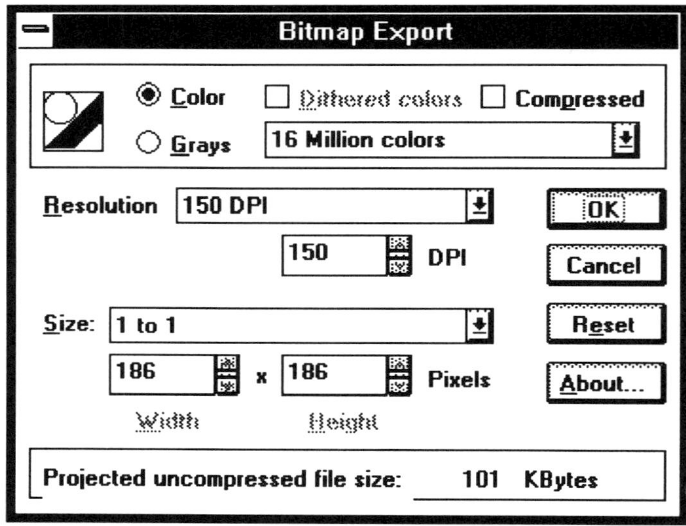

17.14 Bitmap export dialogue box

5   The dialogue box allows you to change the way that the bitmap export works. Set the parameters you want and then click on **OK**. The export will then proceed.

Bitmap Export dialogue box

The dialogue box will be activated whenever you select a bitmap export.

Colour is the first main option. By default, even on monochrome installations, Colour will be selected. You can change the line saying "16 Million Colours" to 16, i.e. 4 bit colour, 256, i.e. 8 bit colour or 16 million, i.e. 24 bit colour. The more colours you use the larger the resulting file will be. Watch the **Projected uncompressed File Size** at the bottom of the dialogue box as you change the number of colours.

Selecting **Greys** will greatly reduce the projected file size. You have the option of using Black and White, i.e. monochrome or single bit, 16 shades of grey, i.e. 4 bit, or 256 greys, i.e. 8 bit. You cannot have more than 256 grey scales.

Dithered Colours is only available when you are using full colour images and using dithered colours for the display. It has some drawbacks, e.g. fountain fills may be banded, but it will produce smaller colour files. Equally if you intend to resize or reshape the exported image in another application then you should not use dithering because you are likely to get a lot of distortion.

Compressed means just that. Any file that is exported as compressed will take up a lot less disk space but it will take longer to save and load. For some formats compression is always used whereas for others it is optional. One thing that you do need to be aware of, many applications that import compressed images will uncompress them as they use them. Given that the uncompressed file can be anything up to three or four times the size of the actual disk file, you must have at least that much free space for temp file storage on your system.

The **Resolution** you are using will make a big difference to the output file. The higher the resolution the larger the file but the better the definition. The line comes with a number of preset values, from 300 to 75 dpi, plus a custom one that allows you to set your own resolution. The line bearing the label **DPI** is only active using Custom resolution.

Size gives the dimensions of the exported image. By default it is 1 to 1 but you can change it to any of the presets or to Custom. The **Height** and **Width** lines only become active with the latter.

The button labelled **Reset** will return all the settings in the dialogue box to what they were when you opened the dialogue box in the first place.

About gives you information about the filter being used.

Finally, the **Projected uncompressed File Size** gives you an indication of the size of the exported file. The figure is only an estimate, albeit a good one.

Remember that a bitmap is a fixed resolution so that if you take the image into another application and resize or reshape it you will get distortion occurring. Generally, you can reduce bitmaps in size without too much hassle and you will lose less clarity than you will if you enlarge them.

A full size bitmap can be huge, taking up several megabytes of disk space. For example, the Star we created earlier exported as a 16 million colour image at 300 dpi will be over 15 Mb!

When using fountain fills in bitmap images, the setting you have in the Preferences dialogue box is what controls the number of stripes in the image itself.

VECTOR EXPORT

CorelDRAW also allows you to export images in a variety of vector formats, i.e. Abode Illustrator, Computer Graphics Metafile, AutoCAD DXF and Encapsulated PostScript. Which one you use depends on what you want to do with the exported image. Each option has its own associated dialogue box.

1   Open the **File** menu again and click on **Export**. You'll get the same export dialogue box as before but this time select **Encapsulated PostScript**. Give the file a name, again the extension is added automatically. The dialogue box closes and then you get another.

EPS EXPORT

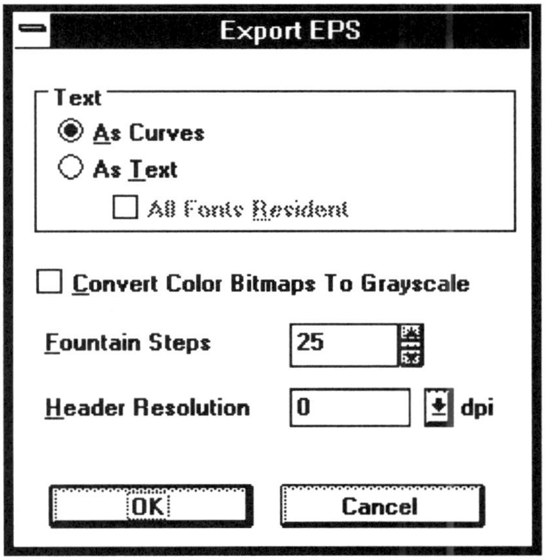

17.15 EPS Export

The dialogue box allows you to set the various parameters for the exported file.

Text as Curves converts any text in the image to curves. This is the default.
Text as Text retains the text information as text in the image.

All Fonts Resident is only active if you have used Text as Text. You should only use this if you know for certain that the fonts used for the text in the image are already downloaded or resident in the printer that the file will be output to - otherwise you'll run into problems.

Convert Colour Bitmaps to Greyscale does just that and saves disk space in the process. It is worth doing this if you intend outputting the finished file on a monochrome printer.

Fountain Stripes sets the number of bands that will be used for the stripes. It overrides the setting in the Preferences dialogue box and elsewhere. The higher the number of bands the smoother the transition in the fountain fill but the large the file will be.

Header Resolution is worth turning on. What it gives you is a little thumbnail of the image that you can then see in other applications. If you leave it turned off then all you'll get is a grey box once you import the file into another application. The higher the resolution the better the thumbnail but the larger the final file becomes.

---

2   Click on Cancel. Then open the **File** menu again and click on **Export**, select **Computer Graphics Metafile** as the file type. Click on **OK** and again you get another dialogue box.

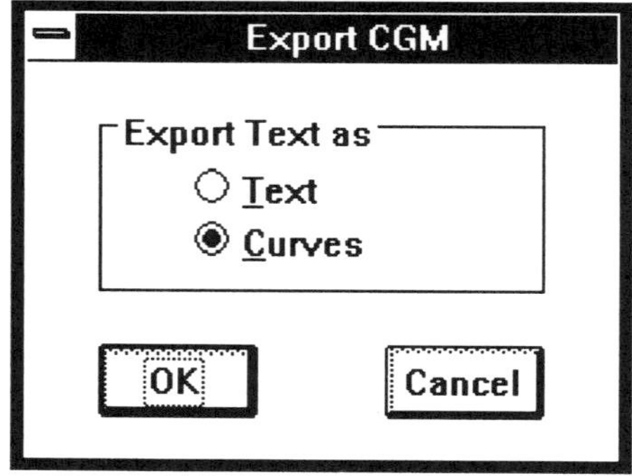

17.16 CGM Export dialogue box

3   The dialogue box only has two options. The first, **Export Text as Text**, will create smaller files and the text will be editable in other applications. The second, **Text as Curves**, can create very large files and the text is not editable. However, the latter is usually preferable. One problem with CGM is that you cannot have true curves. All curves will be converted to polygons, albeit a huge number of lines.

4   Click on **Cancel** again. Open the **File** menu again and click on **Export**, select **Adobe Illustrator** as the file type. Click on **OK** and again you get another dialogue box.

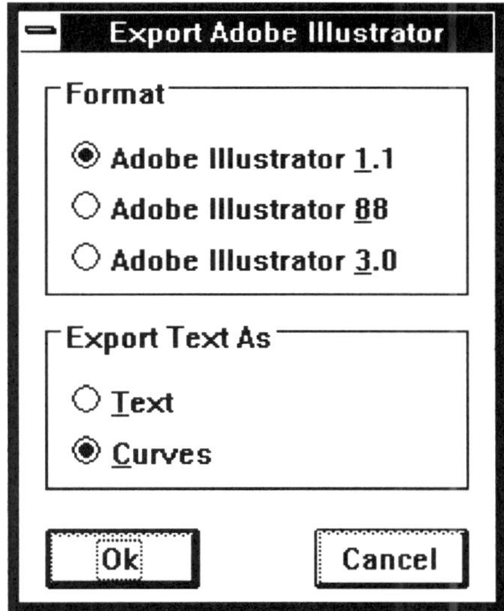

17.17 AI Export dialogue box

5   The dialogue box carries the same text export options as CGM along with the facility to select which version of Adobe Illustrator you want to export to.

6   Click on **Cancel** again. Open the **File** menu again and click on **Export**, select **AutoCAD DXF** as the file type. Click on **OK** and again you get another dialogue box.

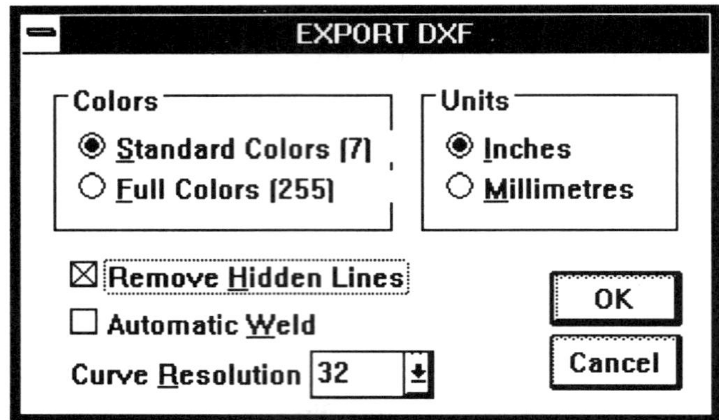

17.18 DXF Export dialogue box

DXF EXPORT DIALOGUE BOX

As with the EPS export, this dialogue box allows you to set a variety of options.

Colours gives you two options. The first is 7, i.e. the standard number of colours available in DXF, and it is selected by default. The second is 255 and it can only be used on certain systems so it is as well to check the actual output device options before you select this.

Units allows you to specify whether the image measurements should be in inches or millimetres. By default it will be the former.

Remove Hidden Lines means that the export effectively ignores any lines that are hidden behind objects or other lines. It is on by default.

Automatic Weld operates in the same way as Weld does in CorelDRAW itself. Objects will be welded automatically if possible.

Curve Resolution will affect the overall size of the file produced. By default it is set to 32. The higher the resolution the cleaner and smoother the curve but the file will be large and take a long time to process. A lower value will give you polygonal curves but be smaller and much faster.

7   Try the different export facilities and compare the various outputs. You will find that some exports work better than others in some applications. For example, PageMaker cannot display EPS files properly so it is worth using CGM files with with program.

18. Contours

Contours is another new feature in CorelDRAW 4. It's a bit like blend but it works with single objects rather than two. Contouring allows you to create a series of additional objects based on a single object, you can contour text, regular shapes or lines. However, you cannot use contouring on groups of objects. The contour is a dynamically linked object so any change to one part of it affects the whole.

1   Clear the page. Draw a large rectangle, say 250 mms by 150 mms. Press **Ctrl-F9**, or open the **Effects** menu and then click on **Contour**, to bring up the roll-up.

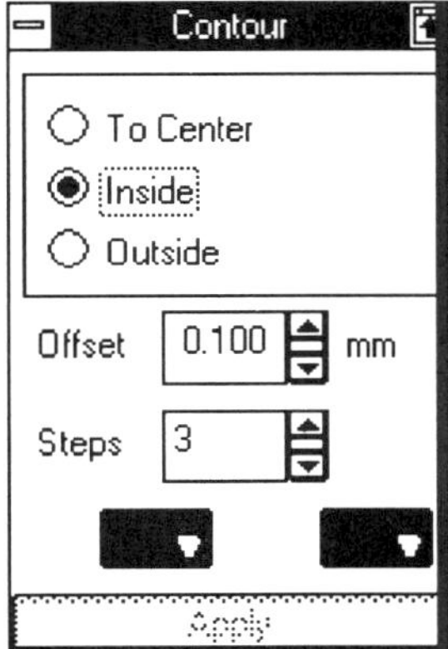

18.01 Contour roll-up

2   With the rectangle selected, click on **Apply**. You'll get three new rectangles appearing inside the original.

3   Select a different outline colour and fill colour in the roll-up and then click on **Apply** again. The new rectangles will assume those colours.

4   Click on **Outside** and then on **Apply**. The extra rectangles appear on the outside of the original.

5   Now click on **Centre**. The Steps line will be greyed out and you will get as many additional rectangles as it is possible to fit appearing inside the original. Again they will use the outline and fill colours you have set.

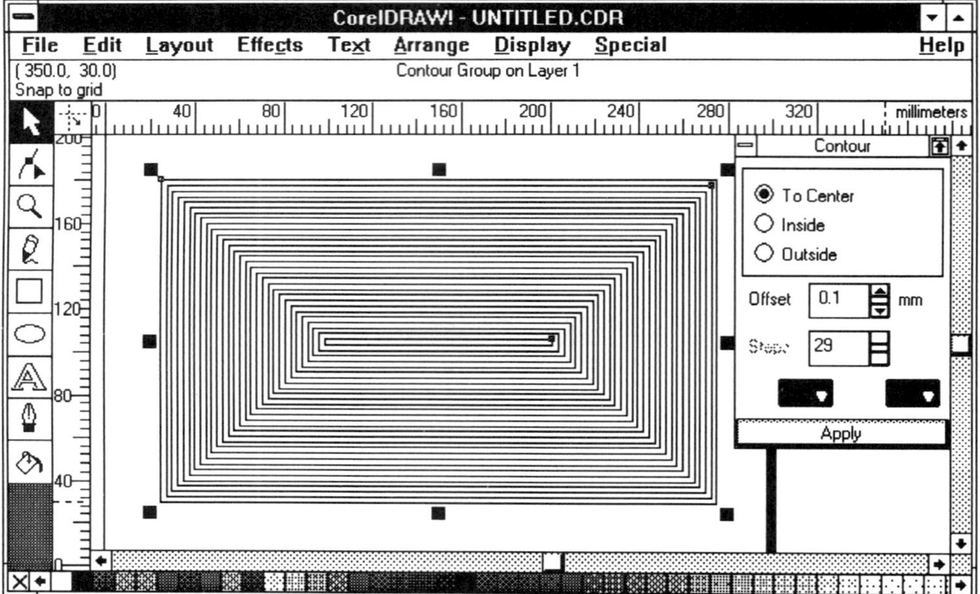

18.02 Centre steps

Contour Roll-up

The roll-up is deceptively simple considering as it contains only four basic commands, but the effects you can generate with it can be astonishing.

The first part of the roll-up controls where the contours appear:

> **To Centre** will add as many additional shapes as it can until it reaches the centre of the original object. The extra ones are controlled by the value in the **Offset**.

Inside will add extra shapes inside the original but you can set the exact
number depends on the value you set with the **Offset**.

Outside places the extra shapes outside the original, again according to
how many steps you've asked for and using the value in the **Offset**. For
obvious reasons the extra shapes get bigger.

The value in the **Offset** controls the distance between the shapes that will be
produced. One thing you need to be aware of though is a slight oddity when
using millimetres. An offset value of 0.1 mms produces offsets that are actually
5 mms, 0.2 mms will give you 10 mms offsets, 0.3 mms gives just over 15 mms,
0.4 mms gives a fraction over 20 mms, 0.5 mms gives 25 mms and so on. It
works fine in inches by the way.

The number of **Steps** is the number of additional objects that you want to
create and it is only available when using Inside or Outside. CorelDRAW will
work out the steps for itself when you use To Centre - it actually places as many
additional shapes as it can given the offset value. When you are using Inside
the offset also takes precedence over the number of steps and it will only place
as many steps as there is room for.

The two buttons at the bottom allows you to set the **Outline** and **Fill** for the
extra shapes. They will blend slightly from the original object colour to the
final colour. The colours you select are actually applied to the final additional
object and the intervening steps will blend between the two.

CONTOURED TEXT

You can create some weird and wonderful effects using contours with text.

1   Clear the page. Place some Artistic Text on the page, e.g. your name. Fill the
     text with white and give it a thin black outline. Open the **Contour** roll-up, click
     on **Outside**, use an **Offset** of 0.3 mms and 3 **Steps**. Click on **Apply**. You should
     get something like this:

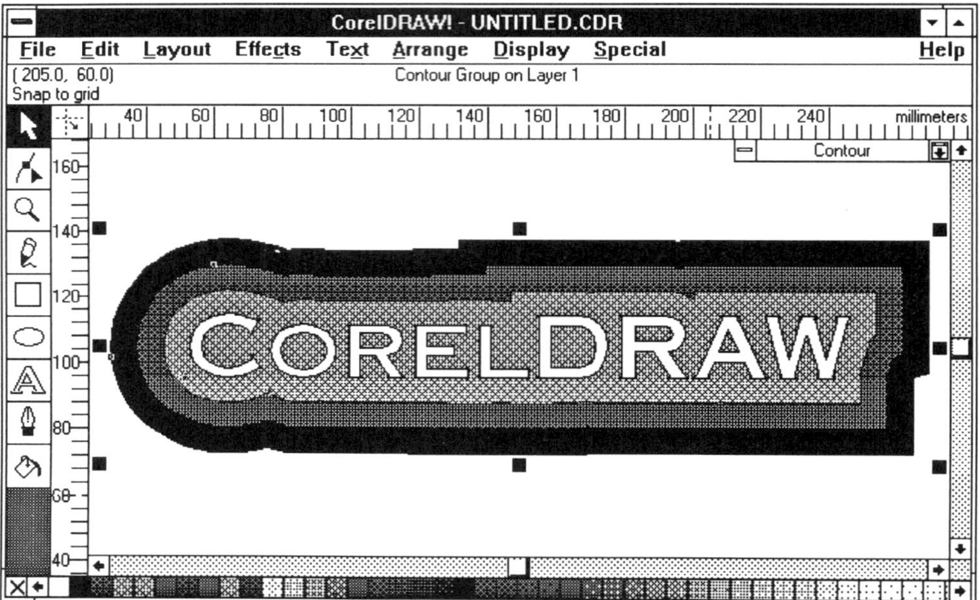

18.03 Contoured Text

2   Contouring text to the inside doesn't really work very well - unless you are
     using very large text. Try using a very large, e.g. 720 points, individual letter
     and then contouring that to the inside. You have to play with the steps and the
     offset to get the effect you want but you can get things like this:

336

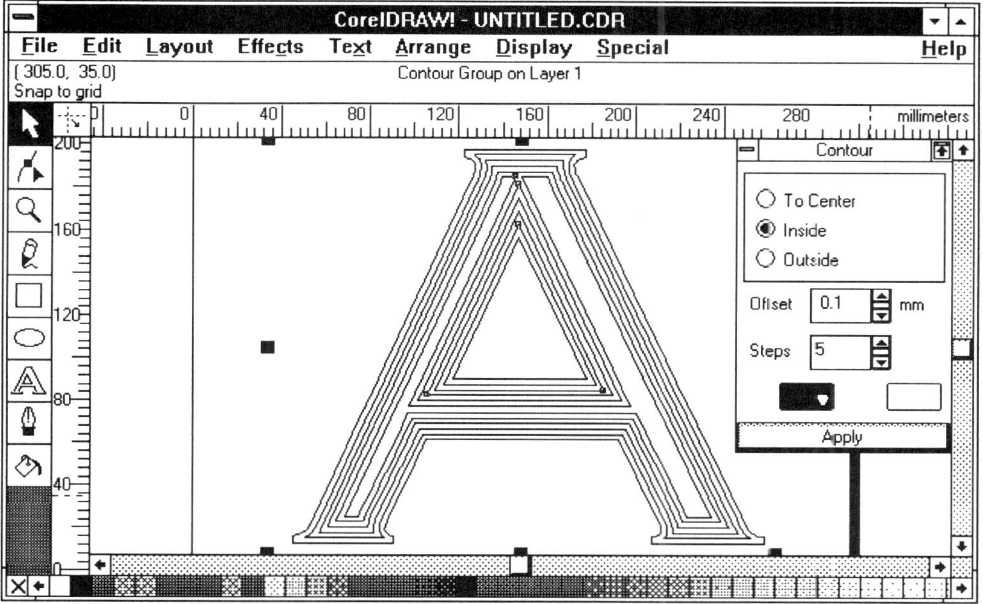

18.04 Letter contoured

3   Equally with very large letters you can use **To Centre**. This will give you the same kind of effect as the previous step but the program determines the steps.

You can also contour shapes that contain fountain fills or other fills. The additional objects will try to blend using the same colours from the original to the final additional shape. You can get some very beautiful images in this way. However, contouring a filled object needs resources and takes time. Play with the contour and discover its capabilities.

19. STYLES

Because CorelDRAW 4 now has DTP capability, you can use styles to quickly and easily change text. You can also use styles for graphics though. Being able to define your own styles and use them can save you a lot of time and effort. A style may consist of just about anything, outline, fill, effect, text attributes, and they are very easy to create.

1   Start a new page. Draw a series of eleven squares, each 25 mms to a side. Outline each in turn with different line thicknesses, the first one with 0.2 points, the second with 1 point, the third with 2 points and so on until the final one had an outline of 10 points. Deselect all the squares.

2   Press **Ctrl-F5**, or open the **Layout** menu and click on **Styles Roll-up**, and the roll-up will appear.

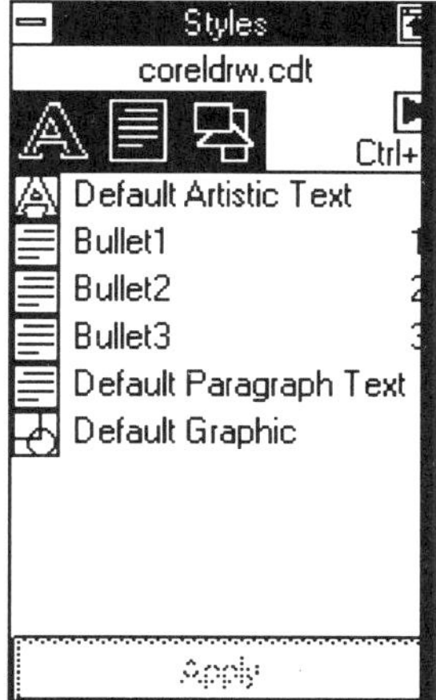

19.01 Styles Roll-up

3   Arrange the roll-up and it will move to the top right hand corner of the screen. Open it out again and you see that it contains a number of predefined styles - mainly text based but there is one called Default Graphic.

4   If you click on any of the squares on the page then the text styles in the roll-up will vanish and you'll be left with Default Graphic. Don't click on Apply or the square will change to bear the default attributes you have already set for graphic objects.

5   Click on the square that has the 1 point outline to select it. With the right mouse button click and hold on the square. The **Object Menu** will appear after a couple of seconds. Click on Save As Style and a large dialogue box appears.

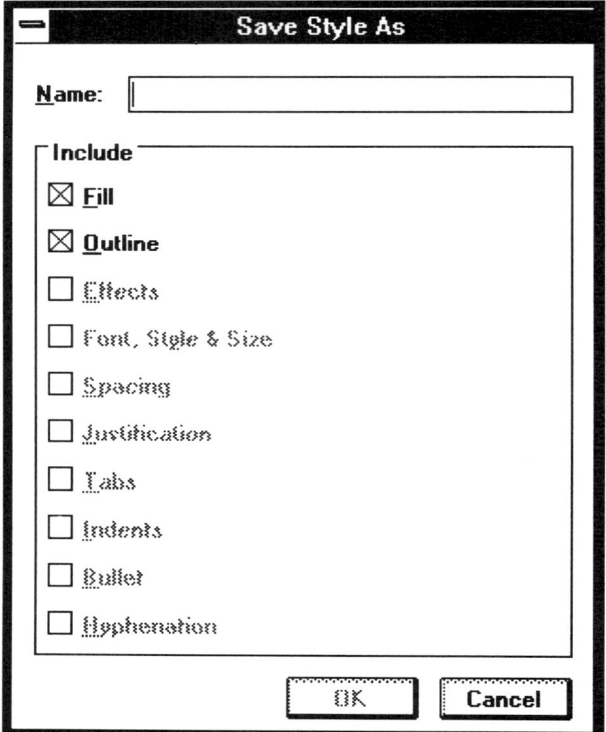

19.02 Save Style As dialogue box

6   Give the Style a name, e.g. 1 Point Outline, and deselect Fill. Then click on **OK**. The new style will be added to the roll-up. Do the same thing for all the squares on the page, naming each one x Point Outline where x is the line thickness. You should end up with the roll-up looking like figure 19.03.

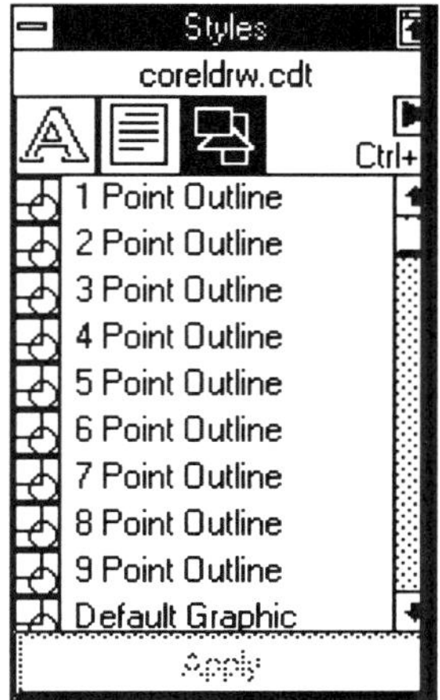

19.03 New Graphic Styles

7   To apply any of the new styles, simply select the object you want to change, select a style and click on **Apply**. The program does the rest for you.

8   You can create graphic styles that include any outline attributes or any kind of fill that you wish. It means that if there is a graphic format that you need very often you need only create it once, define it as a style and have it available.

9   To delete a style, select the style you want to remove by highlighting it, click on the arrowhead in the roll-up and when the drop down menu appears, click on **Delete Style**. Be warned you do not get a request to confirm the deletion so if you selected the wrong style by mistake you'll have to recreate it.

STYLES ROLL-UP

The Style roll-up contains the names of all the styles that currently exist in a particular template. You can have a number of templates and have access to all of them. The roll-up is divided into three main areas.

Immediately below the roll-ups title bar is a name, e.g. CORELDRW.CDT. This is the **Template** that is currently in use. Below that are three icon buttons, each of which is a toggle. You can have any of the buttons turned on or off.

341

The first, bearing a large A, is for **Artistic Text Styles**. When it is turned on, the artistic text styles are shown in the roll-up.

Next to that is the **Paragraph Text Styles**. If the button is depressed then those styles are shown.

Finally there is a button with graphics on it, this is the **Graphics Styles**. When it is on the graphic styles are visible.

To the right of the buttons is an arrowhead that will cause a menu to drop down bearing the following commands:

Load Styles will bring up a loading dialogue box in which you can select any of the existing style templates to load. CorelDRAW 4 comes complete with 15 pre-created styles you can use, including the default one, and you can create as many as you need or have disk space for.

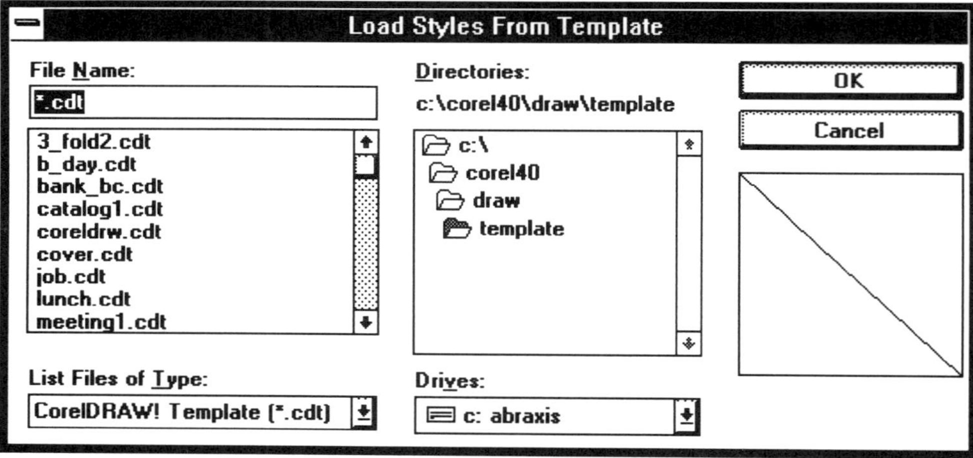

19.04 Load Styles dialogue box

Save Template brings up a dialogue box that allows you to create new template files. These are normally stored in the \TEMPLATE sub-directory. If you click on **With Contents** then the contents of the page are saved as well as the styles.

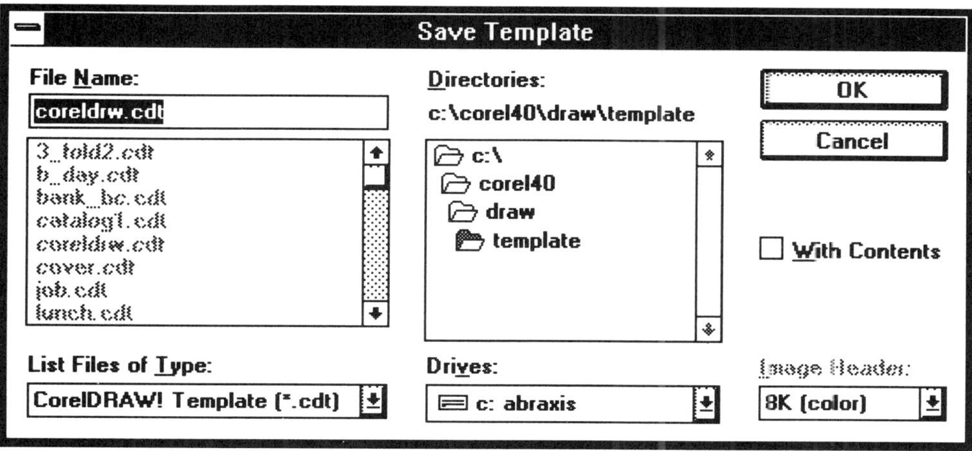

19.05 Save Template dialogue box

Set Hotkeys is only active for Paragraph Text styles. It allows you to set key combinations for the various styles. The program is already set to use **Ctrl-1** for Bullet 1, **Ctrl-2** for Bullet 2 and **Ctrl-3** for Bullet 3. In the dialogue box you can change any or all of these and assign additional combinations for extra styles. You can even do it automatically: clicking on **Auto Assign** will start assigning the keys from the first style to the last in the order they are listed.

Delete Style deletes the currently selected styles. Be warned you are not asked to confirm the deletion.

Find is a very useful way of searching for images or text that have had a style applied to them. Highlight a style in the roll-up and then click on Find. CorelDRAW then searches for the first object it can find that bears that style. Once it has found it, you have to reactivate the command (which will now say Find Next) to find subsequent usages. If you have selected a style that has not been used then nothing happens.

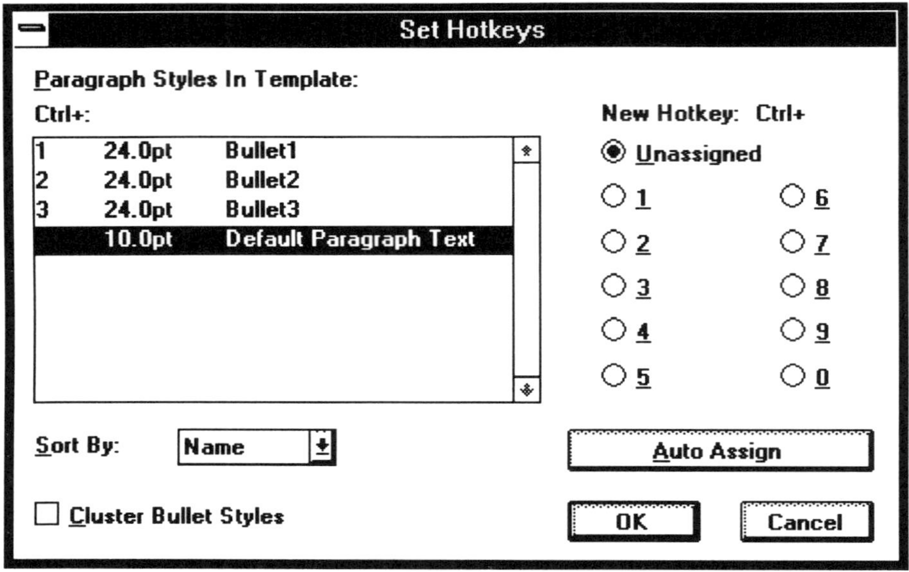

19.06 Set Hotkeys dialogue box

Finally there is the **Apply** button.

TEXT STYLES

You can also have as many text styles as you want or need and you create them in the same way as graphic styles.

1   Select the **Artistic Text** tool and place some text on the page. It will appear in the defaults you have already set.

2   Open the Text roll-up, **Ctrl-F2**, and change the text. For example, make it a different font and a different size.

3   Now click and hold on the text with the right hand mouse button. In the object menu click on **Save as Style**. You'll get the Save Style As dialogue box and this time you'll have some extra parameters that you can set. Give the style a name, e.g. the font and size, and then click on **OK**. The style is then added to the Styles roll-up.

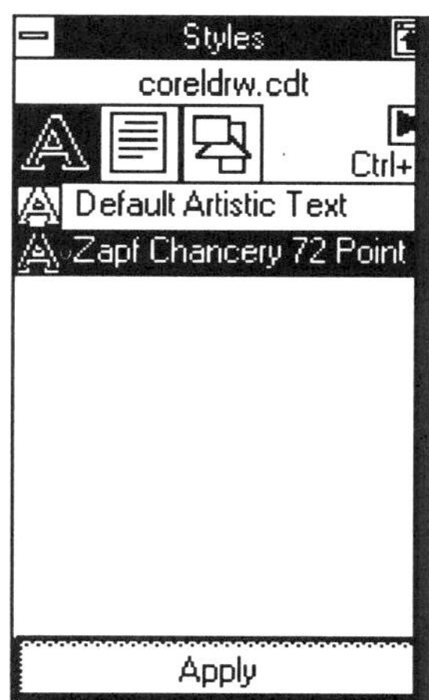

19.07 New Artistic Style

4   You can create as many styles as you need and save them as a template if you wish.

5   Activate the Paragraph Text tool, **Shift-F8**, and place some text on the page. It will appear in the Default Paragraph Text style. Make whatever changes you wish and then save it as a style. If it is a style you will use frequently it is worth assigning it to a key combination.

Object Menu

The Object Menu allows you to do things with styles and objects. There isn't room in this book to cover all of the facilities so this is just an overview.

Save As Style brings up the dialogue box that allows you to set the characteristics and attributes for the style you want to create.

Update Style will bring up a dialogue box that allows you to amend the details and characteristics of the selected style.

Revert to Style will take the selected object and undo any changes you have made to it by reapplying the named style characteristics.

Apply Style pops out a menu that bears the possible style names for the object that you have selected. It's the equivalent of applying a style from the roll-up except that you only get the applicable styles.

Overprint Outline is for colour trapping in colour separations. The command is a toggle and applies to specific objects.

Overprint Fill used for colour separations as above.

Data Roll-up will bring up the Object Data roll-up and database. The full use of this is, unfortunately, outside the scope of this book but it will be included in the Advanced Guide.

20. Fonts

CorelDRAW 4 comes a huge number of fonts, over 750 of them, and they are available to you in both TrueType and Adobe Type 1 formats. When you install the program you only get a limited number of fonts, roughly 100 of them. If you want to install the remainder you must have a CD-ROM because that's where they are. You cannot have the extra fonts otherwise.

Adding TrueType Fonts

There is a special installation program on the CD-ROM that allows you to install extra fonts. It's called FONTINST and you'll find it on CD-ROM Disk 1. It only installs the TrueType fonts, you have to do the Abode Type 1 fonts differently. You can run this program at any time to add additional fonts to your system.

1   Run Windows File Manager. Log on to the CD-ROM drive and double click on **FONTINST.EXE**. Alternatively, using Program Manager and do **File, Run**. and then enter **[CD-drive]:\FONTINST.EXE**. You'll get a little message box telling you that the program is being initialised and then the first set window appears.

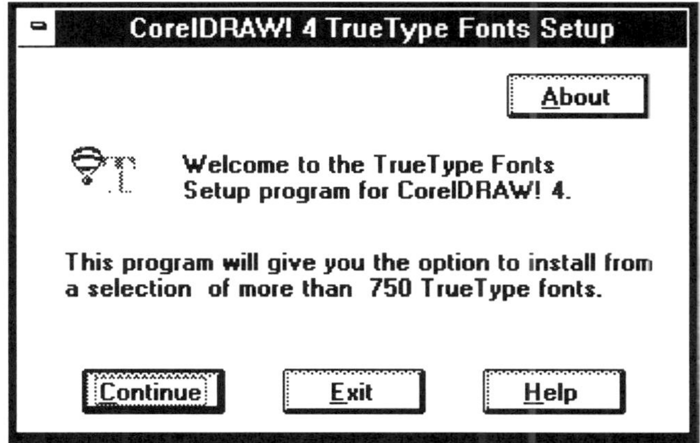

20.01 Font Installation start

2   Click on **Continue** and you'll get a second dialogue box that allows you to set the destination path for the new fonts. Set the path to be whatever you wish. Normally you would place TrueType in the **WINDOWS\SYSTEM** directory but because there are so many of them you are well advised to place them into their own separate location.

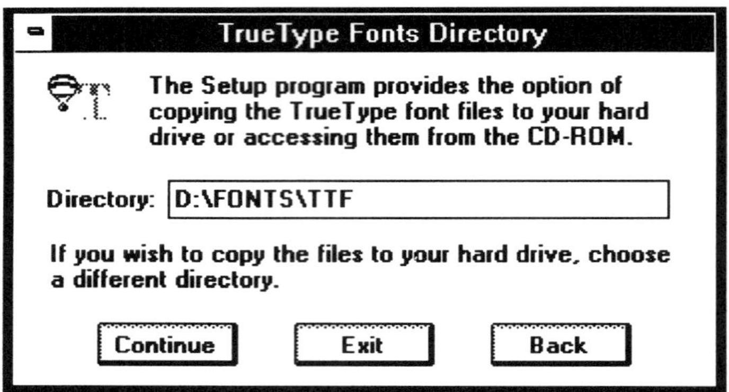

20.02 Set Path dialogue box

3   There will be a slight delay and then another dialogue box appears. In this you can set which fonts you want to have installed. To know what is in each category check the front of the Clip-Art manual where all the fonts are listed. To select a category just click on the button beside it. As you add more fonts so the **Space Required** will be reported along the bottom of the dialogue box. If you installed all the fonts you would need a minimum of 36,568 Kb or nearly 36 Mb!

TrueType Fonts Selection

Select the font groups you want to include or use Customize to choose using font names. The Font Groups are described in the Corel Libraries Catalog.

- [ ] Basic
- [ ] Casual
- [ ] Design
- [ ] Formal
- [ ] Education

- [ ] Fun
- [ ] Presentation
- [ ] Printer Fonts
- [ ] Publisher
- [ ] Signs

- [ ] Technical
- [ ] Template
- [ ] Theater
- [ ] Upgrade 3
- [ ] Assorted ------> Customize

Fonts Selected
0

Drive: Space required: Space available:
C: 0 K   19290 K

Continue   Exit   Back   Help

20.03 Selection dialogue box

4   If you want to install all the fonts - which means you either have a huge hard disk or are given to grandiose gestures or both - then you can click on **Assorted** and then on **Customise**. You then get another dialogue box wherein you can select all the fonts there are.

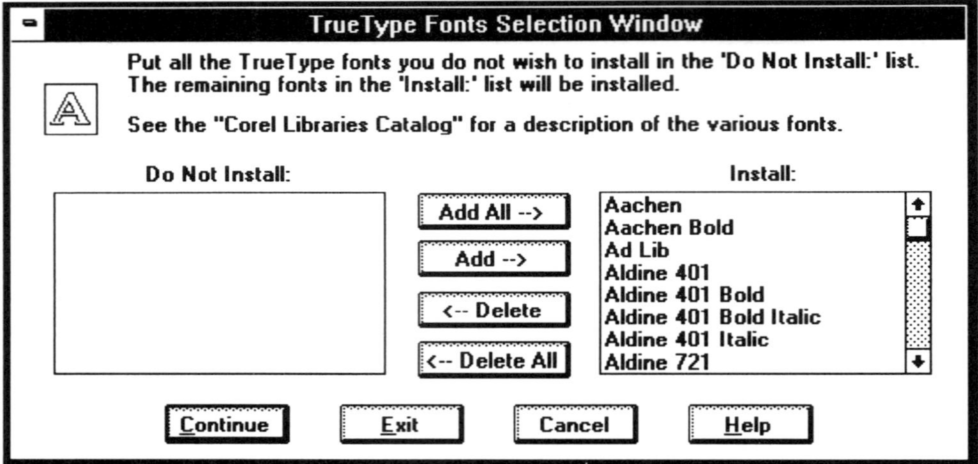

20.04 Customised selection

5   Once you have the fonts selected, click on **Continue** and the process begins. You'll get a message box telling you how far the process has gone as the fonts are added.

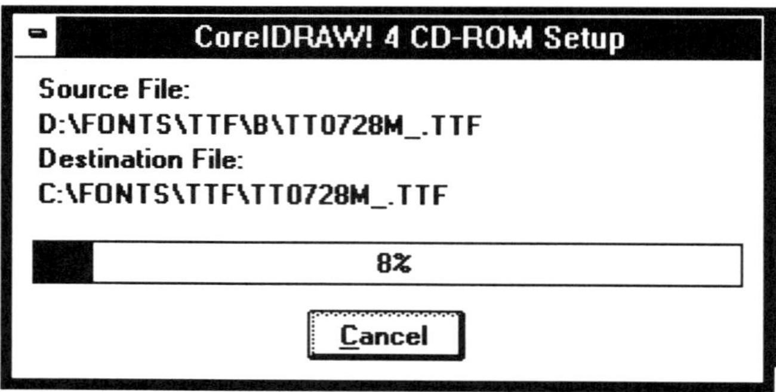

20.05 Adding fonts

6   Finally you get another message box telling you that the process is completed. Click on **OK** to close the program. The fonts will have been added to your WIN.INI automatically as part of the process.

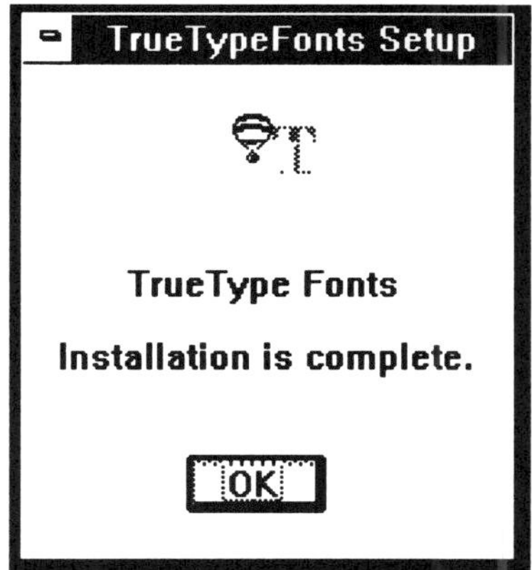

20.06 Process Complete

7   You can then remove any fonts you don't want or need using Windows **Control Panel, Fonts**.

ADDING ATM FONTS

There is no rapid installation process for Adobe Type 1 fonts so you have to do it manually. By the way it helps if you have Adobe Type Manager 2.5 when it comes to using these. Don't try adding fonts to Type Manager directly from the CD-ROM, it takes too long and ATM doesn't like it much.

1   Open Windows **File Manager**. Log in to the **\PSFONTS** directory on whichever drive it is on.

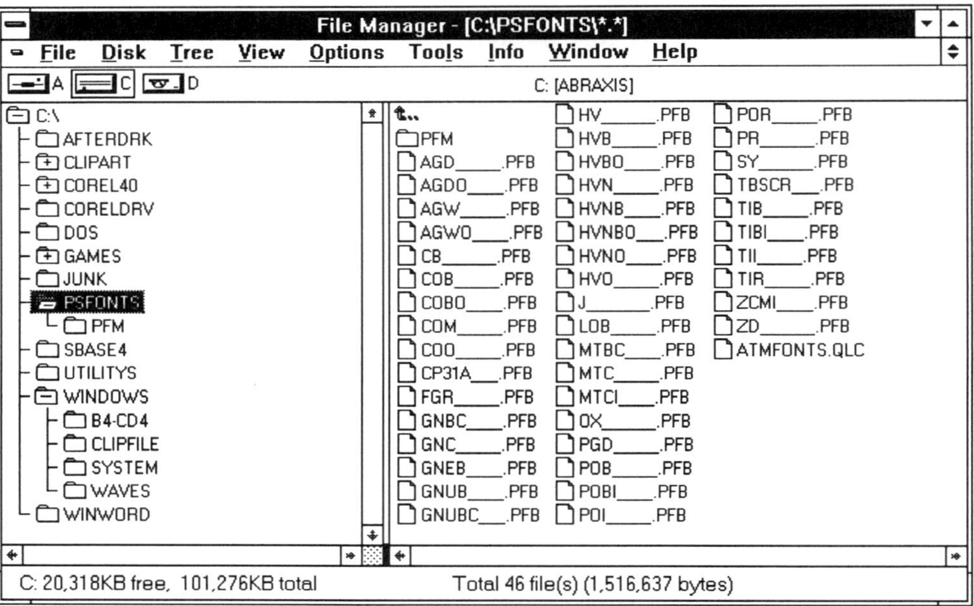

20.07 File Manager

2   You need CD-ROM Disk 1 in the drive. Double click on the **\FONTS** directory and it will open up to display three sub-directories. **ATM** contains the Adobe fonts, **TTF** contains the TrueType fonts and **WFN** contains the symbols. (By the way, 16 of the symbol libraries are only available as TrueType fonts.)

3   Double click on **ATM** and you'll get the next series of sub-directories. All the fonts are stored in alphabetical directories, e.g. all the A's together and so on.

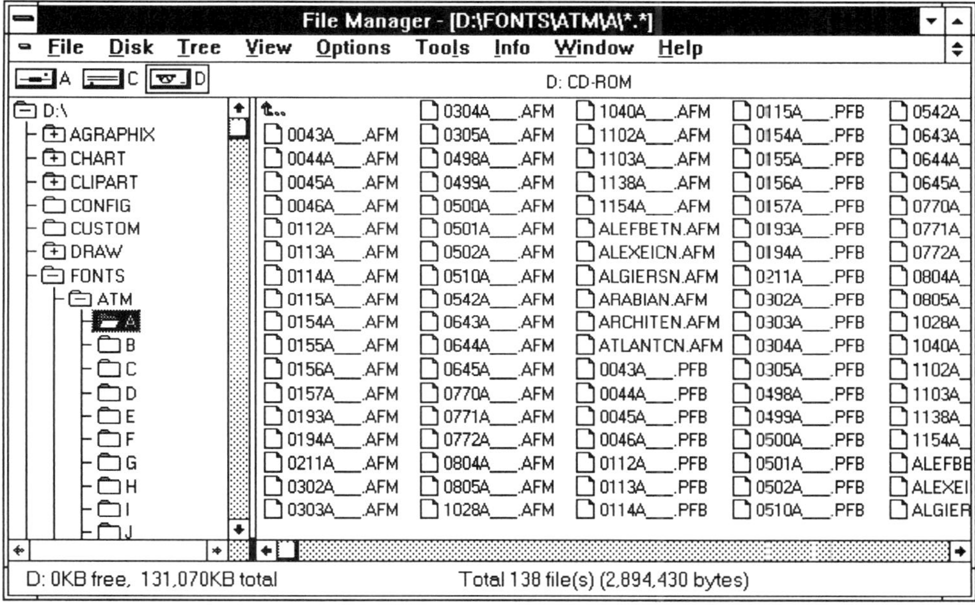

20.08 Correct directory

4   Log on to whichever sub-directory contains the files you want. You'll find that there are AFM, PFB and PFM files in each one. You don't need the AFM fonts for Windows so you can ignore them. Select the **PFB** files of whichever fonts you want to add to your system and then drag them to the icon for the drive that contains the PSFONTS directory, e.g. Drive-C. Release the mouse button once you are over the icon and the files will be copied to the correct drive and directory.

5   Once that is completed, select all the corresponding files with extensions of **PFM**. Press **F8** and you'll get a dialogue box. One the second line, labelled **To**, type **[drive]\PSFONTS\PFM** and then hit return. The files will be copied to the correct directory.

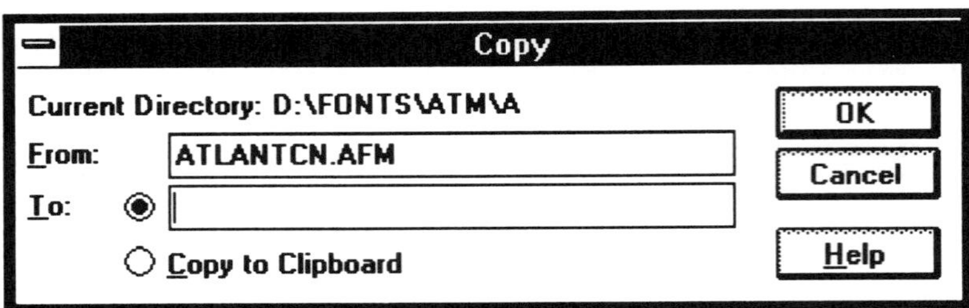

20.09 Copy Files dialogue box

6   Once you've copied all the files you want to your hard disk, run **ATM**. Click on **Add** which brings up a dialogue box. In the Directories window click on **[PFM]** and the available fonts will be displayed. Select the ones you want and then click on **Add** for the fonts to be added. If you use a version of ATM earlier that 2.5 you have to reboot Windows, otherwise you don't have to.

Font Notes

Thanks to CorelDRAW people these days probably have more fonts than they have ever had before and it is arguable about whether or not they need them. Certainly for the vast majority of people there should be no need to have more than about half a dozen fonts installed on your system and ready for use. By all means have the others available but don't have them loaded.

If you were to install all 750 plus fonts that is supplied with CorelDRAW 4 as TrueType fonts you are going to run into horrendous problems on two counts.

a. The WIN.INI file cannot exceed a certain size, 32 Kb to be precise. Well, it can but it will ignore anything that goes over that limit. Because the fonts are usually listed in the middle of the file and program definitions are listed at the end you may well find that some of your program won't work - because they are beyond the 32 Kb limit.

b. Windows itself will take forever to load and run because you have the fonts installed. Your resources will drop through the floor and everything will slow down to a snail's pace - even on the most powerful machine.

The answer is to load the fonts on to your system but then be selective about which ones you actually have installed at any one time. If you need a particular font, install it, use it and then remove it. It's a bit more fiddly but it is much cleaner and neater.

ATM fonts are easier to handle and don't eat your resources in the same way but even with these you should only add the fonts you actually need at any time, use them and then remove them again.

By the way, never use Courier as a font. It is the default for all PostScript printers and so if it appears on your print out you know that something has gone wrong.

There is a rule of design that says you should not have more than six fonts on any one page - and don't forget that a font can be a printing effect, a size, a weight or any combination of these. It is a good rule to stick to because it teaches disciplined design.

When it comes to using fonts CorelDRAW will look for them in a hierarchical order. Firstly it looks for TrueType fonts, secondly it looks for Adobe Type 1 fonts and finally it searches for WFN fonts. So if you had all the TrueType, Adobe Type 1 and the old WFN fonts loaded - granting that only some of the fonts are available as WFN fonts - CorelDRAW will never find the Adobe and WFN ones. It will find the TrueType fonts and stop there.

So the moral of the story is decide which font technology you want to use and stick to it. Don't bother loading the other technology because either it or the old one will be redundant. Besides which, with disk space at a premium you don't need to waste the space.

DEFINITIONS

The following are some basic definitions about typefaces, fonts and DTP.

Ascender

An ascender is that portion of a letter or character which rises above the main body of the letter space, i.e. the upward strokes in b, d, f, h, k, l and t. In fact the letter 't' is referred to as having a semi-ascender because the upward stroke does not rise as high as the other ascending letters. Compare Descender.

Baseline

The imaginary line along which type is laid so that the bottom of the letters or characters, excluding any descenders, is even and true.

Descender

A descender is the term applied to that part of a letter which drops below the main body of the letter, i.e. it is printed below the baseline of the text. Letters which have descenders are g, j, p, q, y and the upper case Q. In some typefaces an upper case J will also have a descender. Compare Ascender.

Desk Top Publishing

Usually abbreviated to DTP. The process of using a computer and software to create text and graphics which can then be imported into a special program, such as PageMaker, and composed to produce either finished documents or Camera Ready Artwork. The term was invented by Paul Brainerd, the creator of PageMaker.

Double Page Spread

Any pair of Facing Pages that are considered and dealt with as a large single page. Used primarily in magazines and newspapers.

DPI

Abbreviation for Dots Per Inch. The basic method of measuring the quality of a laser printer's output. All laser printers are capable of producing a maximum of 300 dpi which is of sufficient quality for their output to be used for the production of printing plates. Some printers can now produce 400, 600 or even 800 dpi, however for the higher resolutions you must use micro-fine toner which is more expensive than normal.

Drop Shadow

An enhancement to a graphic that creates an apparent shadow behind it and so makes the graphic much more dynamic. Drop shadows need not be black, they can be any colour or density. Creating drop shadows in CorelDRAW is easy. Just duplicate the text, fill it with the shadow colour, move it behind the original text and then nudge it slightly down and to one side.

Em

(Sense 1) A measurement used by printers to define a square space. As every point size has an associated Em space it may be any size from 6-Point upwards. The Em is always referred to by its point size, e.g. 6-Point Em, 122-Point Em. Thus a 12-Point em is a square 12 points wide by 12 points high.

(Sense 2) A printers' standard unit of measurement of the width and depth of a page. In this case it always measures one sixth of a linear inch, i.e. 12-Points, so that a page which is 6-inches by 4-inches can be referred to 36 Ems by 24 Ems.

En

Exactly one half the width of an Em (sense 1) used as a measure of the space between words and/or characters. Thus a 12-Point En is 12 points high but only six points wide. Some typefaces, notably Times Roman and Helvetica, within PageMaker use En spaces as the standard for Word spacing.

Facing pages

Any two pages which bear text and/or graphics that face each other. Normally the left hand page bears an even number while the right hand one bears an odd

357

one, e.g. 110 and 111. A double page spread must be facing pages but facing pages are not, necessarily, a double page spread though it usually is.

Font

A sub-set of a typeface. A font means a collection of characters that all bear the same characteristics. For example, Helvetica is a typeface but Helvetica 12-Point is a font. The words font and typeface are the most misused words in computing. They tend to be used indiscriminately and get interchanged without allowing for the fact that both words have definite meanings.

Kerning

A method of manipulating the spaces between individual characters, and occasionally whole words, which is used to enhance the appearance of the text on the printed page. Originally it was special type, used by printers, that possessed extra width on the blocks to allow an increase in spacing, e.g. vertical leading. You kern characters in CorelDRAW using the Node Edit tool.

Sans Serif

Applied to a typeface that has no embellishments on the characters. Helvetica is the best known example. This paragraph uses a serifed typeface, Palatino, while the heading is sans serif.

Serif

The little embellishments that appear on some typefaces. Originally developed when letters were carved on stone, the serifs allowed the stonemason to finish carving the letters neatly. Serif typefaces, e.g. Palatino, Times Roman, are much easier to read than sans serif ones, e.g. Helvetica.

Typeface

A set of characters which are all related to each other. Created by a designer and normally covered by copyright. Examples of typefaces are Helvetica, Times Roman, Zapf Humanist. Typefaces contain families, called Fonts , which refer to the size of the typeface. Unfortunately the words font and typeface are the most misused words in computing. The words are not interchangeable because they refer to different things.

21. Menus

In the course of this book you will have used many of the commands that CorelDRAW 4 provides you with but not all of them - simply because there is not sufficient room to cover them all in a book of this length. This chapter give you a run-down on all of the commands available, broken down in menu order.

Control Box

The Control Box is the little square in the extreme top left hand corner of the window. It is common to all Windows applications and each one shares the same basic commands - regardless of the program.

Restore will return the current window or icon to its previous state. To quickly change an icon to an open window just double click on the icon. To quickly close a program just double click on the Control Box because the **Close** command is active by default.

Move allows you to move the window around on the screen using the keyboard. It's actually much easier to do this with the mouse by simply dragging the Title bar - the thing that runs along the top of the window and which contains the program name.

Size allows you to resize and reshape an open window using the keyboard. Again it's much easier to use the mouse, just drag any side of the window to resize it.

Minimise means reduce the window to an icon. You can do the same thing with a mouse by clicking on the downwards pointing arrow at the end of the Title Bar.

Maximise does the reverse of the above. It will expand the window to fill the entire available screen area. You can do the same thing by double clicking on the Title bar or single clicking on the upwards pointing arrow at the end of the Title Bar.

Close shuts down the program.

Switch To brings up a dialogue box that allows you to do different things. You can activate the dialogue box by pressing **Ctrl-Esc**.

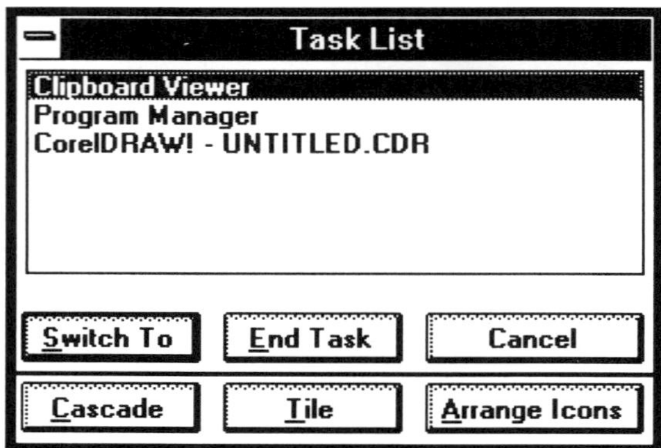

21. 01 Switch To dialogue box

Switch To allows you to switch to another program. Just click on the program name you want to run and then on this button. Alternatively just double click on the program name.

End Task will close an application for you. Just highlight the one you want to close and then click on the button.

Cancel closes the dialogue box.

Cascade will arrange all the open windows into small overlapping windows. At the same time any icons will be repositioned starting at the lower left hand corner of the screen.

Tile will arrange all the open windows so that each occupies roughly the same amount of screen area. The icons will also be shifted as above.

Arrange Icons just moves the icons but leaves the windows alone.

FILE MENU

The File menu is concerned primarily with the input and output of files.

New, which you can activate with **Ctrl-N**, starts a new document. If you have changed the current document then you will be prompted about saving it before the new file opens.

New From Template lets you start a new file using styles from the selected template file. Obviously you have to have created a template first. Template files have an extension of .CDT and the program comes complete with a single sample file called CORELDRW.CDT.

Open loads an existing file. The keyboard shortcut is **Ctrl-O**. Use the dialogue box to find the file you want anywhere on your system.

Save, Ctrl-S, saves the current file to the existing filename.

Save As allows you to save a file to a new filename. It is this command that actually runs when you first save an unnamed file.

Import brings up a dialogue box that allows you to import files in a variety of formats. Just select the file type, the correct directory or disk and then the filename. To import any file type you must have the necessary filter installed.

Export allows you to save CorelDRAW files in a variety of different formats, e.g. for use with other programs.

Insert Object embeds an object from another OLE aware program. The OLE aware programs are listed in your WIN.INI file under the section that says [embedding].

Print activates the print dialogue box. You can use **Ctrl-P** instead of the menu.

Print Merge activates another dialogue box that allows you to merge text from a word processed document with the current file and so produce form letters.

Print Setup produces a dialogue box that allows you to nominate a printer or change the settings of the existing printer.

CorelDRAW 4 - A Users Guide

Exit closes the program.

1, 2, 3, 4 lists the last four files that you saved or had open. You can reload any of these by opening the menu and then pressing **Alt-[number]**.

This is a bit of a hodge podge in every Windows program. Basically it contains the Windows Clipboard commands but it also contains other editing type commands.

Undo cancels your last action. CorelDRAW allows you to set multiple levels of undo and repeated use of the command progressively undoes your actions. A high number of levels though will use up resources and memory. The keyboard shortcuts are **Alt-Backspace** or **Ctrl-Z**.

Redo cancels the undo action.

Repeat re-enacts you last used command or action. You can use this as a shortcut to perform the same action on a number of objects. The keyboard shortcut is **Ctrl-R**.

Cut is the Windows Clipboard command that copies the selected object and then deletes it from the file. The keyboard shortcuts are **Shift-Del** or **Ctrl-X**.

Copy is similar to the above but it just copies the selected object. The keyboard shortcuts are **Ctrl-Ins** or **Ctrl-C**.

Paste copies the contents of the Windows Clipboard into the current file. You can paste as many times as you wish as the contents of the Clipboard do not change until you do another Cut or Copy. The keyboard shortcuts are **Shift-Ins** or **Ctrl-V**.

Paste Special activates the OLE link facility dialogue box. A linked file can be changed and the change will apply to every copy of the file in all Windows applications.

Delete removes the currently selected object(s) from the file. It's quicker to just press **Del**.

"

Duplicate makes a copy of the selected object and moves it by whatever increments you have set in the Preferences dialogue box. The keyboard shortcut is **Ctrl-D**.

Clone is similar to Duplicate but any changes you make to the original object will be applied to all the copies.

Copy Attributes From will bring up a dialogue box, you can use any combinations of the commands it contains to copy those from one object to another.

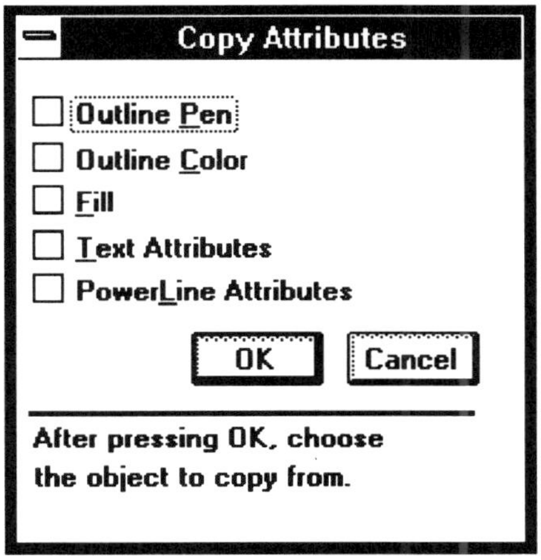

21.02 Copy Attributes dialogue box

Select All is useful as it allows you to select every object in the file even if you cannot see them all.

Object allows you to edit an embedded object.

Links brings up a dialogue box that gives you the current status of all existing linked objects.

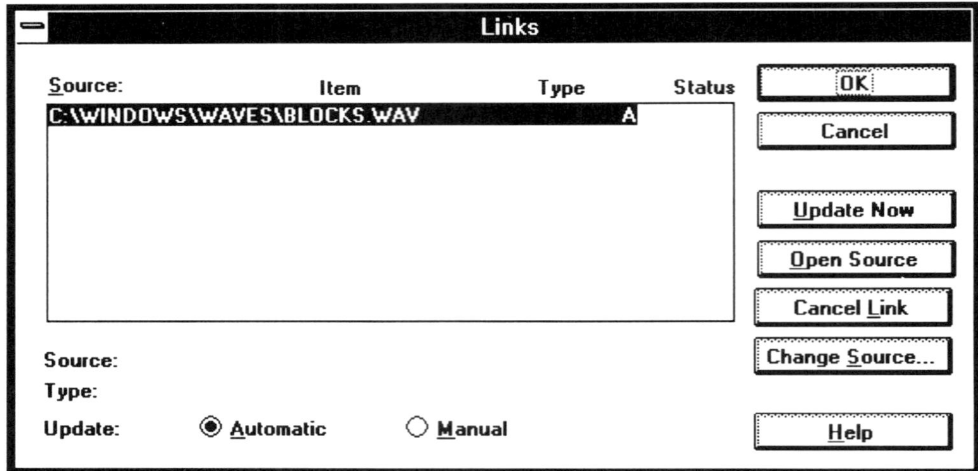

21.03 Link dialogue box

LAYOUT MENU

The layout menu is concerned with the way that the page appears and what it contains.

Insert Page allows you to add an extra page. It brings up a dialogue box that allows you to say how many pages you want to add and where you want to add them. You can use **PgUp** or **PgDn** as keyboard shortcuts.

Delete Page removes the current page. It is only active if you have two or more pages in the document. You'll get a dialogue box that allows you to delete either the current page or a nominated range of pages.

Go To Page allows you to do just that. It brings up a dialogue box wherein you can select the page you want to move to. Alternatively use the page indicator at the left hand side of the palette.

Page Setup is used to set the page size and makeup. You can also access the dialogue box by double clicking on the on-screen page border.

Layer Roll-up brings up the roll-up and positions it roughly where it should be on screen. **Ctrl-F3** is the keyboard shortcut.

Styles Roll-up brings up the roll-up. The keyboard shortcut is **Ctrl-F5**.

Grid Setup activates a dialogue box that allows you set the grid.

Guidelines Setup brings up the Status Bar dialogue box that allows you to add, remove or move guidelines. If you already have a guideline on the page then you can get the same thing by double clicking on a guide.

Snap To pops-out a menu that allows you to set the snap to options:

> **Snap to Grid** makes everything align itself to the grid. You can only move things to the grid points with this command.
>
> **Snap to Guidelines** will make objects snap to the nearest guideline - if they are close enough.
>
> **Snap to Objects** causes objects to align to each other. Each object has a number of snap to points, the exact number depends on the object in question, and other objects can align themselves to these.

EFFECTS MENU

This menu is concerned mainly with the effects that you can generate in CorelDRAW, most of the commands bring up dialogue boxes.

> **Rotate & Skew** allows you to rotate or skew the selected object(s). The keyboard shortcut is **Alt-F8**.
>
> **Stretch & Mirror** allows you to resize a selected object or flip it through either axis. The keyboard shortcut is **Alt-F9**.
>
> **Add Perspective** allows you to edit the perspective of selected objects. It doesn't have a dialogue box.
>
> **Envelope Roll-up** gives you the roll-up. The keyboard shortcut is **Ctrl-F7**.

CorelDRAW 4 - A Users Guide

Blend Roll-up activates the roll-up. The keyboard shortcut is **Ctrl-B**.

Extrude Roll-up gives you the roll-up. The keyboard shortcut is **Ctrl-E**.

Contour Roll-up opens the roll-up. The keyboard shortcut is **Ctrl-F9**.

Powerline Roll-up opens the roll-up. The keyboard shortcut is **Ctrl-F8**.

Clear Effect will clear the most recent effects that have been applied to the selected object, in effect undoing it. It will not necessarily clear all effects.

Copy Effect from pops out a menu that will allow you to:

> **Copy Perspective From** allows you to apply the same perspective to another object.

> **Copy Envelope From** gives you a quick way of applying the same envelope editing to another object.

Clear Transformations cancels some of the effects and transformations that you have applied to an object.

TEXT MENU

This gives you lots of commands that affect the text directly.

> **Text Roll-up** brings up the roll-up. Use **Ctrl-F2** as the shortcut.

> **Character** will bring up the **Character Attributes** dialogue box wherein you can change the definition of any individual character.

> **Frame** brings up the Paragraph Frame dialogue box that allows you to adjust the frame containing the text.

> **Fit Text to Path** allows you to place text on paths in a multitude of different ways. The keyboard shortcut is **Ctrl-F**.

> **Align To Baseline** will align all the selected text to the baseline of that text, i.e. if you moved things it puts them back. The keyboard equivalent is **Alt-F10**.

366

Straighten Text realigns all the text that has been moved, it also cancels any text rotation by resetting characters angles to 0 degrees.

Spell Checker activates the spell checker.

Thesaurus activates the thesaurus.

Find allows you to search for selected words or phrases in a text string.

Replace is similar to the above but it also gives you the option of replacing the designated text string with another.

Edit Text gives you the dialogue box. The keyboard shortcut is **Ctrl-T**.

ARRANGE MENU

This menu is concerned with the how and where of things on screen.

The **Move** dialogue box allows you to move selected objects in very precise increments. You also have the option of leaving the original behind and so effectively duplicating and moving an object in one step. The keyboard alternative is **Alt-F7**.

Align allows you rearrange the object(s) positions on the page. The keyboard shortcut is **Ctrl-A**.

Order will pop out a menu that allows you to move the selected object(s) within the stack on the current layer. There are keyboard shortcuts for each option.

Group will take the selected object and form them into a unit so that any changes or movements made to one will affect the whole. Grouped objects take up more memory than individual objects. The keyboard shortcut is **Ctrl-G**.

Ungroup is the opposite of the above - it restores grouped objects to individual objects.

CorelDRAW 4 - A Users Guide

Combine will take the selected objects and amalgamate them into a single object. Where there are an odd number of overlapping objects you will get a solid, where there are an even number of overlapping objects you will get a hole. The keyboard shortcut is **Ctrl-L**.

Break Apart reverses a combination. The objects are disassembled back into individual objects - all of which will bear the fill and outline attributes of the combined object. The keyboard shortcut is **Ctrl-K**.

Weld is similar to combine but different in that the lines of the overlapping objects are erased so that the selected objects now have a single outline.

Separate breaks the dynamic link between blended, extruded, fitted and contoured objects.

Convert to Curves takes the selected real object, e.g. an ellipse, rectangle or text, and turns it into a Bezier drawn object. The keyboard shortcut is **Ctrl-Q**.

Display Menu

This menu is concerned with what appears on screen.

Show Rulers is a toggle that turns the ruler on or off. (A toggle simply means it is either on, i.e. it has a tick beside it, or off, i.e. it doesn't have a tick beside it. Most toggle switches will use the tick indicator.) The ruler measurements are set according to the setting in the Grid Setup dialogue box.

Show Status Line is another toggle that controls the Status Bar.

Colour Palette pops out a menu that allows you to set which palette will be displayed along the bottom of the screen.

Floating Toolbox turns the toolbox, normally on the left hand side of the screen, into a free moving sub-window that you can position anywhere on the available screen area.

Edit Wireframe can be useful when you have an image with lots of complex fills or lots of text. Again it is a toggle. In wireframe mode you do not get the full outline and fill attributes being display, everything appears as outlines only. The keyboard shortcut is **Shift-F9**.

Refresh Window simply redraws everything. The keyboard shortcut is **Ctrl-W**.

Show Bitmaps is another toggle. With it turned on, which it is by default, any bitmap you import appears properly. If you turn it off then they appear as grey boxes only.

Show Preview gives you a full screen view of the current file without the CorelDRAW window. To go back to the ordinary window just hit any key.

Preview Selected Only is another toggle. With it turned on the preview screen shows only the selected object.

SPECIAL MENU

This menu contains commands that don't fit anywhere else.

Create Pattern allows you to create either bitmap or vector patterns.

Create Arrow allows you to create arrows that can be applied to the ends of open lines.

Create Symbol allows you to create new symbols - but only if you are using TrueType!

Extract saves text objects as a TXT file that you can then process elsewhere.

Merge Back inserts the text back into the file after it is extracted.

On-Screen Keyboard will only appear if you have a graphics tablet installed. It allows for entering text and accessing the function keys with a pen.

22. MOSAIC

CorelMOSAIC has been with us since Version 2 of CorelDRAW and it has always been one of my favourite Windows programs. It is a graphic file manager and one of the best I have ever seen. Mosaic 4 has been completely rewritten and enhanced and now it's even better than before. Mosaic displays the thumbnail, or header, images that are created with files. You can actually run Mosaic from within CorelDRAW - the Load and Import dialogue boxes contain a button to activate it - but I prefer to use it as a stand alone program.

SETTING DEFAULTS

1 In the CorelDRAW group window double click on the **Mosaic** icon - by the way all the CorelDRAW programs, except CorelCAPTURE and CorelMOVE, have a number of icons you can use instead of the defaults. The window will probably be an odd size, so double click on the Windows background and in the Switch To dialogue box that appears, click on **Tile**.

2 The window will be blank the first time you use it because you have not yet looked at any files. Before you do though it is worth setting the program defaults. Open the **File** menu and click on **Preferences** and you'll get a dialogue box.

3 The **Orientation** you use depends on yourself. By default, Mosaic is set to use Landscape but you have a choice of Portrait, Square or Custom.

4 The **Thumbnail Size** you set depends on your monitor and the resolution you are using. On a standard VGA 640 by 480 resolution monitor, a thumbnail size of 75 is fine and anything larger limits your field of view. If you are using a better resolution then you can increase it. The thumbnails are displayed in pixel sizes so that's what you are setting.

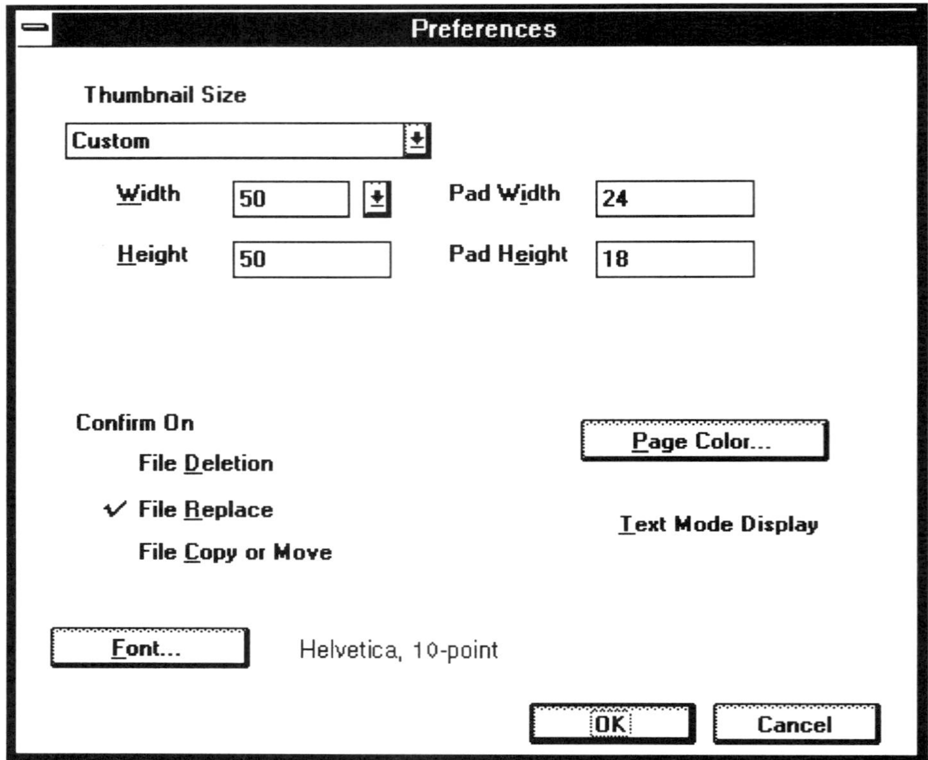

22.01 Preferences dialogue box

5   You can set the program to ask for confirmation of **File Deletion**, i.e. every time it deletes a file; **File Replace**, whenever you are replacing a file with the same name; or **File Copy or Move**. Personally, I leave just the middle one turned on.

6   Click on the button labelled **Paper Colour** and you'll get another dialogue box that allows you to set the background colour for the screen display.

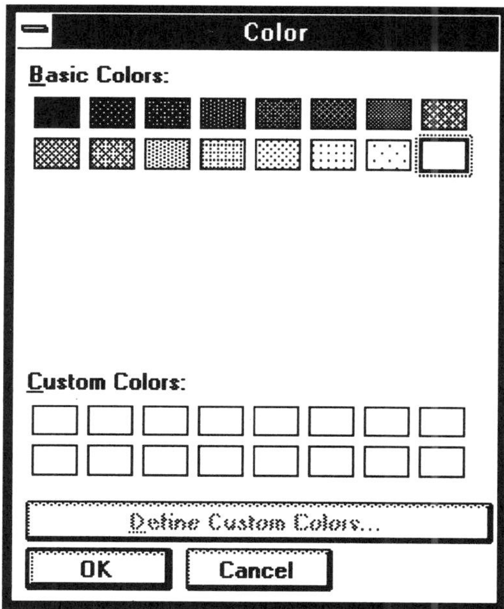

22.02 Screen Colour dialogue box

7   If you turn on **Text Mode Display** then you don't get the thumbnails being displayed, you get the filename and details instead.

8   Click on the button labelled **Font** and you'll get another dialogue box that allows you to set the font that will be used for the thumbnail names on screen. It's worth using the MS Sans Serif here because it's quick and easy to read.

9   Once you've set all the preferences, click on **OK** to close the dialogue box.

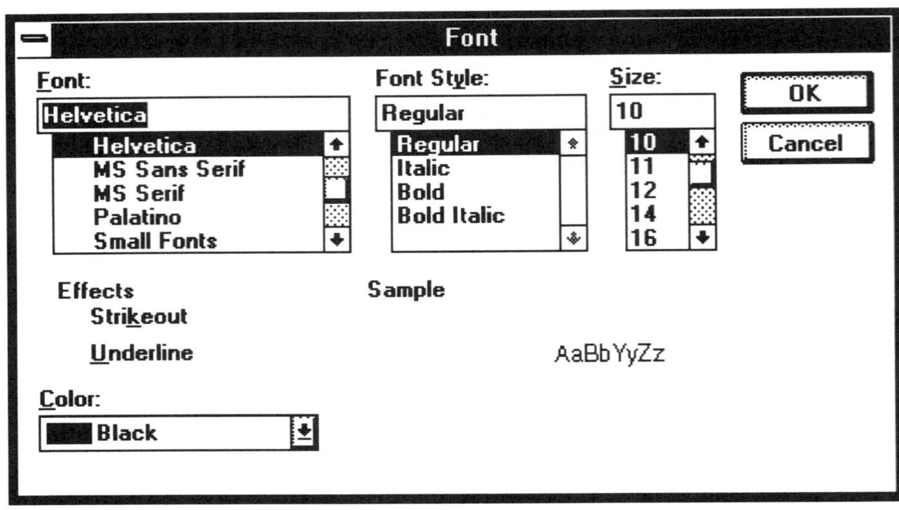

22.03 Font dialogue box

10   Open the **File** menu again and click on **Print Setup**. You'll get another dialogue box. Set the printer that you want to use and then close the box.

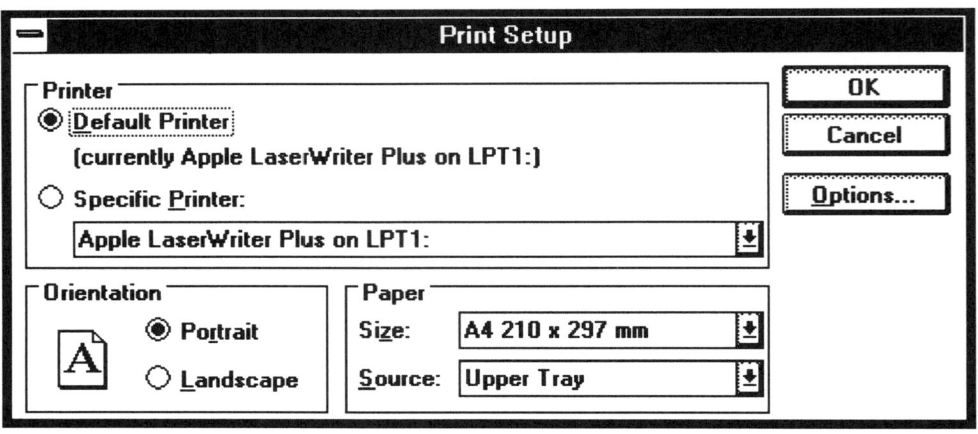

22.04 Printer Setup dialogue box

11 Open the **File** menu yet again and click on **Page Setup**. This dialogue box allows you to set the appearance of the pages that can be printed from Mosaic.

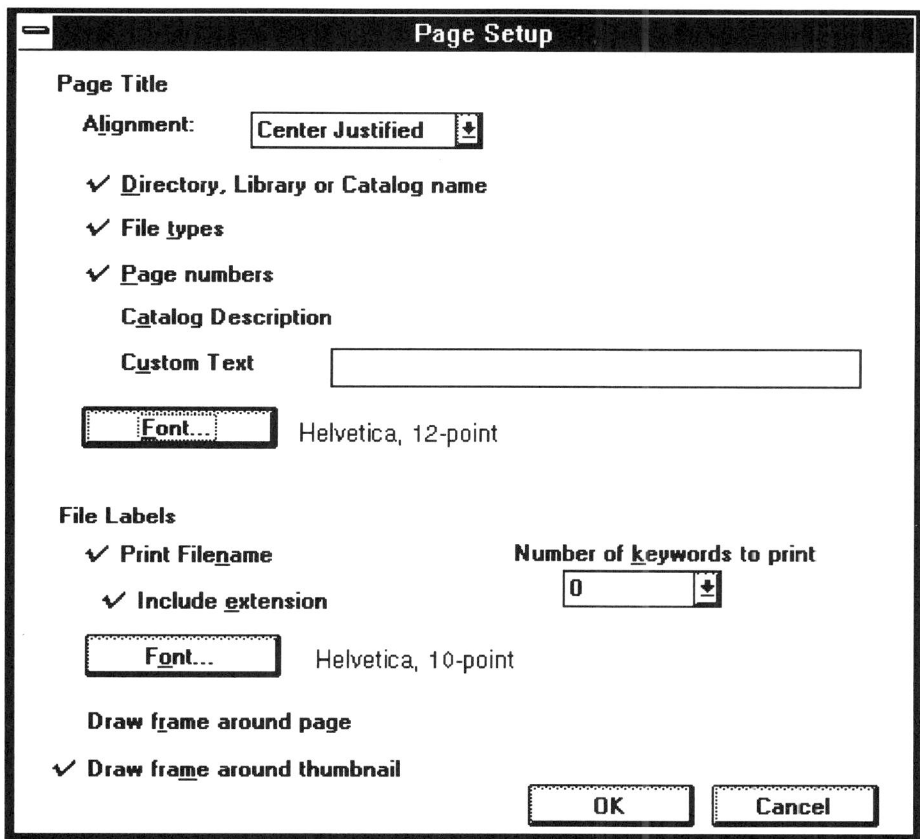

22.05 Page Setup dialogue box

12 Set the parameters for the printed page any way you wish. The **Alignment** determines where the page title, and you get one on each page, will appear. It is always a header. The next few lines define what will be printed by way of descriptive detail which is included with the title. **Directory, Library or Catalogue Name** is just that, the location of the files. **File Types** lists the types of files. **Page Numbers** gives you a page number on each page. **Catalogue**

Description prints the full description of the catalogue - which you define. Finally, **Custom Text** is a text string, of whatever you wish, that will be printed on each page.

13   Clicking on either **Font** button will give you the same sort of dialogue box as before, in Preferences, that allows you to set the printer font. Don't use MS Sans Serif for either of these though because you want a printer font.

14   **File Labels** are just that, the details that will be printed below each file. You can include the name and the extension if you wish. You also have the option of printing the **Keywords** that have been assigned to the files - always assuming there are keywords with the files in the first place.

15   The final commands are **Draw Frame around Page**, which prints a border on the page, and **Draw Frame around Thumbnail**, which border the image itself. Bear in mind that if you use borders then the print out will take that much longer to do.

16   Finally close the dialogue box in the usual way.

That's all the preferences set. The program will remember them all when you close it down.

USING MOSAIC

Mosaic 4 allows you to look in and display the contents of a number of different directories all at the same time. The first time you log into any directory though there will be a delay while Mosaic assimilates the information it contains. The more complex or more numerous the images the longer the delay for obvious reasons.

1   Press **Ctrl-D**, or open the **File** menu and click on **View Directory**. You'll get a dialogue box appearing that allows you to select a directory.

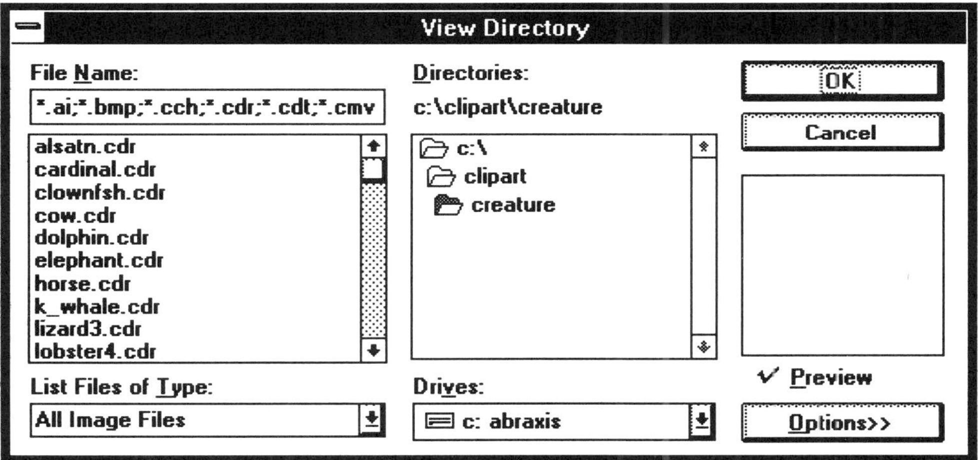

22.06 View directory dialogue box

2   Log into any directory that you know contains graphic files. You'll get a small sub-window appearing and gradually it will fill with the images in the directory. To see the full extent of the available space, maximise the window.

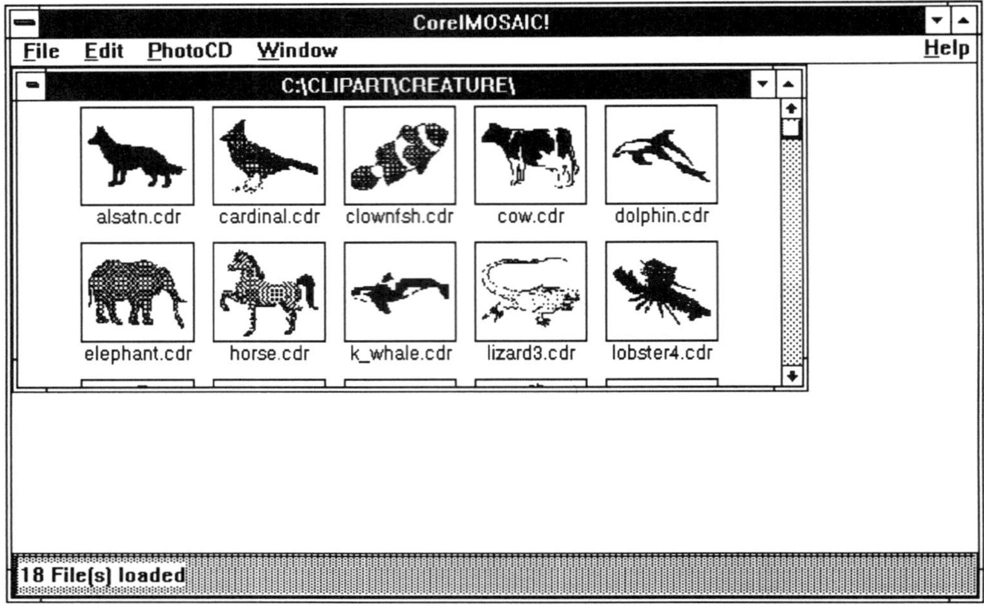

22.07 Files displayed

3   Open another directory and once the files are loaded, open the **Window** menu and click on **Tile Horizontally** or just press **Shift-F4**. You can continue opening windows and viewing directories as long as you have space on screen to do so.

4   If at any point you get a little balloon and a camera being displayed instead of the image, it means that that particular image doesn't have a header and so you cannot see it.

5   You can use Mosaic to compress the images on your system - provided they are CorelDRAW graphics. Select the images you want, using the standard Windows **Shift** and **Ctrl** key actions. Open the **File** menu and click on **New Catalogue/Library** or just press **Ctrl-N**. You'll get a dialogue box.

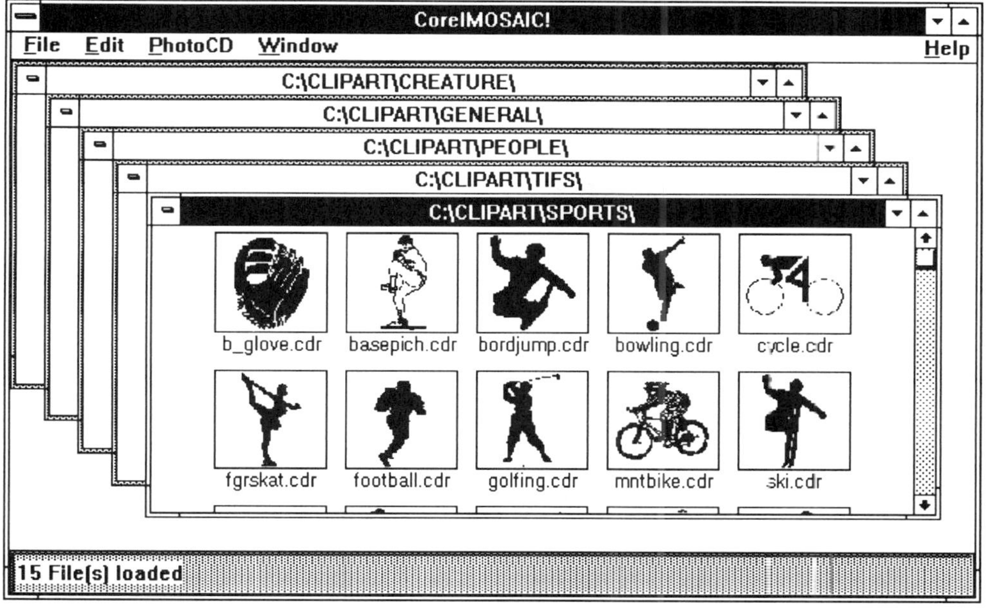

22.08 Sub-windows tiled

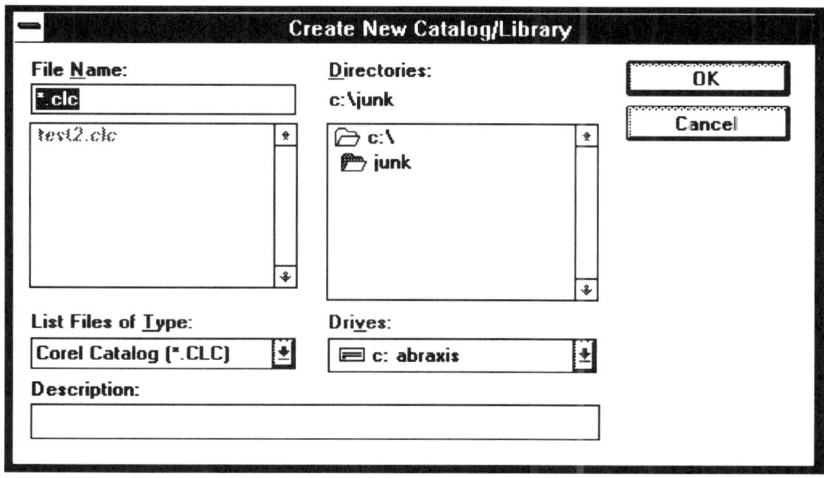

22.09 New Library dialogue box

6   A **Catalogue** contains just the thumbnails and the description, including keywords, of the files but not the images themselves. A **Library** contains the actual images as well. The files in a library are compressed to take less disk space but you have to have enough space in the first place to make the library file. Once you have done so you can delete the original files. Select Library for now under **List Files of Type**. Set a directory where you want the files to be placed. Give the file a name and then click on **OK**. The library will then be created. Note that this is just the basic library file - it is still empty.

7   You now have another sub-window bearing the new library file name. Close it. Open the **Edit** menu and click on **Insert Files**. You get a dialogue box that allows you to pick the library that you want the files inserted into. Select the one you have just created and they will be added to the file.

8   Before you delete the original files, open the new library to make sure that it has been created properly. Press **Ctrl-O** and in the dialogue box select the library that you have just created. If the files are present then you can delete the originals. If they are not then you need to recreate the library.

9   To delete files from Mosaic, just select them and then press **Del**. If you have **File Delete** selected in the **Preferences** then you will be prompted before each file is removed, otherwise you won't. Be warned, Mosaic deletes files PDQ. I have just deleted the entire Creature sub-directory contents in less than half a second.

10   Once the files are in a library you can expand them again whenever you wish. Open the Library file so it is in a sub-window. Select the files you want to expand. Open the **Edit** menu and click on **Expand Files**. You'll get a dialogue box wherein you can set where you want the files to be expanded to. Set the destination and click on **OK**. In a matter of second the files are expanded into the directory you selected.

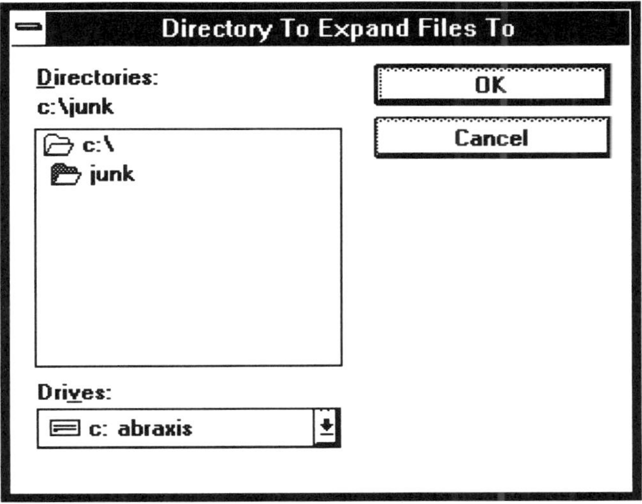

22.10 Expand Files dialogue box

PRINTING

1   You can print files directly from Mosaic in two different ways, either the files themselves, in batches if you wish, or just the thumbnails. Select some files and then Open the **File** menu and click on **Print Files**.

2   CorelDRAW will run and the first of the selected files is loaded. The Print dialogue box appears - once only - and you make whatever settings you wish for the whole batch print process. Click on **OK** and the first file is sent to the printer. The second is loaded and printed and so on until all have been sent. CorelDRAW then closes automatically.

This is a handy way to print lots of files, say overnight, without having to sit there watching them. However, you must remember that all the files are printed with the same orientation and whatever settings you made in the print dialogue box. Don't mix landscape and portrait images.

3   The other way to print the files is to print just the thumbnails. Select the files again. Open the **File** menu and click on **Print Thumbnails**. You'll get the same kind of print dialogue box that you get in CorelDRAW. (By the way you can print thumbnails from library files.)

4   Set the parameters and then click on **OK**. The thumbnails will be sent directly from Mosaic. This is very useful because you can create your own printed catalogue of the Clip-Art that you have on your system.

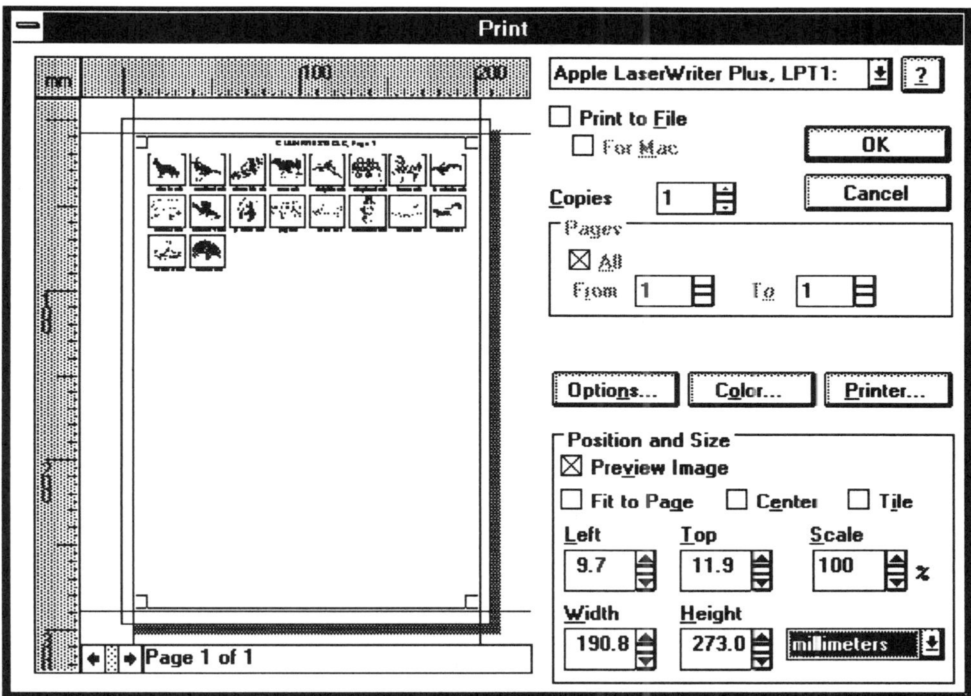

22.11 Print Thumbnails

To deselect files you can either click on it again or use the **Clear All** command in the
Edit menu.

FILE INFORMATION

Your catalogues can contain information and so can the individual files.

1   Select an open Catalogue window. Open the **Edit** menu and click on **Edit Description**. You'll get a dialogue box. Type the descriptive detail that you want and then click on **OK**.

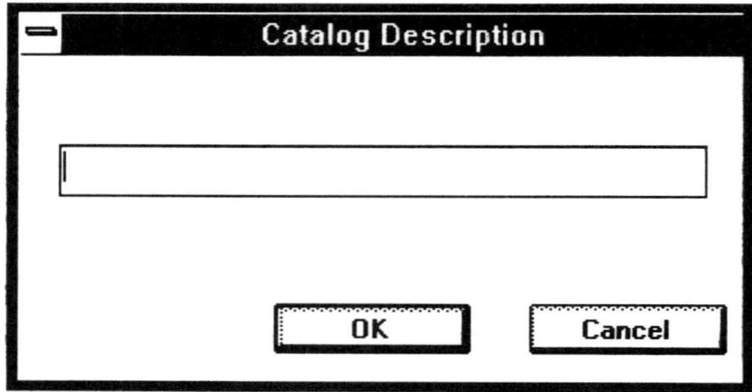

22.12 Edit Description dialogue box

2   For individual files you can amend the keywords that are associated with it. Select a file and then open the **Edit** menu and click on **Keywords**. You will get a dialogue box.

3   The dialogue box lists the existing keywords in the order they were added originally. You can delete any of these by highlighting them and then clicking on **Delete**. To add new words, one phrase at a time, type the word on the top line and then click on **Add**. When you are finished click on **Done**.

4   You can get full information about any file, or selection of files, by pressing **Ctrl-I** or open the **Edit** menu and click on **Get Info**. You'll get a large dialogue box that shows you a larger image of the file and gives you the full information about it, including the colours and the fonts that were used.

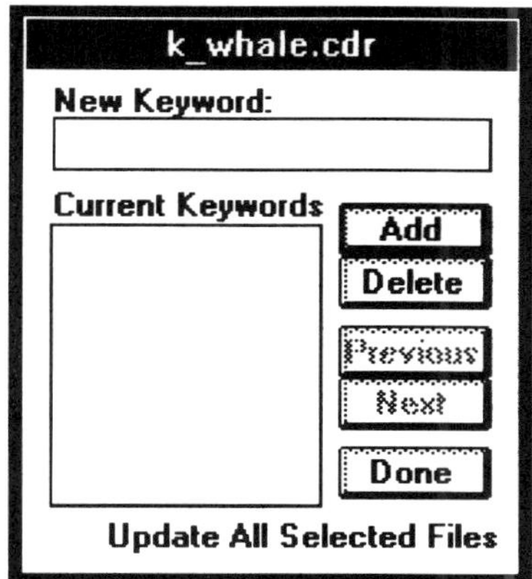

22.13 Keywords dialogue box

5   If you have selected multiple files you can page through them using the **Next** and **Previous** buttons. If you click on **Cycle** you'll be presented with all the files one after the other in a continuous loop.

6   Click on **Cancel** to close the dialogue box.

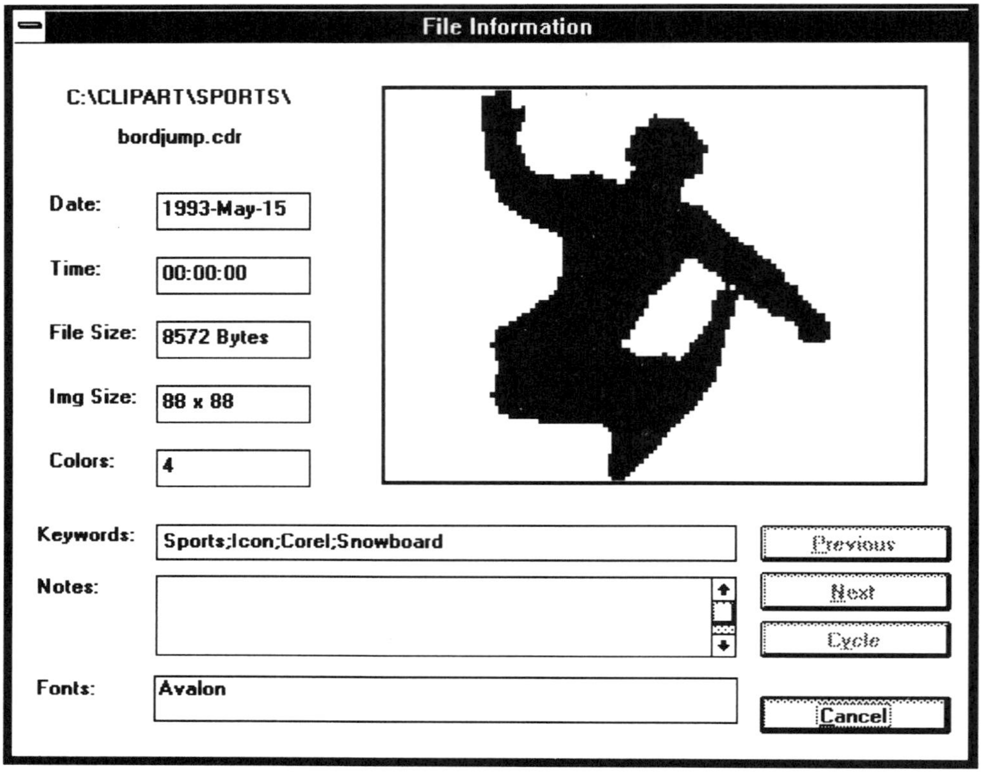

22.14 File information dialogue box

Changing files

CorelMOSAIC allows you to quickly and speedily convert files from one format to another in a single action.

1   Select a number of files. Open the **Edit** menu and click on **Convert from CorelDRAW**.

2   CorelDRAW will run and the first file is loaded. The **Export** dialogue box appears. Set the parameters that you want, e.g. the export type, and the file is exported. The second is then loaded and exported in exactly the same way with exactly the same parameters, and so on until all the selected files have been exported.

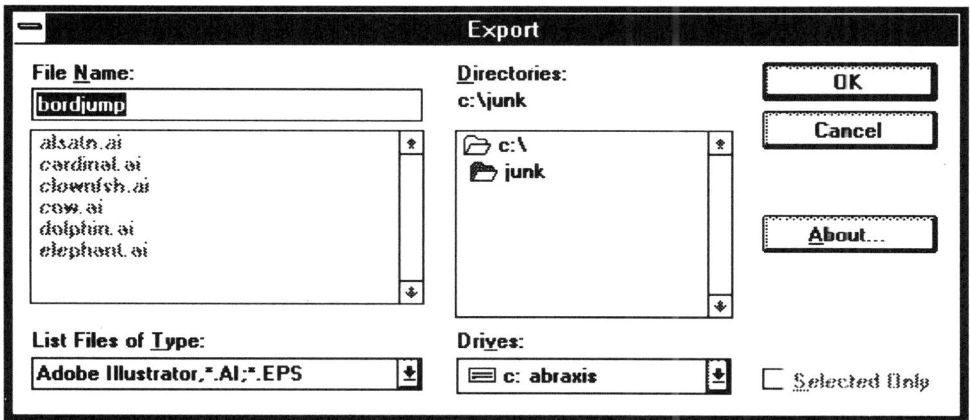

22.15 Export dialogue box

3   Once all the files have been exported, CorelDRAW will close automatically and you'll go back to Mosaic.

4   Alternatively you can load individual files into CorelDRAW and then export them manually yourself. Select the file you want to treat. Open the **Edit** menu and click on **Import into CorelDRAW**. CorelDRAW will run and the file is imported for you. You can then do with it whatever you need or wish to.

PHOTO-CD

CorelMOSAIC 3 was the first Windows program that allowed you to look directly at Kodak Photo-CD discs - even before the product was launched. Mosaic 4 also has that capability. The difficulty is getting a CD-ROM drive to look at the discs in the first place! There is a problem which has only just come to light in the U.K. because Kodak have only recently launched their new product here.

Kodak Photo-CD is a revolutionary process that takes your ordinary 35 mm photographic images, whether they are slides or ordinary film, and converts them into digital format. (You can still have normal prints or slides as well.) These converted images can then be put onto the Photo-CD which can store at least 100 images. There's only 36 images on a roll of film so the idea is that you take your first roll in and have all or just selected images from that put on the CD. The next time you have a roll of film you want developed you take the CD back again and have all or some of those images added to it. You can carry on doing this until the disc is full and then you simply start another disc.

You can read Kodak Photo-CD discs in a normal CD-ROM drive provided that the disc is a single session one depending on the type of CD-ROM drive that you have. In other words you must have a fairly modern, i.e. less than two years old, drive.

The big problem is Multiple Session Photo-CD discs. To use these on a computer you need a CD-ROM drive that is a Mode 2, Form 1 XA drive. At the moment these are few and far between but most of the manufacturers are due to bring them out in the near future.

For example, I can read single session Photo-CD discs in my drives but if I try to read a multiple session one then I run into a stone wall.

Kodak do make their own player which is capable of showing the Photo-CD images on an ordinary television screen but it cannot be coupled directly to a computer because it has the wrong kind of output. You could use a video grabber board and get at the images that way but that is a very expensive method of doing so given the price of video grabber boards.

Mosaic is, in that sense, ahead of its time because it already has the capability to read from and view the Photo-CD images. You can then convert those images into a form suitable for use with CorelDRAW or its related programs - or at least you could if you could read the disc. In a year's time we won't have any problem but until we all get the new CD-ROM drives we're stuck.

If you can read the images from the Photo-CD then you can do all the usual things with them in Mosaic after you have run the Convert Images command on them. You cannot use the images directly as they are.

MOSAIC MENUS

New Catalogue/Library creates a new, blank library or catalogue file. Files have to be added with the Insert Files command from the Edit menu. The keyboard shortcut is **Ctrl-N**.

Open Catalogue/Library opens a new sub-window to display the contents of the selected file. The keyboard shortcut is **Ctrl-O**.

View Directory allows you to log into any directory and display the graphic files it contains. The keyboard shortcut is **Ctrl-D**.

Delete Catalogue/Library allows you to remove catalogues of library files from your hard disk.

Print Files causes CorelDRAW to run. Files are loaded and you set the print parameters once only. The first file is printed, the second is loaded and printed and so on. Allows for batch printing, however all files should be the same orientation.

Print Thumbnails prints the actual thumbnails of the images in the selected directory.

Print Setup identifies a printer to the program.

Page Setup sets the parameters for the printed page used when printing thumbnails.

Preferences allows you to set your preferences for the screen display. The keyboard shortcut is **Ctrl-J**.

Exit closes the program. The keyboard shortcut is **Alt-F4**. You can get the same effect by double clicking on the Control Box in the top left hand corner of the window.

EDIT MENU

Select by Keyword allows you to select files on the basis of the keywords you input in the dialogue box.

Select All highlights all of the files, even the ones not visible, in the current window.

Clear All deselects all highlighted files.

Insert Files allows you to add files to an existing library or catalogue. Files in libraries are compressed to save disk space.

Expand Files, which only applies to library or catalogues, will unpack the file and restore it to its original uncompressed state. You can select where files are uncompressed to.

Update Catalogue updates the thumbnail and file information in the selected catalogue.

Edit will open the Corel application best suited to handle the selected file, e.g. EPS files are opened in CorelDRAW, PCX files are opened in Photo-Paint. You can use the shortcut of double clicking on a selected file to get the same effect.

Convert from CorelDRAW allows for batch conversions of files. Files are loaded into CorelDRAW and then exported one by one to the selected format.

Import into CorelDRAW runs CorelDRAW and loads the file into the program.

Delete removes selected files from the hard disk or from a library file.

Extract Text is the same as the command in CorelDRAW. The file will be loaded into CorelDRAW and the text extracted.

Merge Back Text is the same as the command in CorelDRAW.

Keywords allows you to change the keywords of the selected image.

Edit Description allows you to change the description of the catalogue file.

Get Info displays a large dialogue box giving you an image of the file and all the data about it.

Photo-CD Menu

View Kodak Photo-CD allows you to look at a Photo-CD - provided your CD-ROM drive is capable of doing so.

Convert Images allows you to change the Photo-CD images into other formats that can be handled by computer programs.

Window Menu

Cascade arranges the open windows so that they overlap each other. The keyboard shortcut is **Shift-F5**.

Tile Horizontally arranges the open windows into horizontal bars.

Tile Vertically will arrange the open windows so that each occupies approximately the same amount of screen area. The keyboard shortcut is **Shift-F4**.

Arrange Icons neatly sorts the window icons within Mosaic into order.

Numbers gives the number of the current open windows.

23. CORELTRACE

CorelTRACE is the program that will allow you to convert bitmap format pictures into true vector images. It is fast, reliable and accurate. Version 4 of the program is now even better, more user-friendly and nicer to use.

1   Double click on the **CorelTRACE** icon. The program window will appear and will probably need resizing. Reduce all other applications to icons, then double click on the Windows background. The Switch To dialogue box appears.

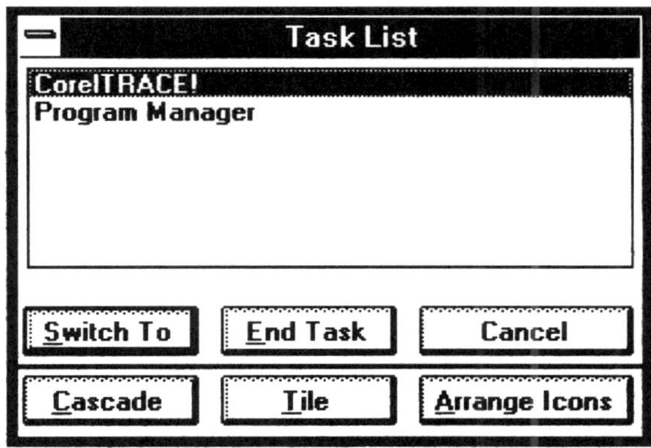

23.01 Switch To dialogue box

2   Click on the **Tile** button to make the Trace window expand but still leave the icon visible.

3   Press **Ctrl-O**, or open the **File** menu and click on **Open**, and a dialogue box appears.

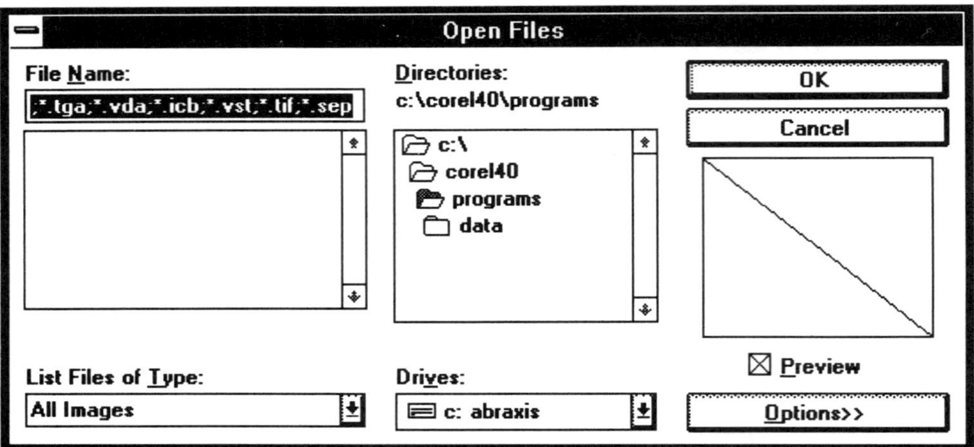

23.02 Open dialogue box

4   Log in to the Clip-Art directory and then in **\TIFS**. This contains some TIF images that are supplied with CorelDRAW 4, mainly for use with Photo-Paint but they will work just as well here. You will then get the available files being displayed in the box on the left hand side. Click on any one of these.

5   If you then click on the button labelled **Options**, the dialogue box will open out to give you details of the file you have selected, including the size, colours, date, etc.

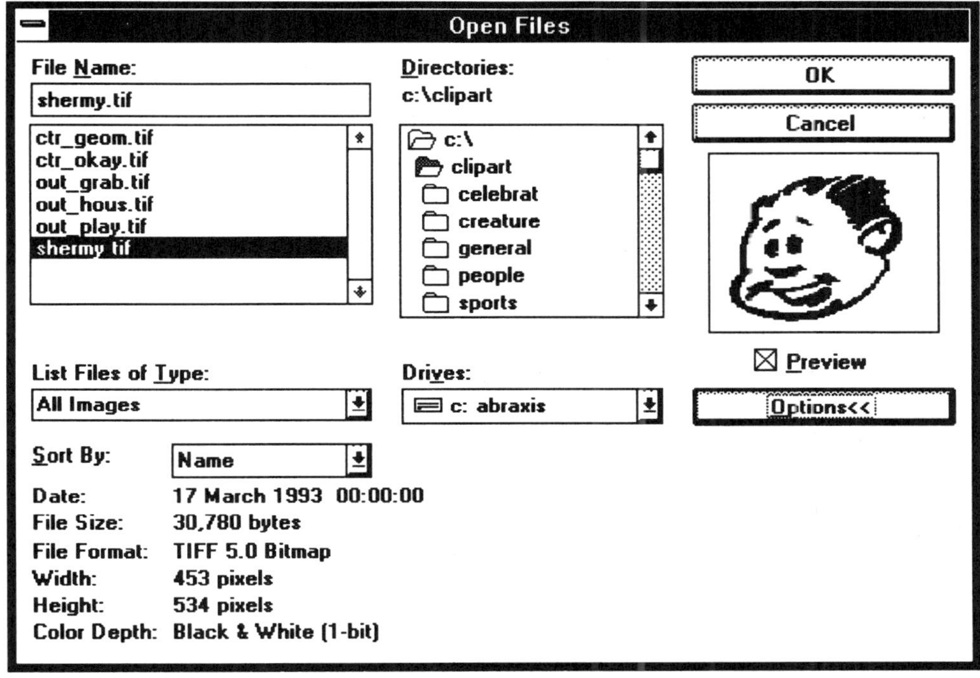

23.03 File details

6   Click on **OK** and the file will be loaded into the left hand portion of Trace.

23.04 Bitmap loaded

7   Having now got the image you can trace it to convert it. Trace normally works by following the lines between colours but you can adjust the way it does so. Do a simple trace first. Just under the Menu bar is a series of buttons. The first is for a roll-up, the second is the first trace option. Click on this and the image is traced, a bar graph appears in the bottom right corner of the screen as it does so. You'll get something like this:

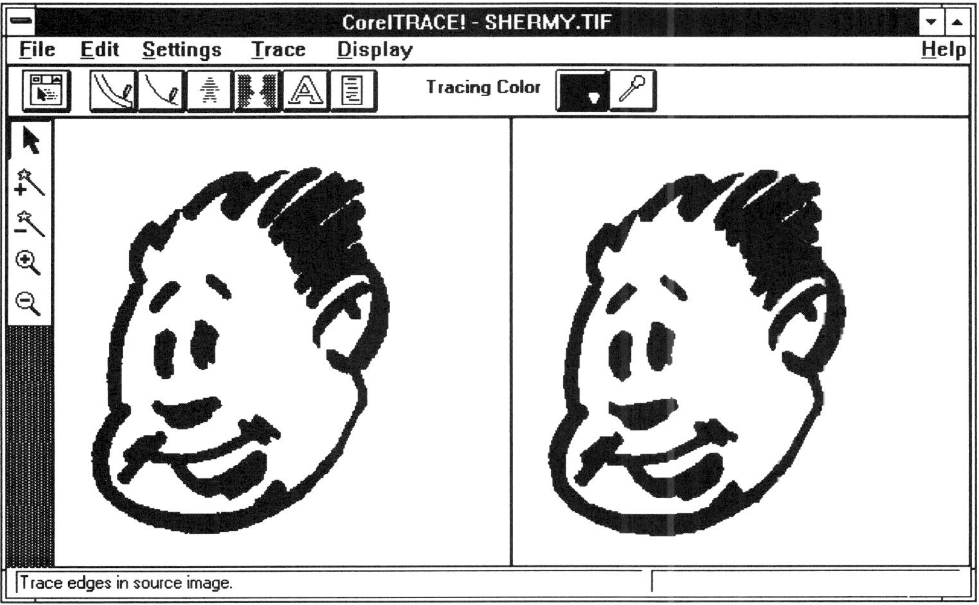

23.05 Image traced

8   If you examine both images closely you will find subtle differences between them. The original image, on the left, is a bit blocky around the edges of all the black areas. The traced image is smoother but actually has slightly less definition. Some of the lines are cleaner while some areas are slightly wider.

9   Having traced the image you now have to save it. Open the **File** menu and click on **Save Trace** or just press **Ctrl-S**. The image is saved. But where to? It's saved back to the same directory that it came from, but the file now has an extension of .EPS. The filename remains the same.

10   A better way to save files is to open the **File** menu and click on **Save**. A drop down menu appears. Click on **Trace As** and you'll get a dialogue box. This allows you to use alternative names, but not the file type, and/or to set a destination path.

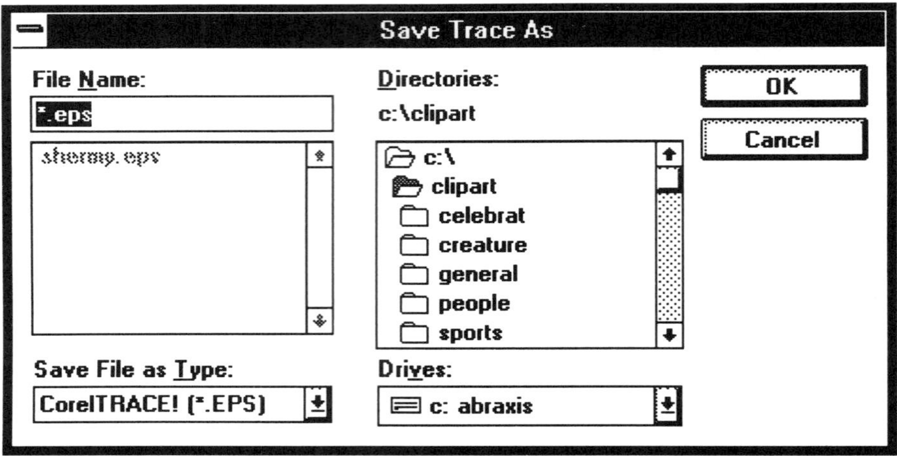

23.06 Save Trace As dialogue box

11   Let's try different tracing techniques. The first file was traced using normal outline tracing. Click on the second button in the button bar and the trace will be redone. It will take slightly longer but the end results looks the same. Save the file with a different filename.

12   Now click on the third button - the one that bears a funny human figure. This is the woodcut trace and it produces slightly weird effects. Save the image, again with a different filename.

On the next page are four images, the top left is the original TIF file, the top right is the Normal outline, the bottom left if the Centreline trace and the bottom right is the Woodcut outline.

Trace Menus

We have neither the time nor the space here to fully cover the capabilities of CorelTRACE so here is a brief rundown of the available commands and menus.

File Menu

Open allows you to load a bitmap image from any location on your system using a dialogue box. You can search for bitmaps in specific forms by changing the file type line if you wish but the dialogue box normally shows all the possible bitmaps files. The keyboard shortcut is **Ctrl-O**.

Save Trace will save the traced image to the same directory that the original file came from with the same filename but it will have an extension of .EPS. The keyboard shortcut is **Ctrl-S**.

Save causes a pop out menu to appear bearing the following:

Trace As which allows you to use alternative filenames and/or directories.

Text As allows you to save traced text because CorelTRACE has OCR (Optical Character Recognition) capability as an ASCII text file. Again you can use alternative filenames and destinations.

Image As allows you to save the original bitmap image in a different bitmap format.

Acquire Image allows you to select a scanner to use to scan in a new image. You must have a scanner connected and have the necessary driver installed as part of the CorelDRAW installation.

Exit closes the program. The keyboard shortcut is **Alt-F4**.

Edit Menu

Undo undoes the last action. The keyboard shortcuts are **Ctrl-Z** or **Alt-Backspace**.

Cut will take the selected area and cut it to the Windows Clipboard. The keyboard shortcuts are **Ctrl-X** or **Shift-Del**. In all the Clipboard functions it is the image in the right hand window that is used, not the original.

Copy will copy the traced image to the Windows Clipboard. The keyboard shortcuts are **Ctrl-C** or **Ctrl-Ins**.

Paste allows you to paste in from the Clipboard. The keyboard shortcuts are **Ctrl-V** or **Shift-Ins**.

Clear removes the traced image completely. It is not copied to the Windows Clipboard, just deleted. You can use **Del** as a shortcut.

Edit Image applies to the original image. It will run a Paint style program, e.g. CorelPHOTO-PAINT, and allow you to edit the image before tracing it.

SETTINGS MENU

Load will bring up a dialogue box that allows you to load a file containing settings for the Trace program. At the start there is no such file - you have to create one.

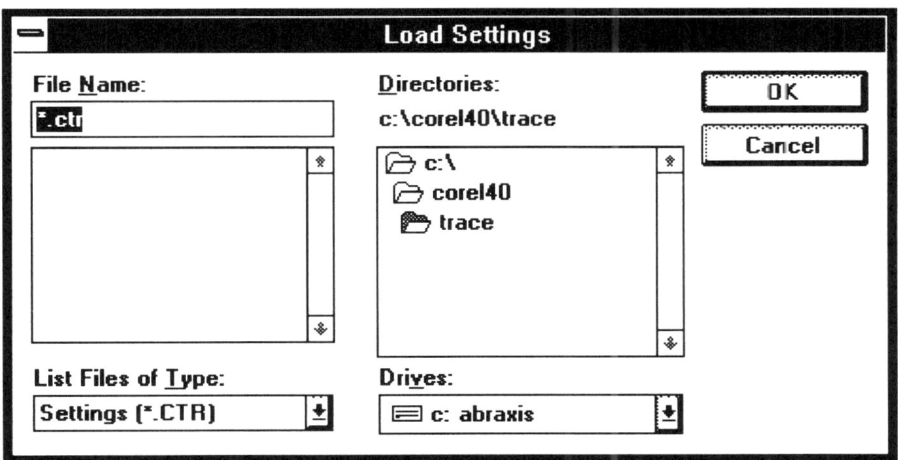

23.07 Load Settings dialogue box

Save As allows you to save a custom setting configuration file.

Modify will pop-out a large menu containing a variety of commands that you can alter:

> **Image Filtering** allows you to specify the settings for dithering, colour inversion, monochrome inversion and colour reduction. The settings affect how the program reads the original source file.

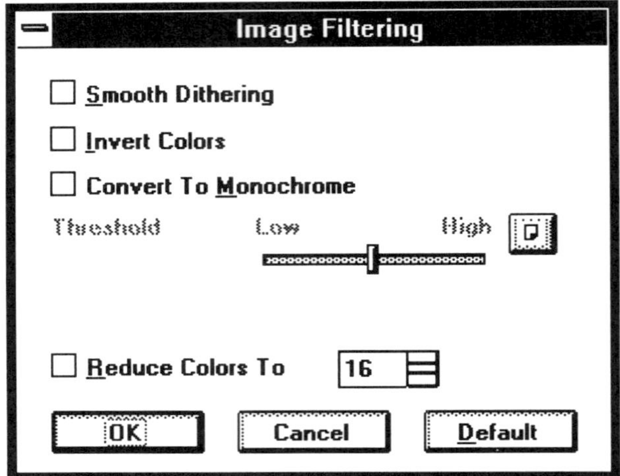

23.08 Image Filtering dialogue box

> **Colour Matching** sets the colour tolerances for the Wand tool and for overall tracing tolerance, i.e. the way that Trace distinguishes objects in the original file.

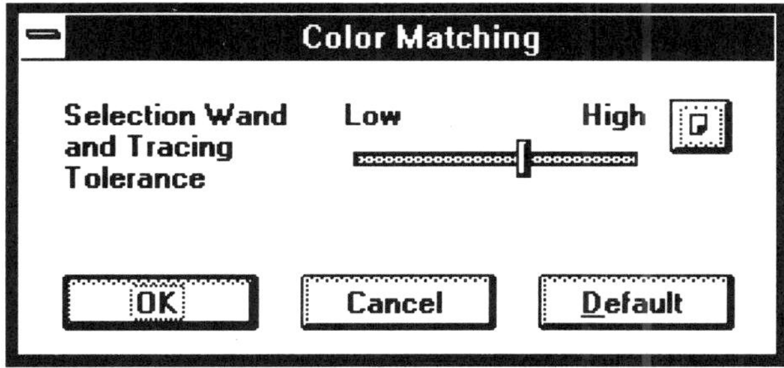

23.09 Colour Matching dialogue box

Line Attributes directly affects how the trace is performed. The first four options range from Very Loose to Very Good. Changing any of these will affect how the trace itself is performed.

Line Attributes

Curve Precision — Good
Line Precision — Good
Target Curve Length — Very Long
Sample Rate — Fine
Minimum Object Size — 5 pixels

OK   Cancel   Default

23.10 Line Attributes dialogue box

Centreline Method adjusts the way that centreline tracing is performed. When you use centreline tracing the trace follows the middle of lines rather than the edges.

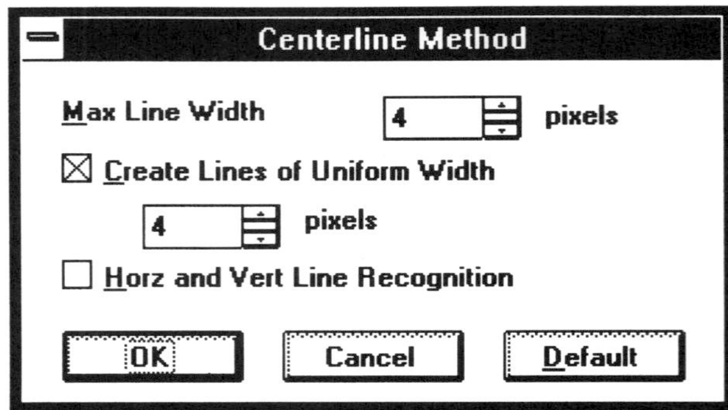

23.11 Centreline Method dialogue box

Woodcut Style changes the way that woodcut tracing is done. You can generate all kinds of different effects by adjusting the values here.

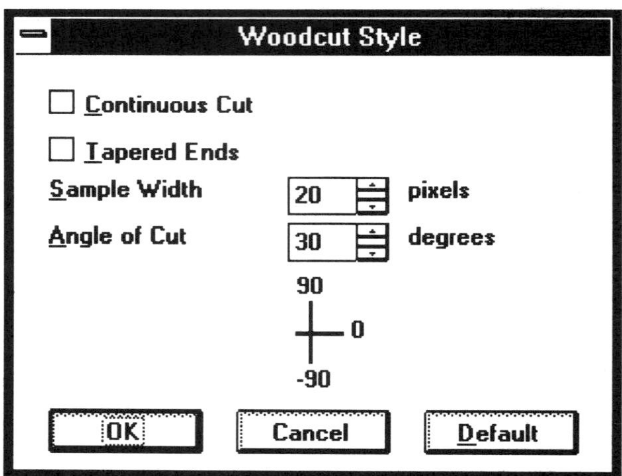

23.12 Woodcut Style dialogue box

OCR Method allows you to set spell checking and the document source.

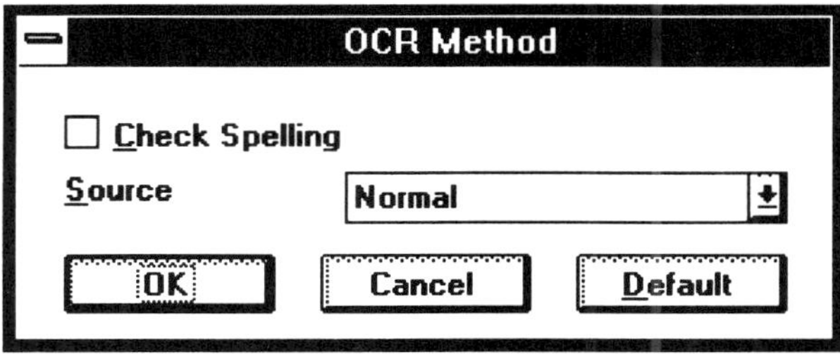

23.13 OCR Method dialogue box

Batch Method allows you to set the parameters for batch tracing of files. You can use Trace to convert a batch of selected files rather than individual ones and you set the options for that here.

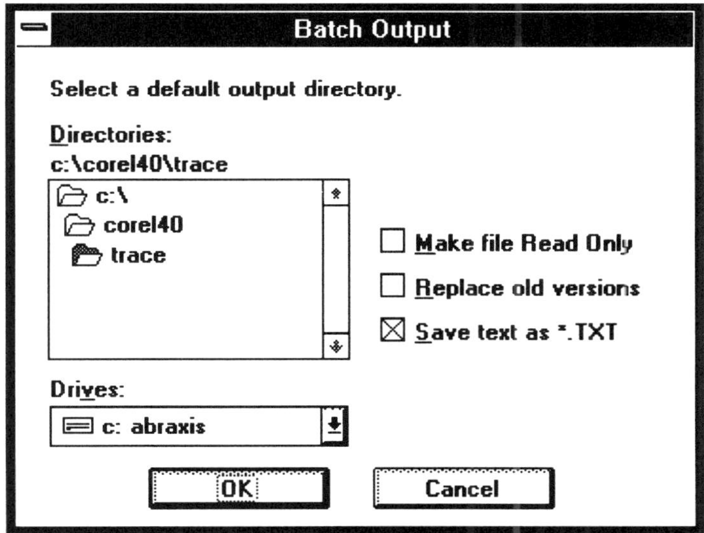

23.14 Batch Output dialogue box

Default Settings changes everything back to the original default settings.

Trace Menu

Rather than using the buttons you can trace an image using the commands directly. The first is **Outline** which traces around the edges of the shapes. For example, if you trace the letter O you will have two objects, the first is the outside of the shape filled with black, and the second will be the inside of the shape filled with white.

Centreline tracing is different. It follows the middle of the lines in the original file. For example, the letter O will consist of a single line that has thickness but no fill. This works best for technical images.

Woodcut produces snazzy images that look as if they have been carved with chisels. You have to play with the parameters to get the effect the way that you want it.

Silhouette traces selected areas and produces silhouettes of them. You must have selected an area of the image first to use Silhouette tracing.

OCR will trace and convert scanned text to vector images so that it can be used as normal text in CorelDRAW.

Form traces scanned forms so that the text appears as text but all other details appear as images.

DISPLAY MENU

Image Info brings up a dialogue box that gives the details of the original image.

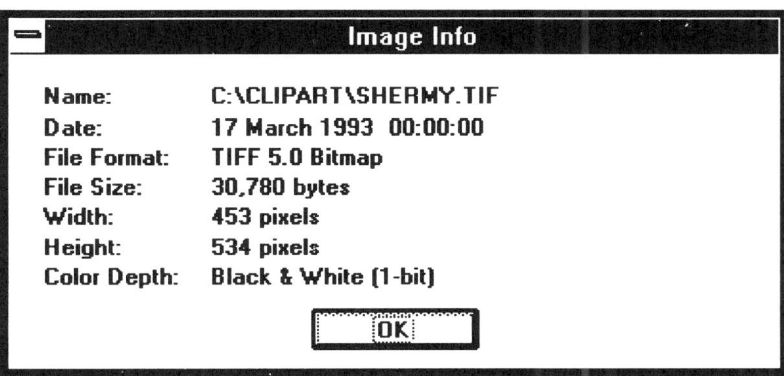

23.15 Image Info dialogue box

Trace Info gives the same kind of information for the traced image. It will give you the number of objects and the total number of nodes that have been produced. Different tracing methods give different results.

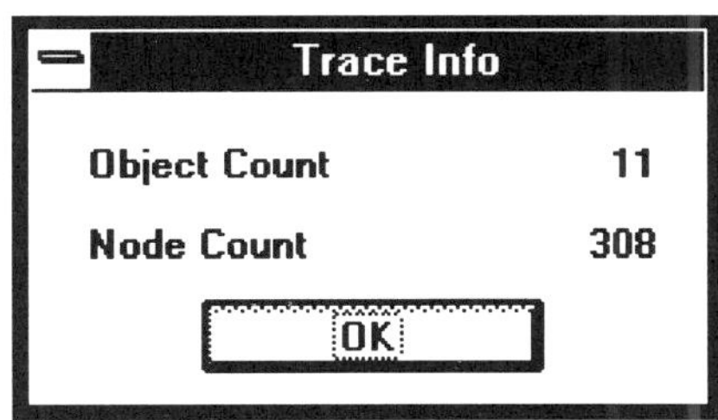

23.16 Trace Info dialogue box

Refresh Window simply clears and redraws both windows so that the images are clean.

Clear Marquee removes any selection area.

Trace Tools

CorelTRACE provides you with a series of tools and buttons to save you having to use the menus. The tools are on the left hand side of the window.

> **Pointer Tool** functions the same way as the tool does in CorelDRAW in that it can be used to define an area to trace. Just drag a bounding box on the original image around the area you want traced rather than the whole image. It is only when you have done so that a Silhouette can be traced.
>
> **Magic Wand Plus** is used to select a colour range.
>
> **Magic Wand Minus** deselects a colour range.
>
> **Zoom Plus** magnifies the selected area - if it is possible to do so. With some images they will have been magnified as much as possible already.
>
> **Zoom Minus** reverses a magnification.

Trace Buttons

> The first button activates the **Batch Processing** roll-up. You load images into this and then trace the whole lot - using only one set of parameters - in a single session. Once you have the images loaded click on **Trace All** and all the images are traced and saved in a single operation.

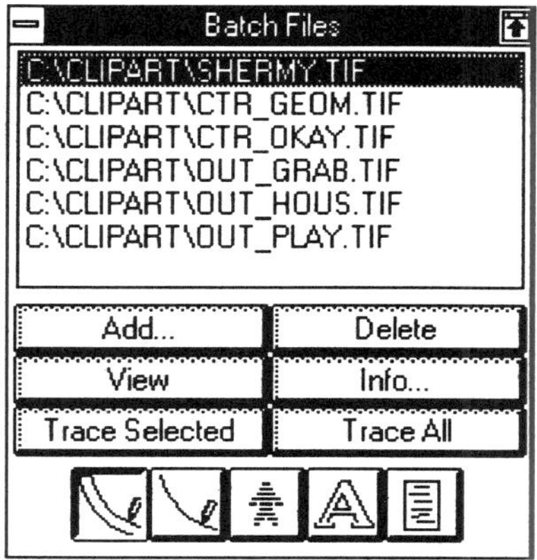

23.17 Batch Trace Roll-up

The tracing buttons are:

> **Trace Outline** which bears a double sloped line and a small pencil.

> **Trace Centreline** which bears a single sloped line and a small pencil.

> **Trace Woodcut** containing a human shaped figure or tree shape.

> **Trace Silhouette**, only active if you have selected an area, containing the classic faces/candlestick image.

> **Trace Text** bearing the large letter A.

> **Trace Form** with a funny rectangle and lines in it.

Tracing Colour will pop out the palette that allows you to set the colour that the trace will be performed in.

Eye Dropper allows you to pick a source colour from the original image that will be used for doing the trace.

24. CorelCHART

CorelCHART has been greatly improved and enhanced since the launch of the original version with CorelDRAW 3. The new version has been completely rewritten, improved and enhanced. The program will allow you to create charts in a huge variety of formats and styles using data that you have either entered manually or imported from other sources. We don't have room here to do more than take a quick overview of the program - after all it is a fully fledged Windows Application all by itself.

1   Double click on the **CorelCHART** icon and **Tile** in on the window. You'll get a large window that is essentially blank. Open the **File** menu and click on **New** and a dialogue box appears:

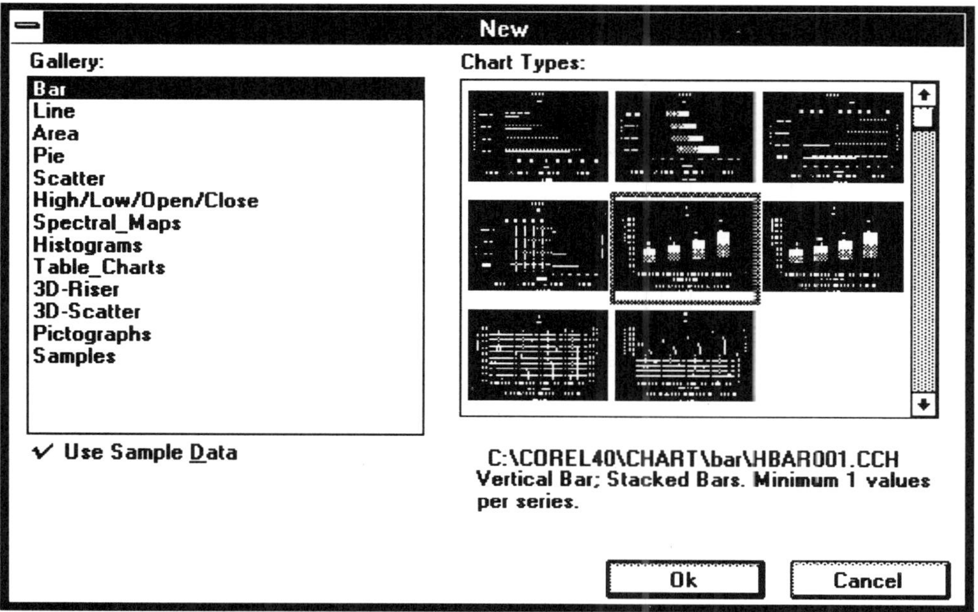

24.01 New Chart dialogue box

The dialogue box is divided into two main areas. On the left is the list of the basic chart types that can be produced and on the right are the possible variations of those types. As you change type so the variations change. All told CorelCHART can produce a minimum of 52 different chart variations but you can further enhance and change these to produce almost unlimited variations.

2   For now you want **Bar,** then click on the central image in the right hand side of the dialogue box. Make sure you have **Use Sample Data** turned on and then click on **OK**. The chart will then load for you using the sample values. (I've had to amend the colours and things to get a good illustration because I'm grabbing it off a monochrome monitor.)

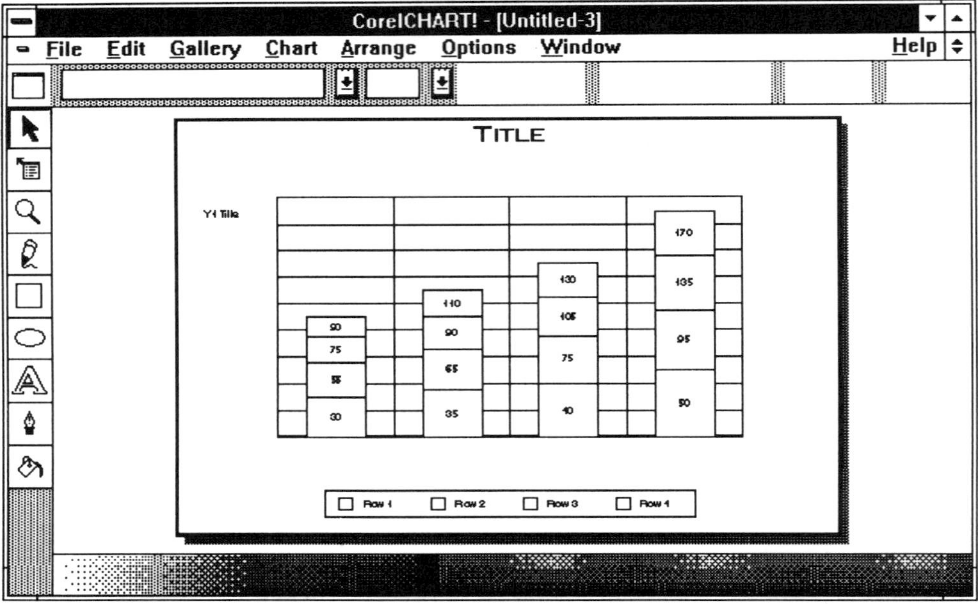

24.02 Chart Loaded

3   The first thing to do is set the main defaults. Open the **File** menu and click on **Page Setup**. Alternatively you can double click on the page border. You will get a dialogue box.

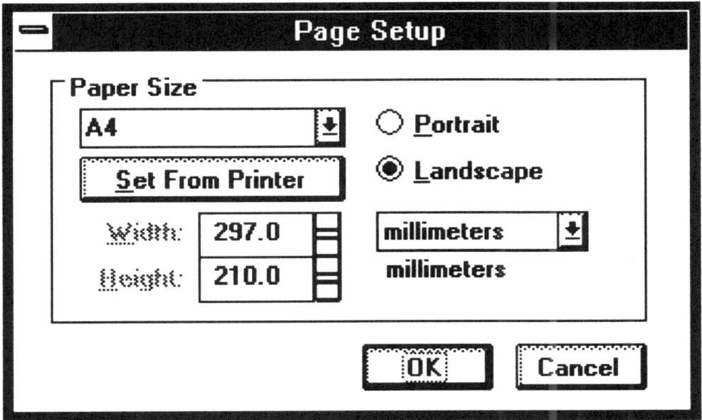

24.03 Page Setup dialogue box

4   A quick way to set the size to the paper size you are using is to click on **Set from Printer**. That will get the basic information from the printer driver and change the values in the box accordingly. The only other thing you then have to do is change the orientation. Charts work better on Landscape pages rather than Portrait ones. Once you've made the change click on **OK**.

5   The chart size will change automatically to reflect the new size. Now you can resize the chart itself. Click on the frame for the charts and you'll get the handles appearing. Drag these around to get the basic chart to the size and shape you want. As you do so the bars within the chart will change to maintain their aspect ratio to the chart itself.

6   Click on the **Legend** box along the bottom of the screen and resize that in the same way. You should end up with something like this:

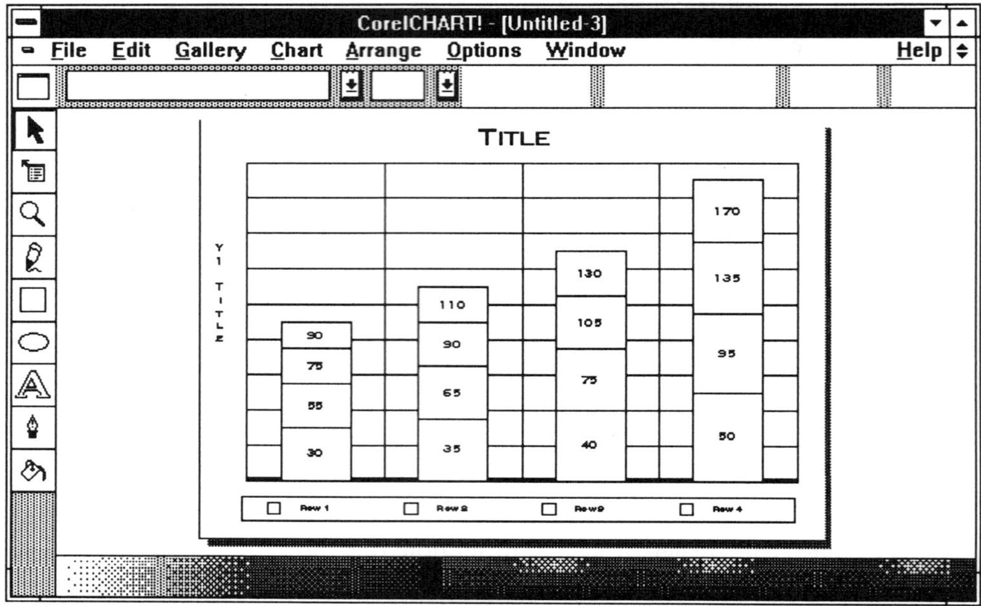

24.04 New size and shape

7   You can change the colours of any of the areas by clicking on the one you want
     to change and then using the palette along the bottom of the screen in the same
     way as you do in CorelDRAW.

8   Let's change the chart type itself. Open the **Gallery** menu and you'll get a long
     menu listing all the chart types. As you highlight any of these so you'll get a
     pop-out menu showing the different sub-types. Highlight one of these to see
     what your chart will look like. You can spend ages just looking at all the
     different types. For now, select **Bar, Side by Side** and you'll get this:

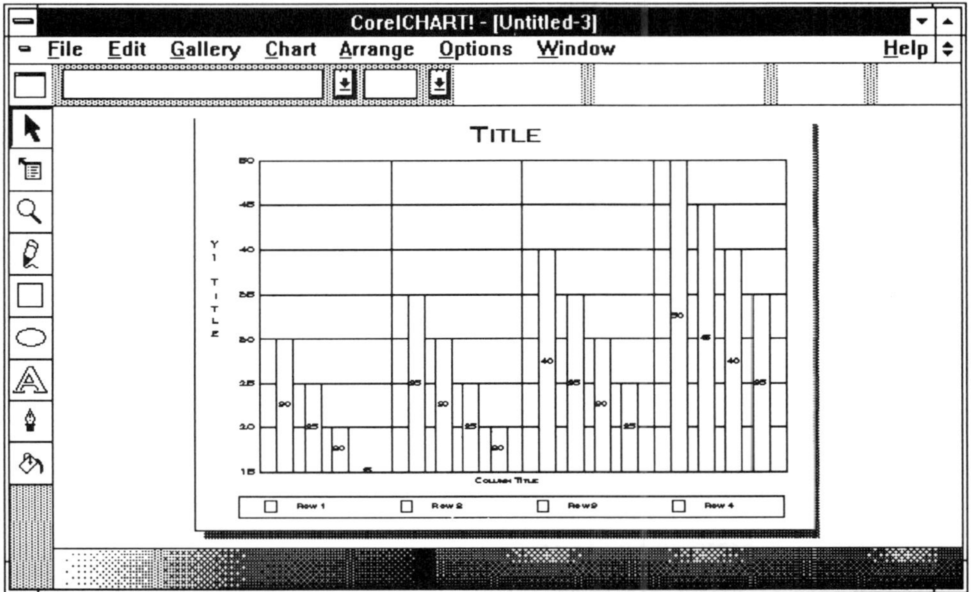

24.05 Bar Side by Side

9   The bars are a bit narrow. Click on any one of them with the right mouse button and you'll get a status menu. Click on **Bar Thickness** and you'll get another pop-out. It should be set to **Default**. Change it to **Major** and the bars thicken up.

10   That's got the chart looking more or less decent but now we need to add the actual text instead of just the headings. Click on the odd icon just above the Pointer tool button and you'll move to the **Data Manager**.

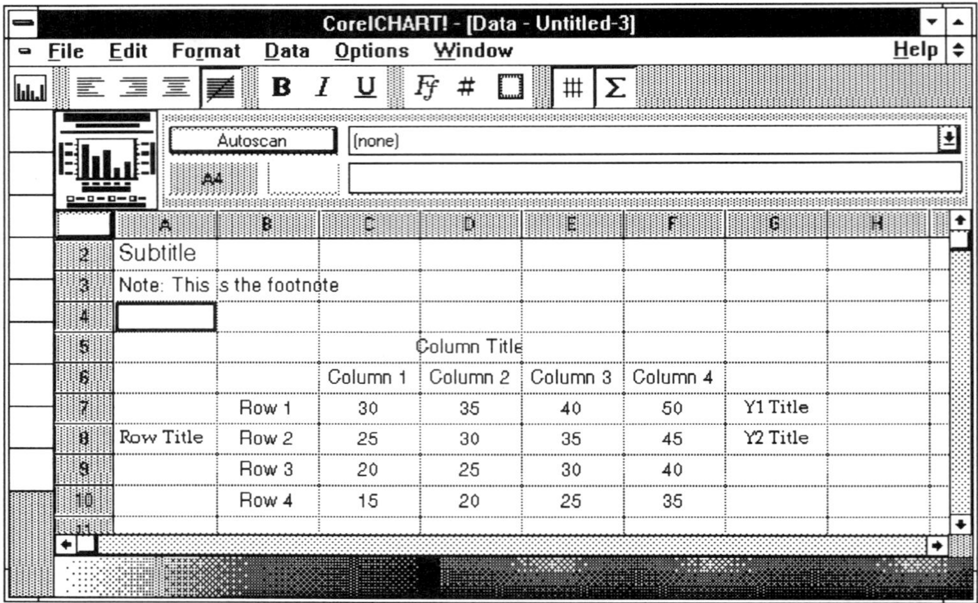

24.06 Data Manager

11   At present the various headings are given rather than text for the headings.
     Click on any cell in the data manager that contains a heading and then just type
     what you want the heading to be. When you have finished press **Enter** to place
     the text in the cell.

12   You can also change the values in the data range, i.e. the numbers, if you wish.
     Then click on the **Chart** icon at the top left hand corner of the screen and you'll
     go back to the chart, which is now changed.

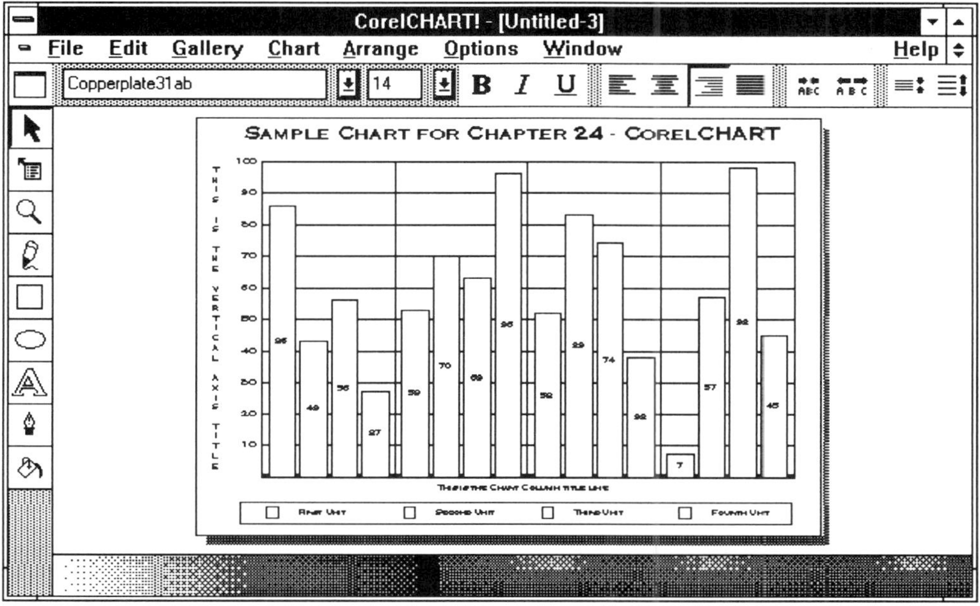

24.07 Chart Changed

13 Click on the bar values with the right hand mouse button. A pop-out menu will appear saying **Data Values** and there will be a tick beside **Show Data Values**. Click on it to turn it off and all the numbers vanish from the bars.

14 Now select any of the bars. Click on the **Fill** tool which will open out to be the same as the one in CorelDRAW. Give the bar a fill of your choice. You can even use the roll-up as you would in CorelDRAW. All four bars of that category will change at the same time. Fill the other with different patterns.

15 Try filling the chart area itself with one of the textures. You can produce some really nice effects. You can even fill the entire paper background.

16 To change the font for any of the text, select it and then change the font and/or size in the relevant box. You can change the outline and fill of the text in the same way as you do in CorelDRAW. You can end up with something like this:

CORELDRAW 4 - A USERS GUIDE

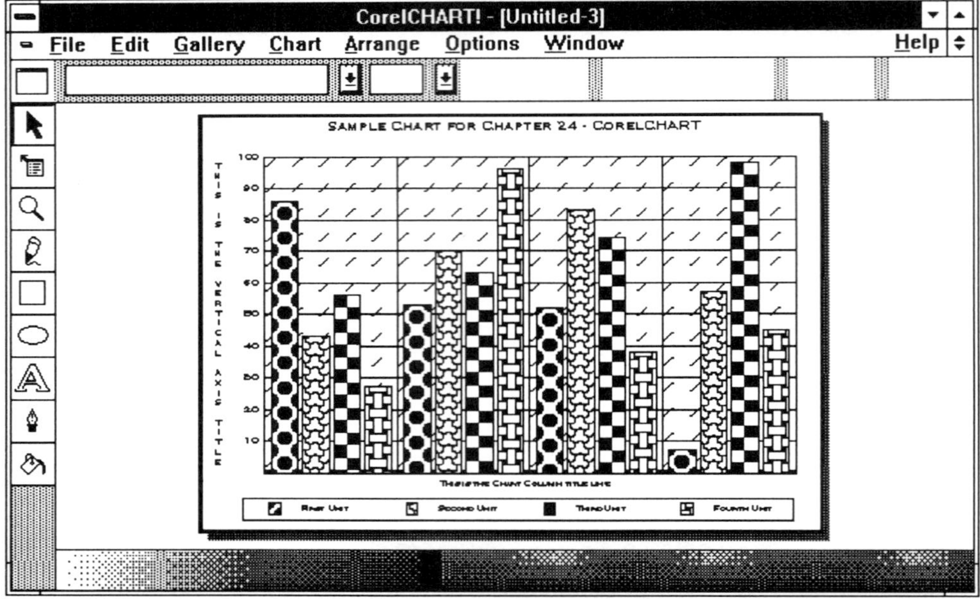

24.07 Chart filled

CorelCHART is really meant to be used in colour and thus the examples that I can produce for this book are very limited. Play with the program and see what you can do. You can have lots of fun just playing with the possible fills and colours.

For all that though, CorelCHART also has a serious side. The Data Manager can function as a true spreadsheet. It can import data from a variety of other spreadsheets and sources. You can then use the charting capabilities of the program, which are far more interactive than any other program, to bring the data to life.

One thing you need to be aware of is that CorelCHART is resource hungry, in the same way that all the CorelDRAW applications are, and you need to have adequate amounts of memory and resources available to run it at optimum levels.

25. PHOTO-PAINT

CorelPHOTO-PAINT, like all the CorelDRAW suite bar one, has been improved and enhanced for the latest release. The tools have been streamlined and rearranged, the program now uses roll-ups and generally it is much more user friendly.

Photo-Paint allows you to do things with bitmaps files that almost defy belief. Once again there isn't room in this book to cover even a few of them and so this chapter is going to provide the briefest of overviews. The program, along with the others in the suite, will be fully covered in the companion book to this one, CorelDRAW Applications.

1   Double click on the **CorelPHOTO-PAINT** icon. **Tile** the window once it opens. What you will have is a blank window with two roll-ups in the top right and the toolbox down the left hand side.

2   Before you do anything else, check your system resources availability. Fortunately Photo-Paint has a built-in utility that will do this for you. Open the **Special** menu and click on **System Info**. You get a dialogue box with the information.

Current Operating Statistics				
CorelPHOTO-PAINT!				
Image name:				
		Horiz	Vert	
Image:	None			
Screen:		640	480	2 Colors
Printer:	Apple LaserWriter	300	300	DPI
Computer Memory		Installed	Remaining	
RAM (DOS):		640 KB	17 MB	
(Virtual):			17 MB	
Disk:		98 MB	18 MB	OK

25.01 System Information

3   Load an image. Photo-Paint is shipped with some samples that you can play with. Open the **File** menu and click on **Open** or just press **Ctrl-O**. You will get a dialogue box.

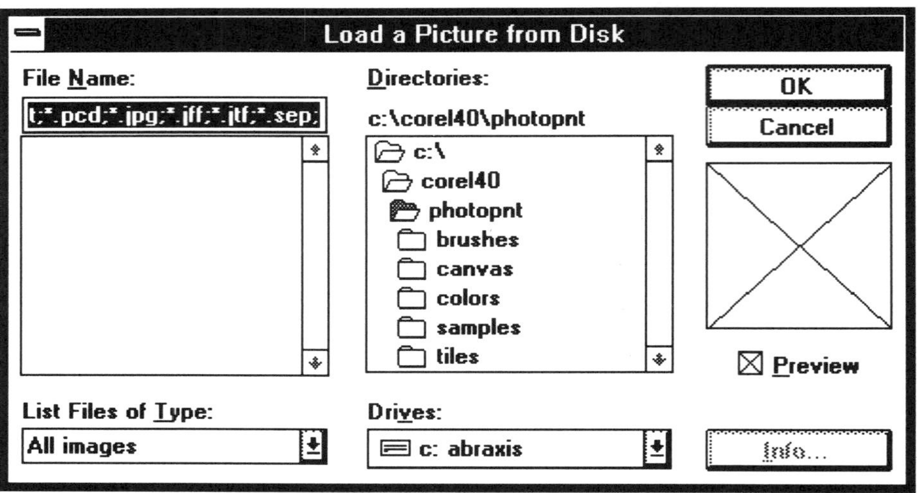

25.02 Load dialogue box

4   Log into the **\Samples** sub-directory and you should find that it contains three files. Double click on **APPLE.PCX**. The image will be loaded into a new sub-window and all the tools and roll-ups become active.

25.03 Image loaded

5   Having got the image in, you can now do just about anything you like with it. And probably a few things you won't like. The question is "Where to start?" because there is simply so much you can do. Open the **Effects** menu and click on **Emboss**. You'll get a dialogue box.

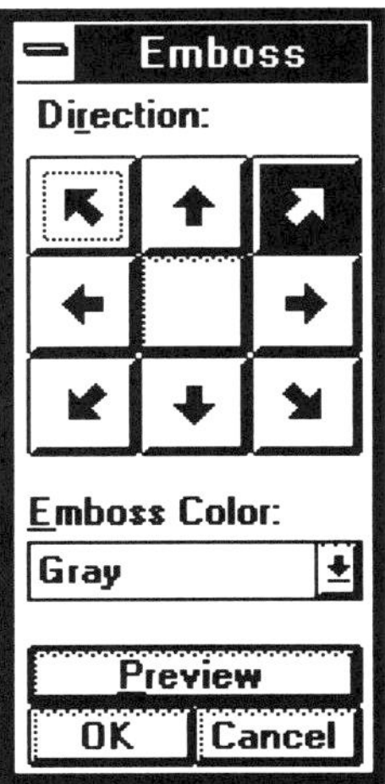

25.04 Emboss dialogue box

6   Move the dialogue box to one side and then click on **Preview**. Watch what happens to the original image. It hasn't actually changed yet - this is just a sample of what could happen. Play with the angles of the embossing and the different colours available, previewing each one, until you find one you like and then click on **OK** to apply it.

7   Try duplicating the apple, using **Ctrl-D**. You'll get another sub-window bearing a copy of the original image each time. Use different embossing settings for each one. You can arrange the windows using the Windows menu.

8   Open the **Effects** menu again and click on **Psychedelicize**. (Who invents these words?) You get another dialogue box. Play with the values and Preview each one. You can get some really weird effects with is one.

25.05 Embossed Apple

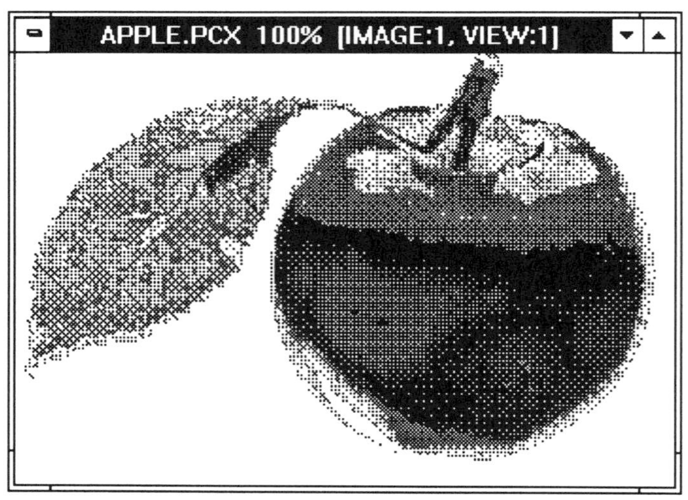

25.06 Psychedelicized apple

9   Try the **Solarise** command, again in the **Effects** menu, both on an 'untreated' apple and on one that you have applied other effects to.

10   Let's do something different. Reload the original apple if you don't already have an unchanged copy of it. Roll out the **Canvas** roll-up. Click on **Apply** using the default pattern. The apple is partially obscured. Change the **Transparency** to 90% - the higher the value the clearer the original image is - and click on **Apply** again. The canvas is a transparent fill that allows you to create textured images, you can even blend them to the original image to produce astonishing effects.

11   To get back to the original apple, click on **None** and then **Apply**. To load other canvas patterns click on Load and you'll get a dialogue box. As you click on each pattern in turn you can have a preview of what it looks like. When you find one you like double click on it to load it. Some canvases are quite small and they will be tiled in order to fit the image.

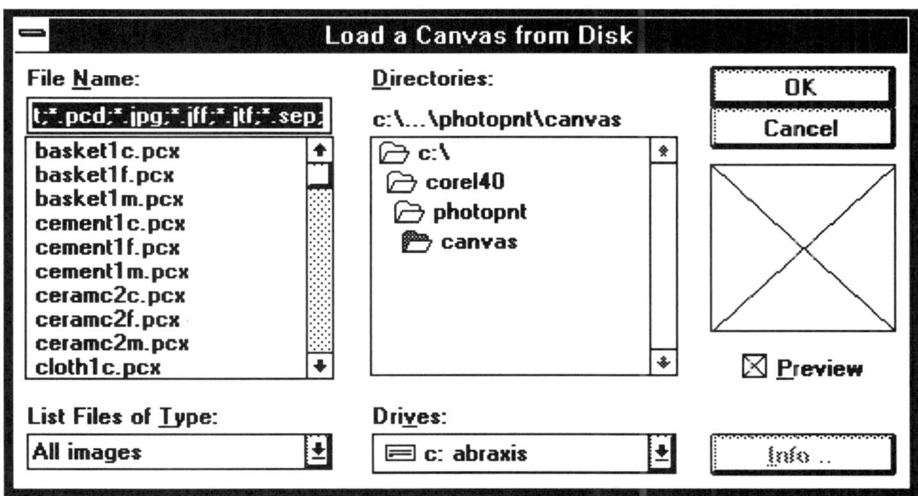

25.07 Load Canvas dialogue box

12   Talking of tiles. Press **F7** to bring up the **Fill Settings** roll-up. Click on **Load Tile** and you get a dialogue box. (You cannot use tiles as canvas or canvas as tiles by the way.) Select a pattern you like.

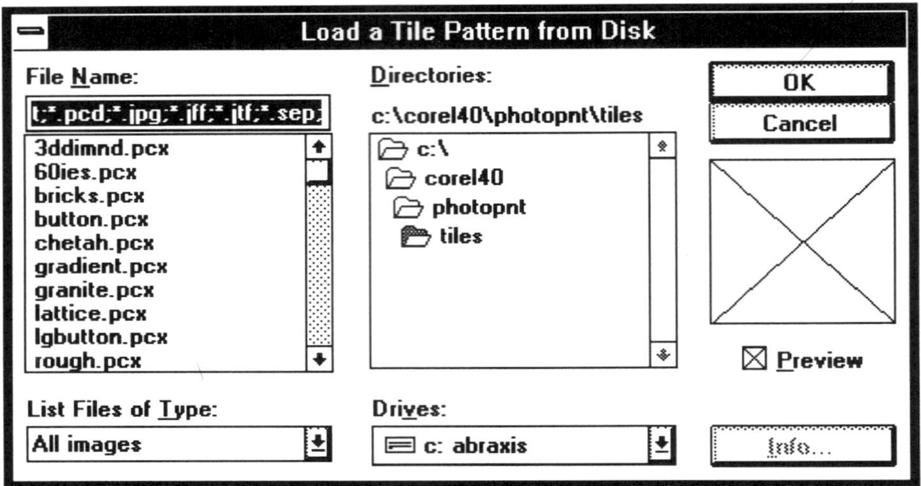

25.08 Tile Load dialogue box

13   Now click on the **Fill** tool, hold the mouse button down and when the fill tools appear click on the checkerboard pattern. Move the cursor on to the background area of the apple image and click once. The area will be filled with the pattern - but the apple itself won't.

You have to play with Photo-Paint to discover all that it is capable of - assuming you have a year or two spare. The effects can be very gaudy or incredibly subtle depending on your mode and inclination. Quite simply, you can do things with bitmap images in Photo-Paint that you only dream about in other programs.

26. CORELSHOW

CorelSHOW is a screen presentation program, which allows you to generate and develop slides shows that can viewed on a computer monitor or via a large screen projector. You can incorporate images from any of the CorelDRAW suite of applications plus animations from Autodesk Animator or Quicktime for Windows. You can also print the slides as paper, ordinary slides or OHP slides. CorelSHOW gives you total control over the presentation, everything from the background, the colours, the transition effects and timing.

1   Double click on the **CorelSHOW** icon. The window will open maximised. The first thing you see is the copyright notice followed by a dialogue box.

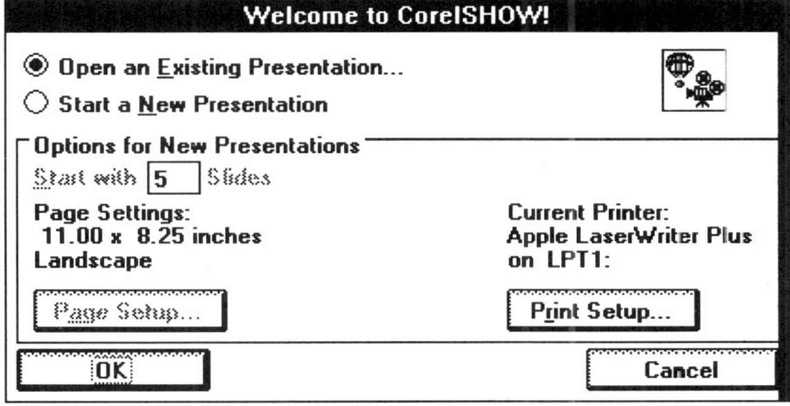

26.01 Opening dialogue box

2   At this point you cannot open an existing presentation because you haven't created one yet, so click on **Start a New Presentation**. The options for setting the number of slides and the page size now become active. Click on **Page Setup** and you get another dialogue box.

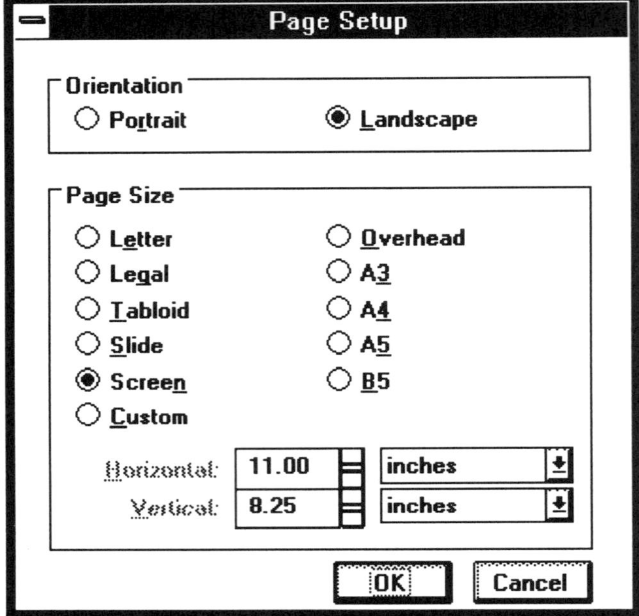

26.02 Page Setup dialogue box

3   We want a page that is in millimetres so click on **Custom**. That makes the page measurement boxes active. Change the inches to millimetres. Then click on **A4**. You want a **Landscape** page. Click on **OK**. The dialogue box closes and you go back to the first one.

4   Because it is set for 5 slides, click on **OK**. You then get the CorelSHOW window proper.

426

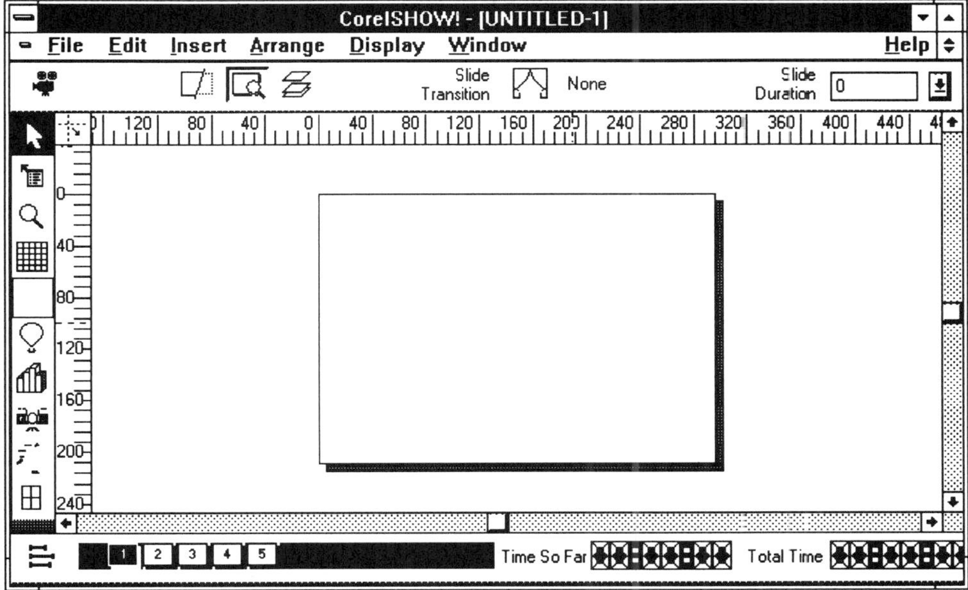

26.03 CorelSHOW

CORELSHOW SCREEN LAYOUT

This window is slightly different to the ones you are used to but only slightly. Along the top is the usual Title Bar and below that is a line with a series of buttons and icons.

Far left is a little **Camera**. That runs the slide show once it has been created.

Next is the **Background View** which allows you to edit the background of the slides.

Next is the **Slide View** which gives you a view of all the slides in the presentation. This is the default view that allows you to edit individual slides.

Next is the **Slide Sorter**. That will show you all the slides in the presentation as little thumbnails. In this view you can rearrange the order of the slides.

CORELDRAW 4 - A USERS GUIDE

In the middle of the bar is the **Slide Transition** button. That allows you to change the effects between different slides and even parts of slides.

Finally, on the right hand side is the **Slide Duration** that allows you to set the time that each slide will be on screen.

Down the left hand side of the window is the toolbar giving you, from the top down:

The **Pointer** tool.

The **Pop-Up** tool, similar to the one in CorelCHART. It allows you quick access to various commands for the slides.

The **Magnifier** tool

The quick access to the **Background Library**. That will activate a dialogue box that allows you to select a background for the slides.

The next three buttons allow you to activate the **OLE links** to CorelDRAW, CorelCHART and CorelPHOTO-PAINT.

The penultimate tool allows you to insert an **Animation** file.

Finally there is the button activating the links to other **OLE** aware programs on your system.

Across the bottom of the screen there is:

Firstly, in the lower left hand corner, the **Timelines** button. This allows you to co-ordinate the times for the slides.
Next are a series of buttons that contain numbers which correspond with the number of the slide currently being viewed. You can switch to another slide by clicking on the appropriate number. If you have a lot of slides this area also contains arrows.

Finally there are two digital windows. The first gives the **Time so Far**, i.e. when you change to slide x it will tell you how much time will have elapsed when you get to this slide in the actual presentation. The next gives the total time of the whole slide show.

428

5   Let's make a slide show. The first thing to do is place a background. Click on the **Background Library** button and you get a dialogue box.

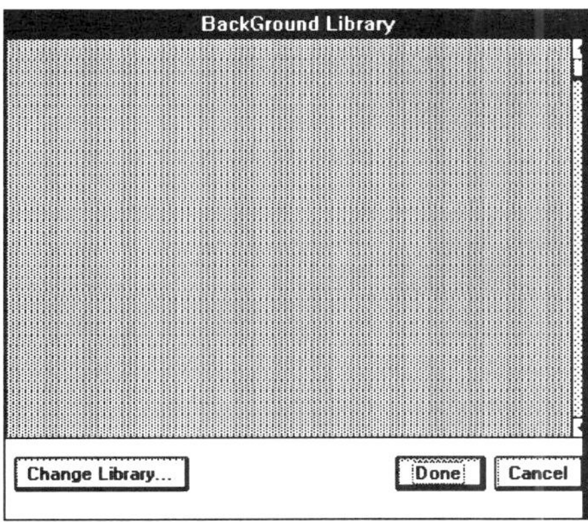

26.04 Background Library dialogue box

6   The dialogue box is currently blank because you have no library loaded. Click on **Change Library** and you get another dialogue box.

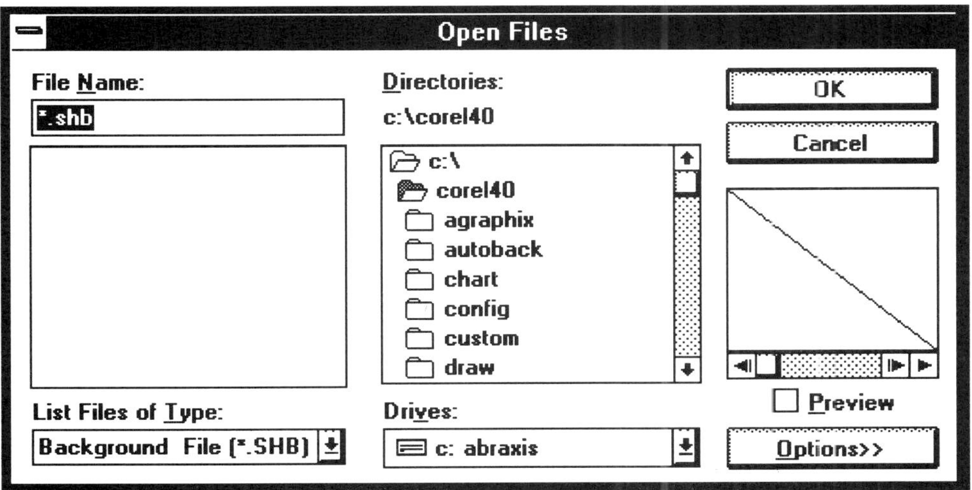

26.05 Change Library dialogue box

7   Log in to the **\SHOW\BACKGRDS** sub-directory and double click on **SAMPLES.SHB**. You'll then go back to the previous dialogue box which now contains something.

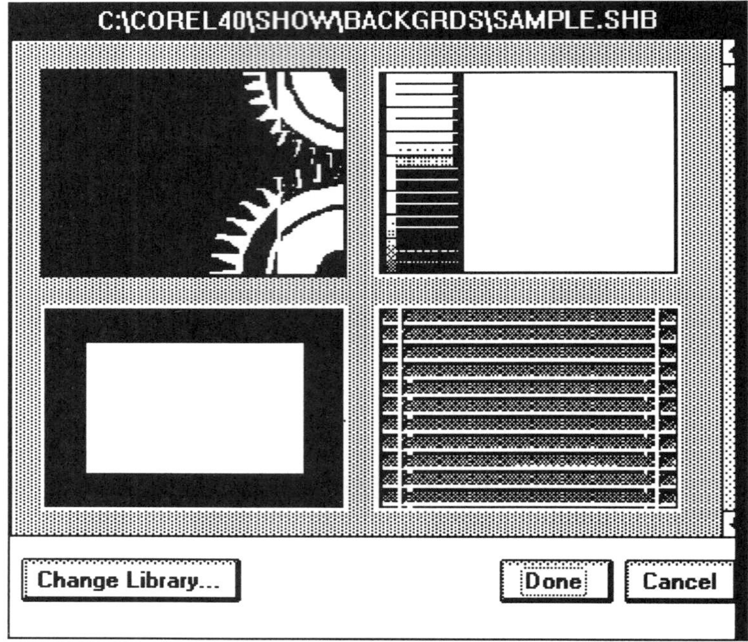

26.06 Libraries loaded

8   Pick a library of your choice by clicking on it and then click on **Done**. The background is applied to all the slides in the presentation. You cannot have different backgrounds for each slide.

9   Now to add some transition effects. Look at the **Transition Effect** at the top. At the moment it says **None**. Click on the icon and you get a dialogue box.

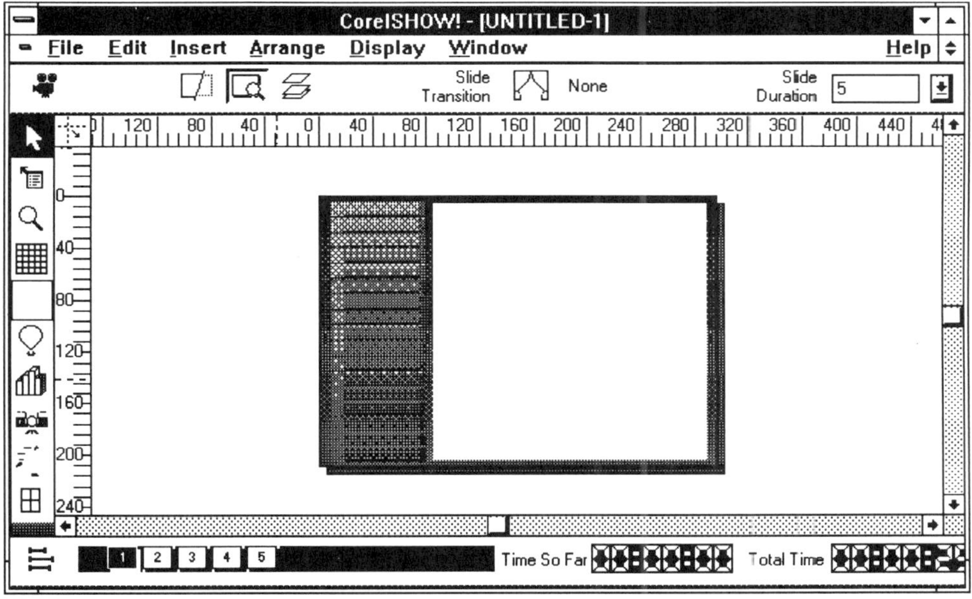

26.07 Background in place

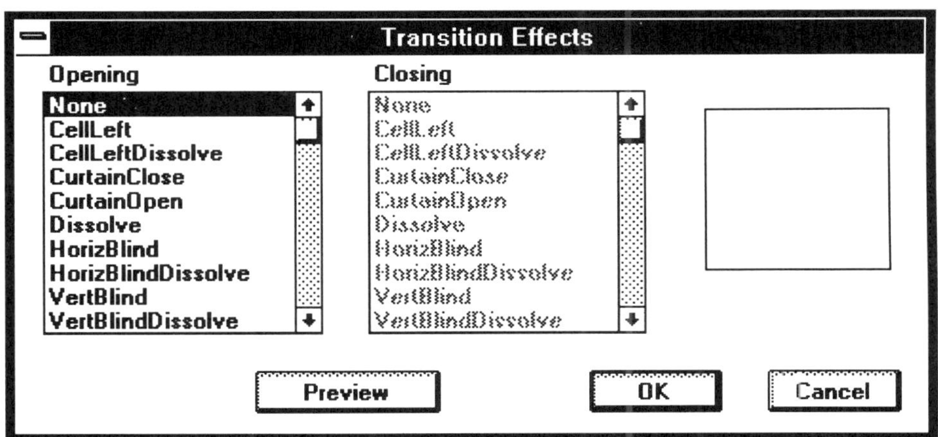

26.08 Transition effect dialogue box

10   You can set an effect for how the slides open. Each slide can have a different effect. Click on an effect and then on **Preview** and it will show you an example of what the effect looks like. All told there are 21 possible effects, including None. Use whatever effect you wish.

11   Click on the button for slide 2 and apply a different transition effect to that. Set different effects for the other slides in the presentation.

12   Now to see what the whole thing looks like so far. Click on the Camera icon in the top left of the window. You'll get a message box telling you that the slides are being generated. The slides are actually being created at this point because up to now they exist as pages.

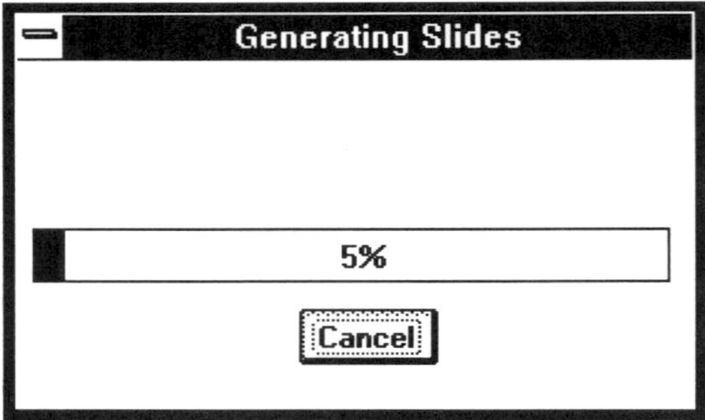

26.09 Generating slides

13   You then get a dialogue box asking you if you want to start the screen show. Click on **OK** and it will run, each slide will be on screen for 5 seconds - because that's the default time and you haven't changed it yet. Between each slide the transition effect you set will appear. To stop the show at any point press **Esc**.

14   So far so good. If you don't like the transition effects, change them and run the show again. To change the time for a slide, click on the **Slide Duration** arrowhead and select a time from the pop-down menu.

15   Let's add an image from CorelDRAW to the first slide. Click on the CorelDRAW OLE button. You'll get a cross hair cursor. Drag a bounding box on the slide

432

with this and as soon as you release the mouse button, CorelDRAW will run. Draw a circle for example and give it a fill of some description.

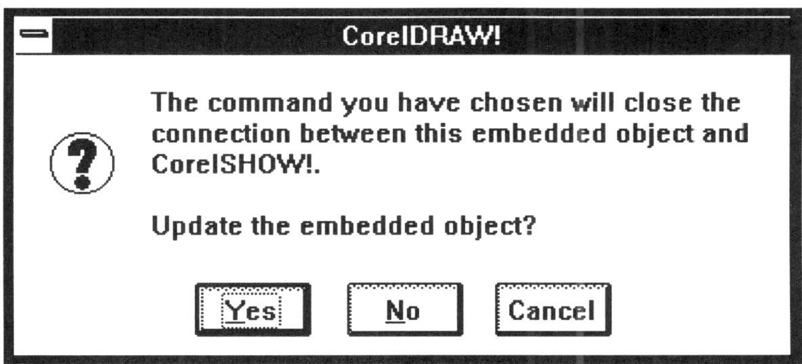

26.10 Return dialogue box

16   Open the **File** menu and click on **Exit & Return to CorelSHOW**. You'll get a dialogue box. Click on OK and you return to CorelSHOW and the circle you drew now appears on the slide.

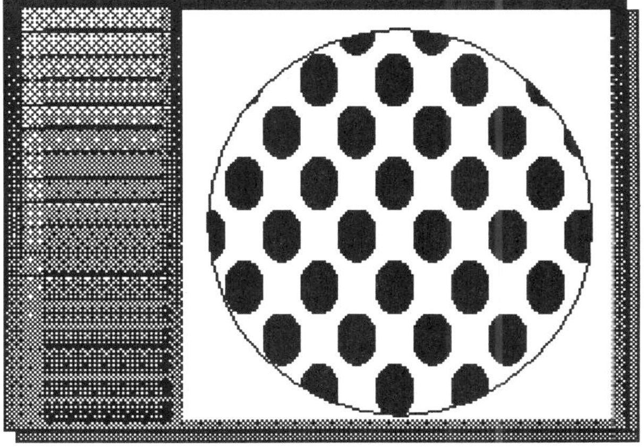

26.11 Image in place

17   At this point it is worth saving the presentation. Open the **File** menu and click on **Save** or just press **Ctrl-S**. You get a large dialogue box in which you can assign keywords and apply notes. Give the file a name, add whatever keywords and notes you want and then click on **OK**.

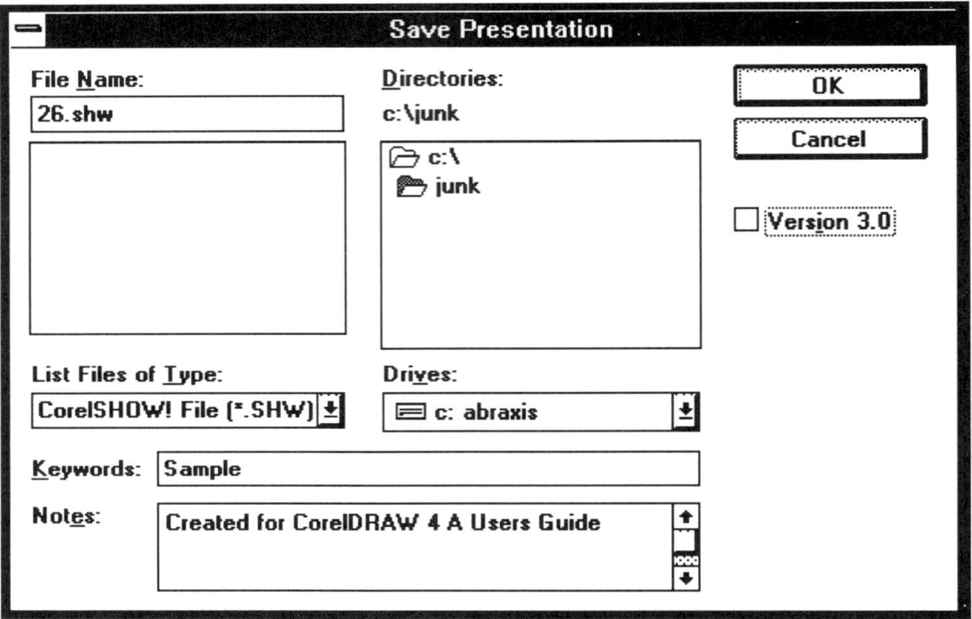

26.12 Save dialogue box

18   Move to slide two and add a CorelDRAW image to that in the same way that you did before. Do the same for the other slides except the last one. Save the file again.

19   Let's add an animation. Make sure you are on the last slide. Press **Ctrl-A** and you get a dialogue box that allows you to load a file. Change the file type to **CorelMOVE** and log into the **\MOVE\SAMPLES** sub-directory. You'll find that there is a file called **SAMPLE.CMV**. Double click on this.

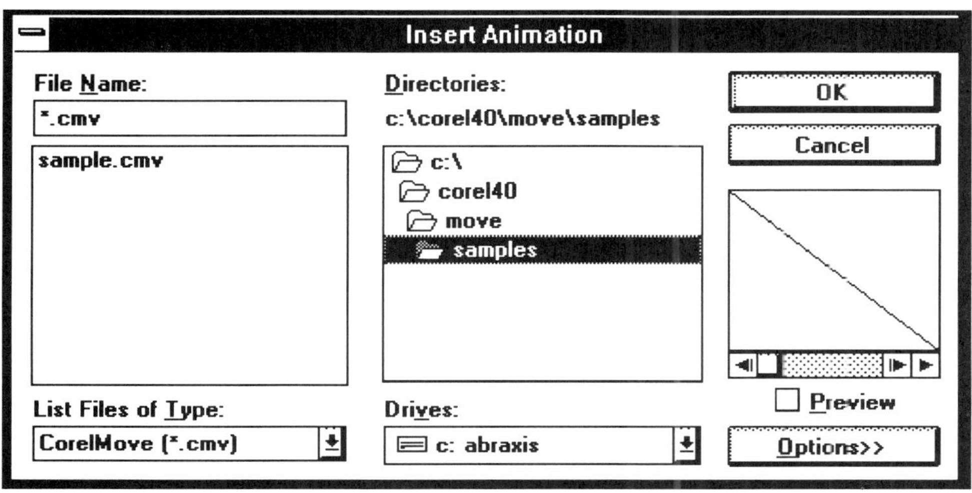

26.13 Load animation dialogue box

20 The animation will be loaded as an object. Because of that you can move it around and centralise it on the page. Because you are using an animation you don't really want the background. Open the **Edit** menu and click on **Omit Background** and for just that slide you won't have one.

21 Save the file again. Now run it by clicking on the camera icon. When the show gets to the animation that will run normally.

You can have lots of fun with CorelSHOW, you can even include sounds if you wish, but you have to play with it to discover its full range of features. There isn't room here to do more than take a brief glimpse at these.

Show is resource hungry so take care with building large presentations. If you intend building a show of more than about two dozen slides you should change your Windows swapfile to be a temporary one rather than a permanent one. Equally you need to have lots of contiguous disk space for the temp file storage because you can generate huge, i.e. over 30 Mb, temp files especially if you include lots of animations.

27. CorelMOVE

CorelMOVE is a completely new program for CorelDRAW 4. It is an animation program that allows you to create two dimensional cartoons. You can include all kinds of images and sounds in these. The program mimics the traditional frame by frame animation that is the classic way of producing everything from the original Felix the Cat (remember him?) through to the most comprehensive special effects in today's multi-million dollar movies. You can't create the equivalent of the latter with CorelMOVE but you can generate something similar to the former.

Before you start using CorelMOVE you have to be aware of some specialist terms and their meanings:

> An **Actor** is the thing that moves, usually a figure of some description. Actors are usually multiple cel creatures (see below) but they don't have to be.

> The background through which the Actor moves is the **Stage**.

> A **Prop** is something that has a single capability, e.g. something that an actor uses in a single cel.

> A **Cel** is a single frame. Originally a cel was a single piece of paper or plastic. An animation consists of a number of cels that when run together make the animation.

On the CD-ROM there are hundreds of cartoons that you can use for and with CorelMOVE, see the Clip-Art book for them all. You'll find them on pages 461 to 472 inclusive.

CorelMOVE brings you the concepts and discipline of traditional animation combined with the power of computers to allow you to create your own animations quickly and easily. (What's the betting that the Annual Design Contest has a category for animations next year?)

We don't have room here to do more than take a cursory glance at CorelMOVE but the program will be covered in depth in the companion book, CorelDRAW Applications. As with CorelSHOW, Move can be resource hungry so make sure you have enough free space on your hard disk for the temp files. Don't forget that if you want to use sound in your animations then you must have a sound card installed on your system.

1   Double click on the **CorelMOVE** icon. It will probably be a odd shape and size when it opens so it is worth tiling it. The window will be blank until you either load an animation or begin to create one.

2   Open the **File** menu and click on **Open** or just press **Ctrl-O**. You'll get a dialogue box.

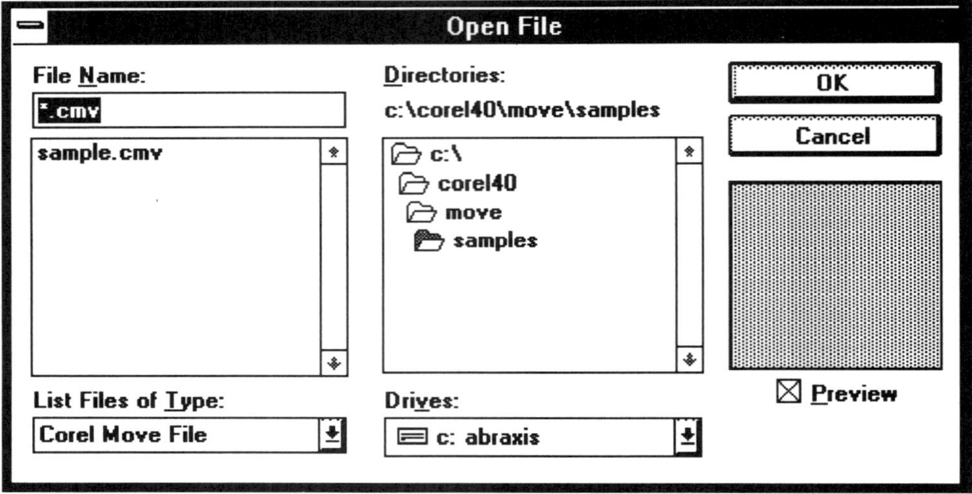

27.01 Open dialogue box

3   Log in to the **\MOVE\SAMPLES** sub-directory and double click on **SAMPLE.CMV**. Once the file is loaded you'll be able to see the full Move screen.

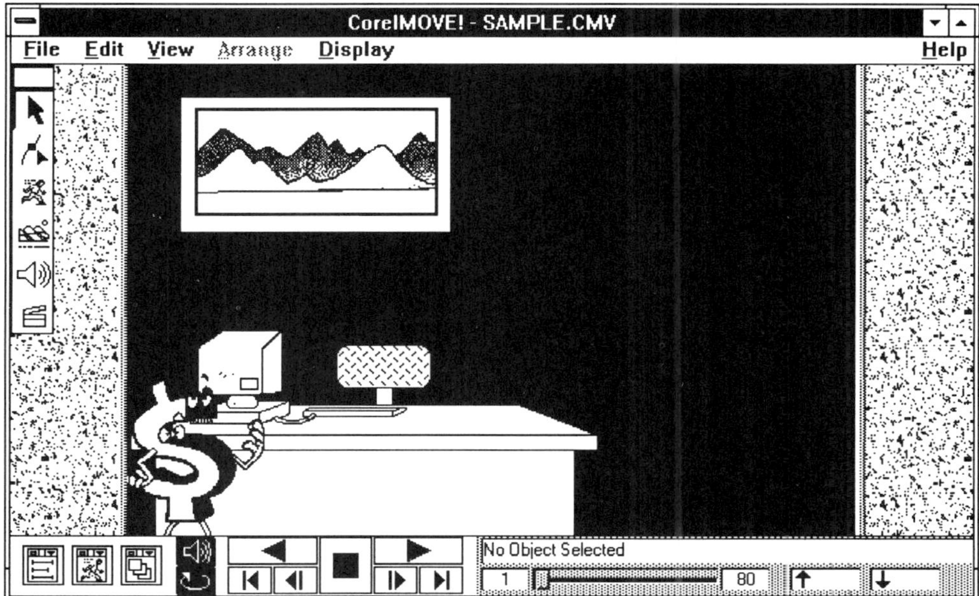

27.02 Animation loaded

CorelMOVE Screen

The windows contains the usual Title Bar and Menu Bar along the top. Down the left hand side is the toolbox containing:

The **Pointer** tool, used in the same way as in CorelDRAW.

The **Path** tool. This looks like the Node Edit tool of CorelDRAW and in one sense it works in the same way but in others it doesn't. The Path tool is used to add, create or change points along the Actor's path.

The **Actor** tool that allows you to place an actor on to the current cel.

The **Prop** tool which allows you to place new props on the current cel.

CorelDRAW 4 - A Users Guide

The **Sound** tool that enables you to add sound to the animation. Sounds have to be in WAV format for use with CorelMOVE.

Finally there is the **Cue** tool used for adding cues to the animation.

Along the bottom of the screen is a long series of icons and buttons which together make up the CorelMOVE Control Panel.

The first activates the **Timelines** dialogue box. Clicking on this will bring up a roll-up that shows you the various times and inter-activities of the slides. The display is dynamic and so the data about any prop or actor can be modified here.

The second is the **Library** button which activates another roll-up. This is used to store and thereafter retrieve objects that can be used in the animation. You can assemble all the elements you need for your animation here and then use them as necessary. It's quicker and faster doing this rather than having to import all the elements as and when you need them but it does require a bit of forethought.

The third is the **Cel Sequencer**. Again it will activate a roll-up which allows you to select when and where the actor appears.

Next is the **Sound Toggle**, bearing a loudspeaker cone. It is either on or off.

Below that is a **Loop** button. This is another toggle and when it is on the animation runs over and over until you stop it. If you turn it off then the animation runs from the first cel to the last and then stops.

Next are a series of **Playback Controls** that function in the same way as VCR controls do. They allow you to move backwards and forwards through the animation, move one cel backwards or forwards or jump to the beginning or end of the whole animation.

Beside those, and running the remaining width of the screen, is the **Status Bar**. When you select things on screen the information about them will appear here. Currently because nothing is selected it says No Object Selected.

Beneath the Status Bar are:

The current **Frame Number**.

The **Frame Slider**. You can drag the button on this to move through the animation if you wish rather than using the VCR controls.

The **Total Number of Frames** in the entire animation.

The **Current Object Movements**. These are only active if you have selected an object in the cel. The first box tells you when that object appears and the second one tells you when it vanishes.

---

4   With the Pointer tool selected, click on the **Play** button - the one with the large right pointing arrowhead. The animation will run. The little figure jumps up on the desk and a series of balls fall from the ceiling.

5   To stop the animation click on the **Stop** button - the one with the large square. This animation doesn't have any sound by the way.

6   Go back to the first cel. The quickest way is to click on the on the button that bears a left pointing triangle against a vertical line, i.e. |<.

7   Select the **Path** tool and click on the little Dollar figure.

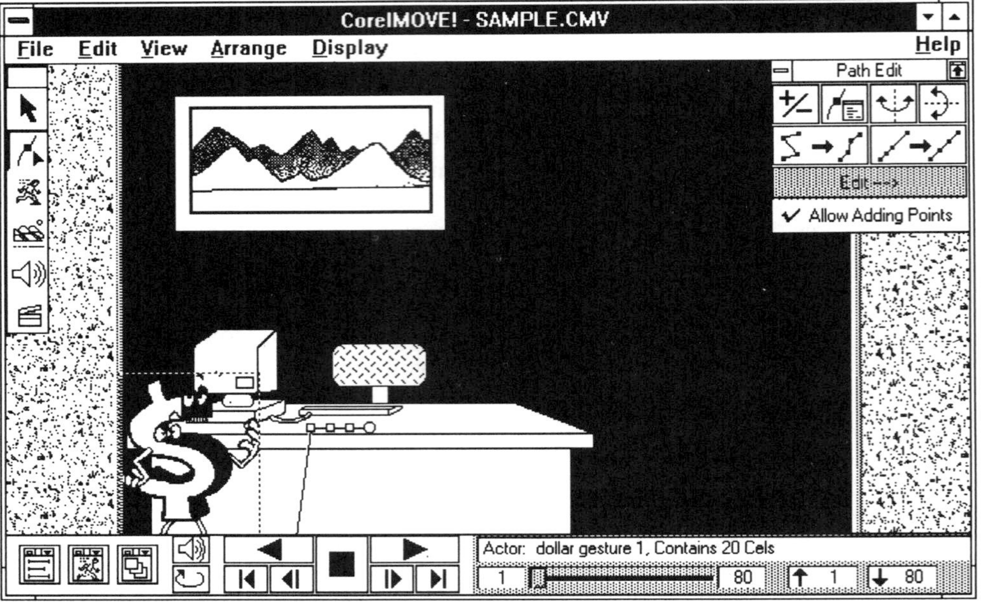

27.03 Path available

8   You get the **Path Edit** roll-up and you can see a bounding box around the figure plus a line with some nodes. The lines and nodes are the actual path that the figure takes. Notice that one node is round rather than square: that's because it is the final position.

9   Turn off **Allow Adding Points** in the roll-up. With it turned on you get a new node everywhere you click anywhere.

10   Move some or all of the existing points around the image - anywhere - to get something like this:

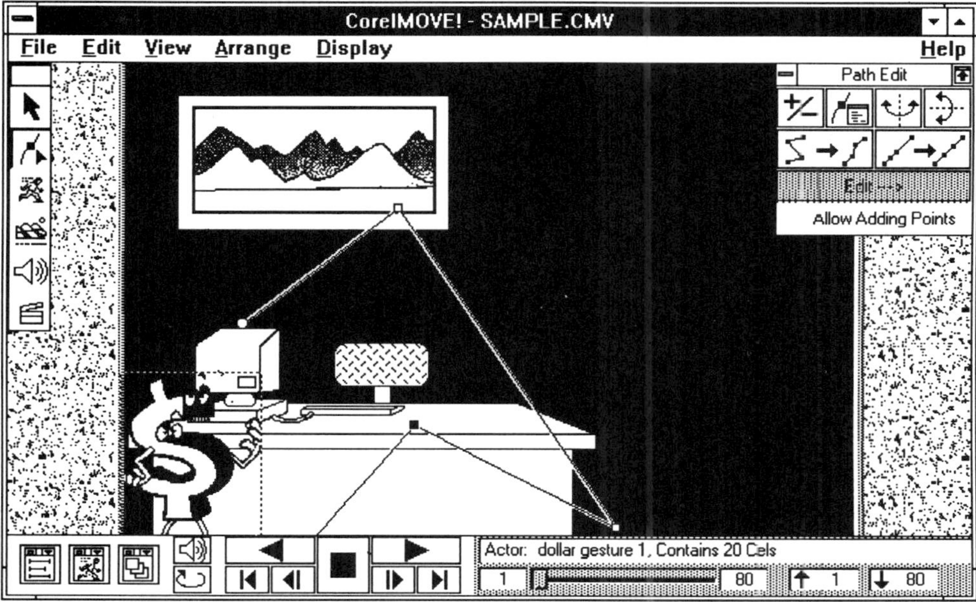

27.04 Path moved

11   Now run the animation again. The little figure flashes around following the new path. One problem, CorelMOVE doesn't have an undo facility. So if you don't like what you have done you have to reload the original file. When you do so you'll get a message box asking if it should save the changes. Click on **No**.

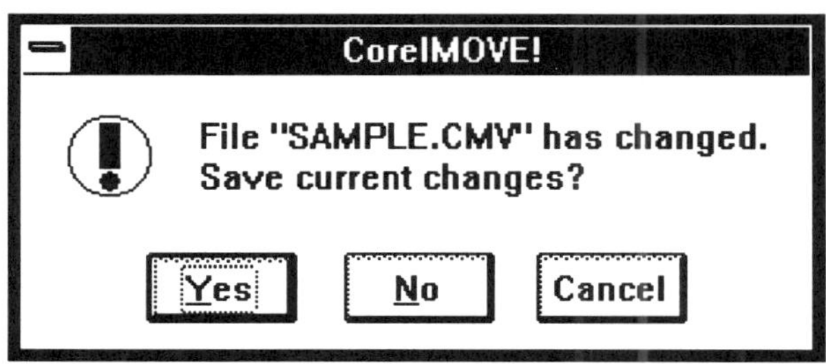

27.05 Save Changes dialogue box

12 Once you have the original file loaded again, continue playing with it. For example, click on the picture above the desk and move it to the other side. Now run the animation again.

13 The balls falling from the ceiling are now obscured by the picture. Use the **Arrange** menu and move the picture to the back. Run the animation again.

14 You'll now find that there is text appearing and running over the picture. Stop the animation and then click on any of the text items. Press **Del** and you get a message box. Click on **OK** to remove the text.

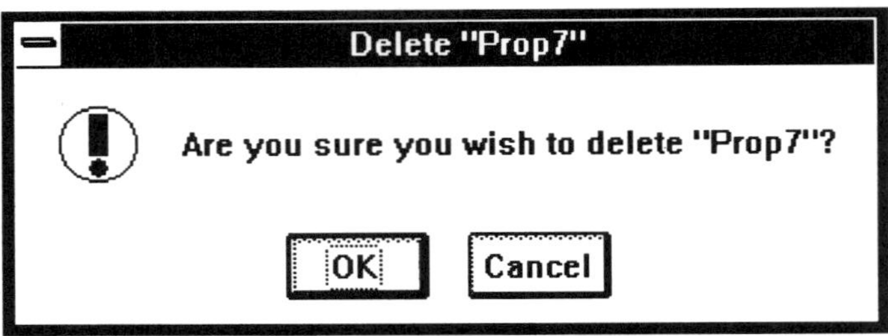

27.06 Delete Prop dialogue box

15 Move the balls over to the left hand side of the window and instead of having them in a straight line make it jagged or a curve. Run the animation again.

16 Play with the sample some more. Rearrange things some more, change the path of the actor and generally get the feel of the program. Once you have discovered the way that various tools work you can begin to create your own animations.

A1. SHORTCUTS

CorelDRAW provides you with a host of keyboard shortcuts plus some mouse shortcuts that allow you to run commands, access dialogue boxes and perform actions. These are often far quicker than using the mouse but they do take a some remembering. All menus can be accessed by pressing Alt-underlined letter. To use a menu command you then press the underlined letter of the command you wish to use. For example, to Select All you press Alt-E, which opens the Edit menu, and then press A for the command.

TOOLS AND BASIC ACTIONS

F1	Activate Help.
Shift-F1	Activate Context Sensitive Help.
F2	Magnifier, allows you to select any part of the image to magnify.
F3	De-magnify, effectively the reverse of the above.
F4	Fit to page, i.e. show (if possible) everything in current document.
Shift-F4	Display full page in window and ignore anything off the page.
F5	Select Pencil tool.
F6	Select Rectangle drawing tool.
F7	Select Ellipse drawing tool.
F8	Select Artistic Text tool.
Shift-F8	Select Paragraph Text tool.
F9	Switch to full screen preview mode - any key cancels.
Shift-F9	Switch to wireframe mode, i.e. don't display colours and outlines.
F10	Select Node Edit tool.
F11	Activate Fountain Fill dialogue box.
Shift-F11	Activate Uniform Fill dialogue box.
F12	Activate Outline Pen dialogue box.
Shift-F12	Activate Outline Colour dialogue box.
Spacebar	Switch from current tool to previous one.

POINTER TOOL SHORTCUTS

Ctrl	Stretch or scale selected item in 100% increments.
Ctrl	Constrain movement to horizontal and vertical axes only.

Ctrl	Rotate or skew in increments as set in Preferences.
Down	Nudge selected item(s) down, in increments set in Preferences.
Esc	Deselect all objects.
Left	Nudge selected item(s) to the left, in increments set in Preferences.
Plus	Leave duplicate of object when stretching or rotating.
Right	Nudge selected item(s) to the right, in increments set in Preferences.
Shift	Hold down to select multiple objects.
Shift-Tab	Select objects in reverse order.
Tab	Select items in the order they were added to the page.
Up	Nudge selected item(s) up, in increments set in Preferences.

NODE EDIT TOOL SHORTCUTS

F10	Select tool.
Ctrl	Constrain movement of nodes to multiples of 90 degrees.
Ctrl	Constrain movement of Perspective handles to horizontal or vertical.
Ctrl	Constrain movement of text to nearest baseline.
Ctrl	Move opposing Envelope handles in equal and opposite directions.
Ctrl-End	Select last sub-path of selected path.
Ctrl-Home	Select first sub-path in selected curve.
Del	Delete selected node(s).
Down	Nudge selected text character down in increments set in Preferences.
End	Select last node on selected path.
Home	Select first node on selected path.
Left	Nudge selected text character left in increments set in Preferences.
Minus	Delete selected node(s).
Plus	Add node at selected position.
Right	Nudge selected text character right in increments set in Preferences.
Shift	Allows selection of multiple nodes.
Shift	Move opposing Envelope handles in opposite directions.
Shift-Ctrl	Move corner and side handles of Envelopes in opposite directions.
Shift-Ctrl	Move opposing Perspective handles in equal and opposite directions.
Shift-Ctrl	Select all nodes on current path.
Shift-End	Toggle selection of last node on selected path.
Shift-Home	Toggle selection of first node on and off.
Shift-Tab	Moves current nodes back along the path.
Tab	Moves current node selection along the path.
Up	Nudge selected text character up in increments set in Preferences.

PENCIL TOOL SHORTCUTS

F5	Select tool.
Ctrl	Constrain tool to increments set in Preferences.
Shift	Erase as you backtrack over a path being drawn.

RECTANGLE DRAWING TOOL SHORTCUTS

F6	Select tool.
Ctrl	Constrain tool to draw squares.
Shift	Draw from centre outwards.
Shift-Ctrl	Draw squares from centre outwards.

ELLIPSE TOOL SHORTCUTS

F6	Select tool.
Ctrl	Constrain tool to draw circle.
Shift	Draw from centre outwards.
Shift-Ctrl	Draw circles from centre outwards.

TEXT TOOL SHORTCUTS

F8	Select tool in Artistic Text mode.
Shift-F8	Select tool in Paragraph Text mode.
Backspace	Delete previous character.
Ctrl-C	Cut selected text to Windows Clipboard.
Ctrl-End	Move text cursor to end of text.
Ctrl-Home	Move text cursor to beginning of text.
Ctrl-Ins	Copy selected text to Windows Clipboard.
Ctrl-V	Paste text from Windows Clipboard.
Ctrl-X	Copy selected text to Windows Clipboard.
Del	Delete selected characters or next character.
Down	Move text cursor down one line.
End	Move text cursor to end of current line.
Enter	Insert line break.
Home	Move text cursor to beginning of current line.
Left	Move text cursor to the left.

CorelDRAW 4 - A Users Guide

PgDn	Scroll text down in text dialogue box.
PgUp	Scroll text up in text dialogue box.
Right	Move text cursor to the right.
Shift -Home	Select all the text in the dialogue box from cursor position to start.
Shift-cursor	Select or deselect character one at a time in text dialogue box.
Shift-Del	Cut selected text to Windows Clipboard.
Shift-End	Select all the text in the dialogue box from cursor position to the end.
Shift-Ins	Paste text from Windows Clipboard.
Up	Move text cursor up one line.

DIALOGUE BOX SHORTCUTS

Alt-letter	Move to designated area of dialogue box.
Cursor keys	Select possible actions with options buttons.
Enter	Close dialogue box - equivalent of clicking on OK.
Esc	Close dialogue box - equivalent of clicking on Cancel.
Letter	Scroll to first item beginning with selected letter.
Shift-Tab	Move to previous option.
Spacebar	Select or deselect option button.
Tab	Move to next option.

MAJOR ACTIONS

Alt-Backspace	Undo last action(s).
Alt-Enter	Redo last action.
Alt-F4	Close CorelDRAW.
Alt-F7	Activate Move dialogue box.
Alt-F8	Activate Rotate and Skew dialogue box.
Alt-F9	Activate Stretch and Mirror dialogue box.
Alt-F10	Align to Baseline.
Ctrl-A	Activate Align dialogue box.
Ctrl-B	Activate Blend roll-up.
Ctrl-C	Copy selected item(s) to Windows Clipboard.
Ctrl-D	Duplicate selected item(s) and possibly move them at the same time.
Ctrl-E	Activate Extrude roll-up.
Ctrl-F	Activate Fit Text to Path roll-up.
Ctrl-F2	Activate Text roll-up.
Ctrl-F3	Activate Layers roll-up.

Ctrl-F5	Activate Styles roll-up.
Ctrl-F7	Activate Envelope roll-up.
Ctrl-F8	Activate Powerline roll-up.
Ctrl-F9	Activate Contour roll-up.
Ctrl-G	Group selected items.
Ctrl-Ins	Copy selected item(s) to Windows Clipboard.
Ctrl-J	Preferences dialogue box.
Ctrl-K	Break apart combined objects.
Ctrl-L	Combine selected items.
Ctrl-N	Start new document.
Ctrl-O	Open an existing file.
Ctrl-P	Print current file.
Ctrl-PgDn	Move selected item(s) down one level in stack.
Ctrl-PgUp	Move selected item(s) up one level in stack.
Ctrl-Q	Convert to curves.
Ctrl-R	Repeat last action.
Ctrl-S	Save current file.
Ctrl-T	Activate Edit Text dialogue box, either artistic or paragraph.
Ctrl-U	Ungroup items.
Ctrl-V	Paste item(s) from Windows Clipboard.
Ctrl-W	Redraw entire window display.
Ctrl-X	Cut select item(s) to Windows Clipboard.
Ctrl-Z	Undo last action(s).
Del	Delete selected item(s) from page.
Plus	Duplicate selected item(s).
Shift-Del	Cut selected item(s) to Windows Clipboard.
Shift-Ins	Paste item(s) from Windows Clipboard.
Shift-PgDn	Move selected item(s) to bottom of stack.
Shift-PgUp	Move select item(s) to top of stack.

MOUSE SHORTCUTS

Character Attributes	Double click on any character node.
Grid Parameters	Double click on a ruler.
Guidelines Setup	Double click on any guideline.
Page Setup	Double click on Page Border, the grey area around the page.

A2. USING CLIP-ART

CorelDRAW comes complete with a huge number of images called Clip-Art. These are images that someone has spent time creating, colouring, revising and refining. The images are then given to you so you can use them within your own artwork in some way. But there is a catch.

All clip-art, unless it specifically says otherwise, is covered by Copyright Law. There are tomes and tomes about this one subject because it is exceedingly complex. Far too complex to go into in anything other than broad detail here. Essentially it means that any image you create belongs to you and you therefore have copyright of that image. And the same thing applies to clip-art. The people who create the clip-art images own them!

I've just looked up the definition of copyright and this is what I got:

> Copyright is the statutory right of the originator to have exclusive control of an original design or production. The copyright holder may reproduce the work or licence others to do so. In the case of licensing the copyright holder receives a payment or royalty for each copy. Copyright extends for the lifetime of the originator and then for 50 years after their death. Books, plays, musical compositions, sound recordings, video recording, films, works of art, computer software may all be copyrighted.

For example, I own the copyright of this book and all the illustrations it contains and I get a royalty from the publisher for every copy of it that they sell. The same thing applies to Clip-Art.

Look in the front of the clip-art catalogue, on the second page. It tells you that Corel Corporation has licensed for distribution the clip-art images from a number of companies. The important point to notice is the words "licensed for distribution". That means that Corel Corporation does not own the images - the companies specified do. In this case the companies are Totem Graphics, One Mile Up, Techpool, Micromaps and Image Club. Then just to confuse matters further, Corel Corporation employs its own artists who also create images for you to use.

450

Typefaces and fonts are also copyright. For example, the name Helvetica is copyright by Linotype-Hell AG or one of its subsidiary companies. That's why many printer manufacturers use Swiss instead of Helvetica. Swiss is owned by a different company and they don't charge as much for it - or so I've been told. The printer manufacturers have to licence the typefaces from the copyright owners. That cost in turn is passed on to you because it is included in the cost of the printer.

But back to clip-art. Corel Corporation grant you a licence, in turn, to use the clip-art images for your own exclusive use. For that matter, Corel licence you to use their software - you do not own it! Not many people realise that. In fact you might be surprised to learn that you don't own any software other than that which you write yourself. But suppose you take a piece of clip-art and incorporate it into something you are doing yourself and in the process you modify and change that image. What then?

The answer to that is - Nobody knows for certain. There has been a case going through the American courts about just such an issue for the last ten years and it is no nearer to being resolved. What happened was that someone used a clip-art image of a red car and changed it to blue. The image is therefore not the same as the clip-art image, so what happens to copyright in this case? Given the nature of American law it could be decades before they hand down a definitive ruling.

However, on a purely personal level think that there is a moral point here. Take the case of the red car. The person who used it did not draw the car and surely that is where the work lies. Anyone can change the colour of it but very few people have the skill to draw the thing in the first place. Therefore I believe that it is immoral to use clip-art images and pass them off as your own.

Don't get me wrong, I'm not saying that you shouldn't use clip-art. By all means do so, after all you've been given it to use, but have the courtesy to say thank you when you use it.

As far as Corel are concerned they allow you to use the clip-art that comes with CorelDRAW for your own purposes, which includes business purposes. So you could do a poster for which you get paid, for example, and use clip-art in it. That's okay. What you cannot do is sell the clip-art to anyone else - because you don't own it.

A3. OUTPUT

The companies on this list all have facilities for outputting CorelDRAW files in their native format directly from PC. The list is not meant to be definitive - they just happen to be the companies that I know about. The list is for your information only and it is entirely up to you to check the services for yourself.

**Ascobra Ltd., Hill Farm, Byslips Road, Studham, Beds. LU6 2ND
Tel: 0582-872716**

A slide bureau based near Luton. They produce slides directly from CorelDRAW files, including those containing large bitmaps.

**Direct Signs (Northern) Ltd, 191 North Road, Darlington, Co. Durham DL3 0NF
Tel: 0325-351092**

Offer a Dye Sublimation Service printed on to a variety of sub-strates, e.g. material, metals or ceramics. The service is the same as that offered in the CorelDRAW catalogue by Image graphics in the USA - Direct Signs are the European agent.

Multicopy Imagesetting Bureau, 384 Buxton Road, Great Moor, Stockport, Cheshire SK2 7BY Tel: 0742-582292

A imagesetting bureau that offer output to a Linotronic 300 with a resolution of up to 2540 dpi. Can accept all major DTP programs as well as CorelDRAW.

On the Shelf, Ember House, Hersham Green, Walton-on-Thames, Surrey KT12 4HG Tel: 0932-254787

A complete presentation service including 35 mm slides, colour prints, OHP transparencies, etc.

Output Specialist PC Bureau, Whitfield House, 81 Whitfield Street, London W1A 4XA Tel: 071-631-5349

This is actually the production arm of Saatchi & Saatchi and their complete operation brochure is huge. Basically it says that they can output anything to anything! Ask for their brochure yourself.

Quorum Technical Services Ltd., Sandford Park Trading Estate, Corpus Street, Cheltenham, Glos. GL52 6XH Tel: 0242-584984

Photo-studio, typesetting, data conversion and printing services. The company use CorelDRAW themselves and so have a lot of expertise.

Teleset Ltd., 1st Floor, Charlton House, Chester Road, Old Trafford, Manchester M16 0GW Tel: 061-873-8282

One of the first imaging bureaux to use PC's directly. They have been using CorelDRAW since version 1.0 and so they have a lot of expertise.

The Paperworks, 16 Prebendal Court, Oxford Road, Aylesbury, Bucks. HP19 3EY Tel: 0296-399740

Output to Linotron, to A3 size, and Varityper 4990 for colour work. They can also output to a Tektronix Phaser III. They can also take Mac files and output them via PC - which is a nice change!

A4. COMMON Q&A

This chapter contains some of the most common questions that people ask about CorelDRAW, all versions, in general. It doesn't contain printing questions because they are included in the Chapter 8.

WHAT ARE THE MINIMUM SYSTEM REQUIREMENTS FOR RUNNING CORELDRAW 4?

This is the commonest question ever asked. The absolute minimum that you need is an 80386 with 4 Mb of RAM, Windows 3.1 running in VGA mode, a Windows swapfile (virtual memory) of at least 10 Mb and a minimum of 6 Mb of contiguous disk space for the temp files. (Please don't use any kind of disk compression program.) That will run the program - just! But you must have the operating system and Windows properly configured.

Far better would be an 80486 with at least 8 Mb of RAM. (If you have 16 Mb you can use a Ramdrive for temp storage for but with only 8 you cannot.) Windows 3.1 is essential and a 17" monitor, or larger, at 1024 by 768 resolution is very nice. The Windows swapfile wants to be around 15 Mb and you should allow between 10 and 15 Mb of contiguous space for the temp files.

CAN I INSTALL THE CORELDRAW MODULES SEPARATELY OR DO I NEED THE WHOLE SUITE OF PROGRAMS?

You can install any part of CorelDRAW or the associated modules that you want or need. Just use the Custom Setup and select the parts you want. As a precaution you should always back up your WIN.INI and SYSTEM.INI files first.

DO I NEED TO HAVE THE CORELDRAW DIRECTORY ON THE PATH?

No, Windows handles all that for you - though you do need Windows itself on the path. By the way, you must have Windows 3.1 to run CorelDRAW 4.

454

EVERY SO OFTEN MY MOUSE GOES HAYWIRE. WHY?

I don't know! It happens to mine occasionally too. I've tried everything from taking the mouse to bits, cleaning it, reinstalling, all sorts of things. I've come to the conclusion that the fault is to do with the level of compatibility between so-called Microsoft compatible mice and real Microsoft ones. (The fault never occurred when I used a Microsoft mouse.) Generally though the simplest answer is just to reboot the machine. In 99 cases out of a hundred the problem goes away when you do that.

I HAVE A PROBLEM WITH FOUNTAIN FILLS ON MY POSTSCRIPT LASER. I CAN'T GET RID OF THE BANDING NO MATTER WHAT I DO.

The 'fault' is not really a fault as such. The problem arises because you are trying to push the capability of the printer too far. On the majority of lasers you are limited to 300 dpi and you'll find that there is little difference between 128 fountain stripes and a higher value. There is nothing you can do about it except use a higher resolution printer. Alternatively have you considered using the banding as a special effect?

I'M TRYING TO JOIN TWO LINES TOGETHER BUT I CAN'T GET THE NODES OF BOTH LINES TO BE VISIBLE AT THE SAME TIME. WHAT DO I DO?

Before you can join the lines together they have to be part of the same object. Select both lines and then combine them with **Ctrl-L**. If you now switch to the Node Edit tool you will see that the Status Bar says Curve: x nodes on 2 sub-paths. It is only when you have two sub-paths that you can join the nodes together. Remember also that you can only join nodes when they are at the ends of lines - you cannot join them in the middle of a line.

WHENEVER I TRY TO PRINT A PARTICULAR IMAGE ON MY PRINTER IT KEEPS THROWING UP A LIMITCHECK ERROR. WHAT'S HAPPENING?

The image is too complex for the printer to handle. Try playing with the PSComplexityThreshold value in the CORELDRW.INI file. By default it is set to 1500 but you can increase it all the way to 20,000 - not that I suggest you do.

CorelDRAW 4 - A Users Guide

Try doubling the value and see if the problem goes away. Unfortunately if you increase the value too much your image will be less detailed, especially if you have used lots of fjord-like edges, but you can't have everything. Alternatively you could try adding more memory to the printer itself.

I want to play music CD discs on my CD-ROM from inside Windows. Is there any particular program you would recommend?

Definitely. On the Corel Artshow CD-ROM disc there is a wonderful little program called CD-Audio. This is fully programmable and you can set it to play your CD discs in just the same way that you would a normal CD player. (In fact it's better because it's easier to use.) I use it all the time and I think it's wonderful - especially as you get it for free!

There is a new Artshow disc every year and it contains all the entries for each year's design contest. It also has a whole host of interesting goodies on it and it comes complete with a full colour, coffee table book.

What is the design contest?

It's an annual competition, that also has monthly prizes, that Corel created for all registered users of CorelDRAW. There are a number of categories and monthly competitions. The winners from each month go on to the Grand Final that is held in Ottawa every May. The total prize value each year is over $1,000,000 - One Million Dollars! - and the winner gets, amongst other things, a 2 kilogram bar of gold! Full details are available from Corel.

CorelDRAW is running very slow and I have to have the CD disc in the drive for it to work. What's wrong?

You've installed CorelDRAW to run directly off the CD-ROM - or someone installed it that way for you. Reinstall it using SETUP to run it off your hard disk. CorelDRAW actually works better if you install it on a hard disk because CD-ROM drives are about ten times slower than a hard disk.

456

I don't want to use TrueType but CorelDRAW installs them anyway. Can I remove them?

Yes, delete all the fonts with extensions of .FOT and .TTF from your WINDOWS\SYSTEM directory. See Chapter 2 for details of installing fonts. If you want to use the Adobe Type 1 fonts instead you have to have access to a CD-ROM drive in order to get them. The ATM fonts are not supplied on the floppy disks unfortunately.

When I turn on Show Grid I get little blue dots on screen but they're not set right. What's happening?

Your monitor is not capable of showing the grid at its true resolution (none of them are) so all you get is an impression of the grid. There's nothing you can do about it because the limiting factor is the size of the pixels on screen. Why bother turning it on in the first place though? If you use Snap to Grid the cursor will stick to the grid even though you cannot see it.

How do I get the rulers into millimetres?

Change the measurement system in the Grid Setup dialogue box to read millimetres instead of inches.

Does the registration card have to go back to Canada?

At present, yes although Corel are looking at using national postings. The registration card is in the front of the manual and this year for every card that is returned Corel Corporation will donate $1 to any one of four international charities. Doesn't sound like much but when you consider the total number of CorelDRAW users world-wide that an awful lot of dollars. So send your cards back!

A5. FLYING ELVISES

The final page, people, and it's a fun one. If you want to see just how many people are involved in producing CorelDRAW and its associated programs, there is a way to find out.

1   Open the **Help** menu and click on **About CorelDRAW**. You will get a dialogue box that gives you the Version number, who the copy is registered to and the amount of free disk space you have.

2   To the left of the version number is a little Corel balloon. Double click on this and the dialogue will change dramatically. Down at the bottom is another balloon.

3   Now, you can either wait to see what happens or you click and hold the left mouse button.

4   While what's happening is happening - and I'm not going to tell you - click with the right mouse button.

INDEX

C

E

F

G

H

I

CorelDRAW 4 - A Users Guide

N

O

P

R

T

U

CoRELDRAW 4 - A Users Guide